BERYL IVEY LIBRARY

Camelot and Canada

# Camelot and Canada

## CANADIAN–AMERICAN RELATIONS
## IN THE KENNEDY ERA

ASA McKERCHER

OXFORD
UNIVERSITY PRESS

## OXFORD
UNIVERSITY PRESS

Oxford University Press is a department of the University of Oxford. It furthers
the University's objective of excellence in research, scholarship, and education
by publishing worldwide. Oxford is a registered trade mark of Oxford University
Press in the UK and certain other countries.

Published in the United States of America by Oxford University Press
198 Madison Avenue, New York, NY 10016, United States of America.

© Oxford University Press 2016

Library of Congress Cataloging-in-Publication Data
Names: McKercher, Asa, author.
Title: Camelot and Canada : Canadian-American relations in the Kennedy era /
Asa McKercher.
Description: New York, NY : Oxford University Press, 2016. |
Includes bibliographical references and index.
Identifiers: LCCN 2016001625 (print) | LCCN 2016002585 (ebook) |
ISBN 9780190605056 (hardcover : alk. paper) | ISBN 9780190605063 (Updf) |
ISBN 9780190605070 (Epub)
Subjects: LCSH: United States—Foreign relations—Canada. | Canada—Foreign
relations—United States. | United States—Foreign relations—1961–1963.
Classification: LCC E183.8.C2 M364 2016 (print) | LCC E183.8.C2 (ebook) |
DDC 327.7307109/046—dc23
LC record available at http://lccn.loc.gov/2016001625

9 8 7 6 5 4 3 2 1
Printed by Sheridan Books, Inc., United States of America

*This one's for Dad.*

*Qualis pater, talis filius.*

# Contents

# Acknowledgments

A book such as this one is hardly the result of individual effort alone. Thus, first, I would like to acknowledge the financial support of the John F. Kennedy Library Foundation and the Social Sciences and Humanities Research Council of Canada. While doing fieldwork on other projects I also conducted research for this book, and so I thank the Lyndon B. Johnson Foundation and the Dwight D. Eisenhower Foundation. As well, the expert help of Sharon Kelly and Stephen Plotkin at the Kennedy Library, Sharlaine McCauley at the LBJ Library, and Herb Pankowitz at the Eisenhower Library was irreplaceable. I thank also the staff at the Mudd Manuscript Library at Princeton, the Massachusetts Historical Society, the US National Archives and Records Administration, and the National Archives, Kew. My appreciation, too, to a host of friends and former colleagues at Library and Archives Canada: Cathryn Walter, Kaelan Murray, Daniel Lahaie, and Marie Blake.

Certainly, I owe many thanks to Susan Ferber at Oxford University Press. A more enthusiastic and kind editor surely does not exist. Len Husband at the University of Toronto Press is a close second, however. For the permission to quote from the papers of Livingston Merchant and of George Ball, I thank the Princeton University Library, just as I thank the family of Richard Wigglesworth for permission to quote from his papers. I am also thankful to the *International History Review, Cold War History, Canadian Historical Review*, and *The Historian* for allowing me to quote from portions of my own work that appeared in their journals. Furthermore, I thank the reviewers of this manuscript for their suggestions and a reviewer for *Diplomatic History* who rejected an article-length version of this study on the grounds that it "would be more fitting as a book"—a criticism I took to heart and one that underlines the importance of that charming aphorism *Illegitimi non carborundum*.

I would be remiss if I did not thank Serge Durflinger both for his early support of this project and, more generally, my academic career. To Galen Perras I owe a great debt, both professionally and personally. I also had the great fortune to discuss my work with colleagues and friends in Cambridge and Oxford: Andrew Preston, Hannah Higgin, Jamie Miller, James Cameron, Tom Tunstall-Allcock, Martin Theaker, Andrew David, Dawn Berry, and Hal Jones. For their advice and their own interest in the Kennedy–Diefenbaker years I also thank Daniel Macfarlane, John Dirks, and Michael Stevenson. Thanks, too, to Robert Bothwell, who very kindly read the whole manuscript and caught some real howlers. Natalie Ratcliffe was an excellent research partner during trips to College Park and Princeton. Lisa and Jonathan Heggie have been two fantastic friends who, throughout my writing process, were unfailingly supportive of me, even if they were not necessarily understanding when—sometimes—I took the position that I needed to write and not drink wine.

Finally, thanks and love go to my family: to Kendall, my sun and stars; to Matt and Monica (and Maria and Mya); to Lindsey and Dan; to my mother, Cheryl; to my other mother, Cathie; and to my father, Brian, to whom this book is dedicated. Dad: you once told me that you never wanted me to become an historian. Sorry. A source of boundless inspiration and support, this book, in a roundabout way, is your fault.

# Camelot and Canada

# Introduction

John Kennedy's inauguration fell on a bitterly cold day, with a blizzard the night before the ceremony having filled the streets with snow. But as the new president rose to deliver his address to the throng in front of the windswept Capitol, the skies, at least, had cleared. Among the dignitaries gathered to watch the proceedings from the huge grandstand ringing the rostrum where Kennedy spoke was Arnold Heeney, Canada's ambassador to the United States. In the midst of his second posting as Ottawa's man in Washington, Heeney had initially expected the day's main event to be a boring affair. Instead, he admitted that it had all been "pretty impressive, in fact very—and the reason was the young man himself, tall, serious, young and really very strong." Speaking of a torch being passed to a new generation of Americans, Kennedy called for a fresh approach to foreign affairs. To "those old allies," like Canada, "whose cultural and spiritual origins we share," the president pledged "the loyalty of faithful friends." But, he cautioned these allies, "united, there is little we cannot do in a host of cooperative ventures. Divided, there is little we can do—for we dare not meet a powerful challenge at odds and split asunder." Throughout his presidency, Kennedy would often find himself at odds with his old allies in Canada. Yet just as often, despite considerable sound and fury and due to the diligent work of diplomats such as Heeney, the close cooperation that characterized US–Canada relations continued. As for the inaugural address, impressed with the new president's rousing call for public service, Heeney judged that the speech would "rank with Lincoln." Moreover, he sensed that Washington "is in for a rapid change—which will be good."[1]

Heeney was not the only Canadian to welcome Kennedy's stirring rhetoric. Toronto's *Globe and Mail* looked to the new president to indicate that American foreign policy would "be more vigorous, more positive, more imaginative then ever it was under" his predecessor, Dwight Eisenhower. Reflecting back on Eisenhower's 1953 inauguration, which had been conducted under a mood of "inflexibly maintaining the status quo" both at home and abroad, the *Ottawa Citizen*'s editors piquantly noted that Kennedy's forerunner had shown little inclination "to work for reform or change, or to work with the forces of reform in the world." Kennedy seemed different. The new president had made clear a desire to "break the bonds of the containment policy" in pursuit of a foreign policy that took seriously "the political and economic battlefield of the world—the only battlefields that count at the moment." Also gushing about the inaugural, the *Montreal Gazette* praised it as "a speech of principles, tempered by a warning and caution," one meant to "inspire not dishearten." Importantly, it had been "an international, not a national speech," which contained a welcome "offer of leadership."[2] A Cold Warrior, Kennedy would continue containment, and only toward the end of his presidency would he show signs of meeting these early expectations.

Still, the press in Canada was not alone in its enthusiasm for Kennedy. In November 1960, 85 percent of University of Toronto students who had participated in a mock election had picked Kennedy over his Republican challenger, Richard Nixon. When the president and his wife Jacqueline visited Ottawa in May 1961, tens of thousands of Canadians lined the streets to catch a glimpse of the couple as they arrived on Parliament Hill, while thousands more followed their every move around the capital. The turnout for the Kennedys—dwarfing the throng that had greeted Queen Elizabeth II during her 1959 royal tour—impressed the US Embassy in Ottawa. Observing that by American standards the "size, warmth, and friendliness of the crowds" in Canada's capital were not unusual, the embassy pointed out that by Canadian standards the crowds had been "extraordinary" and "unprecedented." "The Canadians," recalled one White House aide, "were screaming 'Jackie, Jackie' in the streets and Canadians just don't scream like that normally."[3] The Canadian public's love affair with Kennedy continued well into his presidency. A December 1962 Gallup poll asked Canadians which living person they admired the most. Kennedy ranked first with 21 percent, beating the Pope and Winston Churchill, while John Diefenbaker, Canada's Progressive Conservative prime minister, in office from 1957 to 1963, placed fifth with 3 percent, while trailing even farther behind was Lester Pearson, the leader of the Liberal Party, who was soon to replace Diefenbaker as prime minister.[4]

On a personal level, many Canadians shared these positive assessments. Doubtless reflecting Kennedy's impact upon baby boomers, Lloyd Axworthy, a university student and future Canadian foreign minister, reminisced that Kennedy's inaugural address "was a call to arms to our generation to think new thoughts and challenge the conventional." Despite squeaking out a narrow victory over Nixon in the 1960 election, Kennedy's skill as a campaigner inspired Brian Mulroney, a young Progressive Conservative Party staffer and future prime minister, to write to the White House to ask for advice about campaigning. Enthusiastic about Kennedy for less practical reasons, Canada's septuagenarian governor general, Georges Vanier, was charmed by the president and his glamorous wife. After encountering Kennedy during his 1961 Ottawa trip, a young Canadian diplomat later recalled: "Wherever he went, he radiated dynamic energy, and whatever he did, he gave it his undivided attention. Even when a very junior official like me spoke to him, he looked directly at me, listened attentively, responded decisively, and usually flashed that warm smile." Similarly, Basil Robinson, who worked as the liaison between Diefenbaker and Canada's Department of External Affairs, confided to his diary, "I was enormously impressed with Kennedy's performance—an intelligent and sensitive man with a sense of humour." "I was surprised," he added, "to see how set he was in seeing foreign policy problems in straight Cold War terms."[5] In terms of Canada–US relations, Kennedy's strong commitment to waging the Cold War proved problematic, belying Canadians' hopes that the new president would pursue a less hardline foreign policy. Here was one area—of many as it turned out—where his inaugural warning about the divisions between the United States and its old allies rang true.

Despite the public adulation for the young president in Canada, the Kennedy era was a time of intense friction in Canadian–American relations. It was a short period—just less than three years—during which several factors that were negatively affecting the bilateral relationship can be traced: Canadian aversion to the direction of American foreign policy; Canadian concern over perceived US domination; and various Canadian nationalisms defined, in part, in contradistinction to the United States. These factors were not unique to the Kennedy years. However, during this period they had a profound impact upon bilateral relations, marking a shift from the relative calm of the 1950s, a period when Canadians and Americans lived "parallel lives" and where there was a Cold War consensus, to the deep tension of the 1960s and 1970s and the age of protest.[6] Poor personal relations between Kennedy and Diefenbaker worsened them. The result was that the Kennedy era was one of the most fractious periods in Canada–US relations.

More than half a century after the end of his presidency, it seems appropriate to reassess Kennedy's conduct toward Canada: most archival documents from the period are now available, and the massive literature on the era allows for a fresh look at old arguments and evidence as well as at overlooked issues. Although 1961 to 1963 are at the core of this book, it also highlights the development of Canadian nationalism and of various diplomatic disputes during the latter part of the Eisenhower presidency, a period in Canada–US relations on which little has been written.[7] Analyzing, contextualizing, and explaining the shift from the comity of the Eisenhower years to the conflict of later periods in Canada–US relations, this book employs diplomatic and political papers, press reports, and editorial opinion to explore the views and actions of diplomats and politicians, as well as journalists and academics. As this study focuses, partly, on the practice of quiet diplomacy, the stock-in-trade of Canadian diplomats during the supposed postwar "golden age" of Canada's external relations, it necessarily centers on diplomats and government officials and on Canada–US relations as "seen from above." By focusing on the level of high politics—and drawing in depth from a host of government and private papers—*Camelot and Canada* examines the world in which this diplomatic relationship functioned. These are narrow confines, but they reflect both the way in which quiet diplomacy was conducted and the sheltered world in which policymakers and diplomatists practiced their craft. Indeed, it was these officials' detachment from the wider populace that led to criticisms of quiet diplomacy as the 1960s wore on. Admittedly, such elite-driven studies have their limitations. Beyond a myopic focus on "what one clerk wrote to another" and the prizing of the views of government officials, diplomatic histories offer but narrow analyses of historical events.[8] But drawing on a multiarchival and international source base, *Camelot and Canada* joins a growing number of historical studies of Canada's role in the world that employ a similar focus on elites while internationalizing the study of Canada.[9]

*Camelot and Canada* places the bilateral diplomatic relationship of the early 1960s into context. First, it places this relationship within the more parochial Canadian context emphasizing the growth of different strands of English Canadian nationalism, which contained within them deep uneasiness about the United States. The nationalist tide of the 1950s to the 1970s has been subject to increasing historical scrutiny from a host of viewpoints, but seldom has much attention been paid to American perspectives, despite the United States being, in so many ways, at the root of this phenomenon. Indeed, one can trace the impact of two nationalisms: one, shared by Diefenbaker, rooted in Canada's British past; the other, driven primarily by younger Canadians, a New Nationalism.[10] This study shows how US actions influenced the development of these nationalisms. Within this setting it assesses the Canadian independence debate, and the issue of whether quiet diplomacy effectively made Canada a satellite of the United States. In the Kennedy era—and indeed, since the Second World War—Canada had pursued an independent foreign policy, one that happened largely to dovetail with that of the United States and that supported the postwar order founded on American economic and military might. But Canadian actions were also constrained by a desire not to upset the Americans even as there were strains between the two allies, which only grew along with nationalism. Importantly, *Camelot and Canada* explores American views of Canadian nationalism, thereby breaking out of the narrow boundaries typical of studies of Canadian identity.

Second, this study contextualizes and analyzes the practice of quiet diplomacy and the diplomatic culture that girded the Canada–US relationship. Looking at the actions of Kennedy—as well as Diefenbaker and Pearson—only provides part of the story. Heads of government are busy people, with many issues upon which to focus time and effort. Diplomats, then, are the ones who handle the day-to-day relations between states. This study explores the work of the officials on both sides of the 49th parallel who were responsible for managing Canada–US relations as well as their respective countries' foreign policies, including diplomats in the US Ottawa Embassy and in the State Department, in Canada's Washington Embassy and in the Department of External Affairs, and in various other government agencies in both countries. During the period in question these policymakers practiced quiet diplomacy, implying a reliance on discreet—if frank—consultations and negotiations in contrast to strident public declarations and the airing of grievances. Quiet diplomacy proved useful for the conduct of bilateral relations in that Ottawa was often able to nudge Washington into avoiding measures harmful to Canada; it proved to be an ineffective way for Canadian officials to influence the broader conduct of US foreign policy, but gave them a means of offering advice and venting frustration. Nonetheless, Canada's ability to influence the higher direction of US foreign policy was—and has been—limited, the result of the vast disparity in power between the two countries, as well as Americans' self-assuredness.

Finally, *Camelot and Canada* places Canada–US interaction into a wider international context both of Kennedy's foreign policy and of global politics during the first years of "the crucial decade."[11] Strains in the bilateral relationship were, after all, created by a changing world: the recovery of Western Europe and Japan created fresh economic pressures; the dissolution of European empires, the emergence of a plethora of new states, and rising Third World nationalism created new dangers; at the same time, a vigorous Soviet foreign policy that aimed, in the words of Soviet Premier Nikita Khrushchev, to "bury" the West, raised old fears. As Kennedy had pointed out in his inaugural, he was assuming office at the "hour of maximum danger," and his years in office were among the "crisis years" of the Cold War, when the possibility of nuclear war seemed all too real.[12] How did relations between Ottawa and Washington function within this environment? How did the diplomats, civil servants, and elected officials who managed Canadian foreign policy view and react to Kennedy's vigorous conduct of foreign affairs and to the rapid changes in global politics?

Taking these factors all into account, the result is a work that places the Canadian–American relationship within the broad context of US foreign relations under Kennedy, showing how the New Frontiersmen dealt with their northern neighbors. While the public continues to be enamored with the young president, historians have largely taken a dimmer view of him. Commenting on this "disjuncture," one historian has recently noted that "the historical Kennedy remains elusive, a beloved figure of myth and memory and an inspiration to millions, as well as an all-too-human politician, exploiting the trappings of privilege and power, and pragmatic to a fault."[13] Kennedy's pragmatism might come as news to many Canadian historians, who have tended to typify the president as overbearing and imperious in his handling of Canada—a view of JFK shared by historians of US foreign relations with other countries such as Cuba and South Vietnam. Yet the image that emerges of Kennedy in *Camelot and Canada* is of a policymaker who was indeed pragmatic, and patient, in his handling of his country's increasingly nationalistic northern neighbor.

When, in his inaugural address, Kennedy spoke to his country's old allies, this included John Diefenbaker. Bombastic, passionate, and emotional, he was a politician who excited his supporters and his enemies alike. A *Time* magazine cover story celebrated Diefenbaker as a "prairie lawyer" who brought to politics "the zeal of a successful evangelist." But, it continued, he "is an intense, moody man, sensitive to personal affront," whose "deep-set blue eyes can blaze with anger or fill with quick emotion." Along similar lines, the State Department considered him "serious-minded, vigorous, and self-confident," a "shrewd politician" who was blessed with "rhetorical gifts," which enabled him "to promote his vision of Canada's national destiny with evangelical fervor." Admitting that while Diefenbaker could take positions that deviated from those of the United States, American diplomats judged that, fundamentally, he was a committed ally. Worryingly, however, Diefenbaker seemed prone to a "disappointing indecisiveness" alongside "a lack of political courage and undue sensitivity to public opinion." Ambassador Heeney agreed, recording that the prime minister was generally "hard-headed" about international matters, yet he was also "ruled ultimately (and quite credibly) by political factors."[14]

Historians have shared these assessments of the prime minister. Overwhelmingly, studies of Diefenbaker are unfavorable. He was, apparently, a "renegade in power," a "rogue Tory," and "a bit megalomaniacal, so paranoid, and almost certainly a bit mad."[15] Diefenbaker's character is important. Writing in 1968, a former Canadian diplomat observed cogently that the prime minister's "mounting resentment" toward the president was the "essential key" in comprehending why Diefenbaker came to loathe Kennedy.[16] On this theme, Diefenbaker's biographer has speculated that his subject was motivated by jealousy of the president's youth, wealth, style, and popularity with Canadians, while Basil Robinson recalls that Diefenbaker saw the charismatic president as "a difficult challenge." Two historians have even dubbed it a "Canadian cliché" to contrast the worldly, East Coast aristocrat with the parochial, prairie lawyer.[17]

Alongside these personal jealousies existed an understandable desire by the prime minister to keep power. Having been confined to the opposition benches for almost two decades before seizing the premiership in 1957, Diefenbaker had tasted his share of political and electoral defeats.[18] His survival instincts, combined with his natural populist style, meant that he saw foreign policy through a domestic lens. "When new situations arose in foreign affairs," Robinson reflected, the prime minister overriding concern was with how the issues would play "politically on the home front."[19] That the prime minister was a populist is no secret. Neither is the idea that domestic political concerns greatly affected his actions on the world stage. To the chagrin of hardnosed realists, domestic support is a key ingredient in foreign policymaking the world over. As Pearson, Diefenbaker's great political opponent and Canada's foremost statesman, once quipped: "Foreign policy, after all, is merely 'domestic policy, but with its hat on.'"[20] Yet in Diefenbaker's case, his political instincts often made him overly cautious and extremely suspicious, with disastrous results for relations between Ottawa and Washington.

Just as scholars looking at the Canada–US relationship have been critical of Diefenbaker, so too have they looked dimly on Kennedy. The young president evidently cared little for Canada or for the prime minister's domestic considerations. "It was true," recalled a Canadian journalist who had served in Washington during the early 1960s, "that JFK knew practically nothing about Canada and Canada–U.S. relations when he moved into the White House." Worse, Kennedy likened Canada to "a child nation, sometimes to be chided and sometimes to be patted on the head, but who would agree, willingly or not, that Father knows best." More recently, another journalist has contended that "Camelot was a living nightmare for Canada," while two historians have added that Kennedy, "young and conscious of his and his country's awesome power, had no time to waste on the Canadians" and even sought "to teach Diefenbaker a lesson on how to deal with the power of the American empire." Agreeing, Diefenbaker's biographer concluded that Kennedy was guilty of a lack "of understanding of Canada" and considerable "arrogance" in his dealings with Ottawa.[21]

Oddly, despite the obvious differences in age and background, Kennedy and Diefenbaker had much in common. Both were strident anti-Communists; each was a gifted orator; they shared a concern with alleviating poverty in what was then "the Third World"; neither looked favorably on racism, both doing much to combat this scourge; and they were Anglophiles. Even so, these two mismatched leaders were often at odds with one another. This conflict was not simply because of the personal differences that developed between them. First, whereas Diefenbaker was cautious in foreign affairs, the young president and those who surrounded him were "activist, confident and ambitious," believing that "with sufficient energy, imagination, intellect, and resources, few human problems were beyond solution." They were "action intellectuals."[22]

While Canada and the United States were allied, they had different interests, priorities, and responsibilities: the latter, a superpower, had an enormous global agenda; the former, a self-styled "middle power," was more modest. Ottawa's efforts to maintain an independent course in foreign affairs, complicated by its alliance with Washington, led to disputes over trade with China and Cuba, Southeast Asian security, nuclear weapons, the freedom of Berlin, foreign aid, Britain's entry into the European Common Market, and nuclear disarmament. These disagreements, and the personal dislike between president and prime minister, led to one of the darkest chapters in the Canada–US relationship.

After reaching their nadir in January 1963, relations between Ottawa and Washington recovered when, in April, a new government came to power under Pearson. A consummate diplomat, Pearson had served as Canada's secretary of state for external affairs from 1948 to 1957, the supposed heyday of Canadian foreign policy. During this golden age, Ottawa had supported the development of an international order founded on liberal principles and backed by American power. Canadian internationalism reached its peak in these years as did Ottawa's influence abroad: with Europe and Japan shattered by the Second World War, Canada, by default, had a voice in world affairs disproportionate to its population and importance. In 1959 Kennedy himself paid homage to Pearson as a statesman *par excellence* as well as "the chief architect of the Canadian foreign service, probably the best in the world."[23] Perceptions of Canada's influence aside, caution abounded in Canadian foreign policy. With the Soviet threat to the postwar order, Pearson had helped steer Canada into the North Atlantic Treaty Organization (NATO) and had supported the emerging Cold War consensus. He had no illusions about where Canada stood in the world, reminding a Canadian audience in late 1962: "While we ask the United States to appreciate our position and our sensitivities, we should be careful in trying to understand the position of the United States, in its effort to exercise great power in a way which will bring about peace and security not only for its own people but throughout the world. We must try to understand and appreciate the awful responsibility that rests on the shoulders of an American government."[24] No wonder US officials viewed Pearson as a friend. Nor is it puzzling why they subsequently came to view with alarm the actions of Pearson's Liberal government, which seemed not so different from those of Diefenbaker.

Close allies, Canada and the United States have often disagreed with one another. Abroad, they cooperated in forming the NATO alliance, defending Western Europe, and containing the Soviet Union. However, the atomic specter cast a pall over this cooperation, as did the increasing unilateral militancy of the American response to the communist threat. Hence, Pearson's 1951 lament that "the days of relatively easy and automatic political relations with our neighbour are, I think, over." The issue, he noted, was not "whether the United States will discharge her international responsibilities, but how she will do it and whether the rest of us will be involved."[25] Thus, Canada sought ways of constraining US power and of quietly influencing the conduct of American foreign policy. These efforts led to a "continued tension between conflict and cooperation" with Washington.[26] The Kennedy years were no different from other periods in the postwar era, in which some scholars have characterized the bilateral relationship as a "special relationship," a term derided by some.[27] If not special, there is something exceptional about relations between the northern two-thirds of North America, and a parallel can be drawn with the Anglo-American special relationship. Both relationships grew out of the Second World War, lasted into the Cold War, and were nurtured by military, diplomatic, and interbureaucratic links as well as by shared interests and perceptions of the wider world. Specialness did not "connote perfection or pure harmony," nor did it remove points of "friction and controversy." Instead, it reflected a persistent "desire to work together," even in moments of disharmony.[28] The same can be said for Canada–US relations, especially in the two decades after the Second World War.

In the immediate postwar period Canada's economic and industrial health, military power (the Royal Canadian Navy and Royal Canadian Air Force were, respectively, the fourth largest navy and air force in the world), and geographic position between the United States and the Soviet Union all meant that Washington accorded Ottawa considerable importance. Further, Canada was a vital market for US goods, an invaluable source of natural resources, and a key destination for American investment, meaning that as the Cold War developed, the United States pursued a largely altruistic policy toward its northern neighbor. In turn, Canadian officials desired to maintain the close wartime links that had been established with their powerful and wealthy neighbor, and applauded as Washington spurned prewar isolationism to take an active role in the world.[29] Motivated by these views, Canadian and US policymakers worked constructively with one another and benefitted from the bureaucratic machinery needed to smooth over differences. Taken together, these factors have led to a judgment that "the association between Canada and the United States in the postwar period had perhaps a larger claim to the term *special relationship* than did any other association."[30]

Providing a cogent theoretical analysis of the bilateral relationship in this era, Brian Bow has contended that it "*was* genuinely special, in that it was governed by a distinctive diplomatic culture that shaped the way policymakers on both sides thought about what their interests were and how bilateral disputes could be resolved." In negotiations, diplomats avoided coercive methods and retaliatory measures; instead, they worked quietly and informally to bridge differences.[31] Also emphasizing the existence of a special relationship, economic historian Bruce Muirhead has observed a pattern where Washington treated Ottawa "mildly, often in the face of provocation."[32] Despite the vast disparity in power between the two countries, American officials generally avoided bringing their power to bear in these disputes. The depth and breadth of bilateral interdependence created a system where officials came to view retaliatory measures as being counterproductive because tough action in one area could upset relations in another. Avoiding retaliation and linkage between various issues, Canadian and American officials instead compartmentalized issues.[33] Even so, their deliberations and negotiations could be tense. Yet as Rufus Smith, one of the foremost Canadianists—experts on Canada within the State Department—noted, "the juxtaposition of heated words and calm decisions is perhaps the rule, not the exception, in the history of relations between us."[34] Here was "quiet diplomacy."

Based on a belief that differences in outlook and policy between the two governments were best settled privately, quiet diplomacy offered the Canadian government one of its only means to influence the direction of American policy. Open dissent by Ottawa, the argument went, would not only fall on deaf ears in Washington but also would ruin Canadian credibility with the White House. At the Canadian Institute of International Affairs' 1961 annual conference, held on the theme of "Problems of Canadian Independence," Peyton Lyon, who had recently moved from Canada's foreign service to academe and who was the foremost public advocate of quiet diplomacy, opined that "our credit with the Americans, and others, has its limits. We must be careful not to overdraw by raising too many issues, by squandering our credit on issues of minor consequence, or by speaking from a shaky belief."[35] In the Diefenbaker–Kennedy years, diplomacy was less quiet. Certainly, with its vigorous approach to foreign policy the Kennedy White House had less time for the views of its allies. Added to impatience in Washington was a more confrontational stance by Ottawa in its dealings with its southern ally and in professing, and often charting, an independent course. Canadian nationalism, personified by Diefenbaker, threatened the diplomatic culture governing Canada–US relations. As Lyon would later note in a devastating critique of Diefenbaker's foreign policy, "the loss in Washington of Canada's reputation for integrity diminished its modest ability to influence Western policy, some of which might determine human survival in a perilous age."[36] It is no surprise that the most famous—or infamous—document advocating quiet diplomacy, *Canada and the United States: Principles for Partnership*, which appeared in 1965, was authored by Livingston Merchant, Washington's ambassador to Ottawa from 1956–1958 and again from 1961–1962, and Arnold Heeney, Canadian ambassador to the United States from 1953–1955 and then from 1959–1962. Moreover, it is hardly surprising that Diefenbaker clashed with Canada's diplomatic corps—the practitioners of quiet diplomacy—whom he felt were partisan Liberals, and who disagreed with him over the way in which his domestic priorities seemingly took precedence in diplomatic affairs.[37]

Building on previous scholarship, this book offers, in part, an in-depth historical analysis of how quiet diplomacy and the larger diplomatic culture functioned in the Kennedy years. It highlights another factor that reinforced the view that Canada should be treated in a special manner: the sense among American policymakers that Canadian nationalism was a potent force. In consequence, US diplomats took a patient approach in dealing with Canada and, more often than not, yielded to the Canadian point of view on points of bilateral friction. Shrewdly, in their talks with their American counterparts, Canadian officials often emphasized the potency of nationalism and used the specter of potential nationalist blowback to United States policies to supplement their deft negotiations. Quiet diplomacy's effectiveness made it attractive to Canada's diplomats, while their American counterparts saw it as a means of working around nationalists.

A useful bargaining tool, what quiet diplomacy was unable to do during this period was to give Canada influence over the wider direction of US foreign policy. Ottawa's ability to affect American policy on issues of war and peace was, at best, modest. Canadian advice about how to resolve the Berlin crisis, for example, went unheeded. Some scholars have maintained that the inability to influence Washington through quiet diplomacy showed that in the US capital Canada was "invisible and inaudible."[38] Yet Canada's Western European allies—more powerful than Canada in relative terms—were often as ineffective, thankfully, as it happened, in the case of Berlin, where France pressed the United States to adopt a far more belligerent stance than Kennedy wished to take. Was Charles De Gaulle invisible or inaudible? In this era of United States hegemony and hubris allied advice was easily ignored, even if Americans found Ottawa with Diefenbaker too loud and too visible. For US policymakers at this time, an important question that they posed was what made a faithful, friendly, and unassuming ally like Canada suddenly so hostile? From their perspective, the answer lay in the influence of Canadian nationalism.

Nationalism involves the creation of "imagined communities," a process that is at once inclusionary and exclusionary, in that the quest to create a distinct nation involves limiting membership and preserving the sovereignty of the community against outside encroachment.[39] In Canada encroachment has come from the south, and so nation-building, by both English and French Canadians, has frequently meant emphasizing distinctions from the United States. In political terms, as the historian Frank Underhill joked in 1963, there was a need on Parliament Hill for "a monument to the American ogre," which had been a catalyst for Canada's Confederation in 1867.[40] Whether in military, economic, or cultural guises, many Canadians in the late nineteenth and early twentieth centuries were fearful of the threat from the south. This threat seemed particularly potent for English Canadians who faced "the overwhelming economic and cultural power of the United States, a country with which they share a border, a language, and much culture and history."[41] A crucial element of Canadian nationalism, then, can be seen as being synonymous with anti-Americanism. The latter term is usually meant to imply "the expression of a disposition against U.S. influence abroad," or "an attitude of distaste, aversion, or intense hostility" toward the United States, but in Canada it is reflective of a deep-seated desire simply to be Canadian. Praising the "new spirit of Canadianism" in a 1960 speech, Diefenbaker's justice minister, Davie Fulton, explained that Canadians have always been wary "of the dangers to us of the laws of political, cultural and economic osmosis. We have had to make a conscious effort to remain Canadian and to retain a Canadian control of Canadian destinies."[42] This un-Americanism in Canada has extended back to the American Revolution.

These sentiments had abated somewhat during the 1940s and early 1950s, at least among government officials. Wartime cooperation with the United States had led to peacetime amity. American dollars had flowed into the Canadian economy, fueling the country's prosperity. Canada benefited from the postwar years of US global economic predominance. Despite this affluence, by the late 1950s growing fear over the deepening ties between the two countries meant that nationalism was again viewed in Canada "as a force for progress and reform."[43] American economic and cultural power was wedded to notions of modernism and a sense, in Canada but also throughout the West, both that homogeneity was growing and that the lines between nations were being swept away. Increasing ownership of Canada's economy by US investors and the popularity of materialistic American culture were alarming prospects for increasing numbers of Canadians, many of whom put stock in Canada's more conservative heritage.[44] A series of royal commissions in the 1950s highlighted American cultural and economic domination of Canada.

Against this backdrop, Diefenbaker rose to power in 1957. Throughout his successful campaign that year, Diefenbaker tapped into and stirred up nationalist sentiments. His upbeat message called for massive economic development especially in Western Canada and the North. In a series of "perfervid and almost evangelical speeches" he offered Canadian voters a vision of a strong, prosperous, and independent country set to fulfill its potential.[45] Diefenbaker gave voice to the desire of many Canadians to fashion a distinctive Canadian identity and community—"One Canada," as the Tory leader called it. This desire sprang from a realization that the traditional cultural ties to Britain were giving way in the face of expanded immigration, loosening bonds of empire, and the creep of materialist culture from the south. Moreover, in a Canada still a part of the British world, Diefenbaker emphasized the potent emotional attachment to Britain and to Canada's imperial heritage.[46] So a positive effort to create a Canadian nation was appealing.

But Diefenbaker's message was not entirely rosy. Creating an imagined national community is inherently exclusionary and so his campaign speeches also carried a tinge of un-Americanism. He had, for instance, warned listeners at a political rally that under Liberal governance Canada risked becoming "a virtual forty-ninth economic state in the American union."[47] His exhortations to safeguard Canada against US domination were not new to his country's political discourse, but they were potent as the postwar lull in Canadian anti-Americanism gave way to worries over sovereignty and identity. Nor were such concerns the preserve of Diefenbaker and the Progressive Conservatives. Canada's Liberals may have done much to move Canada close to the United States during the immediate postwar years, but within the party was a sizeable nationalist wing. Nationalism would not die along with Diefenbaker's government. Indeed, a more stridently anti-American strain of nationalism would gain prominence in the 1960s, along with the rise of Canada's New Left and mounting criticism of United States conduct in Vietnam and the rot in American society evident in that country's racial and political violence. Yet culturally and economically, the ties remained. Looking back in 1967 over the past decade, one historian wrote that there had been a realization among Canadians "of a considerable and perhaps growing similarity to the United States in certain spheres, coupled with a strong belief that Canada is somehow different and that the difference must be preserved."[48]

Nationalism involved not simply safeguarding a distinctive culture and economy, but also the conduct of an independent foreign policy. The late 1950s and early 1960s saw the revival of a debate about whether Canada had—or could have—an independent role in the world.[49] Proponents of an independent foreign policy criticized the quiet diplomatists' "overriding concern for kid glove relations" with the Americans, arguing: "surely Canada can aspire to a more significant international activity than just having some influence in Washington." Instead, they urged Ottawa to chart an independent course in the world.[50] Formed in reaction to the Vietnam War and the seeming unwillingness of Canada's government to denounce US conduct for fear of economic retaliation, such views were predicated on a desire for Canadian foreign policy to shift away from its support of the Cold War consensus built around containing communism. Pressure on this score had begun to intensify under Diefenbaker's watch. But Diefenbaker was no neutralist. Rhetorically, he sought to differentiate his policies from those of Washington; in reality Canada often supported the United States, at least on key Cold War issues, less so on more strictly bilateral questions.

What proponents of an independent foreign policy ignored was that a convergence of views with the Americans on the dangers posed by the Soviet Union, support for the postwar order founded on US economic and military might, and a desire to assist its foremost ally did not mean that Canada was a satellite. Rather, it meant that Ottawa and Washington shared similar interests. Despite their doubts about the growing belligerence of US foreign policy, Canadian foreign policymakers were largely "conservative" in their outlook, were certainly anti-Communist, and were definitely pro-Western.[51] Cold War differences between Ottawa and Washington centered on means, not ends. Much to their chagrin, the differences over means served as an indication to American officials that Canada pursued an independent foreign policy—Canadian nationalists may have doubted Canada's independence, but US policymakers had no doubts in this regard. Growing Canadian nationalism only underscored the sense in Washington that Canada and the United States were parting ways.

Much of the nationalist argument for an independent foreign policy in the 1960s was really an argument for a neutral foreign policy, reflecting left-wing revulsion at the excesses of US conduct abroad. The extent to which these views were shared by the broad swathe of Canada's populace is beyond the scope of this study. But in the early 1960s, it seemed to American diplomats that many Canadians supported nationalist goals. And who could fault them for thinking this way? After all, the two main political parties contained their share of influential proponents of nationalism—and Diefenbaker had won a massive majority on a nationalist plank in another general election in March 1958—and the voices of nationalists in the press, in academe, and in the publishing world were growing ever louder. Furthermore, to US policymakers, anti-Americanism appeared to be a growing global phenomenon.

Since, in a sense, they were the targets of Canadian nationalists and because this force was seen to have a negative impact on the quiet conduct of Canada–US relations, this study demonstrates how US officials viewed and reacted to this development. The American appreciation for the influence of Canadian nationalism has largely been overlooked or downplayed. "For a jingoistic and self-obsessed country like the United States," contends historian Bruce Muirhead, "it is odd that its officials seemed unable to understand the attraction of Canadian nationalism for Canadians." For the Americans, nationalism, historian Robert Bothwell insists, was a "minor irritant," with the term "used in the period to explain any and all actions that Washington considered irrational or inexplicable."[52] As for anti-Americanism, a perceptive scholar of this phenomenon argues that it was "understood as an explanation for the source of opposition to U.S. policies abroad"; meanwhile, American self-assurance created a tendency to view such criticisms as illogical and so "not worth taking seriously."[53] Certainly US officials found Canada's developing sense of nationalism irrational, and they were ready to dismiss Canadian criticism; but they in no way saw this phenomenon as an inconsequential annoyance. A standard point made in American briefing material throughout the period was that "the primary problem in U.S.–Canadian relations lies in the evolving nationalist feeling and sensibilities of Canadians confronted with the over-shadowing power and influence of the U.S."[54] On the whole, US officials acted in accordance with this sense of nationalism's primacy. Hence, although the personality differences between Kennedy and Diefenbaker were important, the influence, or perceived influence, of Canadian nationalism was profound. Anti-Americanism in its Canadian form seemed to have definite causal power.

Interestingly, US diplomats drew sharp differences between Canadian nationalism and anti-Americanism, noting that Canadians did not hate the United States, as the latter term would imply. In the autumn of 1960, for instance, the US Embassy in Ottawa, alarmed by reports of growing anti-Americanism in the press, asked the US consulates across Canada to survey local opinion of the United States. The results were reassuring, for they confirmed the views of embassy officials who believed that "there has not been any significant increase in anti-American sentiment in Canada."[55] However, there was growing nationalism. A month after the above conclusion was drawn, the Embassy in Ottawa produced a policy document promoting the view that "the chief problem the United States faces in its relations with Canada lies in certain manifestations of Canadian nationalism which arise from the facts that (1) Canada is one-tenth the size of the United States, (2) most Canadians live within 150 miles of the border, and (3) Canada has no other close neighbors." Often, as an American intelligence report produced in 1961 argued, Canadian nationalism bore "anti-American overtones."[56] And, as the US ambassador observed the following year, "I am satisfied that anti-Americanism just does not exist in the population as a whole. In fact, the reverse is true," with harsh criticisms of the United States confined to "a vociferous minority" in certain political, academic, and intellectual circles.[57] American observers, then, were concerned less with anti-Americanism than with Canadian nationalism, a far more potent force toward which they expressed understanding and sympathy.

The growth of nationalist sentiments injected a consequential factor into Canada–US relations. One of the most important studies on this relationship has highlighted a "psychological-cultural" component to bilateral relations, which "is probably more critical in explaining disputes between the governments" than disparities in military or economic power. This feature manifests "in the well-known American tendency to 'take Canada for granted' and in the Canadian proneness to feel a mixture of envy and ambivalence regarding the United States."[58] The sense of being overlooked by their southern neighbors is a constant refrain in Canada. In February 1957, Frank Underhill famously remarked: "Americans are benevolently ignorant about Canada, whereas Canadians are malevolently informed about the United States." Four years later, Diefenbaker complained to Kennedy that Canadians read "quantities of news about the United States and welcome the President every week via TV into [their] living rooms but that Canadian news gets less treatment in the United States than that from a 'banana republic.'"[59] Malevolently informed about Canadian nationalism, the Kennedy administration spent considerable time on Canadian issues.

But Americans did not see Canadian nationalism as the only driver of Canadian policy. Alongside this phenomenon was a sense that Diefenbaker, especially, was motivated by domestic political concerns, which in turn were influenced by nationalism, two factors that explained the conduct of Pearson's Liberals, too. These twin elements seemed to make Ottawa reluctant to cooperate with and eager to prove its independence from Washington. Nationalism and electoral calculations, US observers felt, could be blamed for Canada's resistance to British entry into the European Economic Community, for Ottawa's delay in arming its forces with nuclear weapons, for Canadian protectionist trade measures, and for the Diefenbaker and Pearson governments' reluctance to take a wider role in Latin America or to cut commercial ties with Cuba and China. This explanatory framework informed the decisions made and actions taken by the Kennedy administration in its dealings with its northern ally. The picture that emerges as a result is of a president more patient and less imperious toward Canada than other historians suggest.

Kennedy's reputation among Canadian historians is not good. For Canada he was, according to J. L. Granatstein, "the first President in the postwar era to use American muscle to achieve his ends," while Stephen Randall has contended that the "activist Cold Warriors of the Kennedy administration had no patience" for the subtleties of Canadian policy.[60] In studies of the Canada–US relationship in this period a contrast usually is drawn between two groups: the State Department, with its collection of Canadianists, professional diplomats who were well-versed with Canada; and Kennedy administration officials who were ingénues when it came to Canadian affairs. Criticizing Kennedy's personal attitude toward Canada as "patronizing and dismissive," two historians have argued that the Kennedy administration put into place a foreign policymaking structure that gave primacy to the White House and National Security Council (NSC), and that lessened the influence of the State Department, "which had been traditionally knowledgeable about, and more sensitive toward, Canadian concerns." Another scholar, meanwhile, contends that "American officials and cabinet members hardly thought it necessary to have a policy for Canada." Bilateral relations suffered because they were "taken out of the hands of State's Canadianist corps" and placed under the gaze of "surprised and impatient U.S. presidents and their NSC colleagues," a process that began with Kennedy.[61] These contentions are either unfounded or in need of nuance.

It is true that Canada was not a former great power like Britain, France, or West Germany, nor was it a rising regional power like Egypt, India, or Indonesia. Nevertheless it was an important country, occupying a significant—indeed unenviable—geographic position between the two superpowers. Further, it provided strategic resources, contributed forces to the defense of Western Europe, and served as an invaluable destination for American capital and goods. Officials in Washington were well aware of these facts and hence of Canada's importance to their own country. "The problem with the Kennedy White House," a recent argument goes, "was that it did not view Canada as a partner, nor the US as a country needing Canada's support."[62] Why, then, did Kennedy seek Canadian support—to name but three examples—over Cuba, Laos, and continental defense? Canada was also seen to have a place in the rapidly evolving transatlantic relationship. "Europe and the United States and Canada," the US secretary of state told a Senate committee in 1962, "can grow increasingly closer together and work as a team on more and more subjects." And as Kennedy explained to reporters several months before his assassination, "I think Western Europe and the United States, and Canada, Great Britain, and the Commonwealth, have a major role in serving as the center or the core of a great effort throughout the world to maintain freedom."[63] Canada did matter to the Kennedy administration, even if it was simply one of many old allies. For this reason, the Americans—including key policymakers in the White House and NSC—adopted an overarching framework, enunciated in numerous reports, memoranda, and policy documents, which called for a patient and understanding approach to relations with a country that easily bristled at any suggestion of American interference.

Despite the primacy of Kennedy's NSC, the State Department was not shunted aside when it came to policymaking toward Canada. Moreover, at Foggy Bottom and at the US Embassy in Ottawa, many of the diplomats who dealt with Diefenbaker's government during the Kennedy years were the same figures who had made policy toward Canada throughout the Eisenhower era. Although comparisons have been drawn between the Eisenhower team's "congenial, respectful and sensitive" stance toward Canadian concerns and the Kennedy White House's "aggressive, and sometime arrogant" position, when it came to Canada, the New Frontiersmen mostly stuck to their predecessors' script.[64] Indeed, along with the professional corps of Canadianists in the State Department, Kennedy administration officials, supposedly heavy-handed bullies, pursued even-handed treatment of Canada, becoming the "tolerant allies" of the Johnson administration.[65]

Certainly, American officials could be arrogant. Writing to the incoming US ambassador to Ottawa in late 1962, Willis Armstrong, one the foremost Canadianists within the State Department, commented: "The more we can keep [Canadian] attention focused on Europe, Asia or some other place, the less we are subjected to morbid mutterings about bilateral affairs." Similarly, in a letter to the president of the American Bar Association, who was due to speak in Canada, Livingston Merchant advised that certain things should go unmentioned. "As you will gather from the line pursued by the President and by us in the Embassy," Merchant wrote, "we are seeking to deemphasize public comment by United States officials on strictly bilateral problems which are admittedly important, but which do not necessarily improve with public discussion in Canada, because of the emotional content which some of these topics impart."[66] However condescending their tone, these were private reflections on Canada—from the professional Canadianists no less—that indicate the amount of frustration that US officials felt when it came to managing the bilateral relationship in a period of growing nationalism. Indeed, given their difficulties with Canada, arrogance was understandable.

No doubt this arrogance is easy to condemn as typical of Americans, firm in their belief both of their own superiority and of their country's exceptionalism. It is undeniable that such ideological views have motivated US officials in their dealings with foreigners, Canadians included.[67] American authorities, in believing that anyone objecting to their views must be beholden to the politics of irrational domestic nationalism, missed the point that the United States could be as much a problem as a solution in the international arena. Charles Ritchie, Canada's ambassador in Washington in the mid-1960s, would complain in his diary that "to the Americans, the irrationality of their allies and their own rationality is an absolute assumption."[68] Yet Canadians, too, saw that in their dealings with Americans their own actions could be irrational, driven, as they were, by emotional and psychological responses. To take but four examples from disparate voices: in late 1960, Canada's United Church complained that "like children, we often show our irritation at being ignored" by Americans; early the next year, Hugh MacLennan, novelist and nationalist, explained that "nations, like individuals, are likely to be neurotic, and Canada's history and location have conspired to qualify here for a pretty high place on the neurotic list," while in a plea for quiet diplomacy, Peyton Lyon admitted that public disputes with Washington were "gratifying to the Canadian ego." Finally, in 1966, historian Frank Underhill noted that Canadians cannot "discuss our relations with the United States in a cool, rational frame of mind."[69] Thus, American diplomats were not alone in perceiving the emotional sources of Canadian policy. Nor were such perceptions out of place, given psychology and psychiatry's postwar popularity. As C. Wright Mills had declared in 1951: "We need to characterize American society of the mid-twentieth century in more psychological terms, for now the problems that concern us most border on the psychiatric."[70]

Regardless of their views on the irrationality of Canadian nationalism, which were neither original nor unique, on the whole, and in spite of their grumbling, when it came to dealing with their Canadian counterparts, Merchant, Armstrong, and other US officials were fair and forthright. As for Kennedy, among historians who study America in the world, the trend of late has been to decry the actions of his administration. One of the president's sharpest critics has argued that Kennedy's actions abroad do "not merit the acclaim" given him by his court historians or by generations of Americans who look back wistfully upon his thousand days in office. It is fair to argue that, writ large, the Kennedy administration adopted an "aggressive, militaristic, confrontational attitude" toward many nations.[71] But what is true for US conduct with Cuba, Vietnam, or British Guiana is not true of Canada. Conscious of Canadian nationalism and cognizant of Canada's independence, American foreign policymakers were careful in seeking out Ottawa's cooperation, which they judged to be important. Indeed, the Kennedy White House was adept at handling nationalists from a variety of countries from the newly independent world. Here, though, a key ingredient was the president's willingness to engage in personal diplomacy with his counterparts from countries as far afield as India, Ghana, and Indonesia.[72] Personal relations also undergirded Kennedy's "special relationship" with British Prime Minister Harold Macmillan.[73] During the early days of his presidency, Kennedy pursued such an approach with Diefenbaker, one that paid few dividends for the Americans and was quickly, and ill-advisedly, abandoned. Even so, the president remained committed to a forbearing policy toward Ottawa. That relations between Camelot and Canada took a turn for the worse is a result of action—or, frequently, inaction—taken in the Canadian capital, not in Washington.

John Kennedy was not the first American president with whom John Diefenbaker dealt, and so for the sake of comparison, chapter 1 reviews the Eisenhower administration's handling of the relationship with Canada from

1957 to 1961. This period saw the revival of Canadian nationalism, a force that contributed to back-to-back electoral victories by Diefenbaker's Tories as well as to increasing bilateral tensions. Dealing with Diefenbaker's February 1961 visit to the White House and Kennedy's reciprocal visit to Ottawa that May, chapter 2 also examines Canadian–American relations against the backdrop of the Cold War's "twilight struggle" in the Third World. Although disagreeing over how to contain communism in Asia and Latin America, Ottawa and Washington shared a common interest in defending the interests of the West, and so they sought to avoid mutual conflict and even aid one another. Common Cold War interests also united Canada and the United States in the summer of 1961, as a crisis with the Soviet Union over the status of Berlin had the potential to devolve into war. As chapter 3 makes clear, Berlin and the related fear of a nuclear conflict led Canada to closely align itself with the United States, but also led many Canadians to champion disarmament and oppose the Canada–US military alliance. These competing forces had a profound impact on Diefenbaker's handling of defense policy, toward which the Kennedy administration displayed patience and understanding—though frustration began to grow.

Mutual frustration and recrimination marked Canadian and American relations over a host of economic questions during the Kennedy period, especially on the important issues stemming from Britain's 1961 decision to join the European Common Market. The fallout from this move, which poisoned the relationship between Kennedy and Diefenbaker, and economic relations more broadly, are discussed in chapter 4. The importance of the break between president and prime minister was made clear in October 1962. In response to revelations that the Soviet Union was installing nuclear missiles in Cuba, Kennedy blockaded the island. With the world on the brink of nuclear war, Diefenbaker refused to back his American counterpart. Yet as is pointed out in chapter 5, throughout this standoff, and in terms of Cuba more generally, Canada offered quiet assistance to the United States. However, the Cuban missile crisis brought to the fore the simmering issue of whether or not Canada would acquire nuclear warheads for its military. Chapter 6 offers an overview of what then became a domestic political crisis in Canada as well as a crisis in Canadian–American relations. The result was the collapse of Diefenbaker's government, for which the United States bears some blame, and a divisive election. Finally, the epilogue deals with Canada–US relations during the eight-month overlap between Kennedy and Lester Pearson, a period that indicated that bilateral tension would continue as would rising Canadian nationalism. In the face of nationalist discontent, as in response to a variety of policy differences with their northern neighbors, the Kennedy administration and the corps of Canadianists in the State Department displayed considerable forbearance, a reflection of the good feeling underscoring the special relationship between the two countries in the era of quiet diplomacy.

# 1

# Good Fences

*Canadian–American Relations
from Eisenhower to Kennedy, 1957–1961*

Visiting Canada for the first time in December 1953 to deliver an address at the University of Montréal, John Kennedy, the young junior senator from Massachusetts, spoke largely in platitudes, raising "the peaceful maintenance of the Canadian–American border," the "indissoluble" ties that bound together the two countries, and Ottawa and Washington's example of international cooperation. In Canada four years later to attend a convocation ceremony at the University of New Brunswick, Kennedy toned down this folksy rhetoric. Instead, he showed considerable understanding of the forces shaping Canadian politics. Only months before, Canada's Liberal government, in power for two decades, had fallen to John Diefenbaker's Progressive Conservatives. Kennedy was not ignorant of this momentous change. In his remarks he praised Diefenbaker's desire to promote a distinctive Canadian identity, noting that Canada had "achieved a national strength and prestige which simply does not allow any portrayal of the country as an appendage of either Great Britain or the United States." Indeed, the country possessed "a national destiny of its own to which it is well and timely to give foremost recognition." Then acknowledging Canadian anxieties with living so close to his own country, the young senator turned to lines from a poem by Robert Frost: "Canada and the United States have carefully maintained the good fences that help make them good neighbors."[1]

More than a cliché about the Canadian–American relationship, Kennedy's acknowledgment of the need for good fences highlights his awareness of the nationalist tenor in Canada. The following year saw the publication of Joseph Barber's *Good Fences Make Good Neighbors: Why the United States Provokes Canadians*, an entertaining but serious travelogue that exposed "the latest ground swell of anti-American feeling" and the danger of American "carelessness" toward Canada.[2] Kennedy's recognition of the growing nationalist

feeling—which had propelled Diefenbaker to victory in the 1957 election—
hardly seems to represent the views of a man "activated by the belief that
Canada owed so great a debt to the United States that nothing but continuing subservience could repay it." Nor did they reflect the outlook of someone
who "was indifferent to Canadian nationalism" or whose "posture toward
Diefenbaker's Canada was that of a president stretching his legs across the
Canadian border and demanding a shoeshine."[3] Rather, Kennedy had summed
up the Canadian zeitgeist. So impressed was he by this speech that meeting
with Kennedy in 1961, Diefenbaker spoke very highly of it.[4] As the young senator had acknowledged, Canada in 1957 was at a crucial point in its modern
political and economic development and in its relationship with the United
States.

At this juncture, the link between Canadian–American relations and
Canada's economic, cultural, and political growth was palpable. In the first
postwar decade Canada had experienced massive economic growth, going,
as one journalist put it, from an "Unknown Country" in 1942 to, in 1957,
"Tomorrow's Giant," a "new world power ... taking shape on the northern slope of the planet."[5] Canada's growth had been reliant upon economic
ties with the United States, and by the late 1950s there was a sense among
Canadians that their country had become too close with the behemoth to the
south. Canadian politicians, academics, and journalists bristled at the extent
of US investment in Canada—the level more than doubling between 1950 and
1958 from US\$3.58 billion to US\$8.33 billion—across a wide range of sectors
from mining and manufacturing to timber and oil and gas extraction. The *New
York Times* would gush that "Canada is burgeoning with earthly riches that can
be transformed into the instruments of war," but many Canadians were worried that despite postwar Canadian prosperity the sale of resources was tying
Canada too closely to its southern neighbor, generating, as a British journalist
living in Canada put it, "attitudes which from across the border may seem like
anti-Americanism" but which were only "the readiest expression of Canadian
nationalism."[6] In a broader context, Cold War fears had led Ottawa to support
Washington's leadership in the bipolar struggle, while during the Suez crisis
of 1956 Canada's Liberal government had sided not with Britain, but with the
United States. Canadian diplomats won rave reviews abroad for their crisis
management at the United Nations, but at home government politicians were
hammered for acting, as one leading Tory put it, as "the United States chore
boy."[7] Concerns among Canadians extended to increasing Canada–US military
ties, to belligerent American Cold War rhetoric, and to McCarthyism. Such
sentiments reflected international trends: Graham Greene's novel *The Quiet
American* (1955) and Eugene Burdick and William Lederer's *The Ugly American*
(1958) were influential critiques of the arrogant nature of US foreign policy,
while Neil Shute's novel *On the Beach* (1957), portraying the horrific reality

of nuclear war, became a stark 1959 film. The late 1950s saw a deterioration of the postwar calm in Canada–US relations and a fraying of the Cold War consensus that had united both countries during and after the Second World War.[8] Summing up Canadian malaise in a speech at Michigan State University in February 1957, historian Frank Underhill observed that every few decades "the fever rises in our blood, we gird up our loins under the leadership of some inspiring prophet-saviour, and once again we save ourselves from the United States." That period was arriving, bringing with it, he felt, "more anti-American speech-making and editorializing in Canada than I have known in my lifetime. We are waiting for the prophet-saviour to emerge."[9]

A gifted orator, John Diefenbaker—the prophet-savior—drew on this unease and its long historical roots. His ascendancy seemed to herald a confrontational era in North America, one that began well before John Kennedy assumed the presidency. There is a tendency to view US policy toward Canada during the Kennedy years as a break from the established pattern. But strains in the bilateral relationship were already apparent when Kennedy took office, as was a distinct American approach to Canadian affairs, one that outlived the 1960 presidential election. Historians have a proclivity to contrast Kennedy's handling of Canada–US relations with that of his predecessor, Dwight Eisenhower. But Kennedy was not "less patient" than Eisenhower, and while the old general certainly "understood how to jolly Diefenbaker along," he oversaw what seemed to observers on both sides of the border to be the deterioration of the bilateral relationship.[10] "As you know," one long serving Canadian diplomat remarked to a White House official in July 1960, "U.S.–Canadian relations are at their worst."[11] Despite diplomats' efforts to quietly resolve bilateral issues from nuclear arms to the embargo of Cuba, when Kennedy took the oath of office six months later he inherited a host of outstanding problems with Canada, a country that was bristling with nationalist fervor. Quickly, the young president became attuned to the style of Canadian–American relations, adopting a patient and understanding approach, reflective of his sense of what made good neighbors.

For Livingston Merchant, the US ambassador in Ottawa, Diefenbaker's campaign rhetoric in 1957 caused considerable consternation. A Princeton graduate, a former Wall Street lawyer, and a State Department veteran, by the time of Diefenbaker's election Merchant had been in the Canadian capital for a year. With the Tories coming into office he sensed that his position was about to become more stressful. On the day after Diefenbaker's win Merchant forecast an "intensification of nationalistic feeling," which could mean that trouble, at least in the economic field, lay ahead. Such foreboding soon gave way to a calmer assessment of Diefenbaker. Merchant left his first meeting with the new prime minister pleased that while certainly nationalistic, the new government was not anti-American and that there would be "no change in the fundamentals of Canadian foreign policy." Secretary of State John Foster Dulles, a dour Cold Warrior, shared this largely positive view. Two days in Ottawa in July 1957 convinced him that Diefenbaker, although certainly quite "Commonwealth minded," nevertheless was "the kind of person we can get along with."[12]

A month into his premiership, the new prime minister, motivated by his Commonwealth-minded outlook, announced a fanciful plan to shift 15 percent of Canada's trade from the United States to the United Kingdom. Looking to this announcement's obvious political overtones, the American ambassador in London sloughed off what seemed an impossible goal.[13] This relaxed assessment was warranted. The proposal was a dud, in part because the British had their eyes set on increasing trade with Europe, not Canada. Diefenbaker's plan also ignored both the facts of geography and the pull of the massive American market. However ill-conceived, the diversion plan reflected the new government's fear of their country's reliance on its southern neighbor. Of course, the Americans were also reliant upon the Canadians. At a meeting of US ambassadors soon after, Merchant underscored that Canada was their country's most important trading partner, with "territory and resources ... essential to our military defense" and "whose influence has been exercised mostly in support of U.S. objectives." But "major and growing problems" were evident as a result of US investment, a $1.5 billion trade deficit in 1956, and "a latent but basic resentment" of American wealth and power. The Diefenbaker government, he continued, preached a "more pro-Canadian" stance that could "merge into anti-Americanism," but that almost certainly would mean that Canada, while remaining an ally, would be "less imaginative, constructive, active and helpful to the U.S."[14] While his judgment of Canadian resentment may have been off-kilter, the rest of his diagnosis was sound. Addressing graduates at Dartmouth College in late 1957, Diefenbaker outlined his broad support of Washington but also his sense of the "inherent dangers" stemming from the fact that Canada's "trading world has become increasingly confined to the United States." In aiming to reduce this danger, he would target the level of American investment north of the border and the trade imbalance between the two countries. He was clear to note, though, that his government "is not now and will not be, anti-American."[15]

Diefenbaker's anxieties over continental integration had been given a public airing when the Royal Commission on Canada's Economic Prospects, chaired by the prominent businessman—and Liberal insider—Walter Gordon, released its findings in a series of alarmist reports in 1956 and 1957, leading Diefenbaker to charge in the 1957 campaign that the Liberals sought to make Canada into "a virtual 49th economic state." The American press, picking up on this "antipathy" toward their country, predicted tough times ahead. "To almost every Canadian," warned *Time*, "the U.S. is an enveloping fact of life."[16] Canadian fears and antipathies dominated the 1957 joint Canada–US committee on trade and economic affairs, which met in Washington soon after the election. Established in 1954, and an exemplar of the close North American relationship, these annual ministerial summits allowed senior officials from both countries to engage in informal consultations. Canada's finance minister, Donald Fleming, an accomplished Toronto lawyer and an influential member of the Progressive Conservative's corporate-friendly wing, dominated the 1957 forum by raising the "substantial problems" existing in the two countries' economic relations. His government "had a mandate to interpret what it considers is the will of the Canadian people," and sensing that Canadians were unhappy with the current penetration of Canada's economy by US capital, Fleming warned that Ottawa intended to act accordingly.[17] Bluster aside, ultimately the Tories proved largely unwilling or unable to take action against American economic interests in Canada, with Diefenbaker going so far as to the sack James Coyne, the governor of the Bank in Canada, whose tight monetary policy was geared, in part, toward discouraging foreign—especially American—investment. The Diefenbaker government's defense of the economic status quo upset Gordon, who would later lead a groundswell of nationalism that stressed Canada's status as a colony of the United States.

At the time, though, it was unclear how successful the Tories would be in their effort to put a nationalistic program into place. Throughout the 1950s the chairman of Eisenhower's Council on Foreign Economic Policy, Clarence Randall, had carefully pushed the notion of a North American customs union. Dulles opposed the idea, emphasizing that it would be untimely to raise the issue given the Diefenbaker's government's "strongly nationalistic motivation."[18] This motivation was on the minds of many Americans at this point. Writing in late 1957, former Secretary of State Dean Acheson lamented that Canadian "resentment against United States public policy and private interests has assumed considerable proportions," while that summer McGeorge Bundy, president of Harvard College and Kennedy's future national security advisor, would tell the Couchiching Conference that given sentiments in Canada, the United States "must respect Canadian interests which may be unwelcome to some Americans."[19] Analyzing the situation for Americans in the influential journal *Foreign Affairs*, Michael Barkway, a reporter for the *Financial Times* and the *Economist*, examined the Diefenbaker phenomenon and its implications for Canada's foreign policy. Canadians, Barkway wrote, were in the midst of rediscovering their history, meaning a rediscovery of nationalism, which stemmed from a belief that ties between Canada and the United States had grown far too close throughout the 1940s and 1950s in contrast to the traditional caution that Canadians had shown in dealings with their southern neighbor. For Barkway, the results of the 1957 election demonstrated that Canadian voters were growing cautious. Observers on both sides of the border could expect to encounter a "restoration of the tension" between a desire for Canadian nationhood and the attraction of the United States. Henceforth there would "be much less pretense from north of the border that Canadian and American interests necessarily march side by side," along with "less inclination to silence legitimate Canadian claims for fear of provoking American retaliation in some unrelated sector."[20] In short, Canada would be much less quiet in its dealings with the United States.

As Barkway's article went to print in early 1958, his observations were only confirmed by the results of a snap election, from which Diefenbaker emerged with the largest majority of seats in the House of Commons to that point in Canadian history. The result led to an outpouring of attention from the American press. The *Chicago Tribune*'s Canadian correspondent reported that Diefenbaker had capitalized on a quasi-anti-Americanism, a "spirit of resentment and jealousy of the United states which has existed on this side of the border since 1776," while the *New York Times*' correspondent in Canada took a more measured view of the "new spirit of Canadian nationalism," which was not anti-American but "an assertive pro-Canadianism." Given the election result, the *Washington Post*, meanwhile, forecast the likelihood of "touchy" relations, and urged Americans to "be more solicitous about opinion north of the border."[21] Soon the *New York Times* would declare that unlike anti-Americanism, Canadian nationalism was "prideful, honest, and healthy," a judgment with which the *Los Angeles Times*' Bill Henry agreed. Diefenbaker, he wrote, "has demonstrated nothing worse than a perfectly natural desire to further the best interests of Canada." More skeptical, doubtless because of its preoccupation with economic matters, the *Wall Street Journal* contended that while it was fine that Diefenbaker was set to pursue positive nationalism, there was "no reason for Americans to forget that anti-U.S. feeling played a role in his election and that this feeling among some Canadians is a serious fact of life that the United States has to contend with."[22] Such comments indicate American awareness of Canada's growing importance, of Canada's relationship with their own country, and of Canadian nationalism's apparent power and appeal. Meanwhile, concerns over growing bilateral friction, or its potential, had led to the formation in 1957 of the Canadian–American Committee, a joint effort by the National Planning Association in the United States and the Private Planning Association of Canada, two umbrella organizations of business groups hoping to keep the Canada–US relationship functioning smoothly. To better understand bilateral relations, in 1959 Assumption University in Windsor, Ontario, just across the border from Detroit, inaugurated an annual seminar series bringing together politicians, diplomats, academics, and businesspeople interested in Canada and the United States. Together, these efforts in which elements of civil society sought to promote a more harmonious relationship between the two North American countries attest to the ferment caused by Canadian nationalism.

Diefenbaker's resounding victory and a more nationalistic Canada did little to mar the prime minister's relationship with the US president. There "was no limit to Mr. Eisenhower's congeniality and friendliness," the prime minister informed his Cabinet colleagues after first meeting the president in October 1957.[23] Over the next three years, the two men developed a friendly, productive rapport, although one that did not prevent a steady deterioration in the bilateral relationship at least at the level of public opinion, thus highlighting the often disjunctive nature of international relations. They worked together on the completion of the St. Lawrence Seaway, a symbolic and economically important project finally begun in 1954 as an effort to create a deep-water channel linking the Great Lakes to the St. Lawrence River and then to the Atlantic.[24] This massive operation, also involving the construction of hydroelectric facilities, was completed in 1959, and Eisenhower and Diefenbaker attended the opening ceremonies, although it was Queen Elizabeth II who formally opened the seaway on Canada's behalf. A more important—if less tangible—development was the signing of the North American Air Defence Command (NORAD) agreement.

Like the Seaway project, which had begun under the previous Liberal government but was completed under Diefenbaker's watch, talks between the Canadian and American militaries over forming a joint command for continental air defense were concluded just as Diefenbaker became prime minister. The threat of a Soviet nuclear attack on North America had resulted in the intertwining of Canadian and American air defenses throughout the 1950s, including the construction of vast lines of radar installations stretching across Canada's north. Despite the asymmetry in power, in negotiations with Washington on these measures, Ottawa had been able to protect its interests.[25] The central goal for both countries, though, was to defend the US nuclear deterrent by providing advanced warning of an attack, thus affording an opportunity both to intercept Soviet bombers and to allow American bombers to deliver a retaliatory strike. Setting up NORAD was the next step in this process. Diefenbaker signed the agreement in July 1957, after only several weeks in office, doing so without consultation with his Cabinet, the Cabinet Defence Committee, or the Department of External Affairs (DEA). NORAD became operational in September that year.

Some observers have contended that Diefenbaker had signed the agreement without fully realizing the extent to which NORAD could limit independent Canadian decision-making during crisis situations. A partnership between Ottawa and Washington was enshrined in the agreement, but in practical terms the United States was clearly the senior partner and the prime target for a Soviet attack. Basil Robinson, a rising star in the DEA who was assigned as a liaison between Canada's foreign ministry and the prime minister, later recalled that External Affairs was stunned both that they had not been consulted and that such an important decision had been made without thought having been given to "the non-military implications" of this move.[26] Alarmed, Canadian diplomats pushed for the arrangement to be formalized to oblige Washington to consult with Ottawa in the event of a crisis. Diefenbaker agreed, and during talks with Eisenhower in October 1957 he won a concession: the president agreed that in an emergency, the commander of NORAD would have to be in communication with both the president and the prime minister. A pledge for consultation then found its way into a formalized agreement, completed in May 1958.[27] Two months later, when Diefenbaker and Eisenhower met in Ottawa, the prime minister underscored Canadians' "wide-spread fear . . . that they were sacrificing sovereignty by turning their squadrons over to an American General." To reassure Canadians, he suggested the creation of a joint defense committee—modeled on the joint economic committee—allowing cabinet members and senior government officials from both countries to discuss defense issues. Given the deep cooperation on defense this was a prudent step, one that acknowledged the need for consultation in an area where disagreements could be damaging not just to bilateral relations, but also to both countries' physical security. Initially doubtful, Eisenhower relented.[28] The Canada–United States joint defense committee first met that December.

Worries over deepening economic ties between Canada and the United States aside, Diefenbaker, conscious of the Soviet threat, was willing to deepen his country's alliance with Washington. These ties were signified not only by the NORAD agreement, but also by the prime minister's decision to acquire new weapon systems: surface-to-surface Honest John missiles and CF-104 Starfighter fighter-bombers, both meant to assist in repelling a Soviet invasion of Western Europe; and Boeing-Michigan Aeronautical Research Center (BOMARC) surface-to-air missiles based at launch sites were to be built in North Bay, Ontario and in La Macaza, Quebec. Designed to destroy incoming Soviet bombers, the Eisenhower administration championed BOMARC as "integral" to continental defense.[29] Eventually, Ottawa would also acquire CF-101 Voodoo interceptor aircraft, meant to shoot down Soviet bombers with tactical nuclear missiles. As Diefenbaker informed the House of Commons in February 1959, the "full potential" of these "defensive weapons" would be "achieved only when they are armed with nuclear warheads." Despite this claim, he was careful to not actually commit to accepting the warheads even as he promised that Canada would play its part fully "in terms both of quantity and quality in deterring and resisting aggression."[30] This disconnect would prove contentious and ultimately fatal for Diefenbaker's government, but is understandable given the momentousness of the decision.

Alongside the prime minister's hesitancy about acquiring nuclear warheads, and beneath the veneer of civility between Diefenbaker and Eisenhower, lurked growing resentment in Canada over the alliance with the United States. Not long after the decision to adopt BOMARC, the prime minister remarked that while he personally liked Eisenhower, he was annoyed by the extent to which Washington was seeking Ottawa's cooperation on joint defense exercises. Diefenbaker was supported by Howard Green, who in June 1959 became secretary of state for external affairs and who believed that to safeguard Canadian sovereignty, the Americans need "not be given all that they asked for" in terms of continental defense.[31] A long-serving MP and one of Diefenbaker's key political allies, Green was also a standard-bearer for nuclear disarmament and for ratcheting down Cold War tension, goals he pursued fervently as foreign minister. These pursuits conflicted with the defense commitments that Diefenbaker had spelled out in February 1959. Green was no neutralist. Rather, he was genuinely concerned over the implications of atomic warfare and the very real health effects of nuclear testing.[32] However, American officials characterized his stance toward the East–West confrontation as "naïve," and they watched him with considerable wariness. Green, the State Department judged, was "sincere, honest, earnest, and a man of strong principles," but also "less flexible" than Diefenbaker, more "sensitive to any implied interference with Canada's independence," and driven by an "almost pacifist attitude." Another senior American diplomat concluded simply that Green was "both stupid and self-righteous."[33] Among Diefenbaker's Cabinet ministers Green was viewed as the chief advocate of an independent line in foreign affairs, and, thus the largest impediment to Canada adopting policies aligning with US foreign policy.

While an important voice within the government, Green also exemplified a movement in Canada skeptical of the military ties between Ottawa and Washington in an era where the threat of a nuclear conflagration was all too real. In parallel with developments in Britain and the United States, the late 1950s and early 1960s saw the formation of Canadian anti-nuclear groups— part of a growing anti-nuclear movement in Western countries—including the Combined Universities Campaign for Nuclear Disarmament, the Canadian Committee for the Control of Radiation Hazards, and the Voice of Women. As one senior organizer of the latter group noted, anti-nuclear activists aimed "to speak out against the tensions of the cold war and the imminent threat of nuclear conflict."[34] Many of their apprehensions were widely aired in 1960, when James Minifie, the Washington correspondent for the Canadian Broadcasting Corporation, published *Peacemaker or Powdermonkey?*, a bestselling polemic capturing the anxiety resulting from the apparent loss of Canadian independence, US belligerence, and Ottawa's support for the Eisenhower administration's foreign policy. Canada, Minifie wrote, possessed a host of attributes that would make it a significant world power, yet such "superb advantages" were "cancelled out" by close alignment with the Americans. Minifie's prescription was for Canada to become neutral. Staunchly anti-Communist, Diefenbaker disagreed with Minifie.[35] Even so, Minifie's views had a growing cachet, with disarmament sentiments playing an important role in the deterioration of Canada–US relations during Kennedy's presidency.

Not all Canadians felt unease over relations with the United States. Arnold Heeney, Canada's ambassador in Washington from 1953 to 1957 and again from 1959 to 1962, confessed in 1959 to being troubled by the "aftermath" of the last two Canadian federal elections, which had left a palpable sense of "suspicion" and "resentment" of the United States. The mood created by the electioneering had mixed with "ignorance" of American domestic and international problems to create a sort of "anti-Americanism," which could "be found in the highest quarters of Canada—in the government, in Parliament, in the press and among people generally." Canadian–American relations, Heeney worried, were moving "into a much more serious phase," one where "the fault is largely—and perhaps mostly—on our side where many tend to equate criticism of [the United States] with patriotism."[36] A Rhodes scholar—like many of his colleagues in External Affairs—Heeney had pursued a career in the civil service, prized smooth relations with Washington, and held deep sympathy for the United States' role in the world. He was the exemplar of the quiet diplomatist: an insider who valued a strong working relationship with his American counterparts. Nevertheless, Heeney was a determined advocate of Canadian interests and viewpoints. A tough negotiator, he put Canada's interests first, prompting one frustrated US diplomat to complain that for all his talk of a mutual harmony of interests between Ottawa and Washington, Heeney exemplified "a brand of nationalism that has a carefully concealed but none-the-less anti-American core," a comment reflecting US officials' predilection to see nationalist sentiment behind any dispute with Canada.[37]

Not that the Americans were wrong to highlight the importance of Canadian nationalism. As early as January 1958, with Diefenbaker's first government in office for only several months, Merchant had told a Canadian audience of his worry over a noticeable "change in mood or climate" in bilateral relations over the previous year. He expanded on this theme in testimony before the Senate Foreign Relations Committee that May, informing lawmakers that "notwithstanding the basic soundness" of bilateral relations, "there is in this rapidly developing nation a growing consciousness of national destiny and nationalism." He was careful to draw an important distinction—as US officials would do throughout the Diefenbaker years—that what was emerging in Canada was not anti-Americanism but "a very powerful Canadianism." This phenomenon had the potential to create problems "if knowingly or unknowingly the United States or its representatives act in ways which appear to Canadians to infringe on their sovereignty." Therefore, American officials needed to "be constantly attentive to this development, and continue to exercise great care in all aspects of relations with this country."[38]

Merchant was not alone in advocating a considerate approach toward Canada. Writing to Eisenhower after the Tories' landslide victory, Dulles counseled seeking to establish "the same mutual confidence and close working relationship" with Diefenbaker's government that had existed throughout twenty-two years of Liberal rule. Yet the administration had to be mindful of "vocal, widespread criticism" of US policy among the Canadian populace, and government officials' tendency both to play up their country's autonomy and to make the United States "the whipping boy for many of Canada's ills."[39] Eisenhower soon arrived in the Canadian capital for a three-day visit in July 1958, which he capped off with an address to Parliament. Memorable for its declaration "that we should talk frankly to each other. Frankness, in good spirit, is a measure of friendship," the president's speech was a vigorous defense of his position on a range of out-standing sore spots with Canada, largely involving economic matters. Touching on concerns that bilateral relations were headed down a rocky path, Eisenhower pointed out that "there is no cause to be surprised or disturbed to discover that occasionally differences arise between us. The distinguishing character of the peoples of the free world lies in the fact that differences between them can de-velop, can be expressed and then amicably resolved." In private, Eisenhower made clear to Diefenbaker his interest in the state of relations, emphasizing the need for "an even closer relationship" between their two governments, one grounded in quiet diplomacy so that issues could be dealt with "informally before they reached an acute stage."[40]

Overcoming problems with Canada was important to Eisenhower, who, as Supreme Allied Commander in Europe during the Second World War, had often found himself managing relationships with difficult allies and overcoming strong-willed personalities. As president, he was reluctant to accept the view that problems with Canada could not be surmounted. At a National Security Council meeting held soon after his return from Ottawa, policy guidelines for Canadian–US relations were presented and debated. The draft document highlighted six problem areas: Canadian dependence on US trade and invest-ment; American trade restrictions' impact on Canada; the Canadian public's ignorance of American policies; the US government's use of Canadian contrac-tors; Ottawa's position on nuclear weapons; and the lack of information shar-ing between Washington and Ottawa on nonmilitary matters dealing with mutual security. Eisenhower rejected the need to study all but the last two items. Furthermore, referring to nationalist sentiment's effect on Canadian policy, he argued that the "whole issue was largely politics," the Progressive Conservatives "themselves did not believe what they said," and therefore Canadian nationalism was not a national security issue. Nevertheless, the NSC resolved to study four of the issues—Canada's dependence on US investment and the Canadian public's misunderstanding of US policy were dropped. The resulting report, NSC 5822/1, was sensitive to Canadian concerns and stood as the official document guiding US policy toward Canada until it was superseded by a new set of guidelines in early 1962.[41]

Unlike Eisenhower, who was content to downplay nationalism, Merchant felt strongly about the matter. Upon returning to Washington in 1959 as as-sistant secretary for European affairs, he used a speaking opportunity at the

US National War College to warn of the dangers of ignoring Canada, which was, he reminded his audience, "a foreign country" and "most anxious to remain so." On this point Merchant was overwhelmingly sympathetic to the Canadian view, pointing to fears that the United States was out to swamp Canada culturally, economically, and politically. However unfounded this sentiment might seem, Merchant warned that it was alive and well and therefore Americans "should watch and exercise mature judgment in our policies, both private and public, which have a prospective impact on Canada."[42] Merchant's use of a forum designed to educate US officials about central issues of American national security indicates the extent to which he viewed the importance of Canada as well as the danger of nationalism. As he had warned his successor in Ottawa, former congressman Richard Wigglesworth: "It's not an easy job—for the country is big and also there is a change in the climate of our relations. Nationalism is on the rise here & the counterpart is criticism of the Canadians' biggest & nearest neighbor."[43]

For his part, Wigglesworth, arriving in Canada in late 1958, sensed at first that Merchant's concerns were overblown. In his maiden speech as ambassador—made, as tradition dictated, to the Canadian Club of Ottawa— he acknowledged the tensions in the relationship, especially on the economic front. But, he noted, "we are moving in the right direction." Both a lessening of electoral rhetoric and attention to Canadian matters by the White House and by Congress were contributing, alongside a decreasing imbalance in trade—falling from $1.5 billion in 1956 to $725 million in 1958—to better relations. In his initial reports back to Washington, Wigglesworth emphasized waning economic nationalism, leading one historian to note that after Eisenhower's July 1958 trip to Ottawa bilateral relations were "fairly cozy."[44] However, despite both Wigglesworth's initial buoyancy and the Eisenhower administration's cautious approach, coziness soon gave way, the result of differences over defense.

In January 1959 planning at NORAD got underway for Operation Skyhawk, a large-scale test of air defenses to take place that October. To create "the most realistic environment possible," the operation would necessitate the closure of North American airspace to commercial traffic while hundreds of US and Canadian military aircraft simulated an attack on the continent.[45] Once plans were formalized, US Air Force officials briefed Eisenhower, who signed off on the operation on August 5. Six days later, American Defense Secretary Neil McElroy broached the plan with his Canadian counterpart, George Pearkes, and talks between the Federal Aviation Administration and Canada's Department of Transport soon began. In this flurry of activity, no one thought to notify Diefenbaker. Railing against Pearkes for this oversight during a Cabinet session on August 26, the prime minister asked how a massive operation could have been planned without Cabinet approval. Acrimonious debate ensued, with critics of Skyhawk winning out and ministers resolving to withhold approval.[46]

Alarmed, Wigglesworth met with Diefenbaker—"much agitated," the ambassador thought—who stated that he was upset on two counts: the late date at which he was made aware of the operation, and potential political criticism in Canada. Many Canadians, the prime minister explained, believed that "military people, primarily US, make decisions which are shoved down [the] throats of Canadian civil officials." Worse, the operation appeared mainly to be "sabre rattling" directed at Moscow. Rejoining that officials in Washington were "mad as hell" that planning had gone forward for six months only to be ruined, Wigglesworth told the prime minister to acknowledge the "dangers of a show of disunity between Canada and the United States," for with Eisenhower due to meet with the Soviet premier, Nikita Khrushchev, Washington needed as much support as was possible. In subsequently reporting on this situation to the State Department, Wigglesworth advised Eisenhower to make a last ditch appeal. As for the prime minister, the ambassador judged that he was sincere in his belief that the exercise would exacerbate relations with Khrushchev. The ramifications for NORAD, he concluded, "could be serious."[47] In reviewing matters with his own officials, Diefenbaker offered no criticism of the United States. Instead, he remarked that in terms of consultation, "the blame lay with the Canadian side," and he was convinced of the need to assert civilian control over Canada's military.[48] Meanwhile, Eisenhower implored Diefenbaker to review his position. Unbowed, the prime minister replied that although he agreed on "the importance of maintaining strong and efficient defences," he would not budge.[49] Skyhawk was cancelled.

Green soon sought to smooth things over with Christian Herter, appointed secretary of state in April 1959. Meeting one another during the opening of the St. Lawrence Seaway they had apparently "hit it off right away," and one reporter saw signs that Herter was more attuned to Canada than his predecessor, for he "recognizes the need to cater to Canada's sensitivity about 'being consulted.'" Skyhawk was an exception on this point, though Green offered Herter his reassurance that Ottawa's position on this incident should "not be interpreted as a change in Canadian foreign policy."[50] Nonetheless, US officials were uneasy. Wigglesworth identified three problems: the poor channel of communication between the civil and military branches of the Canadian government; American officials' lack of awareness of Canadian political affairs; and a "fundamental divergence" between the United States and Canada over "how to deal with the Communist world." Touching on these points in detail he focused extensively on the latter, which he viewed as "the most significant problem" arising from the whole debacle, for it seemed that even if notification of Skyhawk had occurred earlier, it was certain that Green and Diefenbaker would still have withheld approval. The Canadians, he lamented, had a "softer approach" to the Cold War.[51] Skyhawk exposed American concerns about Canada's stance toward the Soviets and its efforts to chart an independent course in world affairs.

As for the Canadians, the issue exposed tensions around the close defense relationship and the lack of consultation. Expecting Washington to ask for a defense exercise the following year, the prime minister soon explained to the Cabinet that cooperation with the United States on joint defense was important; they would simply need to "balance" collaborating with "protecting Canada's interests."[52] When the Canada–United States joint defense committee met at Camp David two months after Skyhawk's cancellation, the Canadians took this track. The incident, Green affirmed, was "water over the dam." But should planning go forward for another exercise, he hoped that both civilian oversight and bilateral consultation would be paramount. With a continental defense system worth $30 billion in need of testing, the Americans agreed to these points, and planning soon went forward with the approval of Canada's Cabinet.[53] Doubts remained. In late March 1960, Diefenbaker told Heeney that public opinion would be "unfavourable" to an exercise, as Canadians evidently believed that "we were yielding too easily" to Washington. Even so, he promised to raise the matter at Cabinet.[54] In the meantime, true to their promise at Camp David, US officials carried out extensive briefings for their Canadian counterparts on what was now dubbed Operation Skyshield.[55] Planning subsequently went forward, with the Canadians withholding a formal decision on whether or not they would participate. International events then intervened.

On May 1, an American U-2 spy plane was shot down over the Soviet Union. With Washington initially denying that the plane was conducting surveillance missions, Moscow produced the plane's pilot as well as wreckage from the aircraft. The timing could not have been worse: a summit between Eisenhower, Khrushchev, British Prime Minister Harold Macmillan, and French President Charles de Gaulle was convening in Paris. Enraged by Eisenhower's unwillingness to apologize for the incident, Khrushchev left the talks. Accordingly, Cold War tension increased drastically. On instructions from Ottawa, Heeney delivered a note of protest to Merchant that stressed the spying revelations' impact on Canadian public opinion.[56] Despite this note, once Khrushchev withdrew from Paris, the Canadians moved to back the United States. Citing the Soviets' espionage activities inside Canada, the Cabinet agreed that the "air espionage programme was a necessary part of the defence of the Western world and that really the only crime was to have been caught." Ministers also expressed collective anger at Khrushchev for having effectively cancelled the Paris summit.[57] In a nationwide broadcast the following day, Diefenbaker made clear that it was "not the time to enter into criticisms or recriminations of our friends," and he reaffirmed Canadian support for the United States.[58] Appreciative of this statement, Eisenhower thanked Diefenbaker for his strong words, while Undersecretary of State Douglas Dillon concluded that the Soviet decision to cancel the summit conference "had considerably modified the 'soft' attitude" in Ottawa. Green and Diefenbaker, he advised the NSC, "had had their eyes opened" by Khrushchev's actions.[59]

Whatever doubts may have remained in the prime minister's mind about Skyshield, the U-2 incident convinced him of the need for the exercise to go forward. Visiting with Eisenhower in Washington in early June, Diefenbaker promised that a decision would come soon; after returning to Ottawa, he secured Cabinet approval for the exercise.[60] Operation Skyshield began early on the morning of September 10, 1960, when three hundred bombers slipped into North American airspace. Hundreds of interceptor aircraft from bases in Canada and the United States scrambled to meet this threat, surface-to-air missiles were readied, and radar systems monitored the incoming attackers. The operation, Green later remarked to Herter, had been "conducted very successfully and without arousing opposition in Canada."[61] Subsequent exercises were held in 1961 and 1962. Ultimately an example of close cooperation between Ottawa and Washington, Diefenbaker's skepticism of the exercise—and Skyhawk—showed his hesitancy about military matters especially once public opposition, or perceived opposition, arose. A similar pattern played out in his handling of military procurement.

Diefenbaker's February 1959 decision to accept BOMARC missiles had been taken in the wake of his unpopular decision to cancel the production of CF-105 Arrow jets. Designed by Canadian firm AV Roe, the Arrow had been an advanced aircraft holding great potential for Canada's aerospace industry. Ballooning costs led to the program's cancellation, and the termination of thousands of highly skilled jobs. The decision touched a nerve, prompting Canada to seek economic benefits from any military procurement deals with the Untied States. Officials in Washington were supportive of Ottawa's position. Since cancelling the Arrow had had a "great psychological impact" in Canada, Neil McElroy felt that the Eisenhower administration had to ensure that the benefits of defense production spread north.[62] The result was the conclusion of a Defence Production Sharing Agreement (DPSA), exempting Canada from the Buy America Act of 1933 by allowing Canadian firms to compete for US defense contracts, and giving the Pentagon access to more suppliers while boosting Canadian industry.[63]

To further assist Canada—and contribute to Washington's overriding goal of having Ottawa assume more responsibility for continental defense—in late 1959 the Americans offered up sixty-six F-101 Voodoos, advanced interceptors worth $187 million, to be delivered in July 1961. Of particular importance was that through cost-sharing measures, Ottawa would need to pay a mere $62 million. The Cabinet demurred. To Diefenbaker, the cost-sharing aspect was politically unpalatable because it went against "the traditional Canadian position against accepting mutual aid."[64] Hoping to overcome this setback, in March 1960 US negotiators hinted at their willingness to supplement the deal by purchasing $150 million worth of Canadian-built CL-44 transport aircraft.[65] Two months later Washington formally proposed a swap: Canada would pay $105 million for the F-101s, with the United States purchasing $155 million worth of CL-44s.[66] American attempts to sweeten the pot reflected their growing frustration with Canada's stance on defense issues.

For Thomas Gates, Eisenhower's new defense secretary, private talks with several Canadian ministers at a NATO conference in April had been "very disturbing." Voicing a belief that "peace and détente are just around the corner," the Canadians had contended that many citizens in their country were concerned by American "'domination' of Canada." The forthcoming meeting of the joint defense committee, scheduled for July, Gates thought, "might be our last chance to attempt to change the Canadian attitude." Equally "disturbed," Eisenhower admitted that "he had never taken this question up with Diefenbaker; perhaps he should do so."[67] A month later, while entertaining General Charles Foulkes, Canada's senior military officer, Eisenhower, referring to defense issues, stated that "Diefenbaker should jam the hard realities down the throats of his people since he commands an almost terrifying majority." The threat of a bomber attack, he continued, "should not be belittled by anybody," and it was "most important" that both countries "act as solid partners and both make some sacrifices."[68] Having long sloughed off his advisors' concerns about relations with Canada, the president had begun to come to grips with what was happening north of the border. Speaking with Herter in April, he had enquired about press and diplomatic reports of the deteriorating bilateral relationship. Surprised and worried that there might be some truth to these reports, Eisenhower suggested that Diefenbaker be invited to Washington and receive the "red carpet treatment."[69] An invitation was extended and accepted, and Diefenbaker was set to travel to Washington at the beginning of June.

Giving an indication of the administration's view of Canada, several days before the prime minister's arrival the NSC examined the state of bilateral relations. Although Douglas Dillon warned that "Canadian nationalism all across the board was increasing in intensity," he was adamant that difficulties could be surmounted through high-level talks with Canadian ministers, particularly on sensitive matters such as Canada's acquisition of nuclear warheads. Supporting the necessity of top-level discussions, Eisenhower added that "Diefenbaker was not difficult to deal with if he were kept informed in advance, even though he was inclined to make impetuous statements and then to refuse to modify them if they turned out to be wrong."[70] In a separate briefing, advisors emphasized to the president that Diefenbaker and his ministers "have been displaying a marked lack of firmness amounting to a softness toward the Soviet threat, coupled with a very noticeable anti-American point of view." Eisenhower agreed, remarking that he was "distressed to admit that a Liberal government in Canada seems more desirable from the American point of view than a Conservative government. The Tories run on a platform of independence of the United States which amounts frequently to antagonism toward the

United States."[71] Despite Ottawa's support over the U-2 affair, doubts about Canada were building.

Hopeful of improving relations, Eisenhower feted his Canadian visitor and engaged him in wide-ranging talks. Addressing the bilateral relationship, the president decried the ability of the press to stir up public anger and morph "potential trouble spots into causes of friction." Diefenbaker displayed little acrimony, agreeing that public perceptions aside, "relations in the past couple of years had been very good and indeed had been unequalled in the past." The two leaders were all smiles, then, and the prime minister secured a promise from the president to address the "unreasonably high" price tag for the F-101s, which was holding up the Swap deal.[72] The issue was soon taken up at the Canada–US committee on joint defense, held amidst the luxurious surroundings of the Seigniory Club resort at Montebello. Providing Washington with the opportunity to engage in the sort of high-level consultations that Dillon had recently lionized, this summit proved frustrating for the Americans, as their differences with the Canadians on a number of issues were thrown into stark relief, belying the rosy aura surrounding the Eisenhower–Diefenbaker summit and raising questions about the extent to which the Canada–US relationship functions at various levels, from the relations between top level leaders to relations at the level of officials and diplomats, to the level of public opinion.

At Montebello the swap deal was a rare point of positive news, with the Canadian ministers indicating a desire to sign an agreement. But on BOMARC, the Canadian side expressed significant doubts that, in a sense, came down to economics. As Donald Fleming explained, "pacifist ideas" were taking hold in Canada, with many Canadians believing that their country had nothing to with the "nuclear deterrent and that for us to get involved in it in any way is both hazardous and an encroachment on our independence." The government was therefore at pains to justify defense spending, particularly since it seemed that the true threat to North America was from nuclear missiles, against which the BOMARC was useless. In response, Gates, who had placed much stock in this meeting, underscored the continuing threat of Soviet bombers and the ongoing necessity of defense against an attack by aircraft.[73] Gates's view was certainly correct: bombers did remain a threat, particularly because of the "missile gap," which strongly favored the United States. However, with the public perception at the time that this gap favored the Soviet Union, critics—not all of who were pacifists, or neutralists like Minifie—were not wrong to note that with the dawn of the missile age, an expensive weapons system like BOMARC possessed a short shelf life. A Maclean's editorial that year had noted that "each [BOMARC] missile, when it works, will probably explode an attacking airplane in dandy style. But if the Russians (who else?) decide on ultimate insanity, why would they bother sending planes over us or at us," when missiles would do the trick. Although he would change his tune by 1963, in 1960 Diefenbaker rejected such views, denouncing *Maclean's* and "long-hairs" for "talking in favour of there being no nuclear defences."[74] Yet even as he spoke in these terms, the prime minister remained demure about accepting nuclear warheads for Canada's nuclear defenses.

In any event, the issue of military procurement was not the only point of friction over Cold War issues that emerged at the Seigniory Club, for a dispute over Cuba was brewing. Following the success of the Cuban revolution in 1959, relations between Havana and Washington steadily deteriorated, especially after Cuba turned toward the Soviet bloc. Responding to the Cuban government's nationalization of American oil refineries, in July 1960 Eisenhower altered his country's sugar quota, a measure that prevented Cuba from selling its largest export to its largest export market. Not content with this step, US policymakers set about debating ways of putting further economic pressure on Havana. Canadian participation would be important, Dillon emphasized to the NSC, because the majority of Cuban currency had been deposited in Canadian banks, and Canada had other economic interests on the island. Agreeing, Treasury Secretary Robert Anderson believed it would be "inconceivable" for Canada to be uncooperative. The NSC had resolved, then, to broach the matter at Montebello.[75]

On Cuba, the summit proved disappointing for Washington. Norman Robertson, undersecretary of the Department of External Affairs, led the Canadian delegation's charge against US policy. One of Canada's most accomplished diplomats, Robertson had served twice as high commissioner in London, twice as undersecretary and once as ambassador in Washington. Admitting that he was affable, accomplished, and intelligent, Robertson's American counterparts held a dim view of his conception of Canada's foreign policy. Foy Kohler, assistant secretary for European affairs, believed that on "crucial" matters such as the confrontation with the communist bloc, Robertson's views were often inimical to those of the United States.[76] Other US policymakers thought that Robertson had a dangerous "preoccupation with Canada's future in five or ten years," making him unable "to think more practically about the decisions of today." Years later, American diplomat Louise Armstrong observed that difficulties with Canada often involved the actions of certain "poobahs" within External Affairs, Robertson foremost among them. "He's a Canadian icon," she judged, "but from the United States standpoint, he was always a problem."[77]

At the Seigniory Club, Robertson certainly challenged the American standpoint on Cuba. Making a pitch for Canadian support, Merchant explained that Washington's course had been conciliatory, but the actions of revolutionary leader Fidel Castro were dangerous and an American response had been necessary—hence, the sugar quota cut. The Canadian delegation was largely unimpressed by this argument: Robertson contended that the recent change in US policy was ill-judged because Washington should aim at allowing disenchantment with Castro to grow among Cuba's populace. Instead, Eisenhower had handed the Cuban leader "a ready-made opportunity to blame the United States for Cuba's troubles and to identify Cuban nationalism with communism to our detriment."[78] In offering the NSC a post mortem of this "very disturbing conversation," Secretary Anderson now admitted that the inconceivable had become a reality: the Canadians were "indefinitely" opposed to adopting economic sanctions. Henceforth, it seemed that Washington and Ottawa would follow separate courses toward Havana.[79]

Differences over Cuba and defense appeared to be symptomatic of a growing gap between Canada and the United States, one that was not bridged by Eisenhower's cordial treatment of Diefenbaker. Capturing growing Canadian concern over the direction of US foreign policy in the wake of the U-2 affair and the clash with Castro, in July *Maclean's* published an alarmist report that the United States had become a militarist country that "rings with cries for more weapons," that "drafts eight thousand young men a month," "where public bomb shelters are almost as familiar as fire hydrants," and where a scaremongering press and the arms industry had left many Americans expecting that a nuclear war was likely to occur.[80] On the latter point, at least, Diefenbaker was in agreement. At a post-Montebello Cabinet meeting, he reported that that Canadian military wanted the interceptors offering under the Swap deal as such aircraft were necessary for defense, and "would effectively placate any United States feeling that Canada was not doing her share." His view, however, was that in accepting the planes, the Cabinet would need to base its judgment on the "world situation," which "was now serious. Only one slip would bring about a world cataclysm." Admitting that the Swap deal was good from an economic perspective and that it might boost employment, he contended that it would be a hard sell to voters who would doubtless point out that the government had already spent vast sums on weaponry that had become obsolete.[81] Diefenbaker seemed of two minds on defense, for several weeks later he reversed himself: the Liberals had come out in favor of accepting interceptors, and so with "the political difficulties" involved in a decision reduced, Canadian ministers approved going ahead with negotiations. But three days later, with the Tory Caucus sensing that the public would be outraged by the Swap deal, Diefenbaker changed his position again and the Cabinet rescinded its previous decision.[82]

This seeming confusion as a result of domestic calculations alarmed several high-ranking Canadians who put great stock in close relations with Washington. Robert Bryce, who as clerk of the Privy Council and secretary to the Cabinet was the head of Canada's civil service, told Willis Armstrong, the US embassy's deputy chief of mission, that the "difficult problems" between their governments in defense could be fixed easily, but that his government was unlikely to offer solutions. Swap, for instance, appeared to be "dead."[83] Armstrong heard much the same thing from Heeney. Whereas economic affairs were quite good, Heeney pointed to differences over Cuba, nuclear weapons, and the East–West confrontation as having a corrosive effect on relations. Blaming "irrational elements" within Canada's government, Armstrong singled out Green, whose actions were causing increasing impatience in Washington. The Americans, Heeney responded, often needlessly provoked people like his minister, who, he admitted, "likes to pluck the odd tail feather from the eagle." The two men then agreed that the situation augured poorly as neither candidate in the current US presidential election—Kennedy and Republican Richard Nixon—were likely "to be as patient and tolerant" of Ottawa's tendency to delay making decisions.[84] Even Diefenbaker had concerns about the apparent deterioration in Canada–US relations, telling Heeney that American militarism, the aggressiveness of US economic interests, the imbalance of bilateral trade, and the impression that Washington was "pushing other people around" all meant that "anti-American sentiment [in Canada] was now worse than at any time in his lifetime." Anxious to keep relations with Washington in good repair, Diefenbaker asked Heeney to bring his concerns to the Eisenhower administration.[85] Focused on US actions as the cause of the anti-US atmosphere—a reasonable position—the prime minister had not accepted any blame for the state of the bilateral relationship, though in several articles *Maclean's* faulted the government for stoking nationalist fires, even dubbing Diefenbaker "the Paul Revere of Canada."[86]

In Washington shortly thereafter, Heeney analyzed this tense atmosphere with Merchant, particularly the "discontent" revolving around "genuine anxiety at the possibility of nuclear war, and, in that context, worry, even distrust, over U.S. military intentions."[87] They subsequently arranged for Green and Herter to review this sorry state of affairs at a meeting coinciding with the opening of the United Nations General Assembly. Hoping to make real progress, Heeney first briefed his minister on Diefenbaker's concerns about anti-Americanism. Admitting both that there was "wide-spread criticism" of the United States in Canada and that the prime minister was more adept than he was at assessing public opinion, Green nevertheless thought that Diefenbaker's sense of anti-US feeling was "exaggerated." Heeney raised his own worry, namely the "gap between our professions and our performance" on defense, but, unsurprisingly, Green disagreed.[88] At the Waldorf the next day, Herter asked Green to comment on "very disquieting reports about serious antipathy and antagonism toward the U.S. in Canada." The situation was "not so bad," the Canadian minister replied. There was simply some natural and unavoidable tension, the result of Canada being "a little country alongside a great neighbour faced with the question of how to avoid being dominated." He touched next upon the "fundamental difference" between Canada and the United States over policy toward the Soviet Union. With Canadians worried over the belligerence of the Pentagon, his government was hesitant to accept nuclear warheads. Hardly reassuring, Green's comments left Herter "genuinely disturbed."[89]

Making his own trip to New York City soon after, Diefenbaker delivered a fiery speech to the General Assembly in which he denounced Khrushchev who had recently made his own fervid tirade against the West. Writing to Diefenbaker the following day, Heeney commended his address and passed on a comment from Merchant that the speech had been "splendid" and that Washington was pleased with the prime minster's defense of the Western position.[90] Diefenbaker's strong public stance against the Soviets was emblematic of the nature of the Canadian position in the Cold War, where support for the United States in the confrontation against the Soviet Union existed alongside doubts about American strategy and tactics.

As for the Swap deal, in early September Cabinet examined a new, "triangular" proposal. The Pentagon still would purchase $155 million worth of CL-44 transports, but in order to pay for the sixty-six F-101s Canada would assume the costs—$105 million over eight years—of running the Pinetree Line, a part of the network of radar stations in Canada's north maintained by the US Air Force, a move appealing to nationalists and the fiscally prudent alike. The Americans seemed supportive, with Secretary Anderson indicating to Heeney that Washington would have to meet Ottawa's position because "nations as close as we were, whose relations were traditionally amicable, should make every effort to avoid difficulties for one another."[91] With the Canadian Cabinet approving the proposal, Eisenhower told Diefenbaker that he was "delighted."[92] But divisions in Washington emerged. In reviewing the Canadian triangular proposal the Pentagon judged that since the CL-44s failed to meet the necessary specifications for transport aircraft, purchasing these planes could not be justified. The State Department countered that the overriding issue was Canada–US relations.[93] There the matter rested until December, when Heeney lobbied both Gates and Herter, arguing, like his State Department counterparts, that there were "larger political considerations" at play.[94] In reviewing the issue, the two US secretaries decided against the proposal. Informing the president of their decision, Herter wrote: "While I believe the decision will put further strain on United States–Canadian relations at a time when economic and other factors are also producing some anti-United States pressures, I am reluctant to recommend that foreign policy consideration should override the judgment of the Defense Department."[95] Eisenhower accepted this advice, leaving a decision to the next administration.

The muddle over the triangular agreement was matched by tension over Cuba. As the dispute with Havana wore on, Washington's divergence from Ottawa grew more pronounced. On October 20, the United States imposed an embargo on exports to Cuba. At the Seigniory Club summit Canadian officials had stated firmly their doubts about the wisdom of Washington's course, but American policymakers, firm in their belief that they were correct, chalked up Canada's divergent position to nationalism. In advance of the imposition of the embargo, Kohler warned Herter that since Diefenbaker was set on using nationalist rhetoric to boost his popularity at home, any American action toward Cuba "which could be interpreted as interference with Canadian sovereignty would have serious repercussions."[96] The Canadians had little desire to support what they viewed correctly as a mistaken policy. Even though Diefenbaker had remarked to Heeney in August that he wanted "nothing done during the remainder of the Eisenhower Administration to exacerbate relations" with Washington, Cuba proved to be an exception. With the embargo about to go into effect, the Americans asked the Canadian government to prevent the transshipment of US goods to Cuba through Canada. Diefenbaker favored only "a minimum compliance" with this request; trade would otherwise continue.[97] Alarmed at the parting of ways on Cuba, Rufus Smith, the US Embassy's political counselor, sought out Ed Ritchie, an assistant undersecretary in External Affairs with responsibility for Canadian policy toward both Latin America and the United States, who had considerable experience dealing with the Americans having served at the Canadian Embassy in Washington during the late 1950s. A stout defender of Canadian interests, in discussing Cuba with Smith, Ritchie pulled no punches, calling American policy "unwise" and adding that public opposition to the embargo in Canada meant that Diefenbaker could not be seen to be collaborating with the Americans even at the risk of opening himself up to criticism from the United States government, public, and press.[98]

Differences over Cuban trade were not unprecedented. Throughout the Cold War, few American allies were willing to support Washington's position of limiting trade with communist countries. Canadians of all political stripes sensibly believed that restricting trade would do little to topple unfriendly regimes and would only generate tension. In the Cuban case, there was a belief too that an embargo would allow Cuba's government to blame the shortcomings of its economic program on outside pressure, and, in so doing, rally support from the populace. Moreover, an embargo would increase Cuban reliance on the Soviet bloc, thus deepening communism's hold on the island. Ottawa's views on economic sanctions were well known in Washington, but the lack of support on Cuba still upset American authorities. Offering the NSC an overview of international reaction to the embargo, Herter dubbed Ottawa's reaction "the most unfavorable."[99] Herter's fears that Canadian exports would fill the vacuum left by the United States were heightened in early December when George Hees, Canada's trade minister, welcomed a Cuban trade mission to Ottawa. In an effort to clarify matters, Diefenbaker publicly outlined Canada's policy toward Cuba. There was, he told the House of Commons, "no valid objection to trade with Cuba," nor was there reason to abandon normal diplomatic relations. In a nod to American concerns, he added that Canada would not "exploit" the embargo, nor would it encourage "what would in fact be bootlegging of goods of United States origin." American reaction to the prime minister's address was positive. In Paris, Douglas Dillon remarked to Fleming that he and other administration officials were now "quite relaxed" about Canada's position. However, any transshipment "would have a very explosive effect."[100]

In the midst of the squabbling over Cuba and the stalled negotiations on Swap, John Kennedy had narrowly been elected president on November 8. Diefenbaker had been hoping for a Nixon victory, expressing, in the summer, his "distaste" for Kennedy.[101] Subsequently, after learning of the results of the election Diefenbaker told Basil Robinson that he was now firmly "against the idea" of cooperating with the embargo against Cuba. He went on to rail against what he saw as an American tendency to pay attention to Canada only when they desired something: "To hell with them." In Robinson's view these statements marked a considerable departure from comments that Diefenbaker had made a few days before the election when he had indicated that Canada "should not long be able to hold off from a more active collaboration" with the United States over Cuba. Kennedy's victory had clearly upset the prime minister. Alarmed by the president-elect's youth, Diefenbaker judged the Democrat to be "courageously rash," adding that "we were closer to war than we had been before." Despite his irritation, the prime minister agreed to Robinson's suggestion that he send a message of congratulations to the incoming president. Two weeks after dispatching this message no response had been received. Annoyed, Diefenbaker asked Robinson to investigate the matter. Making inquiries through Heeney, Robinson learned that a message was on its way, a tardy response that failed to mollify the prime minister.[102] With this discourtesy Kennedy did himself no favors, nor was this the sole instance when he would neglect to respond promptly to a personal note from Diefenbaker.

Other Canadians were more positive about the election result. Commenting on the razor thin margin of victory, Heeney predicted that it would force caution upon the new administration, which would begin its mandate mindful of a lack of overwhelming popular support. Throughout the campaign Heeney had covered the candidates' positions on diplomatic and economic issues, finding that Kennedy and Nixon differed little and predicting that little would change in US foreign policy, though a win by the Democratic candidate offered the "prospect of a fresh and more flexible approach."[103] Drawing on Heeney's reportage, Norman Robertson analyzed the incoming president's likely policies, both generally and in regards to Canada specifically. Bound to offer "bold and vigorous leadership," Kennedy, in Robertson's view, was "evidently aggressive, shrewd and tough-minded" as well as "thorough and calculating." Expecting the new president to focus on foreign relations, Robertson agreed with Heeney that US policies would remain consistent. Happily, he sensed that the new administration would "have much less obsession with communism at home and abroad as being the synthesis or epitome of all problems in foreign affairs." As for Canada, Robertson felt that since Kennedy lacked any discernable "intimate connection" with the country, bilateral relations would be marked by the incoming administration's ignorance.[104]

Kennedy proved, though, to be just as obsessed with the communist threat abroad and on Canada, he certainly lacked intimate knowledge. However, his awareness of the political climate in the country went beyond "the usual benevolent attitude" of most Americans.[105] True, his speech in Montréal in 1953 had shown his familiarity with the common platitudes of "the fraternal friendship" between the two countries, and he had laid blame for bilateral problems on "misunderstandings and misconceptions." But in his speech in New Brunswick four years later, he had indicated an understanding of the force of nationalism, criticized "U.S. domination of Canadian enterprise," and praised Canadian desire to construct "a distinctively national cultural tradition," hence his emphasis on good fences. He had noted his belief that overcoming bilateral squabbles would necessitate leaders "of patience, tact and foresight—dedicated, responsible men who can look beyond the problems of the next election to see the problems of the next generation." During his time in the Senate he had certainly shown a commitment to looking past parochial issues, and on an issue involving Canada to boot. For decades, construction of the St. Lawrence Seaway had been held up due to opposition in Congress. Given concerns that Boston's port would suffer from this new shipping route, no Massachusetts congressman or senator had voted for the project in the six instances in which the issue had been up for a vote since the 1930s. Yet Kennedy voted for the project in 1954, telling his fellow senators that with Canada pushing ahead and with Eisenhower stressing that the waterway was vital to national security it was time to abandon "narrow and destructive" parochialism.[106]

With the Democrat employing similar rhetoric throughout the 1960 campaign, Canadian newspapers welcomed his victory, and compared him favorably against Eisenhower. Shocked by Kennedy's tight win, the *Ottawa Citizen* hoped that he would assemble a strong team that would improve upon his predecessor's record, especially on foreign policy. "During the last eight years," the paper's editors argued, Washington "has sometimes given its friends an impression of not knowing where it was going in the modern world. Perhaps this uncertainty will now disappear, and the strong and enlightened leadership so badly required will now be forthcoming." To the *Montreal Gazette*, the central question that American voters had faced was whether their country's standing had decreased during the Eisenhower years. Soviet advances in the Third World and in rocketry were "many and grievous," and it fell to Kennedy to confront these problems and restore his country's prestige. Thankfully, the president-elect seemed capable of "refreshing national policies," for although he was young, he had "some of the most stupendous prospects the world has ever known, with the chance of grasping the greatest prize of all—the peace

of an anxious and hoping world." Toronto's *Globe and Mail* was more skeptical: Kennedy had not been given a popular mandate, and it seemed that voters had chosen the more telegenic candidate. As for his policies, its editors noted that Kennedy had put forward a mixed bag. Regardless, Canada could take "satisfaction" from his suggestions for "a more imaginative foreign policy."[107] Diefenbaker shared little of this positive anticipation.

In his memoirs, the former prime minister speculated that although unsure of what the results of a Nixon win in 1960 would have meant for American politics, he felt sure "that the course of Canada–US relations would have been a happier one."[108] Nixon might indeed have handled Canadian issues in a better fashion than Kennedy, though once he became president he proved, in fact, to be quite rough in dealing with Ottawa. Furthermore, a number of issues that plagued the bilateral relationship during the Kennedy era had their roots with Eisenhower—would Nixon's handling of Cuba, for instance, have been any less aggressive than Kennedy's own course, one inherited from Eisenhower? As the *Los Angeles Times* noted in early 1961, the new president needed to reverse the "slow deterioration" of Washington's position in Ottawa, while the *Atlantic Monthly* attacked Eisenhower for allowing the "critical deterioration in Canadian–American relations," and in the *Washington Post*, Max Freedman pointed out that when "Kennedy becomes President in January he will find, to his surprise, that he will face many serious problems in Canadian–American relations." Moreover, a December 1960 *Chicago Sun Times* headline declaring "Kennedy Facing Canada Problem" could as easily have read "Nixon." In a similar vein, just after Kennedy's inauguration the *Globe and Mail* reflected harshly on the Eisenhower era. The newspaper was stinging: "Ominous developments at home and abroad passed almost unnoticed. Russia shot ahead in nuclear weapons and rockets, and perfected new techniques of infiltration in the undeveloped countries of the world." Since Eisenhower had offered few effective policies to reverse this negative trend, the "greatest indictment of the departed Administration is the legacy of unsolved problems it left its successor."[109] Canada, then, was one of many issues facing the incoming administration.

Among these problems was the provisioning of Canadian forces with nuclear weapons and Diefenbaker's studious effort to avoid committing himself to actually acquiring such warheads despite his February 1959 declaration that Canada would acquire weapons systems needing these armaments. This political footwork was characteristic of both his political instincts and his growing reluctance to take a stand on defense issues due to divisions within the Cabinet and among Canadians. In November 1960, the prime minister informed Heeney of his sense of growing public opposition to nuclear weaponry. Even so, he thought that Canada would have to acquire the warheads "before long." His only requirement was for "satisfactory arrangements" for joint control.[110] Under American law, nuclear warheads for use by allied governments would have to remain in US custody but both countries could share control of the warheads, thus allowing Ottawa to decide whether its forces would deploy nuclear ammunition. Just days after his comments to Heeney, Diefenbaker made his views public to an audience in Ottawa: "as a sovereign nation" Canada would not acquire atomic weaponry without "equality in control." Mindful of antinuclear sentiment, he added both that without any immediate need for the weapons there was little need to reach a hurried agreement with Washington and that his course would partly be determined by "what happens in connection with disarmament."[111] How firmly the prime minister believed in arms limitation is unclear. When Cabinet debated nuclear policy soon after, he contended that disarmament initiatives, though "laudable," had little chance of success. Then, underlining the importance of joint control and the need to have "the forces of the West, including Canada's, as strongly and most effectively armed and equipped as possible," he highlighted the "necessity for remaining silent" on the nuclear question so as to avoid creating a public perception that ministerial opinion was divided.[112]

The disjunction between public support for disarmament and a strong defense policy would only deepen as Diefenbaker's time in office went on. As the author of an excellent study of Diefenbaker's nuclear decision-making has argued, the prime minister's concern about the "potential political fallout" of his agreeing to requisition nuclear warheads was "reasonable," both because he was "beholden to the electorate" and because he had faced a number of political setbacks during his career.[113] Still, Diefenbaker held a huge majority, although his popularity was slipping and his indecision on the nuclear issue would ultimately prove fatal to his government, a sign that many Canadians would have backed the acceptance of such weaponry. The prime minister, however, had already made what would be a momentous decision when, in October 1960, he appointed Douglas Harkness to be his new defense minister, replacing the retiring George Pearkes. Previously, Harkness had served Diefenbaker as agriculture minister, a good fit for the Calgary MP, and his promotion to the defense portfolio was a reflection of his performance rather than any innate interest in military matters. Upon becoming defense minister Harkness eagerly defended his department's positions, bringing him into continuous conflict with Green; unsurprisingly, US officials labeled Harkness "our best friend."[114] Diefenbaker's electoral worries and his subsequent indecision on nuclear weaponry were only worsened by the drastically divergent views on nuclear weapons held by these two senior minister, a divide found throughout the Canadian government.[115]

Beyond Cuba and defense issues, there were other points of contention between Canada and the United States. After having traveled through Canada in 1960, the *Washington Post*'s Carl Rowan informed readers that he had "discovered that the much-heralded 'undefended border' between the United States and Canada now is being fortified on the Canadian side with a host of cultural and economic artillery." Early the next year, in reporting to London on the state of North American relations, Joseph Garner, the British High Commissioner in Ottawa, asked: "Is Canada becoming a mental and spiritual colony of the United States?" Many Canadians thought so, he observed, hence there was an active effort to preserve "political, cultural and spiritual freedom of action." Nor was Garner alone in asking such questions. In early 1961, the *Saturday Evening Post* asked "Are Canadians Still Our Friends?," while in a week-long series, the *Cleveland Plain Dealer* wondered "Why Don't Canadians Like Us?." Looking first to the American "Blind Spot" when it came to Canada, the paper moved from blaming ignorance to indicting a host of economic factors: the dominance of US investment; United States control of Canadian industry; the role of American subsidiaries in profiting from Canadian resources; and high tariffs, which led to an unequal flow of dollars across the border. The *Milwaukee Journal*, in a similar series, examined the "Dilemma in Canada," or rather it looked at several dilemmas among them Canadians' "underdog neurosis," American indifference, discord between Francophones and Anglophones, and financial and cultural domination from the south. In the autumn of 1960, the *Globe and Mail* had run its own ten-part series on the "Search for a Canadian Identity." Touching on culture, economics, military affairs, and foreign policy, series author Philip Deane had criticized both the Liberals and the Tories for ginning up anti-American sentiment, which has damaged "the international prestige of both major Canadian parties."[116] It seemed evident, then, to many observers that as Eisenhower left office, anti-US feeling in Canada was mounting.

Importantly, Canadian dislike for the United States was also the focus of briefing papers that the State Department's Canada specialists prepared for the incoming administration. These studies, drafted in late 1960 and early 1961, showcased American appreciation for the importance of nationalist sentiment, drawing clear distinctions between nationalism and anti-Americanism. The latter, Willis Armstrong judged, was present internationally but was not a determining factor in Canada, where nationalism was predominant.[117] A career diplomat who had been a Soviet specialist before moving on to dealing with Western Europe, in 1958 Armstrong had been recruited by Merchant to come to the Canadian capital to serve as the Embassy's economic counselor, quickly becoming a keen observer of Canada. Armstrong was well regarded by Heeney, who viewed him as an excellent diplomat possessing strong contacts with officials in Ottawa and Washington alike.[118]

Alongside Rufus Smith, Armstrong drafted the embassy's contribution to the briefing papers for the new administration. Their report, "The Roots of Canadian–American Problems," saw nationalism as the "chief problem" in bilateral relations, the result of geography: Canada lacked other neighbors, its population was a tenth the size of the US populace, and most Canadians lived alongside the American border. Therefore, Canada was left alone to confront "dynamic and powerful economic, political, social, and cultural forces from the United States." Nationalists, who included intellectuals, members of the press, civil servants, and government ministers, were motivated by a desire to combat "this massive pressure" and maintain independence. Since their concerns with sovereignty affected all aspects of the bilateral relationship, nationalist strength was not to be underestimated. As the paper noted, each issue had to be examined "in terms of whether it will array the emotional and irrational nationalism of Canada against the United States (and against Canada's own best interests) or whether it will not." The document displayed a certain arrogance, for Smith and Armstrong judged that since their own country had benign intentions there was little reason for Canadians to worry. Moreover, they failed to make any connection between American actions and popularity in Canada: the nationalist force, they contended, "rises and falls often without objective provocation," in spite of American attempts to placate it. Still, their report counseled a positive approach to Canada, for they concluded that it would be inadvisable to "cease trying to accommodate Canada in every reasonable way—failure to do so would bring far worse reactions." Such grim judgments aside, the report made sure to emphasize that most Canadians were not anti-American: "In their bones Canadians know they are a Western nation, loyal to their allies, faithful in their commitments and reasonable in a crisis."[119]

Viewing nationalism as an irrational and immutable factor that could not be avoided, the Ottawa Embassy's view was that Canada's economic and military importance to the United States—the result of the fact of geography—made this phenomenon disruptive and even dangerous. In a covering letter to the report, Armstrong wrote that any attempt to forecast problems areas with Canada was redundant as the "Canadian reactions to them will be predictable on the basis of the situation described in the first part of the paper"—in essence, nationalism was the lens through which problems could and should be assessed.[120] As the product of two of the State Department's most accomplished Canadianists, "The Roots of Canadian–American Problems" was an important document having a significant impact on the official briefing paper that was prepared for the incoming administration. Additionally, its insights impressed Livingston Merchant enough that in 1962, with bilateral relations becoming increasingly difficult, he ensured that it received wide circulation to the president and other senior administration officials as a way of explaining Canadian actions.[121]

The Ottawa Embassy's views were echoed in the State Department's own analysis, "Approach to Canadian–United States Relations," authored by Delmar Carlson, officer-in-charge of Canadian Affairs—the Canada Desk—and Milton Rewinkel, the director of the Office of British Commonwealth and Northern European affairs. Both men had served at various diplomatic postings in Canada throughout the 1950s, with Rewinkel having recently been Smith's predecessor as the Ottawa Embassy's political counselor. Their study took a broad view, beginning with the observation that in crafting policy toward the Americans' northern neighbors it was vital to account for Canada's "inferiority complex toward the United States, growing nationalism, the tendency to inject relations with the United States into Canadian domestic politics, and the Diefenbaker administration's impulse to exploit these matters to bolster its declining popularity." In words that would be echoed in future briefing notes and policy statements and using the popularized language of mental illness, Carlson and Rewinkel judged that "the essential element" in Canadian problems was "psychological." To deal with Canadian psychoses, they advised policymakers to be constantly on the lookout for signs of nationalism and how this force interacted with domestic politics. In practical terms, this prescription meant that American officials should "exercise great care and patience" with Canada by actively trying "to respect and understand the viewpoints of our Canadian ally" and by ignoring "hypersensitivities which may at times be annoying to us." The paper did not simply advocate taking a passive role. Affirming the necessity of giving "Canada special accommodation," it noted: "We should not hesitate, if our policies are distorted or we are harassed or the occasion otherwise demands, to engage in firm and frank talk to restore perspective."[122] Like the Embassy, the Canada Desk highlighted the importance and prevalence of nationalism—as opposed to anti-Americanism—a force that had to be respected.

Although not involved in the drafting of these reports, Merchant had his own understanding of what lay behind problems with Canada. At a NATO summit in December 1960 he met with Jules Léger, the Canadian representative to the alliance, a former undersecretary of state, and a future governor general. Old friends, the two shared a pessimistic view of the current state of bilateral relations, with Merchant remarking that the deteriorating relationship, in part, was due to Diefenbaker's failure "to attain a sense of genuine security in office" despite his party's landslide majority in the 1958 election. Agreeing, Léger added that over the coming year the Canadian government would become "increasingly election-minded" as pressure built for Diefenbaker to seek a new mandate in late 1961 or early 1962. Their discussion concluded with Merchant's lament that while Washington understood that Ottawa would not always offer its support, he expected that their "special relationship" justified a more assiduous Canadian effort to consult with the United States to "try to reach agreement on the merits of each case." His sense, though, was that the prime minister's increasing insecurity was preventing this dialogue from occurring in any meaningful manner.[123]

As Léger had made clear, anxiety over the state of Canada–US relations was not confined to Americans. Heeney, for one, was alarmed by the mood taking hold in his country, hardly a surprise given his interest in smooth bilateral relations. In November, in separate speeches to the Toronto and Montréal branches of the Canadian Institute of International Affairs, he criticized what seemed to be mounting anti-Americanism. Raising the new "fact of national feeling" toward the United States, he admitted that there were reasons to disagree with Americans, particularly over provocative US foreign policy decisions. Concerns about sovereignty were also legitimate. Nevertheless, he argued that Canadians too often took Americans for granted. Modern alliances, Heeney added, required "some restriction of freedom of decision on the part of the individual allies." Thankfully, the two governments had built up mechanisms for consultation and joint decision-making so that although Ottawa would have to make some allowances for Washington's preponderant power and weighty responsibilities, Canada was in no danger of becoming an American satellite. Heeney's conclusions left American diplomats pleased. The speeches, thought Willis Armstrong, had been a "vigorous blast" against the specter of anti-Americanism.[124]

Beyond advocating looking at Canada's relationship with the United States in a dispassionate manner, from Washington Heeney tried to impart some of the excitement surrounding the arrival of the incoming administration. He saw Kennedy's Cabinet appointments as "cool, competent" and "efficient," with the presence of several Republicans—Robert McNamara as defense secretary and Douglas Dillon as Treasury secretary—a sign of Kennedy's moderation. However much the Cabinet impressed him, for Heeney the "most important ingredient" was Kennedy, whose "drive and energy" would propel the United States "forward toward a 'New Frontier' of the twenty-first century." Commenting on the "important and probably decisive" role that Kennedy was bound to play in foreign affairs, Heeney sensed that the new president was strengthening the White House's ability to manage foreign policy. He also expected that the role of ambassadors would be enhanced so that the new president would be better able to make quick decisions by speaking directly to his representatives abroad. As the post of ambassador to Ottawa was empty—Wigglesworth had died in the autumn—this factor would become important once the position was filled, and Heeney speculated, correctly, that Merchant might be reappointed to the Canadian capital.[125]

The new administration's appointments to lower levels of the State Department and to the Treasury were also applauded if only because a number of officials who had previously dealt with Canada during the Truman administration were returning to power. Responding to a report from the Embassy in Washington about their return, Ed Ritchie remarked to a colleague that he was "fascinated to notice how many of the old characters are coming out of the woodwork." Writing one of these old characters, Harlan Cleveland, who was about to become assistant secretary of state for international organizations, Ritchie welcomed him back: in Ottawa "we have been tremendously impressed by the quality of the people (including yourself) who are being brought into service." Ritchie added a hope "that we shall not try your patience unduly. If we seem a little tiresome at times, I trust that you will bear with us and recognize that in our different ways we are probably attempting to work toward similar ends."[126] Another old character was Adlai Stevenson, perennial Democratic presidential candidate throughout the 1950s and now Kennedy's nominee as ambassador to the United Nations. To a Toronto audience in December, Stevenson pleaded for greater cooperation between Canada and the United States on a host of international issues. Going on to praise the two countries' "fundamental solidarity" with one another, he also spoke of the need for both governments to seek a "fruitful, friendly, and equal" association, and he denounced Minifie and neutralism. Two comments drew a rebuke from the *Globe and Mail*, however. First, Stevenson implored Ottawa to set about "harmonizing" its policy on Cuba with that of Washington. Next, he stated that "the U.S. can't take Canada for granted any longer," an admission that the United States had been ignoring Canadians. Attacking these comments, the *Globe and Mail*'s editors lamented, "if Adlai Stevenson does not understand us . . . what American does?"[127] Stevenson's plea on Cuba was misjudged, but his second point, offered as criticism of Eisenhower, was meant to serve notice that the new administration would seek to rebuild relations with Ottawa. Indeed, an election brief for the 1960 Democratic presidential candidate had noted that Eisenhower had overseen a "precipitous slide toward bad relations" with Ottawa.[128]

Also hopeful of building upon the momentum in Washington, Heeney sought out contacts in Kennedy's administration. Dean Rusk, the presumptive secretary of state, was an obvious target. Having served as a senior State Department official dealing with Asia under Truman, Rusk was well known to many in Canada's foreign service. Two days after Kennedy put forth Rusk's nomination, Heeney wrote him to request a meeting. Recognizing the United States' worldwide responsibilities, the ambassador implored Rusk to take seriously the recent "divergence between Washington and Ottawa."[129] They met in early January and established what would be a friendly working relationship. Displaying some of the ignorance of Canada that so concerned Canadians, nonetheless Rusk evinced an interest in bilateral relations, asking Heeney to explain to him how "the special relationship" between their countries could be maintained and strengthened. Listing the mechanisms for joint consultation that had been built up over previous years, including the joint ministerial committees on defense and on trade, Heeney made sure to broach the outstanding problems between their countries, which fell into two areas, economics and defense. On the latter, Heeney blamed Canadian "misgivings" about some "manifestations" of US foreign policy and American "reservations and worries" about the "wholeheartedness" of Canadian support in the Cold War. The single greatest problem, Heeney said, was nuclear weaponry. Concluding the talk, Rusk agreed to hold a ministerial summit soon so that officials could quickly establish a rapport. He added that he and his son often traveled to Canada for fishing trips; future vacations of this sort might provide opportunities for him to informally speak with his Canadian counterpart. A pleasant conversation, it left Heeney convinced that Rusk was "a pretty impressive fellow" who would be "sympathetic but tough."[130]

Sensibly, Heeney also thought that the possibility of informal access to the American secretary of state would be beneficial. Thus, he felt "surprise and disappointment" when Diefenbaker "dismissed" Rusk's comment as a sign of "condescension," since Rusk "thought of Canada only as a place for fishing and hunting." The prime minister's negativity was unfortunate given that on many bilateral issues, Rusk would prove to be an influential figure within the administration, particularly as the personal relationship between Kennedy and Diefenbaker soured. In this circumstance, the rapport that Heeney established early on proved to be important. He recalled later that Rusk "was unfailingly friendly and put much time and effort into Canadian affairs. Although his schedule became increasingly heavy, he and his wife came on a number of occasions to the embassy for informal evenings. He never failed to see me at the State Department when I asked him to do so on matters of business." On the other side of the fence, Armstrong remembered Rusk as being "perfectly responsive on Canadian matters."[131] The prime minister, inclined to a negative view of the incoming administration, was unappreciative of this early attempt at bridge-building.

Diefenbaker's wariness was on full display only days before the presidential inauguration when he traveled to Washington to see off Eisenhower and to sign the Columbia River Treaty, an agreement on water rights and the development of dams, at a small signing ceremony. Raising with Eisenhower his frustrations with the new administration, Diefenbaker mentioned his "irritation" with Rusk's belief that his exposure to Canada through fishing trips had provided him with an expert knowledge of the country.[132] At a luncheon, the two leaders then exchanged warm toasts, with Eisenhower noting how pleased he was to host Diefenbaker as his last official White House guest and the prime minister praising the president and relating an anecdote about a young Canadian student, who, when asked to name Canada's governor general, replied "General Eisenhower." This child, mused Diefenbaker, had expressed something of the esteem in which Canadians held the president. To Basil Robinson, it seemed that the prime minister's lack of a relationship with Kennedy made this visit with Eisenhower "all the more nostalgic" for Canada's leader.[133] By the time Kennedy took the oath of office on January 20 he had already acquired at least one foreign detractor. "For all the promise of the incoming team," Robinson told Heeney, "there is no doubt that the absence of a personal relationship with the new President is going to introduce an incalculable factor into relations with the United States," and in this regard it was "disturbing" that Diefenbaker had "formed some rather unfavourable early impressions." The *New York Times* offered a different view, noting, despite the smiles between Diefenbaker and Eisenhower, that there was a "new factor in our relations created by a growing Canadian nationalism."[134] These factors, personal, societal, and seemingly psychological would prove important to Canada–US relations as Kennedy began his time in office.

Years later, Howard Green fondly recalled that Eisenhower was "the ideal type of man to have as President of the United States from the Canadian point of view, because you could be dead sure he wasn't going to try to shove anybody around."[135] Good-natured and patient, the former general was adept at handling difficult personalities, Diefenbaker included. In terms of Canada–US relations he pursued a measured course, and, along with Christian Herter, was careful not to overstep the bounds of propriety by forcing a Canadian decision on the Swap arrangement or on trade with Cuba. Taking Canadian amity toward his country as a given, he rejected reports of growing nationalism while affirming the right of the two governments to disagree with one another. This approach reflected not simply Eisenhower's own personality, but also the diplomatic "transgovernmental network" operating on both sides of the 49th parallel.[136] The cooperative disposition of the officials within this network ensured that disagreements were dealt with in a quiet but effective manner. On Cuba, Ottawa and Washington disagreed sharply, but resolved to find middle ground: Canada would restrict trade in certain goods, and the United States would refrain from implementing extraterritorial provisions to target the actions of US subsidiaries. On Skyhawk, the Canadians were concerned that the operation, planned without the approval of the Cabinet, would needlessly ratchet up Cold War tension; the exercise was cancelled, and when the Americans subsequently began planning Skyshield, they did so with full consultations with Ottawa. On continental defense, through NORAD Washington had secured a Canadian commitment to expand security cooperation, while Ottawa had secured an American commitment to a partnership entailing consultations in the event of a crisis.

Yet despite these efforts to remove points of friction, problems remained, including the unresolved question of whether Canada would accept nuclear warheads. Of paramount importance was both the sense in the press and among government officials in Ottawa and Washington that Canadian nationalism was in the ascendant and that Eisenhower had in fact fumbled relations with Canada, leaving Kennedy with a strained bilateral relationship. Eisenhower himself admitted as much in July 1960. Despite Canada's agreement to participate in Skyshield, the positive Canadian response to the U-2 affair, and Diefenbaker's glad-handing trip to the White House, tension remained, and the president "was somewhat surprised" that there were still problems with Canada including the fact that Ottawa had shown "disinterest" with "what we were trying to do with respect to Cuba" and "with respect to the Soviet Bloc-Free World struggle generally."[137] In their briefing papers for the incoming

Kennedy administration, American diplomats in the Ottawa Embassy and in the State Department had highlighted Canadian concerns over sovereignty and independence, while Livingston Merchant was cognizant of Diefenbaker's preoccupation with being re-elected. This mixture of nationalism and populism, alongside the Canadian prime minister's personal distaste for the new White House team, was soon to have a deleterious impact on Canada–US relations, leaving diplomats in both countries to manage bilateral relations and attempt to resolve outstanding issues in an increasingly contentious climate. All of these developments lay in the future, however.

In January 1961 Kennedy entered office receptive to calls for the improvement of Canada–US relations and for a continuation of the Eisenhower administration's patient and forbearing stance toward Canada. By the time of his inauguration the Progressive Conservative government had been in power for nearly four years, the Canadian economy was slumping along, and next to the young president, Diefenbaker looked anachronistic. This contrast explains why many Canadians were attracted to Kennedy. Also, it reflected a larger trend where Kennedy's relationships with the British, French, and West German leaders were also not on the best footing, for "at a time when Europe was ruled by old men, Kennedy's youth was in itself a challenge, as was his rapport with the public."[138] As the new administration was to discover, and as professional diplomats had cautioned, Canadian policymakers shared little of their vigor for paying any price and bearing any burden in confronting revolutionary communism.

# 2

# New Frontiers

*Kennedy in Ottawa and the Cold War*
*in the Third World, 1961–1962*

Within a month of returning to Ottawa as John Kennedy's ambassador to Canada in March 1961, Livingston Merchant took the de rigueur step of addressing the Canadian Club of Ottawa. Reflecting on the changes in global politics since his previous inaugural address to this same body in 1956, he highlighted decolonization in Africa, revolution in Cuba, insurgencies in Southeast Asia, and the development of advanced ballistic missiles, all of which were signs of a more dangerous world. Disputes between Ottawa and Washington over tariffs and trade were important, but it was the Cold War contest, Merchant sensed, that took precedence in bilateral deliberations, for it was the question of how to wage this struggle that exposed potentially dangerous differences between the two allies. His plea was for both countries to devote "more of our time and thought and effort to ensuring that the sort of world in which we can enjoy the luxury of bilateral problems continues to exist."[1] Coinciding with some of the most intense years of the Cold War, the Kennedy presidency marked a period where Canada and the United States began more frequently to disagree about how to confront communism—particularly as this struggle moved into Latin America and Southeast Asia, areas that were then collectively called the Third World.

As for Canadian–American relations, recording his private impressions of Canada in a letter to Ivan White, the deputy assistant secretary for European affairs and former US consul in Toronto, Merchant acknowledged the warm sentiments that he had received since his return, kind words reflective of "an uneasy Canadian conscience." In his estimation, "anti-Americanism has gone wide and deep" but seemed to be "on the turn," the result of the realization by both the Canadian government and the opposition parties that "anti-Americanism and talk of neutralism—talk which they positively have encouraged" had gone too far. But equally important was President Kennedy. "I have always believed," Merchant stated, "that if they were allowed to register ninety per cent of all Canadians would be Democrats." Despite this upswing, problems lay ahead, he felt, because Diefenbaker would become fixated on re-election.[2] Merchant also wrote to the president, informing him that "it would be difficult to exaggerate the number of your admirers in Canada." Then, referring to a trip that Kennedy planned to take to Ottawa in May, the ambassador observed that to Canadians this early visit was "the paying of a particular compliment." For a president so concerned both with his public image and with the US image abroad, such observations were undoubtedly good news, as they were for those policymakers interested in a smooth bilateral relationship.[3]

When Kennedy took office, the situation facing him with Canada augured poorly. Diefenbaker held a negative view of the young president, while the force of Canadian nationalism, with its implications for Canada's foreign policy, lingered. Events over the coming months were to show that Canadian leaders were certainly concerned with maintaining an independent course of action and ensuring that US policy did not impinge on either Canada's own interests or on its sovereignty. In turn, Kennedy, his advisors, and American diplomats recognized the concerns of their northern counterparts and modified their country's policies accordingly. As it moved to deal with matters left over from the Eisenhower administration—the provisioning of Canada's military with nuclear warheads and modern interceptors—and as it sought to put its own stamp on other areas of policy—Cuba and Southeast Asia—the Kennedy administration took care to solicit the assistance of the Canadian government and not exacerbate bilateral relations. Furthermore, Kennedy and Diefenbaker met twice, in February and May 1961, establishing what had the potential to be a friendly but by no means close working relationship.

Although a typical refrain in Canada is that the United States takes its northern neighbor for granted, in its first months in office the Kennedy administration sought active Canadian assistance on several fronts and viewed Canada as an important ally. Like his immediate predecessors, Kennedy waxed lyrically on the "ties that bind Canada and the United States," telling the staff of the US Embassy in Ottawa that these bonds were "so long based in history and common interests, that I am sure that you feel a sense of mutual service to the cause of this great North American continent."[4] Such sentimentality translated into a very real desire to see the two countries stand side by side in Latin America, in Southeast Asia, and in continental defense, with Kennedy carefully seeking Canada's support. As the new administration was to discover, Canadian policymakers shared little of their vigor, instead expressing doubts about the New Frontiersmen's handling of the Cold War in the Third World. Yet allied to the United States, Canada's government sought to balance doubts about the direction of US foreign policy with its obligations and own shared interest in containing communism.

In the wake of Kennedy's inauguration, officials on both sides of the border launched a concerted effort to put the bilateral relationship on a sound footing. In Ottawa, competitiveness took hold: receiving word that the Australian and British premiers were racing to meet Kennedy, Diefenbaker and his diplomatic advisors swung into action to ensure that the Canadian prime minister was the first foreign leader to meet with the new president. Through Heeney, Diefenbaker made inquires about traveling to Washington for informal talks. The Canadian ambassador soon reported back to Ottawa that Kennedy would be "very happy indeed" to meet Diefenbaker for a working lunch on February 20. Basil Robinson later commented: "It said a great deal for Heeney, and for the groundwork laid by Merchant . . . that within three days of the first approach, Heeney was able to report that the president would be pleased to welcome the prime minister at an early date to be agreed." Of course, Diefenbaker had been "a little naughty," Dean Rusk joked, by planting a question about being invited in the House of Commons and thereby forcing a decision.[5]

Announcing the meeting at the outset of one of his first press conferences, Kennedy told the gathered reporters how "important" it was "that harmonious relations exist between two old friends, and therefore I am glad to have this chance to visit with the Prime Minister."[6] However, Kennedy blundered, pronouncing "Diefenbaker" as "Diefenbawker," an error that has gone down in the lore of the period as an early example of the rockiness between the two leaders. Reportedly the prime minister was so incensed over the mispronunciation of his name that he told Robinson that he was considering lodging an official complaint, though no protest was made. Instead, reporters raised the issue with the White House. Advising Pierre Salinger, Kennedy's press secretary, over how to respond to the "flap" over the mispronunciation, Rusk thought it best to blame it on "a slip of the tongue."[7] Kennedy did indeed have a peculiar accent and Rusk sought to ensure that this error did not recur, emphasizing to the president that the prime minister's name was pronounced "Deefen-BAKER."[8]

Despite this apparent fuss as well as the more pressing problems posed by nationalism and the transition to a new administration, Canada–US relations seemed slowly to be improving. Taking up the languishing swap deal with the new defense secretary, Robert McNamara, Heeney underscored that the agreement would be beneficial in terms of joint defense, the DPSA, and joint balance of payments issues. The secretary indicated that he was "anxious to be co-operative."[9] His deputy, Roswell Gilpatric, thus advised the president that with Ottawa attaching "the highest importance" to defense cooperation, Washington needed to focus on working "cooperatively" with the Canadians. Reviewing Eisenhower's failed swap deal, he proposed a new formula under the auspices of the DPSA: the existing swap of 66 F-101 Voodoos for Canada's subsuming of the Pinetree line was kept; the provision that the United States would accept CL-44 transports—aircraft deemed insufficient by the Pentagon—was dropped. Instead, Gilpatric suggested accepting $155 million worth of F-104s, built by Montréal-based Canadair, with Canada paying a portion, $50 million, through the NATO Mutual Aid program. These planes would then to disbursed to the NATO allies.[10] This new triangular deal represented an effort by the Kennedy team to be helpful and constructive in its first dealings with Canada.

Kennedy showed another measure of goodwill, approving—on the same day that he had announced that Diefenbaker would be traveling to Washington—Merchant's return to Ottawa. Commenting on this news in the House of Commons, Diefenbaker opined that this homecoming "evoked universal approval everywhere in our country," a view echoed by the *Globe and Mail*'s George Bain. Merchant's reappointment was "highly flattering," Bain contended, and a reassuring sign because it indicated that the new administration was interested in being informed about Canada by someone who knew the country well and who attached vital importance to good relations with Ottawa.[11] Bain was close to the mark: Merchant had been slated to be sent as ambassador to Paris, but the White House wanted an experienced figure in what was an unexpectedly tense post. Congratulating Merchant, Harvard historian and Kennedy aide Arthur Schlesinger Jr. informed him: "A visit to Canada in December convinces me that Canadian–U.S. relations have not been so bad for a very long time. When I asked what sort of appointment would be welcome as U.S. Ambassador, everyone named you as a model."[12] Given the tough times in bilateral relations Merchant was a sound choice, as he very much personified the special relationship. His advocacy of close relations and quiet diplomacy was a point of criticism for one detractor, who felt that Merchant believed that "Canada cannot pursue an independent foreign policy."[13] Even so, Merchant's impending return and Diefenbaker's pending visit to the White House had created a more positive atmosphere.

In the minds of the State Department officials who briefed the president for his meeting with the prime minister, the overall atmosphere of bilateral relations was still affected by the "evolving Canadian attitude of introspection and nationalism," which was the "primary problem" in bilateral relations.[14] Kennedy had indicated awareness of these developments in his speech at the University of New Brunswick, and in welcoming the prime minister to the White House he adopted a cautious, friendly approach. Diefenbaker arrived by plane and was driven to Canada's Embassy, where he was met by Angier Biddle Duke, the White House Chief of Protocol, who escorted him on to meet the president. Peppering Duke with questions about Kennedy en route, the prime minister "was literally perspiring on that winter day as he talked." Never, Duke later recalled, had he seen "such a man so nervous." Diefenbaker and Kennedy sat for talks in the Oval Office, along with Rusk, Merchant, Green, and Heeney. Here, Duke noted, the president "was terribly courteous and terribly deferential to his senior statesman colleague and couldn't have been more polite …

This reassured the nervous Prime Minister a great deal, and they hit it off as well as possible under the circumstances."[15]

After some perfunctory opening remarks and a *tour d'horizon* of matters in Africa and Southeast Asia, they turned to Cuba, a potentially contentious topic. Diefenbaker made it clear that Ottawa's stance differed from that of Washington for two reasons: Canadian investments had not been aggressively nationalized, and Canada believed in trading with all nations. Still, trade in military items had been forbidden, as had the re-export of US goods to Cuba through Canada. He observed too that his government was not pushing to expand trade with the Caribbean island. Then dismissing any notion that anti-Americanism existed in his country, the prime minister cautioned that it was "perfectly true" that "when Canada disagreed with the United States on policy it would not follow the United States' lead." Evidently realizing that Cuba was one area of disagreement, Kennedy voiced no criticism of the Canadian position.[16]

Diefenbaker's warning proved a good segue to the only divisive issue of the meeting: bunker fuel for Canadian ships carrying wheat to Communist China. In late 1960 Beijing had agreed to purchase 190 million bushels of wheat and 47 million bushels of barley over a two-and-a-half-year period, a big boost to Canada's economy. The only hurdle involved fuel: Imperial Oil, a Canadian subsidiary of Standard Oil of New Jersey, had been asked to supply the oil. The US Treasury Department opposed this transaction on the grounds that the foreign subsidiary of an American company would be fueling trade that contravened US sanctions. In raising the matter Kennedy admitted that he was prepared to authorize the sale so long as the Canadian government submitted a formal request for authorization, but the prime minister explained, understandably, that "Canadians could not understand the United States Government dictating the actions of a Canadian corporation," and so on such a politically "inflammatory issue" he was unwilling to ask the Americans for permission on Imperial Oil's behalf. There discussion rested, with Kennedy stating that as he wished to avoid "embarrassment" he might reconsider his decision.[17]

Over a working lunch, the group then reviewed defense matters. Nuclear weapons were high on the prime minister's agenda: before leaving for Washington he had told the Cabinet that since the stance he had outlined in February 1959 still stood as government policy, his only goal would be to discern "how far" Kennedy would go on joint control. Adding that disarmament sentiments were weakening public appreciation of "the need to have nuclear weapons available," he averred that he did not intend to take a soft stand on defense issues.[18] Diefenbaker repeated this same sentiment to Kennedy, affirming that he would "not accept a policy which will lay upon the United States a responsibility we should carry ourselves." Vowing to cooperate on continental defense, he rejected any lesser role—the opposition Liberals had recently advocated withdrawing from NORAD—as being mere "bird watching." But addressing nuclear weapons,

Diefenbaker asserted that an agreement would not be signed soon on account of international disarmament initiatives; still it would be possible to negotiate a draft agreement "so that there would be no holdup should need arise." On the joint control of any warheads acquired, Diefenbaker agreed with Kennedy's suggestion that the US–UK agreements on control could serve as a model. As for the triangular deal, the prime minister professed support for the new proposal, particularly given its benefits to Canadian industry.[19] After lunch Kennedy and Diefenbaker engaged in repartee on the War of 1812, which left the prime minister alarmed that the president saw the conflict as having been a victorious one for the United States. History aside, Diefenbaker asked Kennedy to visit Ottawa in the spring; the president accepted the invitation. The two men then strolled outside on the White House Lawn, giving the press ample opportunity to snap photos of the two leaders smiling and conversing. Despite the differences over bunker oil, or the assertions of some historians that "from their first meeting, the two men held each other in hearty contempt," this visit was a friendly affair.[20]

On the flight back Diefenbaker was "jubilant," and in remarks to the House of Commons that evening he praised the new administration for its "attitude of the utmost friendliness" and its "obvious desire to assure the maintenance and continuance of the good relations which prevail between the United States and Canada."[21] In private, the prime minister told his Cabinet colleagues that the meeting had begun "with a feeling of strangeness," but had ended with much cordiality. Pleasantly, the new president had agreed to look into the matter of oil bunkering, and had voiced no opposition to a "two key" arrangement on nuclear warheads. The meeting, he told Heeney, "could not have gone better." Relating similar impressions to Robinson, Diefenbaker reversed his previous opinions of Rusk and Kennedy. The president, he now felt, had "a great capacity, a farsighted judgment on international affairs, and an attractive human quality in private exchanges." Dining with the British High Commissioner, the prime minister recalled that when he had praised Kennedy for having expertly managed voters in the American South the president in turn responded: "You did not do so badly in Quebec yourself." This commendation had pleased Diefenbaker greatly, as had the president's admission that as a politician, he recognized that it was only natural that when the prime minister "was in a jam the easy thing was to turn on the anti-American tap," though Kennedy had made sure to underline his hope that the prime minister would never have to rely on this tactic.[22]

The president, meanwhile, has been portrayed as having been far less impressed by his talks with the Canadian leader. Schlesinger would later write that this meeting "had not proved a success" as "Kennedy thought the Canadian insincere and did not like or trust him," with journalist Knowlton Nash relating that the president told his brother: "I don't want to see that

boring son of a bitch again."[23] Certainly the president developed a deep distaste for Diefenbaker, but at the time Kennedy remarked to Merchant that he
"liked" Diefenbaker and that he believed that "on any really important issue"
the prime minister "would be stoutly on our side." Agreeing, Merchant offered
two qualifications: the Canadian government was cognizant of "appearing to
be too closely tied, and hence subordinated" to the Americans in continental
defense; and the president should keep in mind that Diefenbaker "placed great
store on a personal relationship." Whenever there was an important issue necessitating support from Canada, Merchant counseled that sending a personal
message to the prime minister could help to keep Diefenbaker onside.[24]

Neglecting to respond quickly to the prime minister's note of congratulation
following the election had been a misstep, but Kennedy had nevertheless won
over the prime minister. As *Time* observed, Diefenbaker had returned from his
trip to Ottawa "flushed with excitement."[25] Considering both the pessimistic
preconceptions that Diefenbaker had formed prior to Kennedy taking office
and American officials' negative perceptions of the influence of what one reporter called the "new militancy of Canadian nationalism," there is little doubt
that the Kennedy–Diefenbaker summit was, as the *Washington Post* put it, a
"highly successful" introductory session and evidence, the *New York Times*
opined, that Kennedy was set on reversing the "tendency to neglect Canada."[26]
Diplomats from both countries then moved to resolve the two outstanding
issues from the summit: the triangular deal and bunker oil.

Gathering in Washington on February 28, Canadian and American officials
hammered out the details of a triangular deal. The US side made clear that they
were "anxious" to reach an agreement that would be acceptable to Canada, but
that the aircraft industry and certain members of Congress could be expected
to oppose the loss of manufacturing contracts. Wanting to move forward,
the Americans offered to sweeten the pot by increasing the F-104 contract
by $50 million, giving, in total, a $200 million boost to Canadian industry.
Cabinet approved accepting this deal.[27] But a new stumbling block arose: to
get the deal through Congress, the White House had to ensure that the agreement would improve continental security, meaning that the F-101 Voodoos
would need to be armed with missiles carrying nuclear warheads. Adamant
against being hemmed in on nuclear weapons, Diefenbaker told Merchant that
he would wait to press this point with Kennedy during the president's May visit
to Ottawa.[28] This hiccup aside, the White House had shown a desire to be helpful to the Canadians.

The new administration also proved deferential in dealings over Canada's
wheat sales to Communist China. Here American policymakers heeded the
warnings of Canadian officials who emphasized, in a shrewd and effective
manner, that public opinion in their country would turn against the United
States should Washington block this trade. This issue was characteristic of the

differing approach toward relations with communist countries that Canada and the United States had each adopted. Canadian officials saw no reason to cut off trade with other countries simply because of ideological difference, a marked departure from the consensus among US policymakers who favored isolating their enemies.[29] For Canada, a country heavily focused on external trade, there was also an economic interest at play, and with China, this interest was fairly significant, giving the issue added domestic importance. Exports to China were almost exclusively in agricultural products, and with Progressive Conservative support centered partly in the grain-growing region of western Canada, many Tory MPs supported shipping wheat across the Pacific.

At the conclusion of his meeting with Diefenbaker, Kennedy had made a last-minute proposal permitting the fuel sales but requiring the Canadian government to ask permission of the US government. In scrutinizing this formula, Howard Green took exception on the grounds that the problems that existed did so "only on the United States side of the border" between the US government and the parent company, Standard Oil; Imperial Oil should be able to carry on its "normal" business. With Diefenbaker's blessing, he directed Heeney to ask the Americans to immediately permit the oil bunkering and to "avoid any policing measure by United States authorities in Canada."[30] Lobbying by Heeney proved inconclusive, for while the Canadian ambassador defended Ottawa's position that an important "principle" was at stake, White House advisor Fred Dutton countered by raising the domestic political angle for the Kennedy administration, which did not want to be seen to be feeding Communist China.[31] The issue was therefore a significant point of discussion at the annual US–Canadian joint committee on trade and economic affairs, which met in Washington in mid-March and proved to be an opportune moment for Canadian ministers and their new American counterparts to get a sense of one another and to impress upon each other their mutual concerns.

Beyond discussing their common balance of payments problems and various discriminatory trade restrictions and customs matters, the two delegations dealt with oil sales at length. Telling the meeting of the intense public pressure upon his government to protect Canadian sovereignty, Donald Fleming "could not emphasize enough the depth of Canadian feeling on this matter." Addressing this concern, Henry Fowler, the Treasury undersecretary, offered an overview of the existing agreement between Canada and the United States: when Foreign Assets Control regulations might apply to a US subsidiary operating in Canada, informal consultation between the two governments had led to an exemption being granted by the American government. The important issue for Washington was that a legal principle be recognized because the US government could not give up jurisdiction over an American-controlled company. But the Canadians were just as concerned with jurisdictional issues. Canada, replied Canadian agriculture minister Alvin Hamilton, "must maintain a complete watchfulness that her sovereignty is not being impinged." He added that the two countries held "different principles," because "this trade, for the United States, is trade with the enemy. Canada on the other hand, hopes to maintain useful contact with the Soviet bloc on the principle that as long as there is contact, talk and trade, there is no fighting."[32] Disagreement on trade with China aside, the meeting was cordial. Fleming reported back to his Cabinet colleagues that the new administration evidently "would like to improve relations with Canada."[33] Over the coming weeks American diplomats worked closely with Heeney to implement a compromise addressing both governments' jurisdictional concerns.

With grain ships ready to sail to China and with Diefenbaker's instructions to take "a firm stand" both "on principle and in practice," Heeney engaged in tough diplomatic wrangling.[34] In "bluntly" dismissing the arguments of his State Department interlocutors, who contended that legal and political difficulties constrained American action, he countered that since Canada's government viewed the issue as a purely internal matter, bunker oil had become a "laboratory test case involving the proposition as to whether permitting Canadian industry to be foreign-owned was compatible with freedom of Canadian political and economic policy." With this threat of a severe nationalist and protectionist backlash, Washington, unwilling to provoke a serious dispute with Ottawa, permitted the sales to go ahead.[35] Heeney, while certainly inclined to a favorable view of the United States and of the value of close Canada–US relations, certainly was willing to play hardball in defense of Canadian interests, with the favorable result on bunker fuel showing the benefits of quiet diplomacy.

The Kennedy administration had refused to press any further on bunker oil, but in June the Treasury Department did move to block exports to Canada of vacuators, a type of equipment needed to load the grain for shipment. Even though no record exists to prove such an assertion, in his memoirs Diefenbaker wrote that he called Kennedy on this issue, telling the president that if the vacuators were not allowed into Canada then he "would go on national television and radio to tell the Canadian people that [Kennedy] was attempting to run our country." This conversation, the prime minster recalled, effectively ended the good personal relationship between the president and himself.[36] Beyond the fact that Diefenbaker sometimes confused things further by stating that he had flown to Washington to confront Kennedy personally, this recollection seems odd given that when the Canadians did protest the issue, the Americans backed down that same day, with the Treasury agreeing to license the export of the vacuators until a replacement supplier could be found in Canada. In Heeney's view, this volte-face constituted an "extraordinary effort" to accommodate the Canadian position, while Ed Ritchie felt it was "symptomatic of the somewhat better understanding which seems to be developing" between the Canadian and American governments.[37] At the time, Diefenbaker agreed. Announcing this breakthrough to the Cabinet, he argued that it represented "evidence of the desire of the new U.S. administration to meet Canadian wishes."[38] Arguments by some historians, then, that on bunker oil "Diefenbaker had won a small victory, but Kennedy's apparent inability to recognize the importance of the issue to Canadian sovereignty must have been disturbing to him" do not stand up to scrutiny.[39]

Willing to acquiesce on the issue of Canada's trade with China, American authorities were not happy about doing so. As it began to establish its China policy throughout 1961, the Kennedy administration examined whether the horrendous Chinese famine afforded them an opportunity to use food aid as a means of forcing Beijing to alter course in several areas including Southeast Asia. Reports of mass malnutrition in China, one senior White House official told members of the Canadian embassy in May 1961, meant that Canadian wheat sales had "a very real political importance" and should be re-evaluated.[40] Returning to this notion in early 1962, the administration launched an ultimately abortive attempt to have Canada and Australia deny food shipments to China in order to get the Chinese to withdraw support for the North Vietnamese government.[41] So when word of supplementary Canadian wheat sale reached the White House that same year, Kennedy was "not amused," while the president's special assistant for national security affairs, McGeorge Bundy, quipped that since these wheat sales were reversing a Canadian trade deficit, "Diefenbaker will probably be reelected by Mao."[42] Despite its anger, Washington was unwilling to disturb the proverbial Canadian hornets' nest and provoke its northern neighbor into engaging in a potential messy trade dispute.

Trade with the People's Republic of China was one thing, but Diefenbaker was careful not to overstep by recognizing the government in Beijing or support its entry into the United Nations. During their February meeting, the prime minister had remarked to the president that if Washington were to recognize China and abandon Taiwan, then "the position of the free world throughout all of Asia would be destroyed." As for Canada's position, he stated his regret that Ottawa had not recognized Beijing in 1949 because in the current climate such an act would be "construed as a formal act giving political approval to the Chinese Communist regime."[43] There were limits on Canadian policy toward the Chinese, where a clear delineation was drawn between trade and strategic concerns.

Canada also engaged in a careful balancing act over Cuba, which was a far more critical matter for relations between Ottawa and Washington than China policy. In his first meeting with Green after returning to Ottawa, Merchant broached Cuba, prompting Canada's foreign minister to warn that because Washington seemed poised not to exempt Canadian subsidiaries from the Trading with the Enemy Act, he considered Cuba the most pressing issue in bilateral affairs. Green added that Canadians and Americans saw the "Castro revolution differently," at which point Merchant went on the attack, arguing that the "Soviet domination of a country in this hemisphere seemed to me to entail same dangerous implications for Canada as for us."[44] Cuba exposed fissures between an increasingly combative American approach in foreign policy, and Canadians' more measured actions. Throughout early 1961, Diefenbaker's desire to maintain normal ties with Havana was offset both by his desire to have friendly dealings with the new US president and by his awareness of Cuba's increasing orientation toward Moscow. There was a tension on the American side too. Just as the Kennedy administration's approach toward Canada's trade with China acknowledged the importance of Canadian sovereignty, with Cuba, US policymakers were cognizant about a potential dispute over the extraterritorial application of American law. Yet the White House was also intent on strangulating the Cuban economy. Over the first few months of Kennedy's presidency, Washington would seek to balance its relationship with Ottawa with its aggressive policy toward Havana.

In planning to tighten the Cuban embargo, which they had inherited from Eisenhower, members of the Kennedy administration examined expanding these sanctions to restrict United States imports from Cuba. Banning all US–Cuban trade would likely require imposing the Trading with the Enemy Act, making American commercial transactions with Cuba subject to Foreign Assets Control regulations, legislation that could prohibit American subsidiaries operating in Canada from selling goods to the Cubans, a move sure to inflame Canadian public opinion. Hence, Foy Kohler, assistant secretary for European affairs, advised Rusk of the need to exempt Canada. Otherwise, the prime minister and other nationalists would react strongly to infringement upon Canadian sovereignty with anti-US trade legislation. Kohler concluded: "The question thus arises whether the extent of the harassment to the Castro regime which may be achieved by a blanket imposition of the controls would outweigh the resultant serious impact on United States–Canadian relations." Subsequently advising Kennedy to push ahead, Rusk recommended an exemption for Canada.[45]

With the president delaying a decision, Canadian officials were unsure whether the new administration would pursue the same course as its predecessor, which had been reluctant to upset the bilateral relationship over Cuba. Speculative press reports that the White House was set to impose the Trading with the Enemy Act led Heeney to raise the matter while dining with Rusk at the Gridiron Club's annual gala. Revealing plans to implement new trade restrictions, the secretary averred that the White House was "anxious to avoid difficulty for Canada." He wondered, though, would Ottawa be willing to restrict sales to Cuba of machinery and equipment for sugar mills and oil refineries, as well as spare parts for vehicles? First questioning the "wisdom of further economic measures" that seemed unlikely to topple the Castro government, Heeney then argued that Canadians were unlikely to back "a policy for which we had shown little sympathy." However, he suggested that the matter be raised at the joint Canada–US ministerial-level trade and economic conference, which was due to meet shortly.[46]

A meeting on Cuba was arranged on the sidelines of the conference between Rusk, Douglas Dillon, and George Ball, undersecretary of state for economic affairs, on one side, with Heeney, Fleming, Norman Robertson, and George Hees on the other. In earnest tones, the Americans explained that Cuba represented "a source of communist infection" and that sanctions were the most effective means of staving off this contagion. The Canadians offered little sympathy for the view. Wanting to be cooperative, though, Fleming noted that since Canadian exports to Cuba of industrial machinery and truck parts were extremely small, a compromise was possible. Should exemptions from the Trading with the Enemy Act for subsidiaries in Canada trading with Cuba be granted, then he and Hees would be willing "to avoid the frustration of USA policy through any possible exports from Canada" in those items that were of interest to the Americans. This promise, Fleming stressed, should not be taken as any sort of "quid pro quo" for an exemption; Ottawa would simply be helpful. Meeting with Kennedy later that day Fleming and Hees raised this agreement, with the president giving it his own approval.[47] A clever enticement to the Americans as a means to secure an exemption—despite Fleming's avowal, it clearly was a trade-off—it certainly helped that Kennedy felt that the wording of the Trading with the Enemy Act was "very brutal" and that something "less drastic" was needed.[48]

While the president may have wanted a less drastic means of controlling trade, he pushed ahead on a far more extreme course of action, an invasion of Cuba at the Bay of Pigs on April 17 by thirteen hundred Cuban exiles. Originally conceived by the Eisenhower administration, the operation was a fiasco. Debating the future course of Cuban policy at a meeting a week after the exiles had surrendered, the NSC resolved to carry out "all kinds of harassment to punish Castro for the humiliation he has brought to our door."[49] Imposing the Trading with the Enemy Act to shut off all remaining US–Cuban trade was one option. Asked by Kennedy to examine this course of action, Ball and Dillon reviewed the promised exemption for Canadian firms, with Dillon concerned over establishing a precedent for exempting other countries. Strongly favoring an exemption, Ball noted that Fleming and Hees had assured the president that they would "play ball." Without an exemption, he emphasized, the United States would be "in trouble," and "the President had better not go to Ottawa" for his visit in May.[50] Ball won out: when the National Security Council set down a plan of action aimed at Castro's "downfall," it approved exemptions for Canada and the Red Cross.[51]

Respecting Canadian sovereignty, this planned exemption accorded Canada special status, but Dillon, absent from the NSC meeting, remained skeptical and pressed Ball into examining whether Ottawa could get along without an exemption. Raising the notion with Heeney, Ball cited Congressional opposition and explained that even though the Treasury was loath to exempt Canada, it might still be possible to secure an agreement where the Canadian subsidiaries could apply for special licenses from the US government. Immediately attacking this proposal, Heeney argued that not only did it run counter to Fleming and Hees's understanding with the Americans, but that it would create an immense "adverse reaction" among Canadians, who would not countenance Washington's interference in Canada. Alarmed by this forcefulness, Ball spoke with Dillon and repeated the Canadian ambassador's warning that "Diefenbaker would talk about nothing else to the President if we went ahead with this." Dillon acquiesced. In the end, a waiver would be issued for all subsidiaries in Canada and, to make it clear that the United States was not seeking to interfere with Canadian businesses, this blanket waiver would be spelled out in the presidential order authorizing the imposition of FAC regulations, a victory applauded by the Cabinet in Ottawa.[52] It was a victory for quiet diplomacy.

The resolution of the Cuban trade issue pleased Canadian officials, whereas the Bay of Pigs fiasco did little to build confidence in the new administration. Historians have judged that the failed invasion marked the "turning point in Diefenbaker's judgment of Kennedy," and that as a result of the debacle Diefenbaker "concluded that Kennedy had shown he was rash and foolish."[53] The prime minister's position was far more nuanced. Certainly, if the Bay of Pigs instilled in the prime minister doubts about Kennedy's judgment they were short-lived: later that year, as a crisis brewed over Berlin, Diefenbaker voiced no concerns about his American counterpart's handling of foreign policy and instead stood stoutly with Kennedy against Khrushchev. On April 19, with domestic critics circling the White House and with the United States facing a torrent of abuse from the Soviet bloc and from most neutral nations, Diefenbaker confided privately that he was "concerned about Cuba and determined to say publicly that we were disturbed about Communism there." Publicly, without offering actual support for the failed invasion, he condemned the Cuban government for showing "manifestations of a dictatorship which are abhorrent to free men everywhere." Moscow's support for Havana, he added, "revealed beyond doubt the extent to which international communism is prepared to go in consolidating its foothold in Cuba, a bridgehead from which the penetration of the whole of Latin America could be launched." Diefenbaker's sympathetic statement was reportedly widely in the US press and appreciated in Washington.[54] Analyzing the fallout of the attack, the State Department's Bureau of Intelligence and Research noted that world opinion had largely "reacted unfavourably" to the possible role of the United States in the operation. However, apart from expected left-wing criticism in Parliament and in the press as well as some minor public demonstrations, journalistic and government opinion in Canada had been supportive of the United States. Diefenbaker, the report noted, who "had in the past tended to doubt the extent to which Communist elements dominated the Castro regime, came much closer to the US view than ever before." Likewise, Merchant saw the prime minister's hard-hitting statement as a "welcome development," while Kennedy asked the US embassy to inform Diefenbaker of his "appreciation" for the remarks.[55]

Far from indicating a new, more hostile Canadian approach to Cuba, the prime minister was offering his country's key ally support during a moment of weakness. His speech, he told Merchant, was made "contrary to the advice he had received from External Affairs" and "had produced something of a shock" among his diplomatic advisors. He was even upset that his supportive comments had received little to no press coverage in the United States, though in fact this was not the case.[56] Support aside, the prime minister saw the operation as a failure of US policy. As he remarked to Basil Robinson, "he did not wish the United States Government to be left with the impression that they could count on Canadian support for anything foolish they might do with regard to Cuba."[57] Canadian officials duly sought to dampen US expectations that Canada was shifting course. Speaking with Rusk, Heeney underlined that the prime minister's public comments were not words of support for what was "widely regarded in Canada as a serious mistake."[58] Although not pleased by the hapless invasion, Canadian officials offered no public criticism, nor did they take a hard line in private. Meeting with Merchant, Stewart Udall, the US secretary of the Interior, Orville Freeman, the US secretary of Agriculture, and several Canadian ministers in early May, Diefenbaker expressed his "admiration" for Kennedy's "restraint" in not overreacting to the failure of the invasion by attacking Cuba outright.[59] A week beforehand, the prime minister had told Merchant that he was worried "over where the United States goes from here," but he had also taken pains to express support for the United States, adding that he had recently told Cuba's ambassador that "there was one Cuban export with which the world and particularly Latin America could do without and that was the effort to export the Cuban revolution in the form which it has now taken."[60] Diefenbaker's strong words toward the Cuban ambassador were not combined with any concrete change in Canada–Cuba relations, but the prime minister had made clear to the Cubans that while not supportive of the invasion itself, Ottawa stood with Washington, not Havana.

Whereas Diefenbaker offered tentative support for Kennedy, Green took a louder approach. Shortly after the invasion force had surrendered, Fidel Castro and Cuban President Osvaldo Dorticos hinted at a desire to hold talks with the Americans. Spurred on by the possibility that Havana and Washington could negotiate their differences, Green urged Diefenbaker to raise this overture with Merchant. The prime minister refused to support any approach to the Americans. Instead, he sought opportunities for informal talks with Merchant not to raise the Cuban proposal, but to urge caution in US dealings with Cuba.[61]

Undismayed, Green pursued the matter. At a summit of NATO foreign ministers in Oslo in early May, he declared that Canada "deplores many of the practices of the Castro regime," but added that Ottawa hoped "that the possibility of negotiation would not be ruled out."[62] This comment shocked Dean Rusk, who told Green that for Washington, a necessary precursor to negotiations was the elimination of Havana's links to Moscow. Afterward, Rusk implored Kennedy to raise with Diefenbaker Canadian foreign policy's "neutralist tendencies," which were personified by Green. Canada's foreign minister, he warned, was one of those in "the long parade" who wanted to provide "continuous concessions on our part to an insatiable power determined to pursue its world revolution by every available means."[63]

As for Green, he remained undismayed about negotiations. While en route from Norway to a summit in Geneva, he told reporters on his plane that Canada would be more than willing to mediate the dispute between Havana and Washington. As the story broke, Heeney was dining with Schlesinger and other White House officials, who then questioned him as to whether Canada had committed the sin of putting "Castro and Kennedy on the same footing."[64] The next morning, with the *Washington Post* blaring "Canada Set to Mediate Cuba Dispute," Heeney was summoned to the State Department. In carefully stressing that the report of Green's offer remained unconfirmed, the ambassador carefully pointed out that even if it were true, the Canadian minister may not have meant "mediation" in a technical sense, nor did such a policy "represent Canadian policy as he knew it," with Diefenbaker's comments in the House of Commons a better guide to government thinking. However, the ambassador was sure not to "paper over" Canadian–American differences over Cuba. Then asked about the likelihood of Canada joining the Organization of American States, Heeney quickly pointed out that the Bay of Pigs invasion had created considerable discontent in Canada at the direction of US foreign policy in Latin America.[65]

Heeney had touched on an important aspect of the fallout of the failed invasion of Cuba: its impact upon Canadian public opinion. Kennedy's election victory had been widely applauded by many Canadians who hoped to see a new direction in US foreign policy. For instance, criticizing American "brinksmanship" under Eisenhower, *Maclean's* had judged that Kennedy "will be firm but not stubborn, valiant but not foolhardy, flexible but not pliant, a steady hand on the helm of the western alliance." Only a month before the Cuban disaster, one Canadian historian who was often critical of the United States had praised the young president's "cool capacity to stand outside himself and observe his own central performance in the great drama of the 1960s."[66] The Bay of Pigs dashed these hopes. The editors of the *Montreal Gazette* were flabbergasted that Kennedy had pursued a plan "so ill-based on reality." Attacking the White House for its ham-handed intervention in Cuban affairs, the *Ottawa Citizen* pleaded for Washington to seek "better advice about the Cubans than it seems to have been following hitherto." Also questioning American judgment, the *Globe and Mail* observed that the invasion had been counterproductive on several counts: Castro's position was strengthened, Cuba would likely move farther into the Soviet camp, US prestige was battered with "old fears of 'Yankee imperialism,'" and, "most serious of all, the United States has damaged its moral position in the world as a peaceful, law-abiding nation."[67] Unfortunately for American policymakers, these doubts about US policy in Latin America came just as the Kennedy administration was set on asking Canada to take a wider role in hemispheric affairs. The Canadian government, Diefenbaker stated soon after the fiasco, "would not be 'tied up in' any OAS moves in respect of Cuba," an important statement given that Canada's stance toward the Organization of American States emerged as a major issue during Kennedy's visit to Ottawa.[68]

As prime minister, Diefenbaker had pursued a policy of engagement with Latin America, a region that appeared to offer new, booming markets for Canadian exports, thus providing a counterweight to Canada–US trade. When he mounted a state visit to Mexico in 1960, Diefenbaker became the first Canadian prime minister to travel south of the Rio Grande. Supporting the prime minister's southern initiative, Green championed the establishment of Canadian diplomatic representation with all Latin America countries, a feat accomplished under his watch. However, Canadians did not seem all that interested in events in the region. Returning from Mexico, Diefenbaker complained to Green that "Canadians seldom look beyond the United States." Regardless, he maintained: "I am more and more convinced that the political future of the Americas will depend on the OAS. We are losing ground." The cost of membership could be high, but it would be a worthwhile investment likely to boost Canada's commercial prospects.[69] The OAS was the foremost multilateral body in the Western hemisphere, and Canada had long toyed with whether or not it should become a member, fearing that on various issues it would be pitted against either the United States or all of Latin America. Under Diefenbaker and Green's stewardship of Canadian foreign policy, Canada's hesitancy finally appeared to be at an end.

Ottawa's interest in Latin America came just as Washington was itself attaching greater importance to the region as a result of Cuba's revolution and growing unrest among the region's poor and oppressed masses. But whereas Diefenbaker's policy was largely commercial, US officials were focused upon shoring up Latin America as a bulwark against communism. Believing that poverty in the Western hemisphere made the region a breeding ground for Cuban-style revolution, Kennedy sought a program to stabilize the hemisphere, prevent Communist infiltration, and win the Cold War in Latin America. His signature initiative to accomplish these goals, formally announced to a White House gathering of Latin American diplomats on March 13, was the Alliance for Progress, an aid program of massive proportions. As Kennedy reminded his audience, "we North Americans have not fully understood the urgency of the need to lift people from poverty and ignorance and despair."[70] This reference to North America most assuredly included Canada, for administration officials wanted Ottawa to play a role in this effort. Walt Rostow, a renowned advocate of development assistance and Kennedy's deputy national security advisor, had outlined for the president the need to encourage Canadian involvement in aid programs. Canada, as a wealthy and technologically advanced country, could play a positive role in the region both in a material sense and in terms of providing political support to the United States' initiatives, including in the OAS.[71] As early as 1957 Kennedy had himself highlighted Canada as one of several "close allies . . . whose economies can now absorb more international spending and investment," while throughout the 1960 presidential campaign he had emphasized the importance of harnessing Canadian agricultural abundance as a means of feeding the world's poor.[72] To Rostow and Kennedy, then, Canada had an important role to play alongside the Untied States in promoting development and stability in Latin America and across the Third World.

Offering his immediate reactions to the president's proposal, Green told the House of Commons that the government had not yet considered an increase in assistance to Latin America. Going on to affirm his interest in expanding Canada's presence in the hemisphere, he admitted that membership in the OAS would be "a big step," one that government would not take until it was "fairly clear that the majority of the Canadian people are in favour of this being done."[73] This was hardly a decisive statement of support for Washington. Ignoring Green's hesitancy, US policymakers sensed that a Canadian move toward joining the OAS was imminent, a step they welcomed whole-heartedly. With the president's trip to Ottawa coming on the heels of the announcement about the Alliance for Progress, the State Department counseled Kennedy to tell Diefenbaker that the US supported any increased Canadian role in the hemisphere. Even if Canada took different positions than Washington on certain issues, American diplomats felt that "the important point to us is to succeed in having Canada assume responsibilities in this strategic area."[74] Richard Goodwin, an advisor to Kennedy on Latin American affairs, also told the president of the need to urge Canada toward greater participation in this area of the world, particularly through the OAS. Contradictory advice came from Kennedy's military aide, Canadian-born general Chester Clifton. Reporting to the president a conversation that he had had with a Canadian reporter, Clifton warned that the OAS issue was a nonstarter.[75] The matter was settled only four days before the president's departure for Ottawa when Rostow and Heeney met to review the content of the president's speech to Canada's Parliament. Despite his prior sense that Canadians were opposed to OAS membership, Heeney now advised that Kennedy could "tactfully encourage" Canada's entry into the organization. Rostow, in passing this advice along to the president, remarked pithily that Canada appeared ready to take a wider role in Latin America "on grounds other than 'mediating' between" Washington and Havana.[76] Then, on the eve of Kennedy's voyage, the White House received a positive appraisal from the Ottawa Embassy, which noted "growing" interest in Latin America alongside the "increasing" possibility of Canada joining the OAS. Convinced that the time was at hand, en route to Ottawa, Rostow, in a memorandum titled "What We Want from the Ottawa Trip," thus advised Kennedy to "push" Canada toward greater participation in the hemisphere, including OAS membership.[77]

In Ottawa there was much less enthusiasm than the Americans thought. Robert Bryce, who drew up Diefenbaker's briefing book for his meeting with Kennedy, consulted with officials in External Affairs, Finance, Trade and Commerce, and National Defence, and concluded from these talks that Canada was "not yet ready" to join the OAS, nor was the Canadian government prepared to embark on any new aid programs for the region mainly because "our efforts should not be spread too thin." Further, the Alliance for Progress seemed "sensible and constructive," but it was doubtful that many regional governments would carry out the types of reforms demanded by the program.[78] Diefenbaker had already expressed hesitation about the connection between the OAS and Cuba, and Bryce added more reasons to oppose further Canadian involvement in the Latin America.[79] Moreover, unlike the American proponents of the Alliance—who, like Rostow, were a collection of social scientists and modernization theorists—the upper echelon of External Affairs was staffed by a cohort of officials who took a much less technocratic view of world affairs, prizing slow, evolutionary processes.[80] Crucially too, whereas US policy in Latin America was preoccupied with communist subversion, Diefenbaker's policy was less concerned with the Cold War than with establishing new markets. Additionally, the Canadian government was parsimonious with its aid programs, which were focused largely on development efforts in Commonwealth countries. In advance of Kennedy's visit, Diefenbaker remarked to Robinson that with an election brewing, instead of focusing on development aid abroad he was "going to think of Canada for the next 14, 15, 16 or 18 months."[81] Ottawa was not, then, going to embark on any new assistance programs, nor, given the tension created by the Bay of Pigs, did membership in the OAS seem prudent.

Attention, meanwhile, was focusing on Kennedy's pending visit to Ottawa. In advance of the president's trip a National Intelligence Estimate, titled "Trends in Canadian Foreign Policy," was produced. The report's central conclusion was that relations with Canada had reached a "new phase," one "marked by Canadian sensitivity" to increased cultural, economic, and military dependence upon the United States and by a resulting Canadian "determination to pursue a more distinctly Canadian line in foreign policy." This uptick in Canadian nationalism had "anti-American overtones," but the intelligence analysts concluded that the traditionally close relationship between the two North

American countries had not been damaged, with policy differences "not expected to reach such proportions as to cause a major impairment of the present basically good relations with the US."[82] The Embassy in Ottawa offered a similarly positive assessment: since the president personified the nation, Merchant argued that Kennedy's impending visit provided the "best possible opportunity" to win the support of the Canadian government and its people, and despite some nationalist grumblings, the president "had fired the imagination of many Canadians." This popularity offered the chance to advance US interests because "even those who resist American influence in Canada are now well impressed by the new administration and their criticism is muted." Merchant envisaged a dual purpose for the visit: to consolidate pro-American feelings among the populace and to win over Diefenbaker and his Cabinet so that there could be "stronger adherence to our global policies."[83] Written prior to the Bay of Pigs invasion, this assessment was not abandoned by the State Department when it drew up Kennedy's briefing memoranda, nor did Merchant offer a more cautious postinvasion update. The State Department's guidance papers began with the usual observations about Canadian "introspection and nationalism," but also highlighted an uptick in relations, which was the combined result of the president's personality, of Merchant's return to Ottawa, and of the prime minister's friendly visit to Washington, and which provided a basis to establish not a close friendship but a "frank working relationship" with Diefenbaker and to "impress upon him and his government our views and policies on global problems." Repeating in its entirety the Embassy's observation that criticism was muted, the paper warned that this feeling could not be taken for granted because of the ever-present nationalist specter.[84]

US policymakers viewed the president's trip as a key moment to address several issues with Canada, from Latin America to the Canadian government's requisition of nuclear warheads. On the latter, "to promote the security of North America and the NATO Alliance," Kennedy was urged to encourage the Canadian government to "agree before long" to acquire these components.[85] Among American journalists the dominating narrative was that the summit, with its many occasions for public diplomacy and the attendant press coverage, offered Kennedy the chance to allay Canadian upset over American ignorance of Canada other than through lofty but empty rhetoric about "4,000 miles of unguarded frontier, our common heritage, our kindred peoples, and the like." It also afforded him an opportunity to redress the "doubts and misgivings and disappointment and apprehension that have developed in Canada since the fiasco of the Cuban invasion," a debacle that had "upset some who were keenest on Kennedy."[86] Nuclear weapons and Canada's position in the Western hemisphere would emerge as the two issues that received the most attention by the two leaders. Kennedy was to win a partial victory on the first issue, but on the second, he was to learn that there were limits to his charm. Expectations were high that Kennedy would seek support from Diefenbaker, with one reporter predicting that the president would "challenge the Canadian prime minister to follow his example of extending the prestige and glitter of the New Frontier into imaginative new programs."[87]

The trip began warmly enough on May 16 when the presidential plane touched down in Ottawa. A long winter had only recently ended and with Ottawa's tulips in full bloom, "spring and the Kennedys burst upon Ottawa almost simultaneously." Waiting for the president and first lady on the tarmac were Georges Vanier, the governor general, Mrs. Vanier, and John and Olive Diefenbaker. The three men, accompanied by their wives, briefly spoke to the press. Neither the president nor prime minister was an elegant French speaker, a point Kennedy made light of, remarking that after hearing Diefenbaker speak, "I'm somewhat encouraged to say a few words in French," thus apparently upsetting his Canadian counterpart, though Basil Robinson wrote in his diary that Kennedy "pleased all by saying P.M.'s French made him feel somewhat encouraged." The president did praise the prime minister, however, noting that "his counsel and friendship were of great value to us all in the early days of a new Administration."[88] The Kennedys then proceeded to Government House, where, following a short, private meeting with Diefenbaker, the president and first lady each planted a tree, a ceremonial custom observed by foreign dignitaries. While turning over the sod, the president wrenched his back, a wound from which he never recovered.[89] Not dissuaded by the immense pain, the president attended a state dinner that evening and the next morning addressed the staff at the US embassy before taking the short walk to Canada's War Memorial, where he planted a wreath during a brief ceremony. From there the president proceeded with Diefenbaker to the prime minister's office in Parliament's East Block, where a rocking chair had been procured for Kennedy's use. Besides the two leaders, those present were Merchant, Heeney, Bryce, Robinson, Rostow, and Ivan White. According to Robinson, Kennedy arrived "clearly well briefed and sensitive to the Canadian outlook and concerns."[90]

After perfunctory pleasantries were exchanged, the president broached Latin American issues. Citing Cuba as a dangerous "rallying point" for leftists and a source of subversion in the Western hemisphere, Kennedy characterized this area as being among his highest concerns, and so he hoped that Canada would expand its level of participation in the region. Diefenbaker declared simply that "Canadians were farther away today" from OAS membership than previously, adding that Canada would be more influential outside the organization than inside of it. There was further conversation on Latin America, with Kennedy affirming that he had no plans to intervene militarily in Cuba, but that if such a decision had to be made he would consult in advance with the prime minister.[91] The president continued to press Diefenbaker to reconsider the OAS. Declining to address this matter, the prime minister instead raised

Canadian–Cuban trade, stressing that Canada exported only nonstrategic goods and that overall, trade was diminishing. Diefenbaker also did nothing more than simply inquire about Kennedy's plans for the Alliance for Progress. Instead he moved on to the bunker oil issue, thanking the president for the way in which this file had been handled. Again returning to OAS membership, Kennedy added that he hoped Ottawa would at least send an observer to the Inter-American Economic and Social Council meeting to be held in Montevideo in July, but Diefenbaker refused to commit to either appeal.[92]

Acquisition of nuclear warheads was the focus of much of the rest of the meeting. On disarmament, Kennedy contended that pacifism aside, "the average person is reasonable. Canada is in the path of hazard and must accept defensive nuclear weapons." Agreeing, the prime minister revealed his worry at "Canadian sentiment," adding that "the people must be kept aroused to the dangers they face." Diefenbaker also mentioned that it "might be possible" for Canada to take possession of warheads, provided that joint control mechanisms were worked out so that Ottawa would not appear to be "subservient" to Washington. Accepting such weaponry, however, was "politically impossible today" as an "upsurge" of anti-nuclear sentiment meant that Diefenbaker doubted even being able to carry his Cabinet on the issue, let alone the public. But he vowed to Kennedy that he would "make an effort to change public opinion on this question this summer and fall." As for the triangular deal, he indicated that Canada would not accept the condition that the F-101s be armed with nuclear-tipped missiles, with the president expressing "perplexity" that this proposal was causing such difficulties.[93] The two-hour meeting broke up just after noon and a short lunch was held at the prime minister's residence. The president and first lady were then driven through throngs of onlookers to the Parliament buildings where Kennedy was due to deliver an address.

As the Ottawa Embassy had emphasized, this speech was an important element in the public diplomacy aspect of the president's visit north. Commenting on an Embassy draft, Rostow told Kennedy speechwriter Ted Sorenson that two main points required more emphasis: the importance of development aid to Third World countries, and the need to strengthen the Atlantic Community, points that would help to blunt criticism that American "policy has become distorted" by Cuba and Southeast Asia. He further advised that the general theme of the speech should be that "while the U.S. and Canada share many intimate ties and confront an array of special bilateral problems and possibilities, our relations will flourish as we work side by side on the great common problems of the Free World." Canada, in Rostow's estimation, was a partner of the United States, with an important, supportive role to play. Sorensen's draft included a memorable passage drawn from the Book of Common Prayer: "Those who God hath joined together let no man put asunder," a line that alarmed the State Department's Bureau of European Affairs, which requested that it be removed because they believed that it implied a closer union between the US and Canada and so risked drawing the ire of Canadian nationalists.[94] The phrase was retained. But in a nod to nationalist feeling, Rostow, after seeking input from Heeney, urged that the speech should be sympathetic toward nationalist concerns of US cultural and economic preponderance while also taking "the wind graciously out of the sails" of Canadians who feared that their country was "in danger of becoming an American province."[95] Sorensen did not disappoint.

Before a huge audience of Canadian parliamentarians and dignitaries, reporters and the local diplomatic corps, Kennedy made a characteristically emotional declaration: "Geography has made us neighbors. History has made us friends. Economics has made us partners. And necessity has made us allies." Showing sympathy to nationalists, he intoned that although Canada and the United States were allies they were bound to disagree on many issues, to work toward solutions, and to respect cases where agreement could not be reached. "This is a partnership, not an empire," he affirmed. Turning next to his own agenda, Kennedy emphasized the role that Canada could play in the Western hemisphere, one "deserving of your talents and resources, as well as ours," and he stated that all members of the OAS would welcome Canadian membership. On this point, he concluded that "your country and mine are partners in North American affairs; can we not become partners in inter-American affairs?"[96]

Following this stirring address, Merchant hosted a reception at his residence. The meal was followed by a customary round of brandy and cigars and during this postprandial powwow, the president sat between Diefenbaker and Lester Pearson. Years later Merchant recalled that with Kennedy spending an inordinate amount of time speaking with Pearson, and with Merchant and Diefenbaker both failing to interject themselves into the conversation, this affair became intensely awkward. The result, Merchant believed, was that the president's "behavior, unconsciously, had been such to cause a very vain man, Mr. Diefenbaker, to feel that he had been slighted."[97] There may also have been something deliberate in Kennedy's behavior. Before departing from Washington the president had been advised that earlier that year Pearson had tried in vain to meet with him several times when they had both been in New York City. Pearson was apparently "miffed" by this oversight, and so Kennedy's focus on the Liberal leader may have been aimed at soothing him, albeit at the cost of offending the Canadian premier.[98]

The following morning, before Kennedy departed Ottawa, the president and prime minister breakfasted together. In the intervening hours Rostow had spoken to what he described as "the best Canadian civil servants—who are all with us," who had advised that if Kennedy wished to see Canada play a wider role in Latin America, he could ask Diefenbaker to send an observer to the Inter-American Economic and Social Council meeting, a move that did not entail any expenditures on aid or political commitments. The president took this advice. First, though, he again raised the matter of the OAS; again he was rebuffed by Diefenbaker, who did hint at the possibility of sending observers to the summit in Montevideo. In spite of having to fend off the president's advances on the Organization of American States, and regardless of any hurt feelings over Kennedy's impropriety with Pearson, Diefenbaker was still impressed with his visitor, joking to reporters, "I hope that fellow never comes across the border and runs against me." In a letter to his brother, the prime minister wrote that he and Kennedy "got along very well together. The opinion I formed of him when I first met him—a brilliant intellect and a wide knowledge of world events—was not only borne out but intensified as a result of our discussions in the last two days." A week after the president's visit, Diefenbaker repeated similar comments to Merchant.[99] Olive Diefenbaker noticed no hostility between the two leaders and wrote Jackie Kennedy: "It's quite a thing isn't it, when two heads of state can be so comfortable and happy together."[100] Soon after returning to Washington, Kennedy expressed to Diefenbaker his gratitude for the reception that he had received, noting how "much is always said about the special continental partnership of Canada and the United States, and its validity was impressed on me most forcibly during my trip to Ottawa." The prime minister soon responded with a note of sympathy over the president's back injury; he and Kennedy then carried out a series of correspondence over the summer dealing, variously, with Israel, the Soviet Union, Berlin, and Canada's nuclear weapons.[101] It seems too strong to refer, then, to the "rancor of May" or contend that as a result of the visit the president "was furious" and had "no confidence left" in the prime minister—disappointment certainly, but not rancor.[102]

In terms of the broad tempo of bilateral relations, the visit was successful. The Canadian press was certainly impressed by the president and Jacqueline Kennedy, whose visit, *Maclean's* observed, was "the first time the pomp of state and the sparkle of glamour both came to Parliament Hill in the same party." Blaring "Kennedys Hailed by 50,000; Enthusiasm Astounds Officialdom," the *Globe and Mail* gave full coverage to their comings and goings. Across its front pages, the *Montreal Gazette* matched photos of the "jaunty" president and his "attractive" wife with glowing reports of the "enthusiastic crowds" who swarmed to catch glimpses of the Kennedys. The couple also received a favorable review in the *Ottawa Citizen*, whose editors seemed saddened when the president's "cheery wave" brought an end to a "memorable trip." The American press was also pleased. *Time* reported that Canadians, including the prime minister, were "plainly captivated" by the president and first lady. Despite policy differences over Cuba as well as Canadian fears of economic and cultural dominance from the south, the Kennedys had "melted the Canadian ice." Splashing a color photograph of a crimson-clad Jacqueline Kennedy and a member of the Royal Canadian Mounted Police on its cover, *Life* divided its coverage equally between the pomp and circumstance of the visit and its lighter side. Walter Cronkite, meanwhile, hosted "The Kennedys in Canada," a half-hour CBS television program that covered both the ceremonial aspects of the trip and Ms. Kennedy's movements about the Canadian capital. Cronkite reported that the journey had been successful both as a demonstration of warm bilateral relations and as "an indication that the Kennedy Administration understood the problems of Canada more than the previous one."[103] To the US Embassy, the throngs of Canadians and the fawning press coverage were "reassuring" signs of the "basic sense" of Canada's "identification" with the United States. With his "vigorous, eloquent, and thoughtful" parliamentary address, the president had "startled but did not offend Canadians," whose "complacency and smugness [were] salubriously shaken."[104] Observers in the British High Commission likewise judged the visit to be an effective foray into public diplomacy. Kennedy appeared to have tempered "the traditional rumblings of Canadian discontent at the irritations arising from their close proximity to the United States," grumblings that had not lessened thanks to the Bay of Pigs debacle.[105]

Kennedy's visit may have succeeded from a public relations standpoint and, as Schlesinger noted, the "round of talks in Ottawa was civil enough," but in terms of specific policy objectives, the results were more modest. Diefenbaker's promise to seek to change Canadian opinion on nuclear weapons was a welcome development, but no actual commitment to acquire the weapons had been forthcoming. On his return flight to Washington, Kennedy told Heeney, who was on board, that while he wanted Canada to take possession of nuclear weaponry he fully recognized the "political problem involved" and he was content to leave the initiative to the prime minister, comments hardly reflective of a "tendency" on the president's part "to focus only on American concerns."[106] Still, there was action on the triangular deal. Diefenbaker remained adamant that he would agree to the three-way swap provided that the deal not include a requirement that the interceptors be armed immediately with nuclear missiles. With the prime minister refusing to budge on the grounds that this requirement would be politically unpalatable, Kennedy, unwilling to press the point, authorized talks to go ahead without the provisions for nuclear warheads: Canada could accept the aircraft without the nuclear-tipped missiles to go along with them. Expressing to Merchant his "extreme satisfaction" with the president's compromise, Diefenbaker sought and received Cabinet approval for formal talks to proceed, with the Canadian ministers approving a final deal in June.[107] For the United States, the agreement meant that Canada would take possession of modern interceptors seen as necessary for continental defense. As for nuclear warheads, Kennedy had acquiesced to the Canadian leader—a sure sign that he was not out to dominate Canada—but on the understanding that such armament would be part of a later deal. The prime minister, meanwhile, had secured control over the Pinetree line, new aircraft for self-defense, and a $200 million boost to industry.

There was much less compromising over Latin American affairs. On the flight from Ottawa, the president told Heeney that he placed "great importance" on Ottawa becoming more involved in the hemisphere, stressing that OAS membership was not necessary in this regard. It was merely Canada's "presence" that was needed, and the country had "an important and constructive role to play."[108] After receiving Heeney's report of this discussion, Diefenbaker telephoned the ambassador to confirm that "there was no immediate likelihood" of Canada joining the OAS. Despite the Liberal opposition's support of membership, Diefenbaker pointed to correspondence he was receiving from Canadians as indicating "continuing evidence of popular opposition to such a move, particularly amongst 'old Country' elements"—that is, Canadians of a nationalistic outlook who formed the Tory base in vote-rich Ontario. He offered a slightly different explanation to the Cabinet, arguing that worrying events in the region meant that Canada should avoid further involvement. However, Diefenbaker did opt to send observers to attend the upcoming Inter-American Economic and Social Council summit in Uruguay.[109] This move, while hardly meeting Kennedy half way, did show some cooperation between Ottawa and Washington on Latin America. Doubtless Kennedy was disappointed with this partial measure; both Canada's diplomatic stock and Diefenbaker's standing in Washington would have increased with OAS membership. But the prime minister's hesitancy to go all-in stemmed from his doubts about US actions in the hemisphere as well as appreciation for what would be acceptable to voters.

Besides public opinion and worries about US policy in the region, the prime minister may have had another reason to oppose joining the OAS. Two days after Kennedy departed, Basil Robinson recalled, "in a post mortem on the visit, the prime minister brought the paper out, remarking on its repeated use of the word 'push.'" Left behind in the prime minister's office by the president, this paper, Rostow's memo "What We Want from the Ottawa Trip," urged Kennedy to "push" for Canada to enter the OAS, wording likely reaffirming the prime minister's resistance toward membership. To Diefenbaker, Robinson speculated, "this personified the attitude of the Americans: they thought nothing of pushing Canada around. He seemed to be regarding the paper as a sort of trophy, and it was impossible to tell whether he would hold on to it for future display or return it as I had recommended."[110] This document was an innocuous list of talking points, but Kennedy's repeated insistence on the OAS during his talks with Diefenbaker and in his speech may have come to look like pushing. Certainly, it contributed to the prime minister's eventual deep dislike for the president. The Americans were not yet aware that something was amiss, though by July word was leaking out as British diplomats reported rumors that Rostow had said something to offend Diefenbaker.[111]

The prime minister's desire not to be pushed reflected his judgment of the domestic situation surrounding OAS membership In the wake of Kennedy's speech in Ottawa. The public appeal to Canada to join the organization was certainly a mistake. Although he felt that the president's plea had been "couched in delicate, indeed flattering terms, those calculated to avoid disturbing Canadian sensibilities," in his memoirs Heeney took the blame for having suggested to Rostow that the OAS should be mentioned publicly. Also accepting blame, Rostow later conceded that Kennedy had made an error in pushing the matter as hard as he did.[112] Certainly the incident reflected the Kennedy administration's overzealousness, combined with poor judgment on Heeney's part. The original draft of the speech, drawn up by the Ottawa Embassy and the Canada Desk, had implored Canada to take a wider role in hemispheric affairs but had not called for entry into the OAS, text Rostow then changed. As a future ambassador to Canada later remarked, "it's one of the troubles that the White House gets in if they have a bright fellow like Rostow, who thinks he knows more than he does, and they don't bother to consult the Canadian desk where they might have somebody who wouldn't get a Phi Beta Kappa key out of Yale Law School, but who would have goddamn more sense about Canada."[113] Given the feeling among administration officials that Kennedy's very presence in the White House had generated a friendly and receptive attitude in Canada, and Heeney's reassurance on the OAS, it is not surprising that the president pushed so hard on this point, particularly given the importance he attached to Latin America.

Canadians' negative reaction to OAS membership provided the new administration with a valuable lesson. The Ottawa Embassy's initial assessment of the presidential visit had been positive; however, doubts emerged. A week after Kennedy's departure from Ottawa, one senior Canadian diplomat, George Ignatieff, raised Kennedy's speech and cautioned Rufus Smith to "not underestimate Canadian sensitivities about appearing as an American satellite." The Embassy began to pick up further signs of opposition in the press and with no huge outpouring of feeling favoring OAS membership there was "little reason" to expect a decision on the matter, especially given Diefenbaker's "habit of postponing all controversial decisions" and his "consistent effort to avoid any adverse criticism, however weak or ill-founded."[114] Adverse criticism was certainly evident. Green, aware that public and press opinion had previously favored membership in the OAS, wanted to know, in light of Kennedy's appeal, whether there was a trend emerging in the opposite direction. External Affairs responded quickly with two analyses. The first, looking at press reaction, found that with two exceptions, editorials printed after Kennedy's visit backed Canada joining the OAS. The second, prepared in early June, examined incoming correspondence and concluded that while opinion in 1960 had mostly supported Canadian membership, since the Bay of Pigs there had been a "perceptible swing in the opposite direction."[115] As the weeks went on, public opinion remained opposed to membership and editorial opinion, even from newspapers favoring membership, had swung around to a view that a decision be postponed lest it "be interpreted as giving way to United States pressure."[116] Canadians had little interest in hemispheric affairs, and still less interest in looking subservient to the United States.

Understandably, then, Diefenbaker would not budge on the issue, which slipped off of the agenda for the rest of his premiership. The question of membership was debated in the House of Commons in September, with Liberal external affairs critic Paul Martin attacking the government's ignorance of Canada's "responsibilities to our own sister American continents."[117] Several days later, he again pressed the matter by affirming Liberal support for joining the OAS and calling upon Green to indicate the government's intentions. When Green finally responded, it was likely with a degree of disappointment. "One of the least effective ways of persuading Canada to adopt a policy," he explained, "is for the president or head of state of another country to come here and tell us what we should do, no matter if it is done with the best intentions." While admitting "I do not think President Kennedy meant to interfere," Green could not commit to Canadian membership.[118] Rather than reflecting any personal anti-US sentiment, Green's statement was in fact quite accurate.

Kennedy's public appeal for Canada to join the OAS had fallen flat with the prime minister and with many Canadians. Although some historians contend that "Kennedy cared little for Canadian nationalist sentiments and expected Canada to follow the U.S. hard line on Cuba," the president had shown a deep appreciation for Canadian nationalism, both in his speech to Parliament—in many ways a rehash of his remarks in New Brunswick—and in his administration's decisions to back down over Canadian trade with China and Cuba.[119] He had hoped, however, that his advocacy of a policy that Canada seemed to be adopting anyways would be acceptable, not an unreasonable assumption. Yet Kennedy failed to "realize that the surest way to dampen Canadian enthusiasm for any project involving the United States is to appear eager for Canadian participation."[120] There was a limit to Kennedy's influence, charm, and eloquence. Despite the adoring crowds in Canada, the president had been unable to overcome the roadblocks of both Canadian nationalism and Diefenbaker's political calculations. Nor had his actions over Cuba convinced officials in Ottawa that his approach to Latin America was particularly enlightened. Then there was the problem of the Rostow memorandum, a document that outlined the need for Canadian assistance not just in Latin America but also in Southeast Asia. Here, despite Rostow's use of the word "push," Diefenbaker proved to be more amenable to Kennedy.

In Southeast Asia, Washington faced two difficult situations, one in Vietnam, the other in Laos. In 1961 the latter, a small, landlocked country bordering North and South Vietnam, Thailand, Burma, and China, appeared at risk, with a smoldering civil war threatening to turn into a larger conflict. The 1954 Geneva Conference had guaranteed Laotian neutrality and independence from outside interference. However, it was unclear if Laos would remain neutral, because within the country three groups vied for power: a right-wing faction, a neutralist faction, and the communist Pathet Lao movement. The Eisenhower administration had backed the former, which had taken power in a coup, while North Vietnam supported the Pathet Lao, which began receiving Soviet supplies in 1960. The neutralists, meanwhile, had entered into a tenuous alliance with the communists; together, they controlled wide swathes of the country by the time Kennedy took office. The new administration was soon weighing military options, but unlike its predecessor, it also considered the creation of a genuinely neutral Laos.[121] Meanwhile, the United Kingdom and the Soviet Union, which had chaired the Geneva Conference, pushed to begin the summit process anew. This conference, officials in London hoped, would reconfirm Laotian independence and neutrality and forestall US intervention.[122] To help in this process, the British sought to revive the International Control Commission for Laos. Formed by the 1954 Geneva Accords, the ICC was designed to monitor Laos' borders to ensure its neutrality and independence; it had left the country in 1958 after a neutral government had come to power in Vientiane. Three years later, with a conflict raging and with foreign intervention apparent, there was cause to bring back the international commissioners.

Occupying one of three seats on the ICC—which also operated in Cambodia and Vietnam—Canada was meant to provide a Western counterbalance to communist Poland and seek the support of neutral India. Early on into his presidency Kennedy was informed that he should look favorably upon the ICC if it contained Canada and India, two countries that would make it an effective body.[123] In Ottawa, there was both wariness and weariness. Examining the Eisenhower administration's parting actions in Laos, Green told the Cabinet that a new commission "would have very little chance of bringing about a cease-fire unless the Soviet Union and the United States wanted one." The American position was dubious, he continued, because while Laos was meant to be neutral, the United States was training Laotian troops.[124] A month later, during the Kennedy–Diefenbaker meeting in Washington, Green explained that he was less than "enthusiastic over the restoration of the ICC." Even so, Ottawa "was willing to do its duty." The Cabinet soon assented to Canadian participation both in a new conference on Laos in Geneva and in a reconstituted ICC.[125] These moves were welcomed in Washington. Rostow, who was involved in crafting policy toward Southeast Asia for the NSC, believed in the need for Canada to give "strong and unambiguous" support to US efforts at Geneva to control the Laotian border. Chiefly concerned that North Vietnamese supplies were being smuggled to insurgents in South Vietnam via Laos, he contended that the "international community cannot sit 'idly by,' as the saying goes, while aggression in the form of guerrilla war is mounted from outside a sovereign nation."[126] In Ottawa, he urged the president to secure "Canada's active support at Geneva and beyond for a more effective monitoring of the borders of Laos and Vietnam."[127]

Just as Kennedy was arriving in the Canadian capital, the Geneva conference was opening. For Rusk, who headed the US delegation, Canada's support seemed to be in question. In addition to sparring with Green over Cuba at the Oslo NATO summit, they had quarreled over Laos. Green, Rusk complained to Kennedy, had been reluctant to join the Americans, British, and French for talks on Southeast Asia out of a desire to maintain neutrality on the ICC. This reluctance not to attend the "Western caucus" was indicative of the Canadian minister's "relative indifference to far-reaching stakes which free world has in Laotian situation and in general is more like that of neutrals than Western countries."[128] Still smarting from this discussion, at the outset of the conference Rusk told Green that Washington expected Canada to protect Western interests. He would look dimly upon "two neutrals and a communist" sitting on the ICC.[129] This statement alarmed Canadian diplomats. While it was true, one senior member of the Washington Embassy admitted, that the Canadian delegation in Geneva was wary of joining Anglo-American-French talks, this reluctance was purely to ensure that Canada's role as the Western component of the ICC was not apparent "too starkly," thereby prejudicing the Indians against supporting Canadian positions.[130] George Ignatieff, who had accompanied Green to Oslo and then to Geneva, assured Merchant that Green was "not soft-headed or pacifist-minded, but very clear on the matter of the Soviet threat and where Canada's basic interests lie."[131]

Green did indeed prove helpful. Landing in Geneva, he affirmed to reporters that based on its past service on the ICC, Canada had come once again to "build up conditions of security and stability in Southeast Asia." To this end he sought "an independent, unified and neutral Laos."[132] Like the Americans, he was concerned by the ineffectiveness of the ICC, which stemmed from the commission's lack of transportation and its inability to have full access to all Laotian territory. Negotiations in Geneva on these points bogged down, the result of Soviet and Polish intransigence. After this obstruction had gone on for a month Green made a forceful statement, telling the conference that for the commission to "do a useful job" it had to be given authority "with respect to threats to the security of the Laotian state." US officials were pleased with Green's speech, telling him that for the first time they saw "light at the end of the tunnel."[133] Galvanized by this overture, the conference soon approved the reconstitution of the ICC in Laos with authority to monitor both Laotian borders and the ongoing ceasefire. At Geneva, Rostow told Kennedy, the Canadians had been "stalwart" on the issue of crafting an effective commission.[134] Ultimately, the reconstituted ICC in Laos proved ineffective in stemming North Vietnamese violations of the border, though it did help to justify the American commitment to the region, particularly as the situation there worsened.

As for Vietnam, US officials likewise sought an effective ICC—one, Rostow was to tell Heeney, that could "assist in deterring" North Vietnamese aggression.[135] The 1954 Geneva Accords had partitioned Vietnam: the US-backed South Vietnamese were engaged in guerrilla warfare against the Viet Cong, communist insurgents supplied from the North. The control commission in Vietnam was meant to supervise this nonexistent peace. US officials hoped that the ICC would better police the border between North and South Vietnam as well as the Laotian–Vietnamese border, efforts meant to stem the flow of supplies from the Hanoi government to the guerrillas in the South. Throughout Kennedy's presidency, the United States expanded its own role in assisting and arming the South Vietnamese through a Military Assistance Advisory Group. Canadian policymakers held grave doubts about the Saigon government's stability and were worried about the deepening American involvement in the region.[136] Increasing US assistance in the spring of 1961 alarmed policymakers in Ottawa, who subsequently worried both about remaining impartial and about a widening conflict. Washington, though, sought Canadian assistance, chiefly, as in Laos, through the ICC.

During his May meeting with Diefenbaker, Kennedy had highlighted his concern that the control commission in Vietnam was weak and appeared "incapable of dealing with the violations of the Viet-Nam frontiers." As a result, he had increased the personnel assigned to the MAAG above the limit set in Geneva and noted that he wished to increase arms transfers to Saigon. Kennedy then appealed for Canadian help in "dramatizing" Hanoi's actions in violating the 1954 accords by arming insurgents in the South, which would make it easier for the United States to justify its own supplies. Would the Canadians on the ICC, he added, ignore American violations of MAAG? Canada, the president concluded, bore "a special burden" as the West's representative on the commission. Diefenbaker agreed with this judgment, stating that "Canada had a duty to discharge its responsibility on the ICC more effectively."[137] The Canadians followed through by turning a blind eye to US actions and by urging Washington to keep quiet about this increased military aid. After all, Norman Robertson advised Green, "we entirely agree as to the seriousness of the situation in South Vietnam which has led [the Americans] to this decision."[138]

As increased MAAG aid flowed into South Vietnam, in late 1961 Green instructed Canada's commissioners to prevent the ICC from taking "actions which might be embarrassing to USA," all while trying to preserve the commission's "prestige and therefore the effectiveness."[139] The continued introduction of US war materiel made this balancing act difficult. In October, Rostow and General Maxwell Taylor, the president's personal military advisor, toured South Vietnam. Upon their return they issued a report recommending increased economic and military support and, crucially, advised the introduction of 8,000 US ground troops. Speaking with Saul Rae, the political counselor at Canada's

Embassy in Washington and a diplomat who had served on the ICC in Vietnam in 1955, Rostow pointed out that the guerrilla situation was serious and that the "major question" was North Vietnamese violations of the borders of Laos and South Vietnam. The ICC had a role in exposing these breaches. For now, he added, Washington was committed to a diplomatic path, although it would be willing to increase assistance to the South. Rae felt unease, noting that Rostow seemed enamored with guerrilla warfare and that it would not be a surprise one day to find the American bureaucrat in a Vietnamese jungle "clothed in a green camouflage suit and carrying a knife in his teeth."[140] A month later, and only weeks after Green had delivered his directive against embarrassing the United States, Averell Harriman, the assistant secretary for Far Eastern Affairs, informed Heeney that ongoing North Vietnamese violations of the Geneva Accords meant that the Americans no longer saw the limits on aid to be binding. Washington would henceforth increase its military assistance. Harriman hoped to see Canadian efforts toward ensuring that the ICC ignore or play down this increased aid. Canada's task, he admitted with sympathy, was "thankless."[141]

Canadian officials looked dimly upon Harriman's argument. In Ottawa's view, the breaching of the Geneva Accords by one party did not permit another party to violate the agreement. Thus, North Vietnamese aggression did not legally justify massive US arms shipments. This question became a point of contention throughout early 1962, with Rusk pressing for American diplomats to gain Canadian acquiescence.[142] The Canadians stood firm on principle, but gave way in practice. As Heeney explained in early March, Harriman's argument had no basis in international law. However, he expressed to US diplomats that he shared their "anxieties" about Southeast Asia and felt that if Washington judged that "the only way to save Vietnam was to bring personnel and materiel above the limits set by the Geneva Accords, then he would be willing to accept this judgment. He would bless any attempt to save Vietnam." The ICC, though, might have to criticize Saigon.[143] Soon after, Green echoed the ambassador in comments in the House of Commons. It "would be unfair," he stated, "to single out the United States for blame in respect of the situation in South Viet Nam. The provocation, in my judgment, has come from North Vietnam." He professed a certainty "that the Communists have been at the root of most of the trouble" in the country, notably by infiltrating fighters. Hence, "any action that the United States has taken has been in a measure of defence against Communist action."[144] American authorities were thankful for Ottawa's acquiescence and mindful of Canada's position. Canadian officials' steadfastness on the illegal nature of US arms shipments, Merchant reported, "does not by long shot mean they believe our increased aid is wrong." Rather, they were overly concerned with legalistic issues and having to defend these views to the Indians and Poles. To Merchant it was evident both that the Canadians had "gone [a] long way in

[an] effort to be helpful" and that they would go further by doing "what they can" to minimize ICC criticisms of Saigon and Washington.[145]

Ottawa did prove helpful that spring as the control commission prepared a report on violations of the Geneva Accords. A condemnation of Hanoi in the report was vital, Harriman emphasized to Canadian officials. Such a judgment would have a positive impact on political opinion in the United States by justifying continued assistance to Saigon. It would also help Washington defend its position abroad. The White House, Harriman added, was "deeply understanding and appreciative" of Canada for playing its "difficult" part on the ICC.[146] Released in June, the report condemned both South and North Vietnam, criticized the US for introducing personnel, but put the onus for difficulties on the North for its subversion in the South. Implicitly, then, it absolved the Americans for introducing weapons.[147] US officials met this defense of their position with appreciation: Rusk offered words of praise for Canadian efforts on the ICC, and Willis Armstrong indicated being shocked at having to admit that Howard Green could, indeed, be "helpful from time to time."[148]

Through its actions on the control commissions in Laos and Vietnam, Canada assisted its American ally. Even if the ICC failed to deter communist aggression, it served to vindicate the US commitment to the region. Of course, Canada's assistance to the United States helped to facilitate Washington's march to war in Vietnam. This policy of escalation was hardly championed by Canadian diplomats—many would speak out as the American commitment increased later in the 1960s—even if, as Saul Rae put it, "Canadians understand and have real sympathy for US objectives in Vietnam."[149] In the Diefenbaker period, officials from Canada, Green included, offered support for American efforts to shore up Southeast Asian security because the situation in Vietnam—as opposed to circumstances surrounding Cuba—showed a clear case of communist aggression. Nonetheless, these same Canadian diplomats had no desire to see the United States drawn into a ground war in South Vietnam. Ottawa thus found itself "balancing war and peace."[150]

Maintaining a fine balance was indicative of Ottawa's approach to the Cold War. As an ally of the United States, Canada sought to support the Americans in the confrontation against aggressive communist forces. However, Canadian officials did not want the United States drawn into fighting that could risk a wider war that might involve Canada or cost American prestige, lives, and money. Kennedy, too, sought balance: he confronted Castro, sponsoring an invasion of Cuba by émigrés, but stopped short of sending in US forces; he increased assistance to Saigon, but avoided the dispatch of large numbers of American troops, hoping that the small contingent of soldiers and the increased arms would be enough to turn the tide against the communist guerrillas. Canadian officials looked warily upon these moves. Holding different views on what tactics should be employed against communism, particularly in the Third World, Canada had far less power—and far fewer responsibilities—than its southern neighbor.

On tactics, Canadians felt that there was nothing amiss with trading with communist states, even China and Cuba, both of which preached revolution. Still, Ottawa refused to recognize Beijing, nor did Canadian officials embrace Castro. On power and responsibilities, Diefenbaker sought increased involvement in Latin America but stopped short of a political and economic commitment through either the OAS or the Alliance for Progress. Shoring up Latin America against communism, like ensuring Southeast Asian security, was an American responsibility befitting a great power. Canada could play a supporting role, which indeed was what Kennedy and Rostow both wanted. In Asia they were successful in securing Canadian support; in Latin America, they fell short. The president had also sought a greater Canadian commitment to continental defense, again scoring a partial victory: the signing of the triangular deal, but an unfulfilled obligation to accept nuclear warheads. Nevertheless, relations between Ottawa and Washington were good, and those between the president and prime minister were, if not warm, at least civil.

Commenting on the state of Canada–US relations in *Foreign Affairs* in late 1961, John Holmes, a former Canadian diplomat, the head of the Canadian Institute of International Affairs, and perhaps the keenest analyst of Canada's postwar diplomacy, remarked that "our most acute differences are as likely to be about distant places—China, Cuba or Laos—as about tariffs and waterways. There is, in fact, an edge to these arguments about faraway places which make them more of a threat to good relations than are our traditional controversies." In Indochina Canada and the United States had been "seeking the same end," but through different means. Writing for a largely American audience, Holmes made sure to point out that in terms of Cuba the Canadian government was steadfastly "committed to the defense of democracy" and held "no desire to abet the introduction of Communism into the Americas." Ottawa, however, saw Washington's tactics in the region as being highly "unwise." Going on to trace the differences in outlook and responsibility between Canada and the United States—one was a middle power with limited interests, the other a great power with global responsibilities—he touched upon a complex situation that affected Canadian foreign policy. "We are," he explained, "too much concerned with world problems to relax into the happy escape of satellitism," but, at the same time, "we are too deeply engaged in the struggle against totalitarianism to find a way out in neutrality."[151]

Added to the complexities of Canada's position in global affairs was the importance of nationalism as well as Prime Minister Diefenbaker's political instincts. In 1961 these twin factors had played out on issues of trade, Cuba, and the OAS. On the Organization of American States, Kennedy had overstepped. Although Holmes felt that the president's plea had been merely "tactful pressure," it had alarmed Diefenbaker, who was already wary of US actions in the Western hemisphere. Meanwhile, authorities in Washington had deferred to nationalism, or to the threat of sparking nationalist ire, over Canadian exports to China and Cuba, and Heeney and other Canadian officials had expertly—but quietly—used this threat as part of their defense of Canada's position and principles, deflecting US infringement on Canadian sovereignty. Quiet diplomacy proved its worth in these strictly bilateral cases. But Canadian ability to influence the United States was limited on wider issues such as Vietnam. Here, Canadians' quiet advice to the Americans about avoiding a wholesale military commitment went unheeded, and as the war in Southeast Asia expanded, the failings of quiet diplomacy to influence US policy would make the practice a source of debate and criticism in Canada. Of course critics of quiet diplomacy were also reacting to the fact that the Canadian and American governments had a shared interest in not seeing South Vietnam fall to communism. This same common interest in the outcome of the Cold War was evident in the summer of 1961, which saw a tense standoff between the Soviet Union and the West over Berlin. Canadian–American defense relations took on added meaning in this climate, in which Diefenbaker's political concerns soon came to the fore causing bilateral diplomacy to grow distinctly louder.

# 3

# Atomic Anxieties

## *Berlin, BOMARCS, and the Bomb, 1961–1962*

As the Kennedys departed from Ottawa, Douglas Harkness arrived in Winnipeg to address the Royal Canadian Air Force Association. Giving this veterans group an overview of Canada's responsibilities as a member of both NATO and NORAD, the Canadian defense minister warned of the dangers posed to North America by Soviet missiles and long-range bombers and praised Canada's BOMARC missiles and interceptor aircraft, which were both capable of defending against the Russian bomber force. To be effective, however, these weapon systems required nuclear warheads. Mindful of his government's caution on the issue, Harkness pointed out that no decision had yet been made to acquire warheads and that should the government decide to accept them, joint control procedures would be established so that they would be used only when Ottawa saw fit. Hinting that a decision might soon be made, he reminded his audience that Canadians bore a heavy burden to "maintain our defence forces and continue to contribute to the security of the free world." This undoubtedly friendly audience was receptive to the minister's stark message, whereas, in response to Harkness's speech, the *Globe and Mail* argued that nuclear weapons would do little to add to the country's defense, and would instead harm Canadian interests abroad by doing "Canada great damage in the eyes of the smaller and uncommitted nations of the world."[1] Harkness and the *Globe and Mail*'s editors had spelled out two competing views on Canada's defense policy. Throughout the Diefenbaker–Kennedy period, these differing stances caused immense friction in Canadian domestic politics and in Canada–US relations, for the views espoused by the *Globe and Mail* were shared by growing numbers of Canadians alarmed by the specter of nuclear war.

In the early 1960s, the Canadian government occupied an odd position. At once part of the North Atlantic alliance and of a bilateral alliance with the United States, Canada also fancied itself a leading proponent of nuclear disarmament and a leader on this issue at the United Nations. Within the government there was a sharp division between Harkness, who favored a strong defense posture, and Howard Green, an outspoken advocate of nuclear arms limitation; between them sat the prime minister. Attempting to balance the views of these two ministers, Diefenbaker tried, too, to balance his own anti-Soviet inclinations with what he believed to be the growing domestic opposition to a nuclear role for Canadian forces.[2] Thus, Ottawa accepted weapons systems that required nuclear warheads and took a strong stand against Moscow's provocations throughout the 1961 Berlin crisis. At the same time, Diefenbaker put off acquiring the warheads necessary to make this expensive weaponry effective, and he allowed Green to pursue a conciliatory approach toward the Soviets during a series of disarmament talks in 1962. Added to this mix were both changing strategic concepts as well as the prime minister's growing mistrust of Kennedy.

American officials viewed Canada's stance on defense issues with a mixture of understanding and frustration. Recognizing that Diefenbaker paid close attention to voters' views, they were more than willing to give him time to massage public opinion on a question of importance to Washington. Like his predecessor, Kennedy sought to secure the United States deterrent from nuclear attack, which meant a reliance on anti-bomber defenses for North America.[3] In this regard, the new president recognized that Canada was an essential part of the American defense perimeter and saw it as imperative that the Canadian military adopt nuclear weaponry meant to defend against Soviet bombers. Kennedy also saw an important role for Canada in defending Western Europe from Soviet attack alongside its NATO allies. With the tens of thousands of American troops stationed in Europe causing a huge financial drain, the Kennedy administration hoped to build up its allies' military strength on the continent, thus eventually allowing for some withdrawal of US forces and an attendant easing of balance of payments pressure. Moreover, conventional forces could allow for NATO to respond to Soviet aggression in more flexible ways, though the hopeful prospects of limited warfare belied the grim likelihood of a quick escalation to a full-scale nuclear exchange. Hinting at this new emphasis on flexibility in his address to the Canadian parliament, Kennedy had warned of the changing military balance of power on the European continent, with growing Soviet strength threatening NATO, "the world's greatest bulwark of freedom." He had called for increases in conventional forces and had implored the Canadian people to realize that the defense of Europe and the defense of North America were "indivisible."[4]

In the struggle against the Soviet Union, Canada occupied an important and valued place. As Dean Rusk reminded Green in 1962, "Europe simply is not now in a position to defend itself without the help of North America."[5] Canada's importance meant that the prime minister's increasing inability to decide on the nuclear arms question and Green's ongoing support for disarmament together created considerable ill-humor in the Pentagon, the State Department, and the White House, where increasingly, there was a sense that Ottawa was breaking ranks with Washington. In mid-1962, Livingston Merchant complained to a colleague that "the root" of problems with Canada was "the fact that we have all the power and the responsibility. Within the shelter of our power the Canadians and many other relatively weak but articulate friends undertake to criticize and instruct us."[6] But during Kennedy's first year in office Diefenbaker was a solid partner. Despite any supposed doubts about the president's judgment stemming from the Bay of Pigs fiasco, the prime minister supported the United States during the standoff with the Soviets over Berlin, which, unlike Cuba, was the vital front in the Cold War. One of the major events during Kennedy's first year in office, the Berlin crisis was also the backdrop against which Diefenbaker moved toward finally accepting nuclear weapons. Yet driven by his political inclinations, the prime minister backed away from stoutly supporting Washington. Instead, he embarked on a cautious and confusing course with regard to Canadian defense and disarmament policy, in part due to a growing awareness of the bleak realities of the missile age. In reacting to these contradictions and contortions, American policymakers displayed considerable patience and understanding—witness the resolution of the triangular deal, concluded just after Kennedy's visit to Ottawa. Although nuclear issues caused constant bilateral friction through 1961 and early 1962, US officials refrained from forcing matters—their forbearance paid little in return.

Remembered for standing up to Kennedy by ultimately rejecting nuclear weapons, Diefenbaker only arrived at this position late into his premiership. With Merchant in early May 1961 he divulged a concern that opposition to Canada's acquisition of nuclear weaponry was becoming more widespread, and so he asked for time to turn public opinion against the arguments of those "wishful thinkers" who supported disarmament or who foolishly "believed that the Soviets should be propitiated." No wonder, then, that Merchant felt that on nuclear weapons the prime minister was a "strong ally." Reiterating his skepticism about disarmament to Kennedy during the presidential visit the following week, Diefenbaker underscored his concern with the domestic side of the nuclear issue. For the time being, US officials were willing to leave the initiative to the prime minister. Recognizing the tremendous "political problem" facing Diefenbaker, Kennedy remarked to Arnold Heeney that the prime minister was obviously "the best judge of what could (and could not) be done."[7]

With Diefenbaker seen to be the key to resolving the nuclear issue, the White House made Ottawa the focal point for discussions about Canada's nuclear role. As Walt Rostow reported to the president, by establishing a channel between Diefenbaker and the Ottawa Embassy—and ignoring the Canadian Embassy in Washington—it might be possible to lessen the involvement of Canada's diplomats and thus cut Howard Green out of the process.[8] Given Green's hostility to nuclear arms, Rostow's position was prudent, with the value of the Ottawa channel only increased by the importance of the domestic angle to the nuclear

question. On this factor, Merchant judged that Canadian "anti-nuclear sentiment" was "much less then petitions and pickets lead some Government leaders
to believe."[9] But it was the prime minister's perception about the extent of voters'
support for disarmament that mattered. Firm in his belief that anti-nuclear
sentiments were strong, Diefenbaker showed little initiative in the immediate
wake of Kennedy's Ottawa visit. By July, Robert Bryce was complaining to Willis
Armstrong that the prime minister had done nothing either publicly or privately
to "improve the climate of opinion" despite having promised the president that
he would focus on changing public sentiment. A strong advocate within the
government of a Canadian nuclear role, Bryce was one of the prime minister's
most trusted advisors; it is telling that he urged Armstrong to have Merchant
raise this matter with Diefenbaker.[10] The ambassador never pushed the matter,
though, because attention that summer was focused firmly upon Berlin.

It was this crisis that ultimately spurred the prime minister into action on
nuclear weaponry. Not only did Diefenbaker move quickly to establish a firm
Canadian stance in support of Canada's NATO commitments, but also throughout the standoff, with danger escalating, he mounted his public campaign to
pave the way for nuclear weapons in Canada. Moreover, in private, he pushed
for negotiations with the Americans to begin. His actions during the crisis
belie arguments that he pursued an "accommodationist" approach toward
Khrushchev or that he came to believe "that he could not trust Kennedy to
resolve a major international crisis."[11] The president's actions hardly worried
the Canadian prime minister: Kennedy "chose preparedness over provocation"
by putting the Unites States on a high state of military readiness while looking
for a diplomatic way to resolve the situation, a stance supported by Ottawa.[12]
There was some disagreement between the two allies as a result of Canadian
concern at not being adequately consulted by the Americans on efforts to resolve the crisis, and there were later differences over contingency planning.[13]
But because the events surrounding Berlin involved Canada's chief allies and its
foremost enemy, the Canadian government moved decisively behind the United
States, playing a helpful—if marginal—role at least in the initial months of the
crisis.[14] This stout support of the Western position made Diefenbaker's subsequent waffling on nuclear arms hard for the Americans to stomach.

The Berlin crisis had its roots in 1945, when, at the end of the Second World
War, the four principal powers—the United States, the Soviet Union, Britain,
and France—each occupied a section of the German capital, which lay within
the Soviet-occupied half of Germany. The eventual division of Germany into
the Federal Republic of Germany in the west and the German Democratic
Republic in the east, left West Berlin as a small island of freedom toward which
hundreds of thousands of East Germans fled in the hopes of escaping from
communist tyranny. In an effort to steady the GDR and score a victory over the
United States and its allies, in 1958 Nikita Khrushchev threatened to conclude

a separate peace treaty with East Germany, thus granting it de facto recognition as a state and terminating Western access to Berlin. Thankfully, the resulting crisis fizzled out, and by 1959 the situation had stabilized.[15] With a new president in office, the Soviet leader reissued his ultimatum; the result was the first of two grave crises that Kennedy would face.

In their May meeting Kennedy and Diefenbaker had agreed that Khrushchev was likely to provoke a standoff over Berlin, and that in response, a strong stand would have to be taken. A "retreat" by the West, the prime minister had emphasized, would be "the last straw" for neutral nations, which would likely come to doubt whether the United States and its allies were truly committed to defending the free world. When Kennedy admitted to expecting little from his upcoming summit with Khrushchev, Diefenbaker agreed, adding a warning that the rotund Soviet leader was simply "an actor at heart."[16] Khrushchev did not disappoint, browbeating the president and reissuing his ultimatum on Germany and Berlin with a December deadline. Ominously, Kennedy concluded the talks by saying that "it would be a cold winter." In a subsequent note to Diefenbaker, the president informed the prime minister of this development and thanked him for his "positive encouragement" as he faced Khrushchev.[17]

The Vienna summit itself was hardly encouraging. Reacting to the news out of Austria, Green reminded Diefenbaker that "the exposed Western position in Berlin" gave the Soviets the "means of applying pressure" to achieve their ends.[18] In his own assessment, Arnold Heeney reviewed the difficulties facing Canada and its allies in responding to the Soviet provocation: the need to balance a flexible negotiating position with a firm stance on the essential commitment to Berlin; the complication of establishing a single negotiating position across a large alliance; and the necessity of preparing for a military conflict without provoking one. Thus far, he concluded, Kennedy and senior US officials had been "calm and very firm but not provocative."[19] Diefenbaker himself felt the need to be firm. Speaking to a Toronto audience on July 3, he fired a salvo at the Soviet Union. First praising the close links between Canada and the United States—"the closest of partners in freedom's camp"—and then declaring "I have no ear for the lullabies of the neutralist," he noted that meeting Khrushchev's demands would lead the Soviets to "devour one of freedom's outposts," thus striking "a mortal blow to the West." Therefore he urged that NATO work quickly, with full consultation among members, to respond to Khrushchev's provocations with a response that would be flexible but "without appeasement or sacrifice of the pledged word."[20]

The Kennedy administration struck the same balance between flexibility and firmness. On July 17 Washington replied to Khrushchev's ultimatum with a statement defending the Western stance, but leaving the door open to talks and a negotiated settlement. Less rigid in his views on the Cold War confrontation, Green was relieved by the US position, having told Merchant the previous week that "while public opinion at this stage welcomed indications of firmness, it was a question, when the chips were down, as to how far people might be prepared to face nuclear devastation" over Berlin.[21] There was little light between the Canadian and American positions, and in the midst of the brewing crisis, Diefenbaker traveled to Whitehorse to attend a ceremony marking the opening of a communications system linked to a missile detection installation. From this northern outpost, he telephoned President Kennedy and together they christened this transcontinental communications network. Beyond some warm words for one another, the conversation also touched on wider events. Lauding the installation as a sign of "the practical cooperation of the Canadian–American partnership," Diefenbaker went on both to praise the president for his "leadership in the world contest for the hearts of men," and to offer Kennedy a "wish" for "all good fortune."[22] Sentimental prattle perhaps, but for a prime minister mindful of the growing danger over Berlin, his encouragement was genuine.

Two days later, Cabinet debated Canadian policy. Reviewing the recent Soviet provocations, Diefenbaker noted that Kennedy was set on taking a strong stand and that "Berlin must be maintained and the United States had to be supported in this effort." Given the high stakes, even Green, by no means a hawk, took an approach that favored firmness. Canada, he emphasized, was involved in the situation as a member of NATO. However, the alliance's conventional forces were weak, and, addressing a point that Merchant had made to him in talks two days earlier, Green raised the need to contribute more troops to Europe. With the need for balance in mind, he also highlighted the need for negotiation. Ensuing Cabinet debate over what points were negotiable proved divisive, so, bringing discussion to a close, Diefenbaker cautioned that "one could not negotiate successfully unless one was willing to give up something and on Berlin there was nothing that the West could give up." The prime minister clearly favored standing up to the Soviets. As he remarked to the British High Commissioner, he and the Cabinet "were determined to be firm in resisting unreasonable Russian demands," with Green "entirely alone" with his "gloomy" view "and in being so critical of American policies."[23]

Senior American officials were conducting their own reviews of Berlin policy, with the National Security Council formally approving a strategy that mixed a strong stand militarily with a receptivity to talk with the Soviets. During this meeting, Kennedy revealed a fear that military preparations would "not be adequate without an effective allied response" to the American request for a build-up of NATO forces. Equally perturbing was the possibility that Western governments might give disparate responses to the thought of negotiations, with the French and West Germans favoring a far more uncompromising stance than Britain and the rest of NATO.[24] With his policy in place, the president then took to the airwaves on July 25 to explain it. Spelling out the legal basis for the Western position in the city as well as the moral responsibility to defend West

Berliners, he warned that Khrushchev threatened to spark a war "through a stroke of the pen." Next, Kennedy outlined his efforts to put his country on a firmer military and civil defense footing. Despite this dark tone, at several points the president underlined his willingness to negotiate. As with Canada, his position balanced firmness and flexibility. "We will," he said "at all times be ready to talk, if talk will help. But we must also be ready to resist with force, if force is used upon us. Either alone would fail. Together, they can serve the cause of freedom and peace." Pleased with Kennedy's "timely" words, which had "been serious without being threatening," Diefenbaker wrote the president to affirm that they shared a mutual "concern with the Soviet challenge on West Berlin."[25]

The crisis soon worsened: on August 13, the Soviets, fed up with the masses of East Germans fleeing into West Germany, directed the East German regime to erect a wall concretely dividing Berlin in two. External Affairs officials in Ottawa took the move in stride. Given the flow of refugees, Undersecretary Robertson explained to the prime minister, the erection of the wall was perfectly understandable. Further, Khrushchev had tipped his hand by showing that his concern was with the stability of East Germany. There was nothing, though, that Canada could reasonably do at this point.[26] Diefenbaker felt differently. A speech he was due to give to the Canadian Weekly Newspaper Association afforded him an opportunity to harangue the Soviet leader. Borrowing imagery from Kennedy's recent speech, Diefenbaker cautioned that with "the single stroke of his pen" Khrushchev was set on turning millions of West Berliners "over to the tyranny of communist rule." As for the wall, Khrushchev had "closed the gates of Berlin" not against an attacking foe but against the "defiance of those within," a telling comment on the Soviets' inhumane way in dealing with internal dissent.[27]

External Affairs, meanwhile, continued to search for a negotiating position. In a memorandum receiving wide circulation throughout Ottawa and among Canadian diplomatic posts abroad, Escott Reid, Canada's ambassador in Bonn, proposed creating a free city of Berlin, wherein the West's presence would be maintained. Not doubting that the Soviets would find this settlement "distasteful," he judged that the NATO powers could offer the Soviets *de jure* recognition of the Oder-Neisse line—the Polish–East German border, established informally in 1945—as well as arrangements to essentially grant de facto recognition of the East German state. In order for this settlement to be worked out, time and exploratory talks were needed.[28] To get the ball rolling, Reid, never shy about self-promoting, traveled to Ottawa to brief Diefenbaker on his proposal in person. Subsequently, the prime minister brought Reid's plan to Cabinet. Like many senior External Affairs officials, Green was lukewarm toward this bargain, explaining to his fellow ministers that it had little likelihood of being accepted by other Western powers, especially France and West Germany. Discussion turned to military preparedness, and Green, worried about mounting tension, stated that he would direct Heeney to urge American officials not to do anything overtly threatening. Turning to Canada, he argued that the Cabinet should approve the "prudent and necessary" step of putting the country's military into "as efficient a state as possible." Agreeing, the Cabinet endorsed several measures—presented by Harkness—that strengthened Canada's military posture and improved its civil defense system. Further defensive actions were soon approved: the Canadian Brigade in Europe was to be brought up to full strength, the ceiling on the size of the total Canadian military was to be raised from 120,000 to 150,000 men, and the government would attempt to recruit 15,000 more soldiers, sailors, and airmen.[29] Kennedy had asked the United States' NATO allies to increase their conventional forces and Canada responded positively.

As for Green's hope of reviewing with the Americans possible Western responses, Heeney met with senior State Department officials who expressed interest in hearing about Reid's proposal, a comment that spurred Ottawa into action.[30] Although Green was hesitant to support Reid, Diefenbaker was willing to allow him an opportunity to test his idea in Washington, but on the condition that Reid inform the Americans that this plan was Reid's own initiative and did not reflect formal Canadian policy.[31] Heeney duly arranged for his fellow ambassador to speak with key policymakers. A briefing with several mid-level State Department officials proved reassuring, as Reid found that there was a definite inclination on the part of the Americans to pursue a negotiated solution.[32] Meetings with important Congressional leaders only deepened this belief. William Fulbright, the chairman of the Senate foreign relations committee, Mike Mansfield, the Senate majority leader, and John Sherman Cooper, a moderate Republican senator with friendly ties to the president, all emphasized their hopes for a settlement and their support for Reid's idea. Fulbright in particular felt that it would be worthwhile for Canadian politicians to make this position public because such statements would surely "do more good than harm," and Canada, as a minor power, had more freedom to advance creative ideas than did the United States.[33]

Congressional opinion was important, but the decision whether or not to adopt Reid's suggestion would have to come from the White House and so Heeney organized a dinner for himself, Reid, several embassy officers, and an important group of American policymakers comprising Rusk, Charles Bohlen, a renowned Soviet specialist, Foy Kohler, the State Department's point man on Berlin, and McGeorge Bundy, Kennedy's special assistant for national security affairs. Access to the top of the policymaking pyramid in Washington had been secured and it showed something of the importance that the Americans placed on consultations with Canadian officials that they assembled such an eminent group. Although the meal may have been enjoyable, the conversation, centered on the issue of negotiations, was not. Taking turns to emphasize that their willingness to negotiate, Rusk and Kohler explained that their only reservation was around setting down a specific negotiating position for fear that it would be leaked to the press. Bohlen, on the other hand, was pessimistic in the extreme about negotiating their way out of the crisis. Nor did the Americans voice support for Reid's proposal, stressing that Khrushchev would never agree to it. Next, Rusk offered various "disillusioned appraisals of the futility" of negotiating with Khrushchev and predicted that as the West would not accept any Soviet proposals and as the Soviets would not accept Western proposals, the only recourse was war. Realizing that these comments offered little reassurance, Rusk and Bundy were at pains to stress, despite their cynicism, that they would press forward with negotiations.[34]

The dinner ended on this relatively high note, but Reid left feeling ill, a sensation that had nothing to do with the night's cuisine but with his belief that the White House was showing "very little flexibility in their approach to negotiations," which he found "profoundly disturbing." Given that his proposal had been received coolly—Reid could be rather vain—his conclusion is hardly surprising.[35] Heeney was equally "deeply disturbed," albeit because Reid had left the dinner believing that the Americans were unwilling to negotiate. Both through an emergency telephone call to Ottawa and in a hastily written letter, Heeney made it clear to Norman Robertson that he objected to Reid's interpretation of the evening's events, for the Americans did intend to pursue talks.[36] So when Bundy wrote to Heeney the following day to reassure him that Washington would negotiate, the ambassador was pleased. As Bundy explained, "the difference last night was not in purpose, but in estimates of the situation, and we should be very happy to be wrong."[37] Reid's impression of the dinner was little altered. Warning Green and Diefenbaker that officials around the president were overtly hostile to talks with Khrushchev, he did allow that by all indications Kennedy had not yet made up his own mind on the course that the United States should follow and so Canada could "exercise considerable influence by strengthening the hands of those in Washington" who wanted to negotiate with the Soviets.[38]

At this point the prime minister was preparing to give a speech to the Canadian Bar Association's annual convention in Winnipeg, and, with Berlin weighing on his mind, he decided to make the crisis a major focus of his remarks, telling Basil Robinson that he wanted a heavy emphasis placed on explaining why the defense of West Berlin was important enough to risk war. Diefenbaker also wished to lay out tentative possibilities toward reaching a negotiated settlement that went beyond his own recent "exhortations to stand fast but flexible."[39] After receiving the reports of Reid's meetings in Washington, he asked the ambassador to deliver a personal post mortem to him in Ottawa, with Reid then convincing him to emphasize the importance of negotiations in his speech. As the prime minister told Robinson, he had little desire to sit in silence or act as "a tail on the United States kite."[40] The speech was altered yet again, when, on September 1, the Soviets announced that they had conducted a nuclear test, ending a three-year moratorium on testing that had been informally agreed to by Washington, London, and Moscow. Angered by this provocation, the prime minister went on the attack, decrying the highly "disturbing" nuclear test and accusing Khrushchev of making "terror-laden declarations" that showed his "contempt" for international opinion. Regarding Berlin, Diefenbaker raised several questions that had been posed to him by Canadians: Why should Canada risk a war to defend the Germans? Why should Canadians care about Soviet or East German checkpoints in Berlin? Was the West not dangerously "courting war over the question of a rubber-stamp"? To these questions he gave strong, principled answers emphasizing Canada's commitment to European and North American defense and to ensure the nonnegotiable freedom of West Berlin. But there could be negotiation on other points. Canadians, he concluded, had to "prepare accordingly to maintain strong defences," just as the West needed to show "calm resolution without provocative hysteria."[41]

Given that part of his objective had been to win public support, Diefenbaker must have been pleased to see the response of Canadian newspapers. To the *Globe and Mail*, for instance, the speech was nothing less than "one of the best and clearest statements a Canadian Government spokesman has ever delivered on an issue of foreign policy," while the *Montreal Gazette* praised the prime minister's "patient realism."[42] Still, Diefenbaker remained concerned about public opinion, telling Heeney that Canadians continued to have a "misunderstanding of the real issue upon which the NATO countries would have to stand firm." Mentioning "understanding and appreciation" of the president's position, he went on to reveal that he shared with the Americans their pessimism about the likelihood of talks with Khrushchev, asking: "What indeed was genuinely negotiable?" In recording his impressions of this meeting, Heeney pointed out that "throughout, there was utterly no suggestion that Mr. Diefenbaker doubted the sincerity of the U.S. position concerning negotiations, nor was there any criticism whatever of the U.S. attitude in the Berlin crisis."[43] On this central Cold War issue, Diefenbaker stood stoutly with Kennedy.

Criticism did emerge with the White House's decision to embark on its own series of nuclear tests in response to Moscow's abandonment of the moratorium. A fervent opponent of testing, Green, in a discussion with Merchant on August 31, emphasized a hope that Washington would delay any possible test or even the announcement of a test and thereby avoid duplicating the Soviets' "serious blunder." Merchant agreed that the Soviets were making a "great mistake" by angering world opinion and he predicted that his own government would not follow suit. But Merchant was wrong. Kennedy, who had been an outspoken critic of nuclear testing as a senator and as a presidential candidate, agonized over a response, telling Arthur Schlesinger that he was "unconvinced that the military gains will make up for the political losses" and that the notion of testing left him "cold." However, with the Soviet abandonment of the moratorium he felt constrained by a need to look strong, especially in light of Berlin and his stumble over the Bay of Pigs. Thus he announced on September 5 that underground testing would begin, followed by atmospheric testing in the spring.[44]

Privately decrying Kennedy's announcement as "preposterous," Diefenbaker complained that the Americans had not only given no warning to the Canadians but that they had "thrown away" the advantage in world opinion that the West had gained when the Soviets had abandoned the moratorium. In public, however, Ottawa took a supportive stance. "The great tragedy of 1961," Green told the House of Commons, "has been that Soviet leaders have not understood or have ignored the fact that President Kennedy and his top advisers have, from the start of their administration, genuinely desired to bring about a reduction in world tension." Moscow alone bore the blame for the resumption of testing, and although expressing regret at the US move, Green argued that the Americans "could not sit by indefinitely while the Russians were proceeding with their tests." Similarly, Diefenbaker offered no direct public criticism of Kennedy's decision, stating only that as Washington had complied with the moratorium for three years, a delay of several weeks may have been "helpful" in mobilizing global opinion against Khrushchev. In October Canada spearheaded a UN resolution condemning Moscow for testing a 50 megaton bomb, the largest nuclear device ever exploded.[45]

Hurt feelings over nuclear testing did not prevent the prime minister from continuing to condemn Moscow for provoking the Berlin crisis. Diefenbaker had already used the opening of the fall session of Parliament on September 7 to outline the defense measures that the government was taking in support of its responsibility to show "the Kremlin that we will not sit back and allow the world in which we believe to be swept aside by the acceptance of those things that deny every principle of freedom for which we stand."[46] The prime minister's continuing defense of the Western line on Berlin went over well with the Americans. The Ottawa Embassy was pleased that the Tories had "firmly supported" the Western position while criticizing "Soviet aggressive tendencies." Moreover, both the government and the opposition Liberals had harangued Moscow for testing but offered only mild criticism of Washington, in effect giving "strong endorsement" to the president. Rusk, who told Heeney that the administration was "heartened" by Diefenbaker's stance, shared this view, adding that Canada "had been one of the few" members of the alliance to have acted "positively" by boosting troops levels. On this point, American General Lauris Norstad, NATO's commander, expressed to Canadian officials his "personal satisfaction and appreciation" for the strengthening of Canada's conventional military presence in Europe.[47] Then, in a letter to Green, Rusk praised the prime minister's Winnipeg speech as a "telling presentation" and a "comprehensive review of a most complex question." Turning to the comments that Green and Diefenbaker had made regarding the resumption of nuclear testing, the secretary thanked his Canadian counterpart for his "great understanding" of the dilemma in which the administration had found itself. "Canada's stand in these difficult times," Rusk concluded, "is a source of real comfort to us in Washington."[48] Rusk soon arrived in New York, where he carried out a series of discussions with the Soviet foreign minister. These talks lessened the tension and Khrushchev soon withdrew his ultimatum, although the status of Berlin remained an ongoing preoccupation.

Throughout the crisis, and despite the contentious American decision to restart nuclear tests, there had been a surprising symmetry between Canada and the United States, surprising only because of later disputes over defense questions. Diefenbaker had neither criticized Kennedy, except on the issue of testing, nor indicated any disagreement with Washington's mixing of firmness with flexibility. Indeed, Canada had strongly supported its American ally on the main aspects of the standoff with the Soviets. US officials certainly recognized and appreciated this backing. Given the issue's importance, Berlin was the high water mark of cooperation between Ottawa and Washington during the Kennedy years. Canadian policymakers, however, felt considerable frustration that Canada was being kept in the dark about the deliberations going on among the four principal Western powers. In public and in private, Canadian officials from the prime minister on down had stressed that as a NATO member Canada was entitled to better treatment. Having made a robust response to the crisis, Canadians bristled at not being fully consulted on the talks between the British, French, Americans, and West Germans. In a mid-September report to External Affairs on the previous months' diplomatic maneuverings, Heeney made an uncharacteristically critical attack on Washington. Despite promises to keep Canada informed of the deliberations going on within the four-power group, US officials had failed on this point. Due to Canada's "special relationship to the U.S.A, in North America, in Europe and generally," Ottawa was owed more than this token level of consultation. He therefore made strong representations to the State Department, while at the North Atlantic Council Ottawa's representatives spearheaded a protest by the smaller NATO powers over the lack of dialogue.[49] The problem, Green readily admitted, was that alongside France, Britain, and the United States, Canada was merely a "middle power." Moreover, with Western Europe having recovered from the Second World War, "Canada now amounted to very little in the N.A.T.O. picture."[50]

These angry *démarches* paid off. Apologetic, Kohler peppered Heeney with frequent updates on the four power talks and on contingency planning. It was certainly important, Kohler admitted, to recognize that there was a "special Canadian interest" in Berlin, with Canada's membership in NATO and its unique defense relationship with the United States through NORAD established this interest as a fact.[51] Over the coming months, as talks with the

Soviets were carried out, Canadian and American officials carried out their own discussions of Berlin. However, such deliberations did not, nor could not, translate into Canadian influence on US or NATO policy: the Americans and, to a lesser extent, the British, French, and Western Germans were in control. Outsiders, the Canadians held strong reservations about contingency plans for Berlin's defence involving the use of nuclear weapons, a point over which there was sharp disagreement between Canada and its NATO allies.[52]

Assessing Ottawa's preoccupation with consultations, Merchant was far less kind than Kohler. The Canadians, he thought, used protests over the lack of consultation as an excuse to avoid making commitments on fundamentally important defense matters. There were other problems too. In Merchant's view, Diefenbaker's "personal pique" at being excluded from the inner circle of NATO powers presented its own complications as did Green's "special form of escapism" regarding the use of force in international relations. Worse, there was a belief among a number of key members of External Affairs that the United States was "hysterical" in its concerns over national security.[53] Normally quite charitable to Canada, which had been nothing if not helpful over Berlin, Merchant criticisms of Ottawa's stance on defense stemmed from the collapse of movement toward Canadian acceptance of nuclear warheads.

Throughout the summer of 1961, as the tension over Berlin had mounted and as Canada stood foursquare with the United States against the Soviets, the Canadian government had inched closer to meeting its nuclear commitments. At the July Cabinet meeting where he declared the need to support Washington over Berlin, Diefenbaker averred that negotiations to accept nuclear warheads should begin as it was necessary to start the process of arming Canadian forces appropriately. "Canada," he argued, "should not act provocatively but the danger could not be postponed." Challenging this view in a long-winded and heartfelt speech, Green contended that negotiations would be provocative; the matter at hand was not a simple military calculus, but involved "the future of Canada and of civilization." Unsurprisingly, Harkness disagreed with Green. Invited by the prime minister to address the issue, first he stressed that the BOMARC missiles were defensive, could travel only a few hundred miles, and so could not start a war. Next, Harkness noted that he warheads intended for use in Europe were no different than those already held by other NATO forces, and so Canada would not be introducing anything new into the mix. Expanding on this last point and addressing concerns about proliferation, Diefenbaker opined that "it would not constitute any spread of the nuclear powers" if Canada maintained joint control along with the United States.[54] Green's last-ditch attempt to dissuade Diefenbaker appeared to have failed, with the US president soon making his own case to the prime minister.

Against the backdrop of Berlin, Kennedy and Diefenbaker exchanged a number of letters dealing with Canada's acceptance of a nuclear role. On August

3 the president wrote of his preoccupation with "the Soviet challenge to our position in West Berlin," adding that the defense of North America and of the nuclear deterrent served as a bulwark against Soviet aggression. Kennedy urged
setting down an agreement that would then be on hand should the Canadian
Cabinet later give its approval. Referring back to Diefenbaker's assurances in
February and May that negotiations would soon commence, Kennedy acknowledged that "this is not an easy matter for you." In reply, Diefenbaker informed
Kennedy both that he and his colleagues would consider the issue and that
his ministers had been instructed to expedite final preparations for negotiations.[55] Diefenbaker matched this private assurance with a public declaration.
On August 15, in the speech in which he blasted Khrushchev for having erected
the Berlin wall, the prime minister made an encouraging statement: "There are
some in Canada who advocate we should withdraw from NATO in the event
that nuclear weapons are made available for the possession and control of
NATO." This course would endanger NATO and thus "the survival of freedom
itself." After all, he asked, would Canadians truly wish to arm "those who guard
the portals of freedom [with] nothing but bows and arrows?"[56] Pursuing this
line of argument during a Cabinet meeting two days later, he dismissed anti-
nuclear sentiment among the populace.[57]

At a subsequent meeting a defeated Green presented a draft agreement en-
shrining the principle of joint control, which had long been Diefenbaker's concern. In his overview of how the expected negotiations with the Americans
would be carried out, Green told his colleagues that the United States was bound
to assume that by hammering out an agreement, Canada had committed itself
when this was not the case. From the outset, negotiators from External Affairs
would make it clear that the decision to enter into talks did not mean that
Canada had formally decided to accept nuclear warheads. Rather, the negotiations were meant to conclude an agreement that Ottawa would then implement
when and if it saw fit. A more immediate concern, Diefenbaker then added,
was that there was likely to be a press leak about what would be secret talks,
leading the public to assume that Canada was set on acquiring nuclear weapons. Regardless, the prime minister noted that Kennedy felt strongly about the
need for progress to be made on the negotiations; it was therefore important to
proceed. If necessary, he was even prepared to meet the president personally in
order to resolve any sticking points.[58]

Importantly, in staking out his position on nuclear weapons, the prime minister had cited the importance that Kennedy attached to Canada possessing this
weaponry. The centrality of Diefenbaker's personal relationship with Kennedy
to the nuclear question cannot be underestimated. This moment in late August
and early September 1961 was the last time that the president and prime minister were on good terms. On August 21, in the midst of the Cabinet discussions on warheads, Merchant paid a brief call on Diefenbaker. Carrying with

him the prime minister's place card from his visit to Washington in February, Merchant explained that the president wished for Diefenbaker to sign it so that Kennedy could add it to a collection that he was amassing. Merchant, in a note back to the president, recorded that Diefenbaker autographed it with "evident pleasure and alacrity."[59] If this was an attempt to flatter the prime minister, it was yielding positive results. Lunching with Rufus Smith, one senior External Affairs official remarked that the Kennedy–Diefenbaker correspondence was finally breaking "the log jam."[60]

To prepare public opinion for a pending decision, Harkness used a House of Commons debate over defense spending to explain the defensive nature of the weapons that Canada was acquiring and to argue that Canadian forces "should not be required to face a potential enemy with inferior weapons." Perceptively, Paul Hellyer, the Liberal defense critic, observed that Harkness was preparing the public "for the introduction of atomic arms into Canada" by trying to "frighten the Canadian people into submission."[61] Willis Armstrong also saw Harkness's statement, along with Diefenbaker's public comments, as signs, of the long-awaited campaign foreshadowing a "decision to adopt weapons" and even Green seemed to be "more realistic about the world situation."[62] The moment for movement on the nuclear issue did seem at hand. Over the Labor Day weekend, the prime minister had confided to Heeney that groups pressing for nuclear disarmament were tools of the Soviet Union, adding that "in any realistic view, there was no real hope for effective disarmament in the foreseeable future." On September 14, he told the Cabinet that press reports on a change in policy were false and no change would be considered "until the United States had agreed to joint control." But that same day, even with the disappointment over the American resumption of nuclear testing, Diefenbaker wrote his brother to tell him, "the world situation is terrible and people not knowing the situation are loud in their opposition to Canada having any nuclear defence." This view, he felt, was "an ostrich-like philosophy," one "most beneficial to the Communists and of course receives their support."[63]

Days later Diefenbaker buried his head in the sand. A brief story in Newsweek disclosed that Canada was on the cusp of accepting nuclear weapons, with a "straight-from-the-shoulder letter" from the president to the prime minister "expected to resolve the impasse." Then, White House sources unwisely confirmed the correspondence to be true and Canadian reporters picked up the report. The front-page banner headline of the September 20 issue of the Montreal Gazette blared: "JFK Presses Canada on Nuclear Warheads."[64] Learning about the leak, Diefenbaker "hit the roof." Incensed, the prime minister moved quickly into damage control, instructing Heeney to ask Pierre Salinger, the White House press secretary, to decline further comment on the leaked letter.[65] Responding to questions in Parliament about whether there were secret negotiations, Diefenbaker stated that while "discussions with the United States on defence subjects are going on at all times and at various levels," there was no agreement on nuclear weapons; "any rumour to the contrary," he said, "has no foundation in fact." Then going on the attack, he argued that speculation about an agreement stemmed from "those who, desiring one final stand to be taken, are not taking into full regard the international situation nor in the event that it should worsen, the welfare, the future and the safety of Canadians." For a man who had spent several months speaking in belligerent terms about Berlin, this statement was mendacious. That evening, on television and radio, Diefenbaker dismissed certain untrue "rumours and predictions," which had been started for "political purposes."[66] These comments shocked Armstrong, who fired off an emergency report to Washington. Warning that the leak "cannot fail to be quite disturbing" to Diefenbaker and to "others in Canadian Government who are seeking [to] arrive at decision we want," he judged, after speaking with a senior Canadian official, that White House involvement was a "special factor" in the government's postponement of a decision.[67]

As the identity of the leaker remains unknown, one wonders what had been the point of the leak. If it were done to disrupt Canada's acceptance of warheads, then it was a resounding success. If it had been meant to engineer Canada's acceptance of nuclear weaponry—as Diefenbaker had intimated—then it was a grave and foolish error. The prime minister had clearly stressed his concerns with public opinion, of which the White House and the State Department were well aware, and in this period a Canadian federal election seemed likely. Even so, Diefenbaker had told the Cabinet that there would undoubtedly be leaks. Of importance, too, then, was the personal factor: the inevitable leak had involved Diefenbaker's personal correspondence with Kennedy; it had first appeared in a magazine with close ties to the White House; and so the president appeared to have betrayed the prime minister's confidence. Worse, press reports of the leak had made it seem as if Kennedy was pressing Diefenbaker into accepting warheads. Yet regardless of however much Diefenbaker may have been motivated by political concerns, he had spent several months advancing a position on Berlin that he felt many Canadians did not support, thus demonstrating that he could leave his populist instincts by the wayside. The personal dimension of the press leak was thus of critical importance.

So that autumn, as Canada's BOMARC missiles were installed at their launch sites, standing useless without nuclear warheads, the Royal Canadian Air Force's F-101 Voodoo interceptor squadrons became operational, again without nuclear warheads for their air-to-air missiles. As one US diplomat would later note, without nuclear weaponry Canada's air force had become "the largest amateur flying club in the world." At a speaking engagement in November and in a series of Cabinet meetings, Harkness underscored the peculiarity of this situation, cautioning his colleagues that they might "soon be in a very uncomfortable position" unless they moved toward negotiating an agreement with the Americans.[68]

Despite this reasonable point, no decision to open negotiations was forthcoming. Harkness's influence was on the wane; Green was now in the ascendant. The lack of a firm government defense policy, one journalist wrote, left the public "uninformed or misinformed, and consequently utterly confused."[69]

In contrast to his defense minister's continued advocacy of nuclear arms, the prime minister, in a speech in which he called for a continuation of a firm stand on Berlin, made no reference to arming Canada with nuclear defenses. He did, though, note that his government had taken remarkable steps toward securing a global disarmament agreement that were "a record for all nations to see."[70] This sudden change of heart is remarkable. Having long attacked advocates of disarmament as being unrealistic, Diefenbaker now cast himself as a champion of arms limitation. It was surely no coincidence that the prime minister's newfound faith in disarmament came just as he needed a defense policy that did not cast him as a vassal of the American president. As he told Merchant in mid-November, negotiations on nuclear weapons were unlikely to begin in the foreseeable future because the leak made it "impossible" for him "to appear to be acting under pressure from Washington." Reporting back to the State Department, Merchant predicted that given the division between Green and Harkness as well as Diefenbaker's "sensitivity to what he considers public opinion," a speedy Canadian decision on nuclear weapons was "improbable."[71]

This situation frustrated the president, who told Merchant that he was "completely unable to understand" the prime minister's position.[72] Relaying this comment to Ed Ritchie, Willis Armstrong—in charge of the embassy while Merchant undertook a special diplomatic mission in Afghanistan and Pakistan—warned that Kennedy "was baffled to understand" why, within a matter of days, the Canadian government had decided that it was not "prepared to use the best possible weapons." As he emphasized, Washington's growing "unhappiness" with Ottawa stemmed from "the disinclination of Canada to make up its mind on nuclear weapons." Although responding that it was essential to understand that the press leak had set things back, Ritchie was quick to agree when Armstrong emphasized that "geography and the fact of the Alliance" between Canada and the United States meant that Washington "had the right to expect Canada either to use nuclear weapons itself, or to let [the United States] use Canadian facilities." Armstrong also singled out Green's preoccupation with disarmament, which was "contributing to a weakening of the Alliance," but he did concede that Green would certainly disagree with this interpretation.[73]

Despite seeming disingenuous, Diefenbaker's Damascene conversion on disarmament was not necessarily out of place. November had seen TOCSIN-B, the most realistic test to date of Canada's civil defense system. The results, hardly reassuring, were a grim reminder for government officials and the public of the realities of nuclear strategy.[74] Moreover, at the United Nations General Assembly in September, Kennedy had called for a renewal of disarmament negotiations, for a ban on nuclear weapons tests, and for "prohibiting the transfer of control over nuclear weapons to states that do not own them." With the speech placing him into the "rank of world statesman," *Saturday Night* praised Kennedy's sincerity about a desire for peace while being "strong but not boastful."[75] The prime minister also admired the statement, seizing upon it as a reason to hold off on a nuclear decision. After leaving a cabinet meeting on October 6, he remarked to the press that "the Canadian government accepts the principle enunciated by President Kennedy that there should be no extension of the Nuclear Club." When Robinson later asked for clarification as this statement seemed to indicate a change in Canada's position, Diefenbaker stated that Kennedy's speech indicated a "pronounced change" in US policy and so "the public position now taken by the president has killed nuclear weapons in Canada." He then dismissed Robinson's point that ownership would remain with the United States—the two-key agreement on joint control that Kennedy and Diefenbaker had discussed—as a mere "play on words."[76] Commenting on the prime minister's newfound fervor for arms limitation, Robinson later observed that it was most likely just a convenient cover for delay and indecision.[77] However sincere Diefenbaker may have been—and Robinson's observation is astute—from this point on he would never again be such a vocal proponent of arming Canadian forces with nuclear weapons. By pushing Green's disarmament agenda and avoiding a commitment on nuclear arms he fomented a dispute with Washington. After all, if, as he had told Robinson, the nuclear issue was now dead, he failed to make this point clear to the United States government.

Unaware that Diefenbaker was considering a change of heart on nuclear weapons, Kennedy was at least cognizant that the press release had changed the tempo of relations with Ottawa, and so he sought to reach out to the prime minister. At the end of October, General Chester Clifton, Kennedy's personal military aide, approached the military attaché at the Washington Embassy and spoke in broad terms about both the president's desire to maintain relationships with other leaders and Kennedy's concern that his "close personal contact with Mr. Diefenbaker was allowed to slip." While the relationship between the two leaders might have been taken for granted, the president was now "disturbed" that the prime minister had not contacted him for some time; Kennedy wanted "to re-establish their relationship because this is the way that he likes to work." Relaying this conversation to the prime minister, Heeney speculated that the president was trying to repair damage incurred by the press leak, and "was taking this roundabout way" to give reassurance "of his desire for the continuance of a personal relationship," one to which Heeney felt that the president attached "a great importance." Replying to Heeney, Diefenbaker expressed surprise at this overture as he recalled having written the last letter in his series of correspondence with Kennedy, but added that he hoped to soon find a reason to call upon the president.[78] Kennedy has been derided for having been "more responsible than the Prime Minister for the changing tone of bilateral relations," but here was a clear case where he made an effort at bridge-building and Diefenbaker's response, while not hostile, was certainly not warm.[79]

As 1961 ended, the personal relationship between Kennedy and Diefenbaker was rocky and the working relationship between the two governments was also beginning to show signs of strain. In a year-end look at Canadian–American relations, the Canada Desk's Delmar Carlson highlighted the negative influence that Diefenbaker's "procrastination" was having on bilateral affairs.[80] At the same time, Carlson was working with Milton Rewinkel to produce policy guidelines on Canada for the Kennedy administration's use, part of a department-wide initiative to prepare such documents for each country. Their first draft was completed in November. Commenting on it, Merchant emphasized the growing importance of nationalism, a force that "tends to increase during political crises or at election time." With an election nearing, he predicted little action by the Canadians on the host of outstanding issues and he cautioned that in this climate, "almost anything done or said by the United States will evoke a sharp response."[81] Still smarting from the fallout of the press leak, Merchant's frustration with Canada was mounting, though he continued to advocate for forbearance in dealings with Ottawa.

Completed in March 1962, *Canada—Guidelines for Policy and Operations* was the first of these State Department documents to reach final form and it highlighted US officials' recognition of and concern with nationalism in Canada. Its central advice was a call to both expand governmental cooperation and "deepen mutual understanding" of Canadian–American "economic and military interdependence." In short, it called for an affirmation of a special relationship between Ottawa and Washington. Yet there was no patter about harmonious relations. Instead, the document recognized that this relationship was looked upon dubiously by increasing numbers of Canadians. Given this "ever present nationalist sensitivity," United States officials were advised to treat Canada "as a major and independent associate of the U.S." Above all, American officials were warned to avoid infringing upon Canada's sovereignty, taking Canadians for granted, or overlooking Ottawa's "vital economic interests." Nonetheless, the paper recommended that US policymakers "should not hesitate, if our policies are distorted or misinterpreted, or if the occasion otherwise demands, to engage in firm and frank talks to restore mutual understanding or to protect our legitimate interests."[82] Over the coming months, it proved particularly difficult for the denizens of the State Department and White House to reconcile the catechism to avoid upsetting Canadian nationalists with the need to speak frankly.

With the Kennedy administration reluctant to push the matter, the new year began with little movement on the defense file. Cognizant that Diefenbaker would soon call an election, and worried that pushing from Washington would accomplish little prior to this vote, the impetus among the staff at the Ottawa Embassy was to let the matter rest. The Liberal opposition in the House of Commons thought differently, and, as Parliament reconvened from its Christmas break, the nuclear issue increasingly appeared during Question Period. Hammering at the government for advocating against nuclear proliferation while committing itself to acquiring nuclear weapons, Lester Pearson observed, for instance, that "we are spending millions of dollars for weapons that have no warheads and we are told that when an emergency develops we will then decide," even though an emergency necessitating the use of the BOMARC might last only a matter of minutes.[83] *Maclean's* was also critical of the government for its "perpetuation of indecision." By no means favoring the adoption of nuclear weaponry, it admitted: "There is a case for accepting the BOMARC and the Honest John, and a case for refusing them. There is no case for loading them with blank cartridges, which is what we are doing now."[84]

To meet this domestic criticism, Diefenbaker asked External Affairs for a speech indicating a desire to show the public that "no matter how effectively governments may plan the various aspects of their defense programs, changing circumstances and requirements often necessitate cancellations and requirements often necessitate cancellations and adjustments" with reference to "arms programmes in general and particularly nuclear weapons."[85] In the autumn, the prime minister had remarked to Robinson that he considered the nuclear issue to be dead, and here again, he seemed inclined to oppose taking possession of warheads. External Affairs duly responded with a statement emphasizing the growing missile threat, the declining threat from bombers, and thus the "impossibility of predicting with any certainty what may constitute an adequate defence posture for the future." The statement concluded that it was "imprudent to embark at this time on irrevocable decisions" regarding the acceptance of nuclear warheads. The document's anti-nuclear bent, which heralded a change in policy away from the nuclear commitment, upset Robert Bryce, who dissuaded Diefenbaker from making it public. The statement also floated the notion that rather than be stored in Canada, nuclear warheads for the BOMARC missiles and the missiles for the Voodoo interceptors could be kept in the United States and transferred north in the event of a crisis.[86] Diefenbaker seized on this "missing part" proposal, telling Robinson that "he had no new policy" in mind but would continue to support disarmament and oppose an extension of the nuclear club while maintaining "a potential defence capability" whereby nuclear warheads "could readily be placed at the disposal of Canadian forces" in the event of a war.[87]

The missing part notion offered Diefenbaker the possibility of meeting both Canada's defense commitments and the growing anti-nuclear sentiment. Seizing on it as a means of beating back the attacks from the opposition and the press, he told a news conference in Edmonton that his government supported disarmament and would do nothing to extend "the nuclear family."

But then asking how anyone could think it prudent to "to arm Canadians with bows and arrows," he explained that Canada's military had acquired equipment that would "be more effective with nuclear armament," and he then emphasized the missing part formula.[88] Yet complicating things further, in the House of Commons he stressed the importance that he attached to joint control of nuclear weaponry, which was impossible "so long as the law of the United States is as it is at present."[89] Joint control was possible as the prime minister well knew: during their meetings with one another, Kennedy and Diefenbaker had discussed using the existing US–UK agreement on joint control as the basis for a Canada–US arrangement; what was impossible under US law was joint custody of warheads. The point of his comment in the House of Commons, the prime minister admitted to Robinson, was "to place the onus on the Americans." As Robinson privately observed, Diefenbaker was seeking "to create the public impression that the degree or type of joint control which the Americans could offer under existing legislation, was not adequate to Canadian requirements."[90] In seizing on the missing part proposal, and in playing up the issue of joint control, Diefenbaker sought out means of shifting blame and delaying a decision.

Reactions by Canadian newspapers to the prime minister's case were as mixed as Diefenbaker's own argument. To the Montreal Gazette, his position was not "as illogical or contradictory as it may seem." It was certainly absurd that Canada had accepted weapons with no warheads, yet by accepting nuclear arms Canada would be forced to submit control of the weapons to the United States, a potentially humiliating action. Disarmament sentiment, which the government supported, was also an important factor. In sum, the paper concluded that this was "a typical Canadian solution, in that it neither completely satisfies, nor completely denies." Calling for a general review of Canada's entire defense position— Britain had just released a Defence White Paper—the Globe and Mail pointed out an important fact: Canada had accepted the view that "the major threat to our safety lies in an attack from the North cross our territory, aimed at the United States." Canadian policy was designed to thwart such an attack, but the government had yet "to face some of the implications of the situation," namely whether nuclear weapons would be involved.[91] The situation was clear as mud.

As for Diefenbaker's insistence on joint control, American reaction was negative. Reporting on the prime minister's press conference, Merchant cited the nuclear weapons issue as the "greatest single outstanding problem" between the Canadian and US governments; with forces within the government "opposed to dirtying Canadian hands and reputation," there was little resolution in sight. Hoping to spur Canada's government on, the ambassador drafted a letter for the president to send to the prime minister. Admitting that the press leak in September had caused obvious problems for Diefenbaker, this conciliatory message made it clear that Kennedy nevertheless expected a decision to be reached. After all, on several instances the prime minister had given assurances to the president. If, however, he now wished to back away, he should do so unequivocally.[92] This idea was abandoned the next day. In a dispatch to the State Department, Merchant referred to the prime minister's "dismaying" comments in the House of Commons. This "irresponsible treatment of a subject of vital importance" to both countries indicated, in his view, that the Canadians were "farther than ever" from accepting the warheads. Chalking up Canada's position to "ignorance of a complex subject, profound reluctance to face up to a disagreeable subject and an unfortunate propensity to point to the U.S. as an immovable stumbling block," he argued that a letter from Kennedy to Diefenbaker would have little effect, and this proposal died.[93]

In retrospect, the letter from Kennedy to Diefenbaker would have been useful, because it would have given the prime minister the opportunity to back out of the defense commitments. Instead of a note, State Department officials opted for a public statement. At a press conference, Rusk was asked to comment on Diefenbaker's recent statements. Explaining that the decision to acquire nuclear weapons for their own forces was one for Canadians to make alone, he also made clear that American law required that nuclear weapons made available to allied forces remain in US custody, a measure meant both to ensure the security of the weapons and to prevent proliferation. As for the prime minister's concerns regarding control, Rusk affirmed that the administration was ready to implement arrangements "fully consistent with national sovereignty."[94] Although these comments appeared to challenge Diefenbaker, reaction in Ottawa was swift and surprisingly positive. The prime minister admitted to Robinson that Rusk's points were "very fair," while to Merchant he stated "how pleased he was" with the secretary's "very constructive" statement.[95]

The issue then took a turn for the worse when Liberal external affairs critic Paul Martin indicated to the prime minister that he would be questioning him in the House of Commons about an agreement reached between Kennedy and Diefenbaker in May 1961 for Canada to receive nuclear warheads. The information was false, but as a US military official had leaked it to Martin, the prime minister called Merchant in a rage. By the time he and the ambassador met, Diefenbaker had relaxed and the US envoy explained that the White House was equally alarmed and an investigation into the leak was underway. Signaling his understanding, the prime minister "repeatedly expressed admiration" for Kennedy. Merchant then raised nuclear weapons, underscoring that as part of the triangular deal, which involved "domestically unpopular" measures in the United States related to the manufacture of American equipment by Canadian firms, the White House had been forced to sell the agreement to congressional and military authorities by emphasizing its importance to national security. Referring to the fits and starts of negotiations on the nuclear issue going back to the summit between Kennedy and Diefenbaker in February 1961, the ambassador reminded Diefenbaker that as they both knew well, the lack of

Canadian nuclear warheads affected both countries' security. Since the issue remained a "matter of continuing serious concern in Washington," Merchant asked when negotiations might begin. Responding that talks could commence shortly, the prime minister explained that the House of Commons first needed to finish debating budget matters. Cautious in reporting this development to Washington, Merchant wrote that while "some new reason as in the past can, of course, always be conjured up" to delay negotiations, Diefenbaker had "seemed more confident of his ability to carry through than on earlier occasions."[96]

Merchant's hopes were misplaced and also oddly foolish. Not only was an election looming, but also in his recent public speeches the prime minister had underscored the importance that he attached to disarmament and to developments connected to the Eighteen-Nation Disarmament Committee, which convened in Geneva in mid-March. Consisting of a mixed group of Western, Communist bloc, and neutral nations, this conference was set up to conclude agreements on nuclear arms limitation and testing. For several months Green had lobbied hard with the prime minister and his Cabinet colleagues for Canada to take a major role at the summit. With Diefenbaker's blessing, Green traveled to Geneva where, in his biographers' view, he reached "the pinnacle of his career on the international stage."[97] The Americans knew the importance that Green attached to disarmament just as they were aware that it was also important to many Canadians. The previous autumn, Kennedy had remarked to a number of congressional leaders that arms limitation was a "hot issue" in both Canada and the United Kingdom, where public opinion looked unfavorably on any supposed moves toward breaking off talks.[98] As US officials recognized, Canada's geographic position made Ottawa look upon disarmament in practical terms, with a 1961 National Intelligence Estimate observing: "The strongest support for disarmament comes from Canada, which is especially concerned with being caught up in a nuclear war." Canadian views and actions were important, the report noted, because Ottawa "has attempted to create a role for itself as a leader of the 'middle powers,' urging the major contestants into serious negotiations."[99] This spirit was alive and well in Geneva.

While the talks would go on for months—and indeed the committee met through to 1968—for the first few weeks of the 1962 session the foreign ministers of the various countries of the committee attended the conference. On the day before the summit began, Green sat down with Rusk to compare notes and to establish common tactics. The provision of nuclear weapons may have been an ongoing sore spot in Canada–US relations, but both men were equally committed to obtaining a disarmament agreement and test ban. Of course, there was an obvious disparity in power and responsibilities. This factor could be beneficial, Rusk told Green, because Canada's position as a smaller power gave it the ability to work with the eight neutral nations attending the meeting.[100] Green certainly believed that he had a vital role to play. In a stirring speech to the committee he argued that the time was right for real progress to be made "for the survival of civilization."[101] Yet achieving progress proved difficult.

One of the more frustrating and divisive issues at Geneva proved to be the matter of verifying whether the signatories to any treaty were upholding their commitments. The Americans were worried by Soviet opposition to allowing inspections of their facilities, which Moscow believed would infringe on its sovereignty. After one particularly exasperating argument with the Soviet foreign minister, Rusk met with Green and, as the Canadian foreign minister put it to Ottawa, the secretary of state had evidently "felt the need to share some of his private worries with a friend." Washington was willing to try to accommodate Moscow but there was a need for genuine inspections, and if no agreement were made on this point, Rusk worried that it could precipitate a new round of nuclear testing, a comment that made Green recoil. Indeed, the Americans were scheduled to conduct a round of testing in April, and with the deadline approaching, there was mounting pressure on the United States to delay.[102] Having underscored their desire for an effective verification scheme, US officials were alarmed that Green was moving toward throwing his support behind a Swedish proposal for a system with only token inspections. After Green returned to Ottawa, Merchant raised with him his government's consternation at the Canada–US split over inspections. Mindful of Rusk's comments to him in Geneva, Green responded with cautionary words regarding the looming nuclear tests.[103]

Green's uncompromising attitude on verification rankled US officials. Rusk warned Heeney, for instance, against Canada supporting "a vague, indefinite inspection" system.[104] But Green was unbowed, a result of his conviction that the talks in Geneva had reached a "critical stage" where, unless some movement was made, "there might be a renewal of Cold War disputes, with damaging consequences for the conference as a whole." At his insistence, Heeney pressed Rusk on verification. Raising his own anxiety over Ottawa's apparent support for the Swedish proposal, Rusk reiterated that verification was a key sticking point for his government, adding that it hardly seemed unreasonable to see a "gnatsworth" of the Soviet Union. Heeney's avowal that Canada recognized and supported the need for verification therefore cheered Rusk greatly.[105] Mildly reassured, Rusk urged Kennedy to write to Diefenbaker. The president agreed and outlined for the prime minister his position on disarmament, including his hopes for a test ban agreement. Fearing that the Soviets would secure Western acquiescence to an unverified moratorium on tests, and heartened that Heeney had indicated that Ottawa wanted verification enshrined in any agreement, Kennedy told the prime minister that he was relieved. For "some time," he wrote, "I have had an uneasy feeling that perhaps the positions of our two countries were becoming increasingly disparate on the nuclear question."[106] However, Diefenbaker seemed unsure as to whether or not he supported a strict inspection regime. In the House of Commons, the Liberals hammered the prime minister over press reports indicating that Ottawa and Washington were at odds over inspection. After days of criticism, the prime minister finally relented by declaring that any agreement needed a "reasonable means of verification."[107]

Diefenbaker's grudging acceptance reflected policy differences, which were partly influenced not just by domestic politics but also by personal squabbles. In the new year Kennedy had sent the prime minister an autographed copy of *To Turn the Tide*, a collection of his speeches. In February the prime minister replied with several kind words about his meeting with the president one year before, and he extended his congratulations to the president on behalf of Canada for astronaut John Glenn's successful Earth orbit.[108] A month later, Diefenbaker complained to Heeney that Kennedy had failed to respond to this note of congratulations. Rankled by this latest slight, he was loath to respond to the president's note on the disarmament talks. Writing in his diary shortly thereafter, Heeney noted a change in the prime minister's disposition toward the Kennedy administration. Whereas in 1961 Diefenbaker's attitude had been "friendly to the point of enthusiasm," Heeney now found that the prime minister held "little confidence" in the Americans because of his apparent resentment over "their failure to take effective account of Canadian interests," from nuclear weapons and disarmament to Canada's wariness about Britain's entry into the European Economic Community.[109]

The Americans had their own interests. On minor issues, such as wheat sales to China or the triangular deal, the White House had been willing to sacrifice its views in the interests of bilateral harmony. But on major questions affecting national security, there was far less goodwill for Canada. Although Kennedy desired a test ban treaty—and would sign one the following year—he wanted to show the Soviets his resolve, thus putting him at odds with Ottawa. Earlier in 1962 he had remarked to McGeorge Bundy that Washington "should not be bound by the judgment of the British or the Canadians" on the question of testing.[110] True to his word, having already announced that the United States would recommence atmospheric nuclear testing, Kennedy approved a series of tests beginning on April 25. Green, Heeney, and other Canadian officials had urged the Americans not to follow through, but as Rusk reminded them, Kennedy "had a fearful responsibility and played a lonely role. Unless the USA maintained its position vis-à-vis the USSR, the Free World just would not continue to enjoy their freedom to question the USA decisions."[111] As for the disarmament talks, they continued, with Canada's stance toward verification remaining an ongoing source of tension in Canadian–American relations and emerging as a serious point of disagreement later that autumn at the time of the Cuban missile crisis.

The other nuclear issue, the provisioning of warheads for the Canadian military, showed no signs of progress. In Washington in mid-April, Heeney met with Kennedy for what was his farewell call as ambassador. Having originally wanted only to serve several months in the US capital, Heeney was stepping down from his post after more than two years. Fêted at a luncheon, the outgoing ambassador next attended a small ceremony in the Oval Office where Kennedy presented him with a signed photograph. These events had a dual aim: to thank Heeney for his second tour of duty in Washington and to ensure that he returned home "with the best possible recollections," thus maintaining "an aura of the harmonious relationship with the Canadian Government." The president used the occasion to emphasize several outstanding issues: low Canadian foreign aid figures; a supplementary wheat deal between Canada and Communist China; and the stalled talks in Geneva. With rumors swirling that Diefenbaker might soon call an election, Kennedy was particularly interested in hearing Heeney discuss the domestic scene in Canada. The president also expressed his hope that following the election there might be "forward movement" on nuclear warheads.[112] Two days later the Canadian Parliament was dissolved and the long-awaited election was set for June 18. Progress toward resolving the nuclear issue was put on hold indefinitely.

Midway through the campaign Merchant, also stepping down as ambassador, submitted an analysis of the expected course of the election. Concluding that after the vote Canada "would be a stauncher, more consistent, and reliable ally and understanding friend with Mr. Diefenbaker back in power," he based this argument on the premise that "a workable but greatly reduced majority" would allow the Tories "to form a more decisive and self-confident government." The outgoing ambassador believed that Diefenbaker stood with Washington on major issues but that this "has been so far imperfectly translated into policies, action, and public pronouncements." As he often did, he put the blame squarely on the prime minister's "opposition thinking" and sense of political insecurity.[113] What Merchant had not taken into account was that Diefenbaker would fail to win a majority government, which would only make his caution more pronounced. The vote in June saw the Progressive Conservatives lose almost one hundred seats and be reduced from holding the largest majority of seats to that point in Canadian electoral history to a minority government. The result left Diefenbaker despondent—"his morale was ghastly," one Cabinet member noted later—a situation not helped when the prime minister broke his ankle. The ministerial swearing-in "was not a very pleasant occasion," recalled another minister. "Though everything was done with admirable elegance and appropriate solemnity we all knew that something was wrong, desperately wrong, and those who were present looked and must have felt uncomfortable."[114]

US diplomats were equally depressed. No doubt, they predicted, there would now be an increase in the prime minister's "indecisiveness and partisan political motivations." Hence, one State Department official wrote, "there is no basis for us to expect anything very useful, constructive, or positive from Canada in this period and we will be fortunate if we can keep what we have from eroding."

Canadian acquisition of nuclear weapons, the American government's chief bilateral concern, "had now receded out of sight for the foreseeable future."[115] Hoping that the election result would not hamper a resolution of the nuclear issue, Rufus Smith approached Basil Robinson, who was leaving the Prime Minister's Office for a post at the Washington Embassy, and made clear to him that Ottawa's "record on defence policy would colour all the dealings with US officials," who felt "that they have not been squarely dealt with" on the issue. As Robinson correctly surmised, "this theme is too often repeated by US embassy officials to be a casual thought."[116]

American officials, from the president on down, had been repeating the importance that they attached to Canada accepting nuclear weapons since 1959. Cognizant of Canadian feeling on the nuclear matter, recognizing the prime minister's electoral concerns, and appreciating that pushing Canada on this matter would be counterproductive, they had left the initiative to Ottawa. Over the first few months of the Kennedy administration, this tactic had seemed sensible. The prime minister, as Kennedy acknowledged, knew the domestic situation well. Further, Diefenbaker had proven himself a strong ally with his firm stance throughout the tense summer of 1961, when the Berlin crisis threatened war between the Soviet Union and the West. True, there had been some concerns expressed over Washington's failure to consult fully with Ottawa, a constant problem reflective of the disparity in power between the two allies. Canadian diplomats had brought their views on how to resolve the crisis to the attention of their American counterparts, but Ottawa had little influence over the course of events in Europe. However, other US allies faced the same difficulty in influencing policymaking in Washington, thankfully so given that Bonn and Paris were pushing for a much more forceful line over Berlin. Besides Escott Reid's underestimation of the willingness of the Americans to negotiate rather than fight, as well as some disappointment over the US decision to resume nuclear testing, Berlin marked a highpoint of cooperation between the Diefenbaker government and the Kennedy administration. The White House had asked for allied support, and Canada was forthcoming by boosting its troop commitment to Europe, which, unlike Cuba or Southeast, seemed to be the epicenter of the Cold War.

Fear of war that summer had also led the prime minister to begin the process of accepting nuclear warheads for continental defense and for the defense of Western Europe alongside NATO forces, a position he defended in Cabinet. Moreover, fulfilling a pledge that he had made to Kennedy, Diefenbaker carried out a number of speeches meant to prepare the Canadian public for the acceptance of a nuclear role. Yet at the point at which negotiations over accepting these warheads was at hand, the Canadian prime minister, unduly alarmed by a press leak, backed away from these talks. From then on, he moved increasingly farther away from a pro-nuclear position toward Green's anti-nuclear stance.

Principled and noble, the Canadian foreign minister's ultimate aims for disarmament were shared by the American president. Kennedy, though, was trapped by practical concerns for security, the result of the abhorrent logic of nuclear deterrence. It was this same logic that made Canada' acceptance of nuclear weapons, especially those meant for continental defense, a necessity. The problem was that in an age of nuclear crises, the decision to accept such weaponry was not taken lightly. Atomic anxieties lay behind many Canadians' fears of the close alliance with the United States, emerging in James Minifie's *Peacemaker or Powdermonkey?* and in the growing anti-nuclear movement. In early 1962, one contributor to Canada's largest women's magazine asked: "Should we obediently burrow ourselves in the ground like well-disciplined ground hogs? Are we to go calmly about stocking a bomb shelter like a sort of grim concrete cottage?" One of her colleagues soon added that "events of the past few months have forced even the most ostrichlike optimists among us to come face to face with that horrible nightmare of this age of anxiety: the possibility of nuclear attack."[117] Such anxieties were also present in Canadian novelist Arthur Hailey's *In High Places*. Published in early 1962 and set in the near future, the book revolves around an imminent nuclear showdown between Moscow and Washington, which leads the Canadian prime minister to conclude an agreement with the US president to temporarily unify the two countries through a "solemn Act of Union," a step that would move American air defenses northward and create both a customs union and a joint foreign policy. "But outside those areas," the fictional premier assured Canadians, "our national entity and independence would remain."[118] With no control over its foreign and defense policy, what independence remained would be insignificant, the precise fear of those Canadians who saw that this situation already existed in the real world thanks to the close military cooperation between Canada and the United States.

Of course, there were voices in favor of Canada's membership in NORAD, of its acquisition of advanced weapons, and of its role in support of the United States. It was impossible, General Lyman Lemnitzer, the chairman of the Joint Chiefs of Staff, noted in 1961, "to draw lines between Canada and the United States and have effective air defence."[119] The next year, an advisor to Canada's Department of National Defence, R. J. Sutherland, wrote in the *International Journal* in favor of nuclear-tipped BOMARCs, contending: "A bomber is not vulnerable to non-existent defences." As for defense policy writ large, he pointed to the intertwined nature of continental defense. Geography had created an "involuntary American guarantee," meaning that the United States was "bound to defend Canada from external aggression almost regardless of whether or not Canadians wish to be defended." Hence, American self-interest in national security threatened Canadian sovereignty; Canada, then, had to ensure that its weakness would not make it a threat to the United States, with cooperation a means to defend national sovereignty.[120] Also strongly underlining the place of geography, American political scientist Melvin Conant, in a think piece in *Foreign Affairs*, highlighted the importance that successive American administrations had placed on forging "a uniquely close and important defense relationship with Canada." However, US officials had to be cognizant that these close ties had led to "serious and severe political strains" north of the border and conscious of the impact of their actions upon Canada. Canadians, however, had to look to redefine "Canada's role in correct terms—the collective defense of the free world as a whole."[121] However loud dissenting voices may have been, these and other proponents of the status quo were ultimately successful in ensuring public support for the Canada–US defense relationship.

On these issues, Diefenbaker had taken the initial plunge, but he was cautious about going deeper. Reluctant to accept nuclear arms, he also proved unwilling to abrogate his country's nuclear commitment to the United States, though he did consider backing away from a nuclear role, seizing first on Kennedy's desire that the nuclear club not expand and, then on the missing part idea. But he made no mention of his doubts to US officials, instead leading them on with assurances that a decision would come soon. Latent hopes on both sides of the border that Diefenbaker's wavering on this key question would end in 1962 were dealt a blow by the results of the federal election that spring. As Green told Armstrong in mid-July, since the start of the election in April there had been no movement on the nuclear file within the government, and it would be best for Washington to continue to wait for Ottawa to take the initiative.[122] The Americans remained patient even as Diefenbaker seized on Green's disarmament efforts as yet another reason to delay a nuclear decision. For the foreseeable future, Canada would continue to preach disarmament while maintaining weapons systems that, without nuclear warheads, stood useless. This situation, described by British diplomats as "ludicrous," would not be resolved until the following year.[123] By then, however, Diefenbaker would be out of office, the result, in part, of his refusal to accept nuclear warheads and to instead engage in a war of words with Washington. The nuclear issue was not the sole point on which Canadian voters found their prime minister lacking. Diefenbaker also faced public criticism over his handling of the Canadian economy and of Canada's relationship with the United Kingdom, two issues where Washington proved important and where the damage done to Canadian–American relations was palpable.

# 4

# Grand Designs

*Canada–US Economic Relations, Nationalism,*
*and Global Trade, 1961–1962*

In his 1962 State of the Union message President Kennedy focused intently on economic matters. "The greatest challenge of all," he intoned, was "the growth of the European Common Market." Six months earlier, Harold Macmillan, Britain's prime minister, had announced his government's intent to join the European Economic Community (EEC), the customs union comprising France, West Germany, Italy, and the Benelux countries. Addressing this move in his speech to Congress, Kennedy declared that if the United Kingdom were to join the EEC, then "there will arise across the Atlantic a trading partner behind a single external tariff similar to ours with an economy which nearly equals our own." Worried that the United States would be cut off from this massive market, and with his country's existing trade legislation set to expire, Kennedy asked Congress to help him seize the initiative by passing a new trade law. Doing so was of the highest importance, for Kennedy cautioned that a decision whether or not to implement new legislation "could well affect the unity of the West, the course of the Cold War, and the economic growth of our Nation for a generation to come." It was time for a decisive and innovative approach: a five-year Trade Expansion Act granting the president the ability to lower American tariffs on a reciprocal basis, thus encouraging the Common Market to do the same. Viewing this legislation as a cure-all, Kennedy declared, "if we move decisively, our factories and farms can increase their sales to their richest, fastest-growing market. Our exports will increase. Our balance of payments position will improve. And we will have forged across the Atlantic a trading partnership with vast resources for freedom."[1]

Kennedy's lofty proposal was one element of the so-called Grand Design, an Eisenhower-era notion meant to quiet post-Suez strife in the West by knitting Western Europe together with the United States through liberalized trade. The idea had longer roots: since the end of the Second World War Washington had encouraged an integrated Atlantic community, and so it had applauded the EEC's creation as a means of both creating a responsible partner in Europe and tying West Germany into an organization with its neighbors. From an American standpoint it was regrettable that Britain was outside of this grouping, because the British could further stabilize Europe by balancing the French and West Germans. Macmillan, meanwhile, aimed to increase trade with the EEC and so reverse a stagnant economy. Hoping to see a united Europe, Kennedy encouraged this development. In turn, through the tariff-cutting powers that he hoped to win, the president planned to bind the Common Market to the United States via extensive economic links. The US economy, struggling with its balance of payments, would have access to a huge market, and a boost in exports might help to reverse unemployment and pay for American military expenditures as well as Kennedy's increases in foreign aid. Supporters of this plan within the administration also wanted the tariff-cutting powers eventually to be applied to trade with countries beyond Europe. A unified "North Atlantic Community," Dean Rusk told a closed-door session of the Senate Foreign Relations Committee, "would be a nexus of special relationships reaching right around the world, with our relations with Latin America, and with the countries of the Pacific, the British with the Commonwealth, and the French with the French-speaking countries."[2]

For Canada, there was much to support in these plans. The possibility of lower tariffs, for instance, could boost exports, a decidedly positive development for a country looking to diversify trade. Indeed, postwar Canadian governments viewed Western Europe as a potential counterweight to the United States. Closer transatlantic ties had a definite appeal. But for many Canadians, including John Diefenbaker, there was also much to fear as Britain's move into the Common Market threatened the continuation of the Commonwealth preference system, which itself was a counterweight to the US market. Established at the 1932 Imperial Economic Conference in Ottawa, preferences provided access to British and Commonwealth markets that were then protected by high external tariffs. Abolishing this system was a prerequisite for Britain's accession to the Common Market, a development that would confirm the loss of the British counterweight, a process that had been accelerating since the Second World War.[3] Addressing the importance of preferences, Donald Fleming reminded delegates to a conference on Canadian–US relations in November 1961 that Canada was not simply the world's fourth largest exporter, but, per capita, was "the world's greatest trading nation." The Canadian economy was thus "open and sensitive." In real terms, Fleming explained that his country's sales to Britain in 1960 had amounted to $915 million, or 17 percent of total exports. This trade was primarily in raw materials, agricultural products, and manufactured goods, three sectors that the EEC's own tariffs sought to protect. Fleming predicted that if Britain were to abandon preferences and adopt the Common Market's tariff system then more than three quarters of Canada's exports to the UK would be negatively affected by becoming more expensive than goods available from within the EEC.[4] This vulnerability to British moves underscored a fear that shrinking Anglo–Canadian trade would leave Canada's economy even more reliant on the United States.

Canadian nationalists greeted this prospect with little joy. Diefenbaker, for one, had risen to power partly on a wave of public anger at the previous Liberal government's drift away from Britain toward Washington. Criticism of the Liberals for having led Canada "down the slippery slope of economic colonialism" had helped the Tories seize power. Ongoing Canadian concern through the late 1950s and early 1960s over the huge levels of American investment and Canada's growing dependency on the US export market fed into nationalist criticism of the United States for infringing on Canada's "domestic economic sovereignty."[5] Diefenbaker's early, fanciful attempt at diverting 15 percent of Canada's trade from the United States to the United Kingdom was a reflection of his feeling on these matters. Although the Tories had proven unable to shift Canadian trade patterns by fiat, many in Ottawa did not view the possibility of increased dependence upon the US market favorably. Motivated by a belief that Britain's intended move was nothing less than "a turning point in history," Diefenbaker fought against Britain's entry into the EEC, a position that brought him into conflict with the Kennedy administration. Much focus has been placed on the differences between London and Ottawa on the EEC issue as a marker of the "end of empire," with little attention paid to the US angle, despite Washington's obvious importance through the Grand Design.[6]

American policymakers were not ignorant of the effect that London's actions could have on Canada, as well as other Commonwealth countries such as Australia and New Zealand—all key US allies. Early on, George Ball informed the president that he would seek out ways to cushion the impact on these countries of the loss of preferences. But Ball was dead set against any continuation of the preference system.[7] On this subject the Kennedy administration was following a well-established script. Since the 1930s, American officials had sought to do away with preferences. Yet breaking the Canadian–British connection was not the overarching goal for the architects of the Grand Design, who were focused less on this relatively parochial issue than on transforming the postwar world.[8] As Kennedy's ambassador in London mused: "I may yet live to see the US and Canada linked with this great European complex in binds so strong as to create lasting Western unity, with all that would connote for the preservation of Western civilization against aggression from elsewhere."[9] Though sympathetic to the Canadian plight, US officials, convinced of the merits of the Grand Design, thought that Ottawa should not stand in the way of progress. Even so, turning to quiet diplomacy and careful consultations, they sought to assist Canada in adjusting to the expected new reality; Diefenbaker resisted these overtures, loudly at times, vindictively at others.

From Macmillan's announcement on July 31, 1961 that the UK would apply to enter the Common Market, to January 14, 1963, when Charles de Gaulle, the French president, vetoed Britain's application, this issue concerned much of the Canadian government's time, poisoning both Canada–US and Anglo–Canadian relations. Differences over the Common Market also led to the end of the working relationship between Kennedy and Diefenbaker, a situation only exacerbated by Ottawa's handling of an economic crisis in the summer of 1962. Canadian–American disagreement over the nuclear weapons issue eventually brought down Diefenbaker's government, but the Grand Design led to the worsening climate of bilateral relations that allowed the dispute over nuclear warheads to degenerate into a cutthroat battle between Ottawa and Washington. For all the ill feeling generated by these issues, there was still room for diplomatic maneuvering by the guardians of the Canada–US relationship: quiet diplomacy continued to be used, while linkages were avoided. However, the climate within which the careful managers of bilateral relations operated became increasingly tense and very little middle ground existed on which compromise could be built.

Britain's application to join the EEC did not surprise Canada's government. Visiting Ottawa in April 1961, Macmillan had extolled the benefits of membership, assuring Diefenbaker that London would seek to cushion the blow to Canada and the rest of the Commonwealth.[10] When Kennedy traveled to the Canadian capital a month later, he asked Diefenbaker to outline potential difficulties that Canada might face should the UK join the EEC. The prime minister highlighted the loss of markets, particularly for agricultural products. Commiserating, Kennedy noted that the United States would face problems too. But, the president contended, the greater need was to bring stability to Europe, with British membership essential in this regard.[11] Kennedy was not dismissive of Canadian concerns. During his own meeting with Macmillan in April, he had asked whether moves toward greater European cooperation would offer "opportunities not only for the United Kingdom but also for the United States and Canada." London, Macmillan replied, "could use its influence to make a bridge between Europe and North America."[12] With the British prime minister determined to pursue the European option, Canadian officialdom grew agitated.

Responding to a flurry of worried messages from Diefenbaker and other Commonwealth leaders, Macmillan sent Duncan Sandys, the Commonwealth secretary, to consult with Commonwealth governments. Sandys arrived in Ottawa in mid-July. Canadian ministers greeted him coolly. For Donald Fleming, the Commonwealth was a "fundamental factor" in Canada's foreign and trade policy, one worth defending. Doubting that Britain would benefit economically from membership, George Hees questioned whether London could ensure that safeguards for the Commonwealth would be put in place.

Unsurprisingly given his portfolio, Alvin Hamilton underlined the massive damage that he believed would be done to Canada's agricultural sector. Howard Green, examining the supposed political benefits of British membership, wondered how influential London could be when it would presumably have to toe a European—not British—line on international questions.[13] Reporting on the meeting to the British Cabinet, Sandys noted that Canada, along with Australia and New Zealand, had put far more emphasis on the political fallout of British membership in the EEC than they had on the economic impact. Chalking up this anxiety to expected federal elections in Australia and Canada, he added that Canadian worries were heightened by an "additional fear that any loosening of Commonwealth ties would make it more difficult for Canada to prevent herself from being sucked into the economic orbit of the United States."[14] Unperturbed by Commonwealth objections, the British government opted for Europe.

To create the illusion of consultation on this move, Macmillan agreed to a meeting of Commonwealth economic ministers, scheduled to convene in Accra in September. Ottawa's chief objective, Green informed his Cabinet colleagues, would be to "safeguard to the fullest possible extent" access to the British market. Armed with these instructions, Hees and Fleming, Canada's delegates to the summit, "launched a frontal assault on Britain's European aspirations." Their flat rejection of the Macmillan government's plans encouraged the other Commonwealth delegates to speak out against the UK, causing one British delegate to remark to reporters, "they're out for blood."[15] Not everyone in Canada was so sanguinary. The "wailings and lamentations at Accra" earned a sharp rebuke from the *Globe and Mail*, and, in the House of Commons, Opposition leader Lester Pearson attacked Fleming and Hees's "public squealing."[16] A shrewd observer of which direction the political winds were blowing, Diefenbaker was extremely concerned by this "strong critical reaction," telling his Cabinet that he did not want the government to be blamed for upsetting Anglo–Canadian relations.[17] As the months went by Canada's prime minister became increasingly critical of Macmillan. But in the autumn of 1961, hoping to avoid a spat with the British, the Canadians turned their attention to the Americans.

Convinced that the United States had an important role to play in setting global trade patterns, and mindful that Washington was anti-preference, Canadian officials focused on influencing US policy. A chief target was George Ball, who, in November 1961, was promoted from undersecretary of state for economic affairs to undersecretary of state. An economic liberal within the administration, Ball was also the principal proponent of the Grand Design and a committed advocate of economic integration.[18] Although willing to concede to the Canadian point of view on a number of matters—trade with Cuba, for instance—on European integration, he was sympathetic but adamantly opposed to any extension of the Commonwealth preference system lest it harm the creation of a united Europe. His thoughts on economic union also extended to

North America. "Living next to our nation," he wrote later in his memoirs, "with a population ten times as large as theirs and a gross national product fourteen times as great, the Canadians recognize their need for United States capital; but at the same time they seem determined to maintain their economic and political independence. Their position is understandable, and the desire to maintain their national integrity is a worthy objective." His conclusion, however, was that Canada was "fighting a rearguard action against the inevitable."[19] In his dealings with Canadians for the Kennedy administration he largely kept these feelings in check, and indeed his troubles dealing with an increasingly nationalistic Canada only fed his later desire to see the two countries move closer together.

In his fervor for the Grand Design, Ball was joined by Robert Schaetzel, his assistant, who had served in the State Department since the Second World War, dealing primarily with economic matters. In this capacity Schaetzel had gained experience with Canadian issues, having been the American architect of the joint Canada–US ministerial committee on trade and economic affairs during the Eisenhower administration. Canadian assistant undersecretary Ed Ritchie saw him as "an effective operator" who was "quite free in batting ideas around." Still, he could be quite unsympathetic to Canada. Willis Armstrong once recalled how he had tried unsuccessfully to impress upon Schaetzel the fact that Canadians did not like the idea of Britain joining the EEC. Schaetzel's reply: "Well, the Canadians are just wrong, that's all."[20] Schaetzel and Ball were to have an immense impact on bilateral relations because the Grand Design was so important to the growing antipathy between Ottawa and Washington. Conscious of Canadian concerns about an expanded Common Market—even if they felt that Ottawa's opposition was wrong—they sought to assist Canada through the informal consultation mechanisms inherent to the close diplomatic relationship.

During meetings in Vienna just after the Accra summit, Fleming was the first to approach Ball, warning him that Commonwealth delegates believed that the United States was pushing the UK into Europe. Admitting that the Kennedy administration supported an enlarged EEC, Ball vowed that it was not interfering in what was an issue for the British and Europeans to work out together. As to the specifics of Commonwealth preferences, he confessed that the White House "had not really done very much thinking" on this issue and he welcomed high-level talks in order to broaden US thinking and bridge the apparent differences between Ottawa and Washington.[21] Troubled by this discussion, Ball directed Schaetzel to follow up with Heeney in order to relay his concerns over: the "developing split" between Canada and the United States on the EEC; the apparent belief in Ottawa that American officials were pushing for British entry; and the depth of Canadian feeling over the impact of the loss of preferences. On the latter, Schaetzel offered little reassurance, telling Heeney, not incorrectly, that the Commonwealth was not fundamentally an economic organization. Accordingly, preferences could be eliminated without damaging it. Then he outlined the thrust of future American policy: the creation of a dynamic trading network, which would generate innumerable economic benefits for Canada.[22] In Washington's view Ottawa should accept the transition from the Commonwealth to the Grand Design because of the likely benefits that were to accrue. As one White House official—a specialist in Middle Eastern and Asian affairs—advised, the administration had to do a better job of urging Canada and Australia "not to scream so loudly about Britain's entry into the Common Market. They must be brought to realize that political factors outweigh economic in this case, and that their own vital security interests (as well as ours) demand UK entry into Europe."[23] But given nationalist economic sentiments rooted in concerns about a loss of a counterweight to the United States, Canadian officials were not convinced of this trade-off.

The Department of Finance produced for Fleming a scathing study of the US role in trade policy. Beginning from the assumption that since London seemed ready to join the Common Market "at almost any cost" Commonwealth preferences were likely to be eliminated, this report questioned why the United States was not using its considerable influence to protect the Commonwealth. Given that so many key American allies and important developing countries were Commonwealth members, it appeared that the United States was abandoning its role of leadership in the world. Instead, Washington was adopting a "shortsighted," rapacious policy aimed at capturing Commonwealth markets. Canada's only recourse was to push the United States into bringing its influence to bear on the EEC so that Commonwealth economic interests could be accommodated. Should the Kennedy administration adopt a truly "imaginative" approach in crafting new trade legislation that led to a reduction of Common Market tariffs, then it would be in Canada's interest to support the United States.[24] A summation of where Canada's interests lay in relation to changing trade patterns, the document reflected deep-seated Canadian fears about American economic intentions.

Given wide circulation to government ministers and civil service mandarins, this report caused a stir. At the time consideration was being given in Ottawa to Ball's offer to Fleming of talks on the implications of an expanded Common Market, with the groundwork being laid by Schaetzel and Maurice Schwarzmann, the economic counselor at the Washington Embassy. However, at a Cabinet meeting in late October ministers scuttled the summit, arguing that it "might give the impression that the U.S. government was directly influencing Canada's course in Commonwealth matters." As Schwarzmann complained, the Finance Department's report was to blame.[25] Insofar as it accepted the need to seek US help, the Finance report represented an attempt at viewing the Common Market issue in a realistic light. However, in terms of policy guidance, it counseled for little more than simple obstruction—that is, until or unless the United States took a leading role. The report, then, reflected the "inability" of Canadian civil servants to provide policy proposals that could counteract the "disaster" of Britain's entry into the EEC. This vacuum allowed fear mongering about the United States to fester. In this climate, close government-to-government talks were abandoned.

Although suspicions of the United States were growing, Fleming was coming to believe that Washington had a key, positive role to play, thus acknowledging the conclusion of his department's report. Speaking to the Third Annual Seminar on Canadian–American Relations at Assumption University in Windsor in early November, Fleming appealed for help from Washington. First, he spoke in frightening terms of the economic damage that would be done to Canada in the event that preferences were abandoned and that the EEC's external tariff remained. The "trading world," he warned, was about to be "altered in a fundamental way." Worse, the growing "trend to regionalism" was not confined to Europe: Canadians could soon find themselves squeezed by additional trading blocs in Asia and Latin America. What was needed to prevent such a bleak development? "Constructive and imaginative leadership" from Washington. The Americans, Fleming hoped, would lead an "international cooperative effort aimed at finding prompt and effective solutions" to the problems looming over global trade. Should the Kennedy administration develop a "broader, bolder and more forward-looking commercial policy," then the United States would be playing "its proper role" in world affairs.[26] Speaking to the same seminar, Frank Coffin, who as a congressman from Maine had shown great attention to Canadian viewpoints and was now serving as deputy administrator of the US Agency for International Development, offered soothing words. Hinting that the White House would indeed pursue a bold trade policy, he asked that the two governments bring "economic leadership to North America" and jointly work together to lower EEC tariffs. "The ball now is in our court," he implored, "and we won't win by sitting on it."[27]

Fleming's Windsor speech signaled that Ottawa could support Washington, while Coffin's statement indicated Washington's intent of pursuing innovative trade legislation; joint action looked possible. As Heeney and Schwarzmann soon emphasized to Ball and Schaetzel, Fleming had outlined what was expected of the US government if it wished for Canada's support. Assuring the two Canadians that Washington recognized Ottawa's "tremendous concern" over trade, Ball underlined how the administration's plans to cut tariffs would benefit Canada. He also reviewed his long-term thinking, explaining that he foresaw Canada and the United States as "the 'nexus' of three broad communities, the North Atlantic Community, the Organization of American States and then the Western Pacific."[28] Meeting Fleming at an Organization for Economic Cooperation and Development summit in Paris soon after, Ball broached these notions. While much familiar ground was covered, turning to the minister's Windsor speech, Ball affirmed that the White House was indeed set on providing necessary leadership.[29] Worryingly, Fleming also met both with de Gaulle, who confirmed that there was little room for special arrangements for Commonwealth countries, and with Macmillan, who offered little reassurance regarding the protection of Commonwealth interests. Henceforth, Fleming concluded, Ottawa had "to attach considerable importance" to the new trade initiative emanating from Washington.[30]

Fleming's discussions with de Gaulle and Macmillan underscored Canadian reliance on an American initiative. Recognizing Ottawa's parlous position, other US officials briefly considered bringing Canada into a North Pacific Community, tying together Japan and North America. Milton Rewinkel, the director of the Office of British Commonwealth and Northern European Affairs, who oversaw the Canada Desk, engaged in an effort to drum up support within the State Department for the creation of this community, in the hopes that it would "encourage Canada to assume ever increasing responsibility" and that it might blunt "the Canadian tendency toward an unhealthy introspection and excessive preoccupation with relations with the United States." Citing the apparent interest in Asian affairs shown by Diefenbaker and Howard Green—they had hosted the Japanese premier in mid-October—Rewinkel thought the idea would be welcomed in Ottawa.[31] Backing Rewinkel, Robert Schaetzel lobbied Ball for support. Focused on the ways in which Canada might benefit in terms of trade from this arrangement, Schaetzel connected this potential economic windfall to the question of the EEC, concluding that the US could support a move that "in a time of great difficulty" for Canadian officials would create opportunities and also give Ottawa "some outlet for energy other than abuses of the United States and recriminations against the British decision to join the Common Market."[32] Ball warmed to the idea, raising it both with Heeney and with Fleming. However, the notion languished into the new year, until Merchant, learning of it, quickly put an end to the proposal with a warning that "grave damage" would be done to Canada–US relations "because Canadians will think we consider them in the same category as [the] Japanese and that their special relationship with us is of little or no value to us."[33] Relations between Ottawa and Washington were already showing strain, and Merchant was evidently cognizant of not adding another problem to a growing list that included Canadian adoption of nuclear weapons as well as the Grand Design.

Differences over trade were a growing blot on the bilateral relationship. In talks with Willis Armstrong in late November, Ed Ritchie highlighted this growing problem and cautioned him against discounting Canadians' "emotional reactions" to UK accession, the result of "apprehension" at being "sandwiched between the colossus of the United States and the colossus of the United Europe." Seeking to allay Canadian concerns, in early December, Ball told interviewers on the CBC that his government was "not seeking at any time, nor will we seek, any kind of exclusive trading relation with Europe. What we are seeking is a general liberalization of trade in which Canada would participate as the United States would participate."[34] The president's planned trade legislation offered Canadians a glimmer of hope. As Heeney put it, not only did the administration appear ready "to provide the kind of imaginative leadership and initiative in world trade" desired by other countries, but the White House actually had a chance of winning public and Congressional support. Diefenbaker recognized as much, telling Merchant that while fearful about a loss of preferences, he did have "a lively interest" in the president's expected trade bill. In turn, Merchant emphasized Kennedy's firm commitment to liberalizing trade. He added a warning: there was little benefit to the Canadians "digging in their heels" against British plans.[35] Digging his heels in at a meeting of the Hamilton Chamber of Commerce soon after, Diefenbaker, first praising the economic growth experienced by the EEC's members, then declared that future "prosperity should not be realized at the expense of outside countries." Turning to Britain, he made it clear that he would fight to protect Canadian and Commonwealth interests but, unlike Fleming, he made no effort to champion Washington's tariff-cutting, a pattern he would keep to over the coming months. Striking a similarly alarmist note, Green told a gathering of students that the political stakes were "much more serious than the Canadian people realize."[36] These fears drove a wedge between Ottawa and its two main North Atlantic partners, a division that became stark at the joint US–Canada committee on trade and economic affairs conference in Ottawa in January. On the eve of the committee meeting, Kennedy delivered his State of the Union message in which he laid out his trade initiative.

"Canadian ministers," Rusk noted after the conference, were "obviously preoccupied in jockeying for domestic position" in advance of an election. Given Canadians' "sensitivity" and "current sense of frustration," he added, "we felt U.S.–Canadian relations required ministerial confrontation." Douglas Dillon headed a delegation consisting of the secretaries of agriculture, commerce, and the interior, as well as Ball and Merchant. One journalist dubbed it the "most portentious delegation ever to go to Ottawa on economic and trade matters."[37] Beyond discussions of both countries' basic economic outlook, much of the conference was taken up with the deliberations over Kennedy's trade proposals and the Common Market. The State Department's briefing for the US conference delegates underlined the positive aspects of the president's program while underscoring the apprehension felt by Canadians and the concomitant need for using "unusual care and patience," especially in light of a looming Canadian election. Expanding on this point, a second paper, examining Canada's troubled economy and Diefenbaker's faltering domestic popularity, argued that the government "is running scared." Told to be sympathetic to Canadian concerns, the US delegates were also urged to encourage the Canadians to adopt a "broad perspective," and abandon their narrow, parochial focus. As the State Department feared, however, Canada's course of action was likely to be "inhibited by Canadian sensitivities, notably the inferiority complex towards the U.S., and by Canadian nationalism."[38] There was little expectation of Canada's delegates adopting a constructive approach, a prediction that was not wrong as the talks produced more heat than light.

At the opening session, Ball outlined the reasoning behind American support for the UK over Europe. Admitting that there would be economic repercussions for the United States, and acknowledging that Canadians had their own "special problems," Ball believed that such difficulties would be offset by the incredible opportunities that the administration's Trade Expansion Act would create. The Canadian delegation was fundamentally divided over how to respond. Fleming, while acknowledging the political benefits of greater European unity, reiterated familiar arguments about the loss of preferences. He observed, though, that this issue was really the sole area of disagreement between Ottawa and Washington as his government welcomed new trade legislation. At this point, Howard Green intervened. Emphasizing the "great danger" of UK entry, which would reduce Britain's international voice, Green argued that Canada and the United States should both fervently support the United Kingdom as the head of the Commonwealth. Washington, he warned, would "someday discover it has not gained politically from the U.K.'s accession" to the EEC. The meeting subsequently degenerated into a standoff between Green and Ball, with the Canadian foreign minister eventually questioning whether, in addition to an integrated Europe, the Americans desired an integrated North America. Fleming saved the day by jovially asking whether the United States "might wish to become the 11th province of Canada and a Commonwealth member."[39] A hastily called lunch break lowered tensions further, but as Green's comment indicates, a nationalist undercurrent was present.

Once the group reconvened, they took up Kennedy's trade legislation. Ball spoke in glowing terms of the bill, which was *sui generis* "not only in style but also in terminology." Referring to Canadian worries, he offered assurance that Commonwealth countries would benefit from an international environment favorable toward freer trade. This climate "would lead to the benefits of comparative advantage, maximum efficiency and utilization of the entire free world's resources. It would act as a magnet to the rest of the world." Ball's evident enthusiasm was not shared by the Canadian delegation. Fleming, referring first to his own support for low tariffs, revealed skepticism as to whether the legislation could pass through "the Congressional hurdle." Informing the Americans that "many Canadians still remember the Hawley-Smoot tariff"—a piece of Congressional legislation that had crippled global trade at the onset of the Great Depression—Fleming stated that Canada would be waiting "for positive proof" that the Americans sought freer trade.[40] This reference to

Depression-era trade legislation was where the matter rested. Summing up the Canadian position coming out of the conference, Rusk observed that Canada's "suspicions about European integration" and concerns over the loss of export markets had not been overcome. Referring to Fleming's somewhat mixed response, he judged, however, that Canadian policy seemed more "moderate" than it had in the past.[41]

Why had Fleming taken such a hard line, one that marked a reversal of his previous position? In his memoirs, he wrote that he was forced by Green and Diefenbaker to tone down his support for the trade legislation and instead adopt a skeptical position; doing so left him "ashamed and humiliated."[42] Evidently hoping to make up for his humiliation, Fleming used several speaking opportunities to praise the Kennedy administration's initiative. Warning listeners in Winnipeg of the need for "bold and far-reaching" moves to solve looming problems in global trade, he opined that Canadians were "fortunate in witnessing these days the display of just such leadership on the part of the United States." Next, in a report to the House of Commons on the joint economic conference, Fleming described how Kennedy's goal of seeking to expand trade through multilateral tariff cuts was "identical" to Canada's position and so Ottawa "would be extremely interested" in any movement in this direction.[43] Nor was Canada's finance minister alone in his praise for Kennedy's program. A variety of Canadian economists called for imaginative trade policies that included supporting the US initiative or efforts like it. As one Canadian journalist observed, however, the shifts in global trade were "hurtling" Canada "toward the hardest decisions, outside war itself, in the nation's modern experience."[44]

Except for Fleming's occasional statements, the Americans heard little on the Trade Expansion Act from the Canadian government. Ottawa's reluctance to support the trade bill, formally introduced to Congress on January 25, perplexed US observers. They understood Canada's stance on preferences well enough. The problem, Ball told Kennedy, was that for the Canadian government preferences were "politically important." Diefenbaker had captured voters' attention with "a political platform calling for reduced economic dependence on the United States. He held out glowing visions of a vast potential development of industrial exports to the United Kingdom as a means by which Canada might establish its economic independence." The results had proven frustrating for the government, which had largely failed in this effort. The elimination of preferences, then, "would mean the end of the Canadian illusion that it can enjoy industrial growth independent of the United States."[45] Since the Grand Design promised to make up for such losses, American officials expected that Canada, heavily reliant on exports, would be a natural supporter of efforts to liberalize trade. This not unreasonable view rested on two assumptions: a belief that the implementation of the Grand Design was inevitable, and that Ottawa would accept fate and drop its opposition to the UK's accession to the Common Market.

Liberal leader Lester Pearson certainly accepted this stance, telling the House of Commons that "if, in Canada, we do not wish either to face the United States alone or become too economically dependent on it, then surely the best policy for us is to seek economic interdependence within the North Atlantic Community through freer trade." Thus the American government's "positive and farsighted" approach was far preferable to the "negative and sterile" view of Diefenbaker's government. Unfortunately for Washington, Diefenbaker was not forthcoming. Incensed by Pearson's comments, he attacked the Liberal leader for "smearing his country."[46] Over the coming months Diefenbaker largely stuck to this formula, using additional speaking opportunities to play up the importance of the Commonwealth while ignoring the president's trade proposal.[47]

Merchant was displeased with this silence. Speaking with several Canadian Cabinet members in early February, he cited the "somewhat surprising unwillingness" to support the president's trade initiative, which was "in Canada's own interest." However, as he recognized in a report to the State Department, there were two factors that prevented Ottawa from offering support: the expected Canadian election that year and Diefenbaker's predilection for making "periodic declarations of Ottawa's independence from Washington."[48] With the Canadian government refusing to voice support for the president's trade bill, throughout the spring Merchant engaged in a speaking tour in which he sought to explain the need for new, forward-looking legislation, as well as a more unified Europe. He presented the Trade Expansion Act as a forthright effort by the Kennedy administration to respond to the challenge posed by the revolutionary force of communism. Certainly then, Canadians, like Americans, could support the president's "historic and bold initiative" to expand world trade and enrich wealthy and poor countries alike. In sum, tying together and strengthening "the comradeship among all free nations" was an important cause worthy of Canadian support.[49] These paeans to the Grand Design and to the need for Canadian–American cooperation fell on deaf ears in Ottawa. As Heeney pointed out in his own public addresses that winter, Canadian reluctance to support these trade developments was the result of "our old friends, history and geography."[50] The prime minister had these twin factors on his mind, and his existing reservations about Britain and the EEC only deepened as it began to appear that forces inside and outside of Canada were moving against him.

First, as a way to meet its promise to secure some protection for Commonwealth interests, in March London presented Ottawa with a series of proposals outlining a level of preferences to be retained on a limited basis, thus serving as a means to allow Commonwealth countries to transition into a nonpreferential trading system. The British planned to present these transitional arrangements to the EEC to serve as the basis for negotiations. Reviewing this proposal with his ministers, Diefenbaker opined that they were insufficient to protect Commonwealth interests and so he would not support them.[51] Second, the prime minister's anger only increased when Canada House reported to External Affairs that when meeting with British officials in London, Ball had vigorously spoken against a continuation of preferences. To Diefenbaker, it was clear that the Americans sought to destroy the Commonwealth. Ball, he told Basil Robinson, was "interfering too much."[52] Then, the next day, April 19, the long-awaited Canadian federal election campaign began. A week into campaigning Pearson spoke out on trade, telling voters that a Liberal government would "have an even higher aim [than retaining preferences], and that is the creation of a great Atlantic trading community in which the United States, the European Common Market, and all the trading nations of the Free World could be associated." In Calgary, Pearson repeated this sentiment, vowing to "encourage every move to strengthen the economic and to expand the prosperity of the free world by expanding trade."[53] Canada's position toward the Grand Design had now become an unavoidable political issue for the prime minister, who felt hemmed in by the British, the Americans, and the Liberals.

Pearson's showcase of his party's support for the Grand Design came three days before the Liberal leader was due to meet Kennedy at the White House. Weeks before the Canadian election writ dropped, Pearson had been invited to attend a White House dinner for Nobel Prize winners from the Western hemisphere, to be held on April 29. The Ottawa Embassy had informed Diefenbaker of this invitation on April 4; a week later, Pearson had called the Embassy to confirm his attendance and to request a private meeting with Kennedy. Merchant saw an opportunity for the president to use his charms on Pearson, who was "making no public or private sense on defense matters particularly nuclear." However, the ambassador stressed that this discussion "should be worked out with minimum publicity and preferably none lest Diefenbaker and company come to [the] conclusion [that] Pearson is receiving attention in Washington disproportionate to that shown them."[54] This point was further underscored to Kennedy days later, when Heeney cautioned that, as the Liberal leader would be the only Nobel Peace Prize winner at the ceremony, and as the election would be in full swing, discretion was vital.[55] Pearson also arranged meetings with Dean Rusk and Walt Rostow. The secretary of state was pleased to see "an old friend," though he accepted the need for discretion because given "the preelection atmosphere" and the prime minister's "very sensitive mood," it was best to "remove one more thing which Diefenbaker would object to."[56] Rusk's meeting with Pearson was kept quiet, but not so Pearson's visit to the White House.

Pearson and Kennedy were certainly friendly toward one another. As a senator, Kennedy had favorably reviewed a book by Pearson and during the president's visit to Ottawa in May 1961, Diefenbaker had resented the attention that Kennedy had lavished on his political rival. Impressed with the Liberal leader, after returning to Washington the president had asked Pearson to meet with him in the US capital later that same month. Kennedy was due to travel to

Vienna in June to meet with Khrushchev and sought Pearson's advice, a sound move given the former Canadian foreign minister's celebrated meeting with the Soviet premier in Moscow in 1955.[57] This 1961 meeting between Pearson and Kennedy had been kept hidden from the press, which was what the two men attempted to do again in 1962 by meeting in the White House Residence before the Nobel dinner. Pearson later stated that he and the president had been "very very correct," although it begs credulity to think that the two men did not broach the subject of the election. In any case, despite meeting in private, Pearson was spotted leaving the residence by several reporters. Then, throughout the dinner, the president showered him with attention. Jovially referring to a White House tradition, Kennedy told the gathered dinner guests that "Lester Pearson informed me that a Canadian newspaperman said yesterday that this is the President's 'Easter egghead roll on the White House lawn.' I want to deny that!"[58] The friendly rapport between the two men, reminiscent of the president's warm treatment of the Liberal leader in Ottawa the previous year, was noted in the press and subsequently in Ottawa. Photos of Pearson and Kennedy warmly speaking to one another appeared in Canadian newspapers. The visit, one columnist wrote, was a major "coup" for the Liberal leader, who could now return to the hustings with "a sprinkling of new frontier political gold-dust."[59]

Diefenbaker was irate about Kennedy's reception of Pearson. His anger manifested itself when, on the day after the White House dinner, Macmillan arrived in Ottawa. In contrast to the newspaper coverage of Kennedy and Pearson smiling away, photos of the two prime ministers showed them looking dour and upset. No wonder: the two men sparred over the EEC. Downplaying the importance of trade as a unifying force for the Commonwealth, Macmillan argued that this factor was more important for the older members than for the newly independent countries. Feeling betrayed by this attitude, Diefenbaker underlined that Washington "seemed to be considering only the political implications. Canada, and other Commonwealth countries, must concern themselves with the economic consequences. These were likely to be serious." His judgment in these matters, he stressed, was partly predicated on the importance of preferences as an historic means through which Canadians had been able to distance themselves from the Americans. He asked Macmillan, then, "why the United States was so anxious" to do away with preferences, which were "a means" for Canada "of staving off United States domination." The Americans, Diefenbaker bellowed, were on the verge of embarking upon "a new attempt to determine Canada's destiny," with Kennedy and Ball leading the charge. Against this invective, Macmillan could muster only platitudes about the need for the free world to mobilize and unite.[60] Concerned by Macmillan's lackluster response, Diefenbaker told Robinson that he was now convinced that in their talks in Brussels the British were unlikely to safeguard Commonwealth interests. Britain's prime minister was worried too, telling his

Cabinet in London that Canadian ministers were intensely "suspicious" of US motives. Canadians, he lamented, were unable or unwilling to consider the Common Market "dispassionately."[61]

The thought of an American plot to do away with the Commonwealth was a sure sign that Diefenbaker's passions were inflamed. This anger had been building for some time. In March, he had treated Heeney to a rant about the Kennedy administration's "failure to take effective account of Canadian interests." The prime minister had also complained about Walt Rostow's influence on the president, and he had then referred to the memorandum, written by Rostow, which Kennedy had mislaid in May 1961. This document, Diefenbaker said, urged the president to push Canada into joining the OAS and into accepting nuclear weapons, and he told Heeney that "when the proper time came" he would publicly reveal the note and demonstrate to Canadians that the American president was a forceful bully. After reporting this threat to Norman Robertson and Ed Ritchie, Heeney then confided to his diary: "I have rarely, if ever, been so disturbed by a conversation with the head of the Canadian government."[62]

Titled "What We Want from the Ottawa Trip," the so-called Rostow Memorandum—the most infamous document in Canadian–American relations—did use the word "push" to describe the US interest in having Canada join the OAS, take a greater role in Latin America, devote more money to foreign aid, and support US policy in Southeast Asia; it made no mention of nuclear weapons.[63] In fact, the document spelled out a US desire to see Canada participate more in global affairs, with Ottawa viewed in a positive light as a helpful ally. Diefenbaker, though, saw it through a negative lens. Having kept this document secret for a year, the prime minister was now prepared to make his possession of it known to the Americans. The tipping point was the White House dinner for Pearson, which exposed the prime minister's deep fear over Canada's future in a world without a Commonwealth counterweight to the United States.

The fateful day was May 4, when, having spent several days on the campaign trail, Diefenbaker returned to Ottawa. Hoping to pay his farewell call on the prime minister, Merchant, who, like Heeney, was anxious to retire from his ambassadorial post, arranged to see the Canadian leader. Just prior to this meeting, Robinson witnessed Diefenbaker go on "an ungoverned rant about how they [the Americans] were out to get him." When Merchant arrived, Robinson advised him that the prime minister "was in an extremely agitated frame of mind," an accurate warning indeed.[64] For the next two and a half hours the ambassador was treated to what he described as a "tirade" during which Diefenbaker speculated that as his stance toward the Common Market was not in line with American thinking, Washington wished to replace him with a leader who would accept British entry into the EEC. Charging Kennedy with having intervened in the Canadian election by hosting Pearson, he asserted that Canada–US relations would now become the dominant campaign issue. Then Diefenbaker dropped a bombshell: he possessed a document that would prove that the Americans were trying to bully Canada. From this point on, the prime minister declared, his aim would be to present himself to the Canadian electorate as the only leader capable of protecting Canada from the United States.[65]

Merchant was understandably shocked. As Kennedy's meeting with Pearson had simply been a social matter, he told the prime minister, "it was childish to assume that this constituted any effort or intent to intervene in Canadian domestic politics." Switching to a more conciliatory approach, Merchant stated that Kennedy's "respect for [Diefenbaker] was great, and our relations were good." Then warning Diefenbaker that the use of the document would prompt "a serious backlash, if not in Canada, then certainly in the United States," Merchant reminded the prime minister of his "heavy responsibility" as a US ally and NATO member. Leaving, the ambassador received no assurance that the memorandum would not see the light of day, but he did feel that, by venting his anger, Diefenbaker had been calmed. For obvious reasons Merchant kept this information secret, reporting it only in a letter hand delivered to George Ball—the acting secretary of state—via the CIA attaché in Ottawa. Diefenbaker, he reiterated, had been "excited to a degree disturbing in a leader of an important country, and closer to hysteria than I have seen him, except on one other possible occasion." As Merchant reminded Ball, "given Canadian sensitivities, it is in our interest neither to intervene in Canadian domestic elections nor to give the appearance of doing so."[66]

In Washington, the report prompted consultations between Ball and McGeorge Bundy. A possible way of resolving the situation, they felt, would be to have Kennedy meet Diefenbaker at the upcoming World's Fair in Seattle, where the president could give the prime minister the type of publicity that Pearson had received. But deciding that this option was impractical, they opted to bring Merchant to Washington to consult with them personally. Bundy then brought Merchant's report to Kennedy, who was astonished that his meeting with Pearson had been questioned as he had previously met with Willy Brandt and Hugh Gaitskell—opposition leaders from West Germany and the UK respectively—without complaint. Bundy's sense was that "Diefenbaker's relation with the President is not likely ever to be the same."[67] Subsequently, underscoring that he had "no intention of seeking a meeting with Diefenbaker in the near future," Kennedy instructed Merchant to return to Ottawa to tell Diefenbaker that he had not yet informed the White House of the incident because he was reluctant to do so; to remind the prime minister that both governments had a record of the meeting between the president and prime minister, which clearly showed that "there was no improper pressure of any sort"; and to make it plain that even the suggestion of releasing the document to the press "would have a bad effect in Washington." On an upbeat note,

Merchant was told to display empathy for the prime minister's position by emphasizing that Kennedy "recognizes the strains which are characteristic of political campaigns."[68]

Returning to Ottawa with these instructions, Merchant first spoke privately with Robinson, a sympathetic ear and capable, perhaps, of dissuading the prime minister from rash action. Then in the process of transferring to the Washington Embassy after having spent four years assisting Diefenbaker, Robinson was delighted to meet with the ambassador, querying him about life in the American capital. Merchant offered friendly advice, but also spoke of how "distressed" he was about the state of bilateral relations following his recent interview with the prime minister and his worry that Diefenbaker would adopt an anti-American platform in the election. Robinson was left convinced that Merchant "and a large number of people in influential positions in Washington are profoundly worried about the course which Canadian foreign policy has taken."[69] With the prime minister out campaigning, a meeting took place a few days later. Here, Merchant explained that he had acquired a copy of the Rostow memo, which appeared to be quite "unexceptional." Nevertheless, revealing the memo to the public would be "catastrophic" and would do "incalculable harm" to Canada's image in the United States. Responding that he had no immediate plans to wield the memorandum, Diefenbaker then launched into an "emotional sidetrack on the US 'trying to push' Canada around." When Merchant asked what evidence there was to prove this contention, the prime minister, having none, calmed down. In a dispatch to Washington, Merchant reported that although Diefenbaker had been "nervous and in my judgment on verge of exhaustion, I believe storm has passed." To Merchant, the prime minister's outburst and threats were directly related to his insecurity in office; as Kennedy's encounter with Pearson receded away, he believed that Diefenbaker would calm down.[70]

Merchant's observation was astute: despite a draining campaign, Diefenbaker did not publicize the Rostow memorandum, though as he retained the document it continued to cast a pall over Canada–US relations, especially during the 1963 election campaign. It remains unclear, however, why the prime minister tipped Merchant off about the paper. Was it meant to threaten the Americans and dissuade them from reaching out to Pearson? Or was it simply an emotional outburst, reflecting the stresses of the campaign as well as a growing financial crisis, which threatened to spoil the Tories' re-election? In any event, Diefenbaker's outrageous conduct deservedly cost him his relationship with Kennedy, who felt, with good reason, that the prime minister was "a prick," "a shit," and "a fucker." Indeed, the president supposedly spoke of "cutting [Diefenbaker's] balls off," a compliment of sorts given the hyper-masculine climate of Camelot and the penchant of Kennedy administration officials to feminize their opponents.[71]

Given the serious breach in his personal relationship with Canada's prime minister, the president sought to give some reassurance to Canadians. At a press conference in mid-May, he defended his administration's support for an expanded Common Market, arguing that although it might not be in the United States' economic interest to see a larger EEC, it was certainly in his country's national interest to see a "stronger Europe." "What I would regret," he explained next, "would be any effort which would attempt to divide Europe from the United States and perhaps Canada, because I believe that the oceans should unite rather than divide. I do not anticipate that that will come. I think the mutual dependence is so obvious."[72] He also paid close attention to events in Canada. When Merchant made his valedictory call on the White House in May, he found the president taking a "lively" interest in the election. Having gained an "impressive" knowledge of Canada and of the intricacies of Canadian–American relations, Kennedy was keen to hear Merchant's thoughts on the future of the bilateral relationship. In order to "secure a closer harmony of views" on a number of matters and to "straighten out our continental defense relationship," Merchant advised that after the election his replacement should engage in "a long, serious talk" with whomever was prime minister. Doubtful of there being any real improvement in bilateral relations over the short term, Merchant judged that Canadians were coming to realize that "the power of Britain had declined" so that the United Kingdom "no longer presented a refuge and a counter-poise to the power of the United States." Thus, Americans could expect "to find Canada prickly and hypersensitive in the next few years whether under Tory or Liberal leadership."[73] Merchant's deft judgment was reflected in the current of nationalist concern over the Grand Design; his pessimism continued into retirement, the result of his deep frustrations with Diefenbaker during his second ambassadorial tour in Ottawa.

Within a few months of leaving his post, Merchant offered Ball and Bundy further thoughts on policy toward Canada. Acknowledging that little could be done to secure the return or destruction of the Rostow memorandum, he sensed that over time the prime minister, realizing "the enormity of his action," might rid himself of the document. In the meantime, he recommended that Kennedy maintain his "attitude of coolness" toward Diefenbaker, and avoid the re-establishment of a normal personal relationship. He proposed also that in order that relations with Ottawa not suffer, Rusk should pursue "as close a relationship as possible with" Green.[74] Rusk and Green were an odd pair who had clashed frequently over matters of policy, but for American policymakers, dealing with the Canadian foreign minister was seen to be the lesser of two evils. Whether Merchant's first recommendation was a decisive factor or whether it merely confirmed what Kennedy already felt is hard to judge; that the president paid little attention to the prime minister after this incident is certain. As for Merchant's departure, the *Globe and Mail* decried his retirement as "a loss to

Canadians," for the ambassador had been a sympathetic and understanding voice in Washington. However, the *Chicago Tribune*'s Canadian correspondent offered a different take. "For all his diplomacy, charm, skill, and hard work," noted Eugene Griffin, Merchant "seems to have had more friends than influence."[75] Indeed, Merchant and Heeney left their posts at a point where bilateral relations were worsening, leaving one to wonder whether the serious disagreements of late 1962 and early 1963 might have been ameliorated had these two experience envoys stayed on a little longer.

From the summer of 1962 onward, among officials on both sides of the border there was deep anxiety over the bilateral relationship. With the notion of a meeting between Kennedy and Diefenbaker now abandoned, American diplomats debated sending Lyndon Johnson to Ottawa in the summer of 1962. As vice president, Johnson embarked on numerous goodwill tours, and there was an evident feeling that a vice presidential trip north would play well in the Canadian press and could help soothe Diefenbaker's anger toward Washington. Opposed to the idea, however, Armstrong contended that although the vice president and prime minister would "hit it off" quite well, in his view Diefenbaker was a "summit artist" who would consider himself more important than Johnson and so would want to undertake significant discussion. Since it was unlikely that a trip by the vice president would resolve outstanding issues, he recommended that Rusk visit with Green instead. Green, he pointed out, "is as much our problem as is the Prime Minister—or more so."[76] This advice was followed and Rusk traveled to Canada at the end of August to golf and relax at the Seigniory Club resort for what was his first holiday in office. He also managed to fit in a visit to nearby Ottawa, where he and Green held a cordial meeting, just the sort of informal discussion that Heeney had advocated for at the outset of the Kennedy presidency. Rusk, though, had hoped to avoid seeing Green; it took prodding from Armstrong for him to meet with his Canadian counterpart. Their conversation dealt mostly with NATO matters, as well as issues that would arise at the upcoming session of the United Nations. However, Rusk did raise the Grand Design, admitting that while caution was needed, there was "no real alternative to the development of a greater degree of unity in the Atlantic community as a whole." In spite of some disagreement on this point, the meeting went "very smoothly" for both sides. Years later Green would claim that Rusk was "an awfully good chap" and "a good friend of mine."[77]

Meanwhile, personnel changes in Ottawa and Washington throughout the spring and summer of 1962 moved new people into place for the crises that were soon to rock Canada–US relations. In Ottawa, Merchant was gone and Armstrong's tenure as *chargé* proved to be short-lived. In August, after four years of service in Canada, he moved to the State Department, replacing Milton Rewinkel as director of the Office of British Commonwealth and Northern European Affairs, a position giving him oversight over Canadian matters, although that field remained the specific purview of Del Carlson, who retained his post as head of the Canada Desk. Ivan White, Armstrong's replacement at the Ottawa Embassy, was supposed to have been named ambassador to the West Indies Federation, but when the federation dissolved, he was moved to Canada. This move was sound: having previously served as consul general in Toronto as well as deputy assistant secretary for European affairs, White had organized Kennedy's Ottawa visit and had sat in on the president's meetings with Diefenbaker. He was not, however, named ambassador to Canada, and the White House's quest to fill Merchant's post proved to be arduous.

An initial candidate to head the Ottawa Embassy was the long-time dean of Harvard Law School, who eventually turned down Kennedy's appeal. Thoughts then turned to appointing a professional diplomat, including George McGhee, undersecretary of state for political affairs, and William Blair, the ambassador to Denmark, but these two candidates were ruled out, with administration officials judging that whoever went to Ottawa would need to be assertive. "Canada," George Ball emphasized, "is one of the toughest nuts we have to crack. The one who goes has to deal with Diefenbaker and Green." Speaking about diplomatic appointments with several advisors, Kennedy remarked that he was generally wary of most diplomats unless they possessed "cojones."[78] The eventual nominee, named in mid-September, certainly fit this criterion. A career ambassador fluent in French, a long-time friend of both Lester Pearson and fellow Princetonian Livingston Merchant, and a Rhodes Scholar at the same time as Arnold Heeney, Walton Butterworth had been a junior diplomat in Ottawa for two years during the 1930s. Then serving at the US Embassy in London, he worked closely with Kennedy's father, who had been ambassador from 1938 to 1940. Since 1956 Butterworth had been the American representative to the Common Market and to its predecessor the European Coal and Steel Community; thus he was well-versed in the intricacies of the EEC. Quickly establishing himself as a tenacious champion of American positions, his arrival in Ottawa signaled the beginning of a more confrontational approach to Canada by the Kennedy administration. As Merchant reportedly remarked at the time, Butterworth was "just the s.o.b. the Canadians deserve."[79]

Butterworth would not arrive in Ottawa until the autumn of 1962. His first meetings with Canadian officials were not pleasant. For instance, he left Green with an "unfavourable 'big boss' impression" and later engaged Diefenbaker in a lengthy discussion on British entry into the Common Market. With the prime minister adopting a "forthright" attitude, the new ambassador "thought it wise to meet directness with equal directness" and pointed out to Diefenbaker that given that he had just finished a lengthy stint in Brussels and that he been in Ottawa during the 1932 Imperial Economic Conference, he possessed a firm grasp of the preference system and the implications of an expanded EEC. Writing in his report of this conversation that the debate never got unfriendly,

Butterworth's initial impression of Diefenbaker was not kind. "Although vigorous in speech and gesture," the prime minister struck him "as being unwell" and exhibiting "evident signs of palsy or perhaps Parkinson's disease." He added: "I did not get the sense he knew very much about what he was talking."[80] The new ambassador's exasperated attitude reflected general American impatience with Canada, which had steadily increased throughout 1962.

As for changes in Canadian personnel, Heeney's own replacement, Charles Ritchie, arrived in Washington on April 28. Erudite and charming, Ritchie had completed a four-year tour as Canada's representative to the UN, and had served at other top-level posts both in Ottawa and abroad. Holding a more suspicious view of the United States than Heeney—Ritchie hailed from a family of old Tories—he came to the American capital at a critical period when the strains in bilateral relations were beginning to show. However, as a State Department assessment of Ritchie's time in Washington would later note, he had "been consistently cooperative and understanding" as well as "sympathetic with US policy objectives."[81] Prior to departing the Embassy in April, Heeney had organized an informal dinner to introduce his successor to State Department officials. The dinner was dominated by talk of the Grand Design, with little sign that new personnel would introduce new solutions.[82] Indeed, there was a sense of growing estrangement between diplomatic officials. Ritchie, for instance, recalled being "really attacked" by Rusk at a cocktail reception. "Afterward," he acknowledged, "Rusk and I was on very good terms, I think, but it was a most extraordinary outburst and was symptomatic of the really unpleasant atmosphere which the Americans had created." Within this atmosphere, the watchword appeared to be: "Those Canadians, don't give them an inch on anything."[83]

Ritchie presented his letters of credence to Ball at the start of May, but the White House delayed his initial meeting with Kennedy for almost a month, a sign of US frostiness toward the Canadians. Finally presenting his credentials to the president on May 26, Ritchie recorded that Kennedy's "reception of me, while perfectly civil, was, I thought, distinctly cool, and I came away with the impression that this reflected his attitude towards the Canadian government and particularly towards Mr. Diefenbaker. He seemed deliberately to be creating 'a distance.'" The new ambassador was so on edge during the meeting that when Kennedy shooed his young daughter from the Oval Office, Ritchie momentarily thought that the president was urging him to leave. The awkward nature of the new ambassador's relationship with the president did not improve. Confiding to his diary that summer, Ritchie wrote of a "growing sense of my own lack of contact with the President. Apart from the political strain between him and Diefenbaker, perhaps I am myself out of date—Old Hat in the New Frontier."[84]

However much he might have put the blame on his own foibles, Ritchie had problems with the New Frontier and with the policies associated with it. American officials, he told his diary, held a misguided, "negative attitude" toward the Commonwealth, with "any reference to its importance in the world" falling "on deaf ears." He posited several reasons for this negative outlook, including the possibility that the Commonwealth, as a broad, global body, was, by its very existence, in conflict with the proposed vision of how the world would look after the implementation of the Grand Design. Alternately, as a "hangover of British world leadership," the Commonwealth might be a source of enduring American jealousy, or, perhaps like British power, Washington believed that it was in decline. On a darker note, Ritchie mused about a latent reasoning in the backs of American minds: "If the Commonwealth declines or disappears, there will finally be an end to the Canadian balancing act between London and Washington, and we shall inevitably drift further into the American bloc." Such reasoning seemed to explain how Washington could be so indifferent to the position taken by its largest trading partner. Indeed, why else would the Americans "discount as bluff the anti-Americanism now rampant in Canada" unless they had made "the calculation that we have got to give in to them in the end, probably hat in hand."[85] Ritchie's views were deeply rooted in Canadian fears over economic domination from the south, and so indeed were old hat.

Sharing Ritchie's anxieties, Diefenbaker spent much of the remainder of the year attacking Macmillan's plans. While Australia and New Zealand dispatched delegations to speak with officials from the EEC in Brussels, no such effort was forthcoming from Canada. As part of an effort to see if Washington might aid them in pressing London to secure better terms of entry, Canberra also approached Ottawa about jointly meeting with US officials. Raising these initiatives with Schaetzel, Ambassador Ritchie cautioned against thinking that there would be similar moves on the part of the Canadian government. In advance of the Commonwealth prime ministers' meeting scheduled for September, Ritchie lamented, there was unlikely to be any "sudden outburst of Canadian statesmanship."[86] Taking up this theme with Robinson, Schaetzel remarked that he had long been accustomed to a prominent, constructive Canadian voice in world affairs. Now, it appeared that that voice had gone silent. Replying that Canada could hardly be expected to abandon the Commonwealth, Robinson warned Schaetzel against expecting "so revolutionary a change" in Ottawa's position.[87]

Schaetzel's criticism was close to the mark. The foremost historian of Canadian trade policy has pointed out that Ottawa's "lukewarm support" of Kennedy's trade program and "hostility to the reality (rather than to the ideal) of European integration undermined Canada's ability to take advantage of changing opportunities."[88] Certainly, Diefenbaker had ground to stand on: the Grand Design represented a fundamentally new economic system, and its individual parts—British entry into the EEC and the Trade Expansion Act— showed no signs of easy passage, whether through Brussels or Congress. Yet obduracy was hardly an effective substitute for diplomacy, especially so when

Canada risked, as Willis Armstrong put it, being "caught as [the] 'outer one' between two economic giants."[89] Moreover, for over a year, Diefenbaker had resisted overtures from the Americans for quiet talks about cushioning the blow to Canada of Britain's entry into the Common Market.

The Canadian government did finally come around to the idea of looking to the Americans for help. In August, Norman Robertson arranged for a small team of officials from External Affairs, Finance, and Trade and Commerce to travel to Washington, just the sort of low-key talks favored by the quiet diplomatists. He urged the State Department to avoid all publicity lest it seem that the US was "attempting to influence" Canada's position at the upcoming summit of Commonwealth prime ministers. The Canadians were met by Schaetzel, who underlined that the combined weight of the United States, the United Kingdom, and other interested countries such as Canada could win reductions in the Common Market tariff. The Trade Expansion Act would doubtless increase the pressure on the EEC, with Washington prepared to make significant concessions in terms of tariff reductions on a reciprocal basis.[90] This had been the Kennedy administration's position for over a year, but since it now seemed to be the only constructive course for Canada, Ottawa appeared ready to give it support. The Washington meeting, Green told the Cabinet, had been "very successful," because the Americans had affirmed their willingness to make concessions and to adopt a joint approach with other countries. But Diefenbaker was focused elsewhere. His immediate reaction to Green's report was to say that, rather than give consideration to the approach that should be taken once Britain entered the EEC, the Cabinet should consider tactics to adopt at the upcoming Commonwealth prime minister's meeting.[91] He had, however, already offered tentative words of praise for the trade bill at a speaking event that month. Addressing supporters in Regina, he noted that Kennedy's "leadership" on trade "will make possible the realisation of our objectives."[92] Even so, Diefenbaker's objective for the moment was not to champion the Grand Design, but to obstruct London's entry into the EEC. At the Commonwealth meeting in September he savagely condemned Macmillan's government, a verbal broadside that accomplished little. Ultimately, Diefenbaker was saved only by de Gaulle's veto of Britain's application in 1963.[93]

Witnessing the prime minister's desperate struggle, Armstrong was sympathetic. In a letter to Butterworth he expressed frustration with Canadian policy generally, but took an appreciative view of Canada's economic frustrations and its "psychological balancing act" between the British and the Americans, with Britain's turn toward Europe threatening to tip the balance. Canadians, therefore, were "a little lonesome, and in need of a few kind words." His advice was that "as much as we may deplore their hesitations in defence matters, and in a number of political affairs, we are unlikely to gain by handling those questions in the same context as the economic ones."[94] Sensibly, Armstrong was opposed to using American economic leverage to force a change in Canadian policy on the host of outstanding issues. Despite their difficulties with Canada, Armstrong's superiors also believed it necessary to avoid linkage, even though in the summer of 1962, thanks to a Canadian economic crisis, Washington had ample opportunity to bring its substantial power to bear.

Thanks to a floating exchange rate and an influx of US investment, Canada's dollar was artificially high, making Canadian goods more expensive than foreign goods and leading to a significant trade deficit, which did nothing to help the government's persistent budget deficits, nor the country's long recession and high unemployment. On May 2, in the middle of the election campaign, Diefenbaker announced a drastic step: after twelve years with this floating rate, the Canadian dollar would be fixed at 92.5 cents US, a rate guaranteed to decrease imports and increase exports. Within weeks of this announcement, foreign investors, mostly from the United States, became worried about the volatility of the Canadian economy and began pulling capital out of the country. The resulting drop in foreign exchange reserves, and fears of a major balance of payments crisis, led to four days of intense ministerial deliberations in Ottawa. On June 24, six days after the election, these Cabinet discussions ended, and the government announced austerity measures, coupled with the issuance of blanket import surcharges on goods coming into Canada and an end to exemptions on customs duties for Canadian tourists bringing foreign goods into the country. Louis Rasminsky, the governor of the Bank of Canada, also sought aid from the US government, which arranged, through the International Monetary Fund, the Federal Reserve, and the Bank of England, over $1 billion worth of credit. The Americans, Rasminsky would later write to a colleague, had been "as helpful and co-operative as they could be."[95] Yet Rasminsky held concerns about this assistance. During the crisis he had warned Armstrong against using this aid as leverage by seeking a "payoff" on outstanding issues with Diefenbaker. Armstrong responded that his government did not intend to bribe Ottawa, remarking that "it obviously was not in our self interest to have the Canadian financial position deteriorate."[96]

The Kennedy administration certainly had no interest in seeing the implosion of the economy of an ally and major trading partner, even one that was proving recalcitrant on a host of issues. As Douglas Dillon had informed Kennedy, he had put together the credit package because it was "clearly in our interests to move promptly and substantially to the assistance of Canada." Recalling this episode, Basil Robinson was heartened because "despite policy disagreements between the governments and a growing personal rift between the leaders, it seemed that there was still a fund of goodwill for Canada in Washington."[97] This goodwill did not last long. The abandonment of a floating exchange rate undercut one of the central elements in the postwar economic system, while the imposition of the surcharges, along with the halting of exemptions on customs duties, seemed aimed at punishing the United States, which was both Canada's largest trading partner and, thanks to geography, a popular destination for Canadian tourists. In announcing the surcharges, amounting to 5, 10, and 15 percent levies on imports of varying values, Diefenbaker stressed that they were temporary and would "be removed as soon as circumstances permit." However, American officials were not convinced by the temporary nature of the measure, and they became incensed when it seemed that the surcharges would be left in place.[98] To the White House, Canada's government looked highly ungrateful. Additionally, there was a fear in Washington that Ottawa's actions threatened the Trade Expansion Act, centerpiece of Kennedy's legislative agenda and cornerstone of the Grand Design.

On June 21, three days before the surcharges were levied and three days after Diefenbaker's party won its minority government, Ball voiced his apprehensions about Canada's financial policy to Dillon. Having learned that Ottawa was considering putting surcharges in place, Ball wondered whether they might ask the Canadian government to hold off until after Congressional debate on the trade bill had concluded. Dillon thought that there could be little delay: the Canadians were "in a real crisis." The following evening they spoke again. Having been in touch with Donald Fleming, Dillon reported that Canada's finance minister had informed him that surcharges were being considered and that, if imposed, they would be transitory. Later, once the surcharges were put in place, McGeorge Bundy reported to Ball that the president "wasn't very happy." With the Trade Expansion Act winding its way through Congress, Kennedy worried that since it appeared that protectionist motives were behind the Canadian measures, protectionists in Congress might seize on the surcharges as a reason for opposing the trade bill. Bundy, at least, was mollified when Ball recounted the details of the Dillon-Fleming exchange on the temporary nature of these measures. As for potential criticism on Capitol Hill, Dillon and Ball moved quickly, meeting with key lawmakers to dampen disquiet.[99]

American unease grew. In a broadcast address on the austerity program on June 25, Diefenbaker made two points that vexed US officials. First, he appealed for Canadians to support the surcharges until the country's "foreign exchange problem has been solved by an increase in exports or by producing in Canada at competitive prices more of the commodities that we are now importing." Second, he acknowledged that "what is saved on imports will help to balance the foreign exchange situation."[100] Motivated by an "uncomfortable feeling" that Diefenbaker was "being less than straightforward," Ball seized on the prime minister's comments and relayed to Dillon his understanding: that the surcharges were to be temporary; that they were to be substituted by internal taxes; and that they were designed only to create revenue to balance the budget. Why, then, had Diefenbaker made no reference to substitution of the surcharges in his address? Why had the Canadian prime minister cited the surcharges as a way to reverse Canada's trade deficit? Asserting that "this sounds like pure protectionism to me," Ball characterized the surcharges as a direct threat to the passage of the Trade Expansion Act. Indeed, being contrary to the General Agreement on Tariffs and Trade, the surcharges set "a very dangerous precedent," one "unworthy" of an advanced economy. In sum, Ball deemed it "essential that we demonstrate that we intend to take a firm line with the Canadians." Kennedy agreed, instructing the undersecretary of state "to be as tough as possible on the Canadians" in upcoming talks.[101] Ball was correct: the surcharges did violate Canadian commitments to GATT, which allowed only for the imposition of import quotas as a means to temporarily reverse balance of payments problems, and so Kennedy's instruction came at an important juncture. In mid-July GATT meetings were being held and it was expected that the Canadians would ask for a waiver allowing them to continue imposing the surcharges, without penalty, until October 1962.

Adopting this sterner tactic with Ambassador Ritchie on July 6, Ball charged that given the pending Congressional debate on the trade bill the Canadian move was poorly timed. In his view, both the Treasury and the State Department had been led to believe—falsely it seemed—that Ottawa's move had been designed to improve its budgetary situation, that it would have only a limited impact on the Canadian trade deficit, and that the measures were to be supplanted by internal taxes. Responding that the US was "quite mistaken," Ritchie stated that Ottawa had thought that it had made it quite clear that the goals of the legislation were to raise money and to improve Canada's balance of payments position by restricting imports. Adding that the surcharges might be in place for some time, Ritchie said that it was doubtful that new taxes would be levied anytime soon. Next, he asked that Washington consent to a GATT waiver; otherwise, confidence in the Canadian economy would be undermined. Angered by the "protectionist intentions of the Canadian action," Ball nevertheless conceded that in the interest of stabilizing Canada's economy a waiver until October would have to be granted.[102]

Worried that the Canadians were about to "euchre us," Kennedy ordered Ball and Dillon to investigate whether they had been misled or whether there had been a miscommunication. As Bundy—referring to the fallout over the Rostow memorandum—sardonically remarked to Ball, it was important to keep in mind "the President's fondness for Diefenbaker and the reasons for it."[103] Duly clarifying what they had been told, Ball and Dillon concluded that they had been misled and that the "sense of urgency to remove the surcharges earlier expressed to Treasury was decidedly softened in the later Canadian presentations." Despite this view and the sense that "the surcharges will have a progressively corrosive effect in Canada and on U.S.–Canadian economic relations," the Kennedy administration did not oppose a waiver for the surcharges when the GATT Council convened in Geneva.[104]

Criticism of the surcharges aside, Washington refrained from taking retaliatory action, a waiver was granted, and the surcharges were gradually eliminated, with the last ones removed on April 1, 1963. The Americans' unwillingness to either withdraw support for the Canadian dollar or levy their own surcharges, showed their reluctance to undermine the economy of an important ally. After all, Washington had just taken efforts to strengthen Canada's economic position. Furthermore, securing passage of the president's trade bill was a decisive factor in the administration's decision-making, and the need not to stoke protectionism in Congress led to the White House's acquiescence. For greater reasons, then, the Americans avoided provoking a trade dispute with Canada, a position in line both with the Kennedy administration's previous decisions to avoid reacting strongly against Canadian economic policies—trade with China and Cuba—and with the general US policy, in effect since the Second World War, of granting exemptions for Canada. Moreover, linkage between support for the Canadian economy during a moment of extreme weakness and Ottawa's reluctance either to accept nuclear warheads or support the Grand Design was not broached.

The Americans may have been willing to assist an ally and avoid strong-arm measures, but there was still little love for Canada in Washington. As the *Financial Post* had observed perceptively in August, the Canadian government's "enthusiasm" for the Trade Expansion Act was "niggardly when it should have been ebullient. The sad truth is they don't think very much of us in Washington these days."[105] Once the trade bill received Congressional approval in October, Diefenbaker immediately wrote to the president to offer his congratulations as well as his support for tariff-cutting. Also, he suggested calling a Free World Trade Conference to capitalize on this development. Viewing the prime minister's sudden conversion with suspicion, Kennedy thanked Diefenbaker. Then tartly, he asked that the surcharges be removed.[106] In this, one of the last letters between the president and prime minister, Kennedy displayed little warmth for a man who had done little to support both a major goal of American foreign policy and a principal piece of legislation, and who had even threatened its passage.

The surcharges were but one economic issue upon which Ottawa and Washington had disagreed and while there were always points of disagreement, by mid-1962 goodwill was drying up on both sides of the border. In May, the Canadian–American Committee, formed in 1957 and chaired by business leaders, including R. Douglas Stewart, head of Quaker Oats and a former ambassador to Canada under Eisenhower, released a report downplaying fears of a deteriorating bilateral tension and stressing the benefits of North American interdependence. Both "economies today," the committee contended, "are stronger and more prosperous than they could have been if there had been much more restricted opportunities for economic forces to work in a north-south direction."[107] Outside of this circle of business lobbyists, the situation seemed much different. Just two months later, following the economic crisis in Canada, growing tension in bilateral affairs was the subject of a lengthy chat between Green and Armstrong. As Armstrong was due to leave Ottawa to take up his new post in Washington, the Canadian foreign minister had wanted to get a rundown of the American's thoughts on the state of the bilateral relationship. Admitting that there were a number of contentious topics, Green added that it was vital to maintain a "public posture to [the] effect that relations were good." Incredulous, Armstrong replied that avoiding public dissension was advisable but that it had to be accompanied by "candor in diplomatic discussions of unresolved problems" and by "some evidence of progress." His point was that quiet diplomacy had to involve actual diplomacy. A chastised Green responded that "he was sure that Canada had more troubles than anybody and that it needed American help." In disbelief, Armstrong replied that the United States was willing to be helpful, but Ottawa must keep in mind that Washington had problems too.[108]

Green's lament over Canada's plight served as the starting point for a primer for US diplomats dealing with Canada penned by Charles Kiselyak, the Embassy's second secretary. Observing that "in terms of the health and affluence of his countrymen, Howard Green's remark is patently ridiculous," Kiselyak admitted that "here is enough truth—of a kind—in it to warrant inspection." Clearly, Green did "not fear for the lives or welfare of his countrymen." Instead, he was influenced by a "deep and professional concern for the complex of ideas and institutions that is Canada" in light of the nearby presence of the United States. This central factor led many Canadian politicians and intellectuals into being overly "concerned with the definition and preservation of Canada as a unique nation." What this meant in practice, Kiselyak concluded, was that anything that originated in the United States was "viewed with a cold eye."[109] As a summation of the experiences that Americans had had with their Canadian allies on economic matters over the previous year, it was perfect.

In Ottawa, the Grand Design was given a frosty reception. The Canadian prime minister's opposition to British membership in the Common Market and his hesitancy in supporting the Trade Expansion Act reflected differences of policy as well as his abiding worries of being drawn too close to the United States. Diefenbaker had not necessarily been wrong in hesitating to support this plan, for not only did it disrupt traditional economic ties between Canada and Britain and thus threaten nationalistic hopes of steering the Canadian economy away from its reliance on the United States, but its benefit—access to Western European markets—was not a sure thing. Yet he was not right in his handling of the issue—using heedless obstruction—especially once plans for British entry reached an advanced stage. His failure to offer either alternate solutions to ensure access to the European market or more than lukewarm support for the Trade Expansion Act did him no favors. Certainly there were many voices encouraging him to take a more positive stance, just as US officials sought to aid their Canadian allies by seeking a common approach to changing trade patterns. Moreover, the disruption in smooth relations with the Americans and the British threatened Canada's strategic partnerships and the benefits of Canadian occlusion were unclear. Had it not been for de Gaulle's veto of British entry in 1963, the Canadian prime minister might have found Canada in a disastrous position outside of the EEC tariff and neglected by Washington. Moreover, Diefenbaker's position, grounded in a fervent nostalgia for Canada's imperial past, ignored British officials' desire to steer Britain on a new course toward Europe and away from the Commonwealth. Meanwhile, as Diefenbaker's economic experiences in 1961 and 1962 demonstrated, Canada was reliant upon the United States, the result of decades of growing economic interdependence brought about by the logic of geography.

To US diplomats, the reason for Ottawa's unhelpful attitude was plain: a preoccupation with Canada's independence from the United States. As Rufus Smith had predicted in mid-1961, it would be exceedingly difficult "to turn the energies of Canadian thinkers away from chewing their own futility and toward the expanded horizon of the greater sovereignty of Atlantic regionalism."[110] In blaming nationalism, American observers were also not wrong. Diefenbaker had risen to power on promises of expanding Canada's trading horizons beyond the 49th parallel. The Grand Design held the possibility of fulfilling this goal. When Kennedy famously told Americans in July 1962 to "learn to think inter-continentally," he may as well have been speaking to Diefenbaker.[111] But the promise of the Grand Design also carried a likelihood of greater economic association with the United States. Nationalism precluded support for Kennedy's economic program. One wonders if the situation would have been different under Eisenhower, who also supported the creation of a unified Europe and, hence, Britain's entry into the Common Market. Diefenbaker's growing distrust of Kennedy over the president's warm treatment of Lester Pearson contributed to the prime minister's hostility toward the Grand Design, just as American trade policy led to the worsening of relations between the two leaders. The manner in which the prime minister withheld support for the Grand Design was of grave importance. By spurning the chance of working with the Americans to safeguard Canadian economic interests as the Australians were doing and, worse, by personalizing his differences with Kennedy, he irretrievably ruined his relationship with the president.

For all the opprobrium directed at Kennedy—by Diefenbaker and by Canadian historians— he seems to have taken a far less personalized view of Canada–US relations than did the prime minister. As the brouhaha over Canada's import surcharges in the summer of 1962 demonstrated, the president was careful to ascertain the facts of whether or not he had been lied to, doing so despite the prime minister's recent threats to publish the Rostow memorandum. Furthermore, Kennedy supported Canada during that summer's financial crisis, avoiding an opportunity to press for a resolution of outstanding issues. Linkage was off the table, as was retaliation, all in spite of Diefenbaker's conduct. The breakdown in their personal relations—as well as a changing of the diplomatic guard—came at a critical juncture. When visiting Green in Ottawa in August, Rusk had met briefly with Diefenbaker to inform him that Washington was monitoring an influx of Soviet personnel and weaponry into Cuba.[112] Unbeknownst to these three men, among the materiel headed for that Caribbean island were dozens of nuclear missiles. Cuba, long an area of friction in Canada–US relations, was about to become the epicenter of the major crisis of the Cold War, a standoff that would refocus attention in Washington and Ottawa on the dormant issue of arming Canadian military forces with nuclear warheads.

# 5

# Cuban Crises

## Canada–US Relations and Cuba, 1962

Writing to Ottawa in October 1962, Charles Ritchie observed that Canada had "been relatively clear in recent months of direct criticism" from the White House on Cuba, a pleasing turn of events. Although concern at Canadian policy lay not "far below the surface," he reported that Washington's "heavy guns" were trained on other countries such Britain, "whose cooperation would be more instrumental in intensifying the economic pressure on Castro." Still, with the Cuban issue dominating the upcoming congressional election in November, Ritchie believed it was important for the Canadian government to keep quiet about anything which might be perceived as criticism of US policy on Cuba since "every shade of outside sympathy is noted, every sign of reluctance magnified and emotionally assessed."[1] A week later, the American revelation that the Soviets were placing nuclear missiles in Cuba prompted the most dangerous event of the Cold War. Upset with President Kennedy, and convinced that much of the crisis was driven by the midterm election, Diefenbaker withheld support for the United States during the first days of the standoff, a move that generated immense domestic criticism of Canada's leader. Diefenbaker's actions—or, rather, inaction—were the result of the breakdown of the rapport between the two men, with personal differences mirroring divergences on policy: from nuclear weapons and disarmament to Britain's accession to the Common Market. Oddly, as Ritchie had observed that autumn, Cuba had largely ceased to rank among these grievances.

Since mid-1960 Canada and the United States had gone their separate ways on Cuba, with Eisenhower and then Kennedy adopting a combative approach and Diefenbaker refusing to cut ties with Havana. Canada's prime minister had, though, put in place a number of restrictions on exports. Furthermore, he had reacted to the failed Bay of Pigs operation—a stark reminder of the two allies' differing positions—by making a statement supportive of Kennedy. Even so, like many Canadians, he was alarmed by American actions, believing that isolating Fidel Castro's government was counterproductive. The point has been made, then, that "underlying Canadian–American interaction during the missile crisis were profoundly different perceptions of Fidel Castro's Cuba."[2] This argument presupposes that Canada's reaction to the October crisis was a reflection of the Canadian government's own stance toward Cuba. However, rather than a vivid display of differing views of the Cuban revolution, the missile crisis serves to show that Canadian and US policy were in close alignment. Concerns in Ottawa both that Havana and Moscow were becoming worryingly close and that Cuba was an issue damaging the important bilateral relationship with Washington meant that in the months preceding the nuclear standoff, Canada's Cuban policy had hardened. As Ritchie had pointed out in his cable to Ottawa—written just as the Americans were discovering the missiles—in the months immediately preceding October 1962, the United States had focused its efforts on other allies and softened its criticisms of Canada.

The situation had been markedly different earlier that year when US diplomats had launched a concerted effort to change Canada's stance on Cuba, egged on by members of Congress keen to scoring political points against a president who had staked his reputation on unseating Castro. But reluctant to raise nationalist hackles, American officials engaged in tough talk, not aggressive action. Ruling out extraterritorial legislation or linkage to other issues, US diplomats instead preferred quiet diplomacy and the use of their close working relationship with their Canadian counterparts. In reacting to the Kennedy administration's effort to enlist other countries in pressuring Cuba, Canadian officials, despite some nationalist bluster, proved to be helpful allies: adopting a shrewd policy of continuing to trade with Cuba while expanding both restrictions on trade in certain goods and intelligence-sharing with the Americans. Even Diefenbaker saw merit in this quieter approach to defending continued Canada–Cuba trade. But the prime minister was not so quiet during the missile crisis. While it is true both that Diefenbaker failed to immediately stand forthrightly beside Kennedy as he had done over Berlin in 1961 and that he even seemed to question US actions, the showdown in Cuba hardly represented the "nadir" of Canadian–American relations—that would come soon after, during a crisis over Canadian missiles.[3] Once the nuclear standoff began, Ottawa backed Washington, militarily and diplomatically. So did Canadians. As one member of Canada's social democratic party—which did not back US brinksmanship—would lament, "the great majority of Canadians rallied around Kennedy on October 22nd and in the days that followed. The imminent threat of thermonuclear war gave rise to fear which expressed itself as anger and hatred directed against that which they feared: the USSR." Indeed, in reviewing Canada's actions during the missile crisis, it is worth keeping in mind that once the confrontation had abated, Soviet Premier Nikita Khrushchev implored the Canadians to revert back to their "sober and just view" of Cuba.[4] Canada's support for US policy on Cuba, both before and during the crisis, belies the perfervid conspiracy theories that

Diefenbaker's prevarications led the Kennedy administration "to replace his minority Conservative government with one led by Pearson's Liberals."[5] Rather, Washington appreciated Ottawa's quiet help on Cuba, which came despite months of unquiet diplomacy on a host of other issues.

Canada's Cuban policy was based on coexistence. As Norman Robertson acknowledged in early 1962, although "the present Cuban regime" was certainly communist, this reality failed to provide sufficient grounds for breaking diplomatic or trade relations.[6] Kennedy administration officials had been made aware of these views. In his two summits with the president in 1961, Diefenbaker had underscored that Canada sought to trade with all nations even as he made clear that his government had forbidden exports of strategic items as well as the transshipment of US goods through Canada to Cuba. He had added that Ottawa was not actively trying to expand Cuban–Canadian trade. In short, since December 1960 Canada, unlike every other member of NATO, had supported elements of the Cuban embargo through restrictions conforming to the list of items banned by the Coordinating Committee for Multilateral Export Controls (COCOM). Meant to regulate trade between Western and Soviet bloc countries, COCOM did not formally apply to Cuba. Nonetheless, Ottawa was applying the restrictions unofficially.

Even though Kennedy had not voiced criticism of Canadian–Cuban trade in his meetings with Diefenbaker, nor had his administration been willing to provoke a dispute with Ottawa by invoking the Trading with the Enemy Act to target US subsidiaries in Canada, Ottawa's Cuba policy was an ongoing concern in Washington. As the White House moved to isolate the island and to heighten pressure on its economy in 1962, American attention naturally turned to Western trade with Cuba. US officials could not help but notice that while Western European exports to Cuba were declining, Canadian exports were increasing, with the total for 1961 at over $30 million as compared to $13 million in 1960.[7] While Diefenbaker had told Kennedy that Canada was not looking to expand sales to Cuba, it appeared that the opposite was true. For the White House, this trend was worrying, doubly so because of the November 1962 midterm election. As a presidential candidate Kennedy had staked out a tough position on Cuba, but his stumble over the Bay of Pigs left him looking weak, much to the delight of his conservative opponents, who preyed upon this apparent weakness, including his inability to secure allied support for the embargo. For the White House, cutting Havana's economic ties abroad was politically important, just as it was also expected to have a demonstrable impact upon the Castro government's ability to retain power.[8] On this score, in late 1961 the administration launched a covert effort—Operation Mongoose—to use sabotage and assassination to incite an internal revolt against Castro. In setting out goals for the operation, Brigadier General Edward Lansdale, its swashbuckling director, instructed the State Department to explore whether Ottawa could "halt the diversion of vital items in the Cuban trade," and whether the United States' NATO allies, Canada included, could help "to isolate Cuba from the West."[9]

Washington's first target, though, was Latin America. At an Organization of American States foreign ministers' meeting held in Punta del Este at the end of January 1962, American diplomats sought, but failed, to secure an OAS embargo of Cuba. But the conference did result in Cuba's expulsion from the OAS, an important propagandistic achievement for the Kennedy administration.[10] Offering Ottawa a rundown of the diplomatic maneuvering at the summit, Arnold Heeney underlined the importance of the OAS's rejection of Cuba, an outcome that underlined that country's growing isolation from the hemisphere. This result, he warned, could prove problematic in that it put Ottawa's relationship with Havana into stark relief.[11] Heeney's emphasis on Canada's precarious position was important, for seen in retrospect the prime minister's decision in 1961 to turn down Kennedy's appeal to join the OAS was a lucky move sparing Ottawa from having to make a tough choice regarding Cuba at Punta del Este.

As the OAS delegates were meeting in Uruguay, Arthur Schlesinger voiced a blunt, public assessment of Canada–Cuba relations. Inserting foot in mouth during a brief stopover in Vancouver on his way to Tokyo, Schlesinger remarked that "anything that supports Cuba threatens the prospects of democratic success in Latin America." Reporters saw this assertion as an attack on Canada, which could be charged with abetting Cuban revolutionary activities. In the House of Commons, the Opposition inquired as to what was being done to address both Schlesinger's "serious indictment" and "the strong pressure" from the United States; Green responded by chiding Schlesinger. When Canadian diplomats raised the issue with their US counterparts, they were told that the remark had been taken out of context as Schlesinger had not singled out Canada but had "specifically acknowledged" that Ottawa was free to choose its own policy.[12] This ill-timed gaffe undoubtedly reflected Washington's frustration with Canada's Cuban policy; the reaction in Canada showed Canadian frustration with the United States. This same pattern played out days later. Speaking at a press conference in Punta del Este, Dean Rusk raised a hope that Canada, the United Kingdom, and other countries would join the United States and the countries of Latin America in isolating Cuba and that the State Department was set to "take up" allied trade with Cuba, specifically the issue of whether Western money was being used to fund Havana's subversive efforts.[13]

Unimpressed by this criticism, Diefenbaker lashed out in the House of Commons. First, attacking Schlesinger and Rusk, he vowed that as the balance of Cuban–Canadian trade favored Canada, there was no basis for allegations that Canadian dollars were fueling Cuban subversion. Then, allowing that he naturally preferred to co-operate with friendly governments, Diefenbaker asserted that "the decision as to the course Canada shall take should be made by Canada on the basis of policies which we believe are appropriate to Canada."[14] The prime minister's heavy emphasis on a Canadian approach came easily to him. It was also applauded by Canadians. Toronto's *Globe and Mail* dubbed the Punta del Este conference a "fiasco" because Cuba was being pushed further into the Soviet bloc. The paper urged the Canadian government "to keep open the few remaining channels between the island and Western democracy" by not taking part in Washington's effort to "crush an independent State." The *Globe*'s editors also applauded the prime minister's defense of the Canadian viewpoint and "sound considerations of national policy." A similar defense was mounted by the *Ottawa Citizen*, which attacked not only Washington's "oblique but unmistakable" criticism of Canada, but its "mistaken" policies that had succeeded only in causing "mischief." Urging Diefenbaker to continue the flow of trade to the island, the *Citizen*'s editors declared that "trade embargoes settle nothing." Less adamant in its advocacy of Canada's continued trade with Cuba, the *Montreal Gazette* pointed out that since an embargo needed to be total in order to be effective, and as there was little chance of that happening with Cuba, there was little point in Ottawa supporting ineffective sanctions.[15]

Prompted by this sniping over Cuba, Livingston Merchant warned Washington that Schlesinger and Rusk's comments had "generated a flurry" of press coverage, which seemed to indicate that "Canadian support for US policies toward Cuba, never great, has dwindled even further." Analyzing Canada's response to Punta del Este, he stressed the "sad fact" that although Canadians generally applauded the "positive aspects" of US policy in Latin America, such as the Alliance for Progress, they deplored what they saw as Washington's "inept and shortsighted" tactics in dealing with Cuba. Merchant also blamed policy differences on nationalists. Drawing a connection between nationalism and Ottawa's independent stance on Cuba, he added that the "heavily charged preelection atmosphere" in Canada made Canadian politicians reluctant to do anything that "looks like subservience" to Washington. Despite seeing little prospect that Canada would change course, Merchant saw no reason to tolerate open criticism of American policy. Speaking with several Canadian cabinet ministers a few days after Diefenbaker's remarks on Cuba, he noted the measurable decline in Canada's influence in the US capital thanks in part to an "ostentatious divergence" from the American stance toward Castro.[16]

Having secured partial support from Latin American countries, officials in Washington moved to step up the pressure on Cuba by expanding the embargo through an import ban of Cuban goods and the exclusion of all exports save medicine. Taken under authority granted to the president by Congress under the Foreign Aid Authorization Act for 1962 and not the Trading with the Enemy Act, this measure's "one advantage," George Ball told McGeorge Bundy, was that it did not apply to American subsidiaries abroad and so avoided "the Canadian problem."[17] Avoiding a flap over sovereignty with Canada, the Kennedy administration still had its sights set on Cuba's economic links with the West. To this end, Walt Rostow, now chairman of the State Department's Policy Planning Committee, addressed the North Atlantic Council in mid-February, where he argued forcefully for the NATO allies to limit their exports to Cuba by extending COCOM restrictions to cover the island. Unwilling to commit themselves, the delegates to the NAC referred the issue for study by NATO officials.[18]

Beyond this multilateral context, the Americans took a direct approach to Canada's trade with Cuba. Since Canadian officials and the press had Cuba at the "forefront" in their thinking and a number of government officials had made plain their worry over the policy difference between Ottawa and Washington, Merchant advised Rusk to correct "serious misunderstandings" about US policy and perhaps gain some cooperation. Still, with a Canadian election approaching and with Diefenbaker and other members of the government content to blow the "bagpipe of Canadian sovereignty," he was not rosy about changing Ottawa's position.[19] Also pushing for a quiet initiative, at the State Department William Tyler, deputy assistant secretary for European affairs, reminded Rusk that policy differences with the Canadian government stemmed from Canada's general policy to trade with all countries; Canadians' "inexperience" with Latin America; doubts in Ottawa about the direction of US policy; and Diefenbaker's desire to avoid the "appearance of subservience" to the Americans. Like Merchant, Tyler warned against infringing on Canada's sovereignty and of divorcing any linkage between Canadian policy toward Cuba and the position of US subsidiaries operating in Canada.[20] This warning came at an important juncture, as White House lawyers were drawing up an order to implement the Trading with the Enemy Act in a bid to curb the activities of US subsidiaries in Mexico and Canada.[21]

Armed with Tyler's memorandum and hoping to secure Canadian cooperation, Rusk met with Heeney. Urging a reassessment of Ottawa's view of Cuba on account of the dangers that Cuba's government posed to its people, to Latin America, and to Western—and hence Canadian—interests, Rusk added that Canada differed from other NATO countries because of its location in the Western hemisphere. Moreover, with the American public and Congress becoming increasingly preoccupied with the question of Cuba, there was now a "danger" of this outside opinion affecting US relations with its allies. As the Canadian government looked at this question, he concluded, it "would doubtless not wish to complete its analysis without taking into account the situation within the U.S. and Canadian–U.S. relations." In reply, Heeney raised three important points: Canada had a distinct history of relations, or lack thereof, with Latin America; Canadian trade controls regarding Cuba were more prohibitive than those of other NATO countries or even Latin American countries; and Ottawa and Washington held divergent views on trade and diplomatic representation "with governments of whose systems we totally disapproved."[22] Here was quiet diplomacy with an edge.

The results of this *démarche* were mixed. Diefenbaker was not about to bow to Washington, especially with an election looming. Told of Rusk's overture, the prime minister railed that it had taken "a hell of a colossal nerve" on the part of the secretary of state to raise the issue. Reading Heeney's report of his talk with Rusk at a cabinet meeting, Diefenbaker admitted that the Americans welcomed further talks regarding Cuba but that he wanted neither to undertake such discussions nor to review Canadian–Cuban relations. However, parliamentary criticism was building. Paul Martin, the Liberal External Affairs critic, asked whether, given Washington's efforts "to guard against an expansion of communist influence in Latin America," Canada might move to ban exports of certain goods of semistrategic value such as dynamite and automotive parts. There existed, he thought, an "embarrassing situation."[23] Indeed, embarrassment ensued when Cuban Ambassador Américo Cruz told a gathering of students in Montréal that Canada had purchased $40 million worth of Cuban goods in the past year, a figure that was bound to increase; George Hees quickly downplayed Cruz's ham-fisted comment. Sensing that public opinion was shifting slightly, Diefenbaker directed Hees to review the materials that were classified as strategic and nonstrategic with the intent of reclassifying some items of semistrategic importance.[24] This move signaled some backtracking by the prime minister. It also fit with Fleming and Hees's 1961 assurance to Kennedy that Canada would not frustrate the American embargo.

While Diefenbaker reacted to Rusk with mild concern, Howard Green evinced considerable disquiet, a feeling reinforced by Rostow's NATO presentation. To an aide, he admitted that it was of "the utmost importance that we cease treating the Cuban problem as simply one of trade or of relations with Cuba but rather as a highly sensitive issue in Canada/U.S. relations." Skepticism of American policy had made sense in the past but, because the Cubans were "getting progressively more communist-oriented" and were threatening their neighbors, Green felt that a policy shift was needed. He envisioned several important actions: tightening restrictions on goods traded with Cuba to incorporate items with even negligible strategic value; changing Cabinet views; and toning down government statements defending trade with Cuba. On this last point, Green revealed that the prime minister agreed with him that more discretion was needed. Summing up his current feeling, he thought that Canada's Cuban policy was "the most serious problem" in terms of Canadian–American relations because staying the course "might do irreparable harm" to relations with Washington.[25] Far more appreciative of the US position than he had been before—a remarkable contrast to the previous year when he and Rusk had bitterly clashed over Cuba—Green tasked External Affairs with conducting a reassessment of Ottawa's course of action.

To this end, summaries of Heeney's discussion with Rusk were sent to the heads of Canada's diplomatic posts in Latin America along with instructions that comments be submitted to Ottawa. The subsequent submissions were split between those who favored some minor change in Canadian policy—what George Kidd, the ambassador in Havana, termed a "shift in emphasis"—and those who argued for the status quo. All agreed, however, that Cuba posed a mounting threat to hemispheric stability; none argued that this factor necessitated breaking trade or diplomatic relations.[26] Heeney also weighed in on the debate. In discussions with Diefenbaker, Green, and Robertson, and then in a subsequent cable to Ottawa, he urged that existing policy be reviewed "if for no other reason" than to improve relations with Washington. "Cuba," he observed, "continues to cast a deepening shadow upon our reputation here" and was of "pervasive importance" to Canada–US relations. Although not envisioning an abandonment of Canada's current policy per se, he wanted something to counter Americans' "widespread misunderstanding" of Ottawa's stance. An authoritative and unequivocal public statement spelling out the similarities and differences between the Canadian and American positions on Cuba as well as the ways in which Ottawa was seeking to support Washington, would therefore help to restore "the traditionally friendly Canadian 'image'" within the United States.[27]

Heeney was right to be apprehensive over anti-Canadian feeling in the United States. For example, *US News & World Report* had observed that same week: "At a time when the U.S. is appealing for support in a campaign to isolate Castro, Canada's exports to Red Cuba have reached record levels."[28] Earlier that month, the *Dallas Morning News* had made a similar observation: "While the United States is imposing a ban on remaining imports from Cuba, Canada and Great Britain continue to trade in substantial volume with Castro's regime. We should make it clear to these two allies that continued trade with Cuba is not in the interest of our alliance." To Canadian television viewers, meanwhile, New York Republican Senator Kenneth Keating, then emerging as one of Kennedy's sharpest critics on Cuba, stated that he had always regarded Canada as one of his country's "most dependable allies," and so he exhorted Ottawa to "adopt a course which I think is more consistent with the traditional adherence of Canada to freedom, justice and liberty." A month later he again warned Canadians that "a business-as-usual attitude" could not "be squared" with Castro's "aggressive and belligerent steps against freedom," while the *Washington Post*'s resident conservative, George Sokolsky, criticized Canadians for "buying whatever Cuba has to sell and by selling Cuba whatever Castro can afford to buy."[29] A press roundup compiled by the Washington Embassy in mid-March found, for the first time in seven years, that a majority of American papers canvassed held an unfavorable attitude toward Canada; the chief reason cited was Cuba. Heeney, ever mindful of Canada's reputation in the United States, forwarded these findings on to Green with a warning that he sensed that "Canada has been getting an even more critical press than our scan shows."[30]

Taking all of this information into account, Robertson drew up his review of Canada's Cuba policy. To Merchant, the undersecretary had already emphasized his doubts about the Kennedy administration's approach, but he acknowledged that "Cuba must be viewed in the overriding terms of Canada's necessity to maintain close and friendly relations with the United States."[31] His subsequent study sought to strike this balance between smooth bilateral relations and an independent course of action. Beginning with a defense of Ottawa's long-standing practice of maintaining trade relations with all countries, he highlighted that the Canadian government had responsibly put in place effective controls to prevent the sale of strategic goods to Cuba. Robertson stressed, then, that as far as Canada was concerned, Rostow's request to extend COCOM controls to Cuba was redundant. Further, a "drastic change" in the Canadian position, as Rusk envisioned, would likely be seen at home and abroad as Canada "knuckling under" to American pressure. Cognizant of the need to pay closer attention both to Canada–US relations and to the threat of Cuban revolutionary activism, Robertson thought Ottawa might explore increasing aid to Caribbean countries, taking part in the Alliance for Progress, and joining the OAS. Increased intelligence-sharing with the Americans and more stringent trade controls were also viable options. Lastly, adopting Heeney's idea, Robertson advised that a public statement be made with the aim of improving "our appearance in the United States without losing the political advantages for ourselves and other Western countries in a continuation of relations with Cuba."[32]

Robertson's assessment did not advocate for, or herald, a change in the fundamentals of Canadian–Cuban relations, but it did outline a course that was more appreciative of the American stance. Also, as he had pointed out, by unofficially supporting COCOM controls toward Cuba, Canada was already acting in concert with the United States. Discussing several matters with Ball in early March, Heeney revealed that he had recently raised Cuba in a talk with Diefenbaker in Ottawa. The prime minister had indicated his concern that "some things had gone to Cuba which shouldn't have," that he was upset by this evasion of Canadian measures, and that he expected that the forthcoming study of Canada's Cuba policy—which he had initially opposed—would result in a stronger strategic control list.[33] When Green, with Hees's support, presented a version of Robertson's report to the Cabinet on April 10, the Canadian ministers agreed that there was no need to respond to the American request on COCOM, but they affirmed keeping these restrictions in place.[34] Despite the growing worry among some Canadian officials over American public and press criticism of Canada over Cuba, the idea of a formal public statement on the Canadian position stalled.

A superb opportunity for Canadians to clarify their position on Cuba to American lawmakers presented itself when, in early March, a group of congressmen visited Ottawa for the annual Canada–United States interparliamentary meeting. The previous year's conference had touched on Cuba, with the US delegates affirming that because Canada had put in place controls on exports of crucial materials, American criticism of Canada was "unwarranted."[35] In 1962, there was a "noticeable hardening" of the US position. The American delegates argued forcefully that their country was waging total economic warfare against the Cubans, a level of commitment that they hoped would compel Canada to act in support of the United States. An "acrimonious" debate ensued when Canadian parliamentarians responded that Washington's policy, quite simply, was wrong. In the end, the American side admitted both that their government had been slow in tightening its own embargo and that Canada had long given "strong support" to US efforts at containing communism.[36] Not taking part in these deliberations, Diefenbaker had considered mounting a "red-blooded defence" of Canada's position on Cuba at a banquet he was to hold for the legislators. Due to Green's "anxieties" about needlessly provoking the Americans, the speech was abandoned.[37] Given the climate in the United States this decision was prudent, but by no means did it indicate a change of heart for Diefenbaker. Speaking with Harold Macmillan in May, the Canadian prime minister agreed with his British counterpart that "the United States was at present virtually powerless to effect developments in Cuba," and thus the embargo was ineffective. As Diefenbaker then acknowledged, Cuba was growing more aggressive and "at least five countries in Latin American seriously vulnerable to Castro's influence."[38]

The prime minister did envisage, at least briefly, a change of policy based on a matter close to his heart. A strong believer in the sanctity of human rights— he supported South Africa's expulsion from the Commonwealth over apartheid and gave Canada a Bill of Rights—Diefenbaker was monitoring trials of those members of the invading force from the Bay of Pigs who had surrendered to the Cuban government. In the weeks prior to the trials, which were to take place at the end of March, various Cuban–American groups petitioned him to intercede and urge clemency for the accused. Spurred by these representations, the prime minister ordered that humanitarian concerns be raised by the DEA through both the Cuban ambassador in Ottawa and Canada's ambassador in Havana. When Robinson pointed out that with one exception, none of the prisoners were Canadians, Diefenbaker responded that he was interested in the matter because of his humanitarian beliefs. "If Castro took exception to this," he said, "we could break off trade with Cuba." An off-the-cuff comment perhaps, but, in the House of Commons, Diefenbaker voiced his evident concern with the trials.[39]

The White House applauded the prime minister's statement. On March 31, with the trials underway, Willis Armstrong telephoned the Prime Minister's Office to report that Kennedy deeply appreciated what Diefenbaker had said.

Armstrong also passed on a request from the president: would the prime minister consider making a further public appeal for clemency? As a dual Canadian-Cuban citizen was being tried, Diefenbaker had already been mulling the release of a new statement, and so he readily agreed to proceed. However, his own request was that the Americans take every effort to conceal that the president had urged him to speak out.[40] Duly issued on April 1, Diefenbaker's latest statement called on the Cuban government to move the trial from "behind closed doors" and asked that the death penalty not be used against any defendants who were found guilty. Appreciative of this message, Kennedy, in what was one of his last communications with the prime minister, wrote to Diefenbaker to express how "grateful" he was that the Canadian leader had spoken out on an issue in which the president had "a deep personal interest."[41]

As the year wore on, and in contrast to the state of public opinion in the United States, Kennedy was not alone in voicing words of praise for the Canadian government's stance on Cuba. Not only did the administration refrain from implementing the Trading with the Enemy Act, but, during a chat with Green at the Athens NATO ministerial meeting in May, Rusk emphasized his pleasure at Canada's approach toward Cuba, particularly because of prohibitions on trade in semistrategic goods.[42] Merchant, another tough critic, also adopted a softer line. In May, conferring with the US ambassador over several problems in bilateral relations, Robinson observed that the administration had backed away from strong condemnations of Canadian policy on Cuba. This shift was helpful, Robinson commented, because it might dampen public and congressional criticism of Canada. Agreeing, Merchant cautioned that "people in Washington still need to be persuaded of the Canadian arguments."[43]

Why the sudden change in the American viewpoint? The White House had appreciated Diefenbaker's public appeals for the Bay of Pigs prisoners. There was also a growing acknowledgment that Ottawa's export policy was quite effective, especially compared with the positions taken by other members of NATO. In the spring and summer of 1962, NATO's Political Advisory Committee met to discuss Rostow's proposal on COCOM restrictions. While all PAC representatives confirmed that their national governments had banned arms sales to Cuba, the issue of controlling trade in other items was a divisive point, with Western European representatives mounting stiff opposition to their US counterpart's efforts to have alliance members at least agree to unofficially apply restrictions as Canada was doing. The PAC eventually recommended against applying COCOM controls, either formally or informally. This result further underscored Canada's supportive stance.[44] Assessing the outcome, Robert Hurwitch, the State Department's officer-in-charge of Cuban affairs, asserted that Ottawa had made a tremendous effort in "quietly but effectively" supporting elements of the embargo. His wish was that other NATO countries would similarly move to "ensure that they are doing at least this much to avoid assisting and strengthening [the] economic and military potential of Cuban regime." Not all US officials dealing with Cuba shared this rosy assessment. In a July review of Operation Mongoose, Lansdale attacked Canada for continuing to allow essential items into Cuba, a conclusion that ignored Ottawa's supportive ban on semistrategic items.[45] Given Lansdale's delusions about his own capabilities at waging covert warfare against Castro's government, his flawed appraisal is perhaps unsurprising.

Reasonable assessments of Canadian policy were forthcoming from more senior American officials. In testimony before the combined Senate Committee on Foreign Relations and the Senate Armed Services Committee in September, Rusk praised the Canadians. When asked for the administration's reaction toward Mexico and Canada's continued trade with Cuba, Rusk noted sympathetically that while the US government had stressed to these countries the importance of restricting such trade, "this is not something that they find easy to do within their own systems and their own political situation." He went on to reveal a belief that "we have made, I think, considerable headway with the Canadians who have been, I think, more helpful than any other members of NATO." Echoing Rusk in his own testimony before the House Select Committee on Export Controls in October, Ball highlighted Canada's supportive efforts, noting that the volume of Canadian trade with Cuba in 1962 had shrunk to pre-Castro levels. Over the first six months of 1962 Canadian exports to Cuba were $5.5 million as compared to $17.6 million for 1958, the year before Castro took power. The link between this reduction in Canada–Cuba trade and the softening in Washington's position toward Ottawa was no secret. As a September headline in the *Ottawa Citizen* read: "U.S.–Canada Rift Now a Dead Issue."[46]

Canada's shrinking overall trade with Cuba, brought about largely by a shortage of Cuban foreign exchange and not any concerted effort by Ottawa, prompted the Canadian Department of Trade and Commerce to close the commercial section of the Havana Embassy on October 1. Worried that this move presaged a break in relations, Cuba's ambassador, Américo Cruz, called upon Robertson. In replying to Cruz's question as to whether Ottawa was changing its position on Cuba, Robertson was frank: Cuban alignment with the Soviet bloc and "steadily worsening relations" between the US and Cuba had let to "growing uneasiness and anxiety" among Canadians. Furthermore, the standoff between Havana and Washington "inevitably had repercussions on [Ottawa's] intimate relations with Washington." Cruz left the meeting, as Robertson put it, "understanding clearly we were not changing our present policy but without any real assurance as to the future."[47]

The Canadian position on Cuba was hardening partly thanks to the realization that the Cuban issue had domestic political overtones in the United States, but also because Havana's actions were looking increasingly provocative. Since the break in Cuba–US relations in January 1961 Ottawa had put in place what senior White House officials later referred to as "a long-standing exchange program conducted with the Canadian Embassy here in Washington in which reporting on Cuba has received special priority."[48] From Cuba's capital, Ambassador Kidd passed on a wealth of information to Ottawa, some of which was shared with Washington and London. Many of these reports dealt with the Cuban government's arms build-up over the summer of 1962, an effort that involved the arrival of Soviet military personnel on the island. In mid-August Kidd dispatched one such report, which warned of the increasing numbers of Soviet advisors and their close links with Cuba's military. Prompted by Kidd's warnings, Alfred Pick, head of the DEA's Latin American Division, spoke with Ambassador Cruz. As Cruz put it in a report back to Havana, Pick feared that "the Soviets would take control of Cuba, so that in addition to losing [its] sovereignty, [Cuba] would then also constitute a threat to the Americas."[49] While Canadian officials had long been concerned by Havana's ties to Moscow, the increasing links between Cuba and the Soviet bloc in 1962 led to mounting Canadian wariness, prompting Ottawa to step up its intelligence-sharing with the United States and Britain. The aim, Green was reminded that autumn, was to keep up the "the flow of information of a high and valuable character from our embassy in Havana" and thus maintain a "window on a dark courtyard."[50]

Canadian wariness of Cuba only deepened in the autumn as the Soviets and Americans ratcheted up dangerous rhetoric. On September 11, the Kremlin castigated US policy and iterated its strong support for Cuba's security. Commenting on this declaration, Kidd contended that it marked a "new stage" in Cuban–Soviet relations, for it constituted the "deepest Soviet commitment yet made to Castro." Concerned because it seemed logical to expect that Moscow would henceforth demand a greater say over Cuban foreign policy, Kidd also worried that Cuba was now on par with Berlin as a key centre of the Cold War, though Moscow had guaranteed that long-range missiles would not be installed in Cuba, a heartening sign. But with Soviet arms shipments continuing, Kennedy held a news conference on September 13 to warn the Soviet government against introducing offensive weapons—that is, nuclear weaponry—into Cuba.[51] The president's statement was directed at his domestic critics, who, with an election approaching, and with Soviet weaponry pouring into Cuba, were calling on the White House to take aggressive action.

Analyzing the president's predicament, Charles Ritchie evinced a mixture of sympathy for Kennedy and concern over Americans' emotional state. The US attitude on Cuba, he reported, had reached "a new and highly emotional phase," the result of the Soviet military build-up and its effect upon the off-year election. Faced with public opinion that "showed signs of boiling over," the administration was trying to ensure that the American people kept the Cuban issue in "perspective." This effort posed a difficulty for the White House over "how to induce a proper sense of urgency amongst allies without adding to hysteria at home." The administration's resulting statements warning the Kremlin that action would not be ruled out had been necessary, but had left "less room for internal manoeuvre" by the White House while raising "more drastic implications in a miscalculation by Moscow, Havana or Washington."[52] The same day that Ritchie sent this deft analysis to Ottawa, Kennedy was informed that despite Moscow's assurances to the contrary, Soviet missiles were being deployed in Cuba.

After days of tense debate the president and a group of advisors—the Executive Committee of the National Security Council (ExComm)—settled upon a blockade. Less belligerent than an attack, this "quarantine" was ill-designed to force the direct withdrawal of the missiles. Rather, it could prevent more missile equipment from arriving on Soviet ships and allow time for the Soviets and Americans to reach a deal. But it still held the potential to spark a conflict, particularly if Soviet ships did not halt at the blockade line or if Moscow moved either to seize Berlin or pre-empt a potential American attack.[53] It may have been risky, but within ExComm there was a sense that action of some sort was necessary. Discussing the situation during the first day of ExComm deliberations, Defense Secretary Robert McNamara had admitted: "I don't believe it's primarily a military problem. It's primarily a domestic political problem." The statements that Kennedy had made the previous month in response to congressional saber-rattling, he reasoned, had effectively boxed the administration into taking some action to ensure the missiles' removal.[54] With the political situation at home a constraining factor on the White House, both the United States and the USSR soon marshaled their vast militaries, a further ratcheting up of pressure.

The ExComm meetings focused mainly upon how best to confront Moscow and Havana, with little thought given to the role of Washington's allies. During the first day of deliberations, in what was the only point at which Kennedy and his advisors specifically considered Canada, Rusk mulled over using the Canadian ambassador in Havana as a go-between with Fidel Castro, but the idea was abandoned in favor of using the Brazilians instead. Rusk did raise the need to consult US allies; however, Kennedy was dubious, arguing that warning Washington's close allies, "it seems to me, is warning everybody" thanks to the likelihood of leaks.[55] Rusk pressed the issue, highlighting the importance of at least informing important allies of US plans so as not to alienate them or to create a situation where "we could find ourselves isolated, and the alliance crumbling." Relenting, Kennedy acknowledged that there were some "NATO people who have the right to some warning," though at this point he only mentioned Harold Macmillan and Charles de Gaulle.[56] Canada, then, barely entered into American thinking during the crisis.

This neglect startled Diefenbaker. At one point toward the end of the crisis the prime minister remarked to US officials that "if there is going to be an invasion," he expected to be consulted before the fact rather than merely informed.[57] The lack of consultation was the major sticking point, especially given Kennedy's promise in May 1961 to consult with Diefenbaker in the event of action being taken against Cuba as well as the mechanisms for consultation that were enshrined in the defensive pacts that Ottawa and Washington had signed. The NORAD agreement, which was invoked during the standoff, called for consultation in the event that the air defense system was put on alert. Further, in October 1957 Eisenhower had assured Diefenbaker that in a crisis, the commander of NORAD would be in communication with both the president and the prime minister. In 1962 neither type of consultation occurred. Certainly adequate consultations, or the lack thereof, had already been a sticking point between Canada and the United States during the Berlin crisis. That consultation did not occur over Cuba helps to explain why Diefenbaker would embark on a different course than he had done during the standoff in 1961. The prime minister's anger is understandable.[58] But Washington had a firm basis for not consulting with Ottawa.

In crafting their response to the Soviet missile threat, secrecy was paramount for Kennedy and his advisory group, a requirement that meant both that some members of Kennedy's own Cabinet were unaware of the president's deliberations and that no US allies were officially consulted, although, later on, Kennedy did engage in several telephone calls with Macmillan. This secretive approach was intended not only to catch the Soviets off guard, but also to ensure that lengthy debate among the Western allies, and leaks resulting from such talks, were avoided. Timing was important for the White House, which wanted to act before the missiles were operational. Washington's failure to consult with its allies meant that its conduct toward Ottawa was not unique. Still, Canada occupied a particularly important geographic position, a fact recognized by the distinct defense relationship entrenched in NORAD.[59] Likely, Washington took Ottawa's support for granted. Canada, after all, was an ally, one that had given forthright support to the United States over Berlin and had, during recent months, been more supportive than ever on Cuba. However, it is important to recognize, too, that by this point the Americans did not trust Diefenbaker. As one trenchant observer has clarified: "It remains a mystery how Diefenbaker could have expected the confidence of an ally whose basic trust he had violated, sometimes intentionally."[60] Considering the number of events that had occurred over the previous months that cast the PM in a less than positive light in American minds, this argument is quite convincing.

Chief among these indiscretions was the prime minister's threat to use the Rostow Memorandum, which had shredded his personal credibility with Kennedy. Also, on two policy questions, nuclear weapons and import surcharges, Diefenbaker had dithered and deceived his American allies. The latter issue was fresh in the minds of US officials as the surcharges were due to expire in October. On October 11 Diefenbaker had written Kennedy to congratulate him on passage of the Trade Expansion Act, an achievement that Ottawa's import surcharges had threatened. Replying on October 18—in the midst of his deliberations over how to respond to the missiles—Kennedy thanked the prime minister, but then asked that the surcharges be removed.[61] Two days later, with the deliberations still ongoing, the president again wrote Diefenbaker, this time to state his "distress" over Ottawa's decision to support a draft nuclear test-ban treaty containing no provisions for verification. At the time, the UN General Assembly was considering two resolutions: one, supported by London and Washington, called for a comprehensive test-ban with inspections; the other, supported by several neutral nations, was the one Canada seemed to support even though it lacked verification procedures. Writing from New York, Adlai Stevenson warned that a Canadian–American split would likely "attract public notice to our short run disadvantage and to obvious long-run disadvantage of both US and Canada." In his letter to Diefenbaker the president argued that as the Soviets, who supported the latter resolution, would undoubtedly cheat, the American government would not support the unpoliced moratorium. Canada, if it voted for the second resolution, would be siding with the Soviets against the United States. Kennedy warned that Ottawa's position would "only damage, and damage seriously the Western position on an essential issue of Western security."[62] So while a critic of the president has argued that his "disdain for and contempt of the prime minister completely precluded the kind of communication Kennedy had with [Harold] Macmillan," there were justifiable reasons for Kennedy's unwillingness to bring Diefenbaker into his confidence.[63] In addition, the transcripts of the president's deliberations indicate that at no time did he or his advisors give any thought to NORAD or a NORAD alert—this issue was one to be dealt with by the US military and not by the president.

Through Canadian intelligence officers in Washington, External Affairs had already received indications of the nature of the brewing crisis but for the Canadian prime minister, loathed by his American counterpart for his skullduggery over the Rostow memo and his prevarications on important issues, there was no close consultation throughout the coming crisis. Even so, Canada was still an ally and Ottawa ranked among those few governments that were briefed by US officials prior to the president's televised address on October 22. Called to the State Department, Charles Ritchie received a report on the crisis from George Ball, while George Ignatieff attended a briefing for the NATO allies.[64] Meanwhile, like Macmillan, De Gaulle, and German Chancellor Konrad Adenauer, the Canadian prime minister was accorded a private briefing, one provided by Livingston Merchant, who returned to Ottawa from retirement to deliver the president's fait accompli. Two hours before Kennedy spoke, Merchant arrived, accompanied by Ivan White, the US chargé d'affaires, and two CIA officers. Waiting for them were Diefenbaker, Green, and Douglas Harkness. At the outset, the Americans found the prime minister "harassed and worried." He was also confrontational, "brusquely" asking for an overview of Kennedy's speech and stating: "Let us face facts; an election is on in the United States." Merchant's insistence that the president would not play politics with such an important issue seemed to soothe the prime minister as did photographic evidence of the missile sites. At this point, the American note-taker recorded that Diefenbaker "swung around from his original skepticism bordering on antagonism to a more considered friendly and cooperative manner." Green and Harkness also seemed convinced by the evidence: the former was "less shocked and less vocal than would be expected"; the latter was "cheered by the decisiveness of the President's course of action." As the meeting concluded, a pleased Merchant believed that the prime minister "was sobered and upset but ... his earlier doubts had been dissipated and in the end he would give strong support to the United States." Merchant added, though, that "at no point, despite pointed questions, did [Diefenbaker] make a commitment in this regards."[65] Importantly, too, Merchant had made no mention of a NORAD alert.

Once Merchant had departed, Diefenbaker was given a DEA memorandum outlining possible American actions. Because this situation was so dangerous, External Affairs expected that the United Nations would become involved. Canada, then, might urge that the UN "conduct an on-site investigation in Cuba" to confirm the American government's assertion that missiles were being installed. The memorandum cautioned that such a proposal should be made prior to Kennedy's address "as the possibility cannot be ruled out that his announcement may be of measures already ordered against Cuba."[66] Mentioning the UN in his letter to Diefenbaker, Kennedy reported that he had directed Adlai Stevenson to introduce a resolution in the Security Council calling "for the withdrawal of missile bases and other offensive weapons in Cuba under the supervision of United Nations observers." He urged Diefenbaker to instruct Canada's delegation in New York "to work actively with us and speak forthrightly in support of the above program in the United Nations."[67] Clearly wanting Ottawa's support for an American resolution to seek the removal of the missiles, in his televised address Kennedy added that maneuvers at the UN were only one part of his response to the missiles.

Broadcast around the world, the president's address offered words of warning to the Soviet and Cuban governments and demanded the removal of the missiles, some of which could strike "most of the major cities in the Western Hemisphere," from Hudson Bay to Lima. After recounting the clearly false assurances given by the Soviets that no offensive missiles would end up in Cuba, the president also reiterated that he had publicly warned in September that his government would react adversely to the installation of such weapons in Cuba.

Adverse reaction was now to come in the form of a quarantine of the island in order to stop additional shipments of offensive weapons.[68]

Diefenbaker watched the address at home. Contacted by Lester Pearson, he agreed to address the House of Commons on the crisis that same evening. Echoing the president's "sombre and challenging" remarks, the prime minister told the gathered MPs that the construction of missile bases "constitutes a threat to most of the cities of North America including our major cities in Canada." Determined that the UN "be charged at the earliest possible moment with this serious problem," he proposed that should there be "a desire on the part of the U.S.S.R. to have facts," a group of nonaligned nations, acting under UN auspices, could conduct "an on-site inspection in Cuba to ascertain what the facts are." This effort would both "provide an objective answer to what is going on in Cuba" and constitute "the only sure way that the world can secure the facts." Hardly a ringing endorsement of Kennedy's stance, Diefenbaker's statement won him considerable support. Speaking for the opposition, Pearson attacked Soviet perfidy but noted, "I think it is important, as the Prime Minister has indicated, that these international organizations should be used for the purpose of verifying what is going on."[69] The *Globe and Mail* also backed the prime minister and his "statesmanlike attitude." For the editors of the *Ottawa Citizen* it was remarkable that for the first time in ages, Canada's parliamentarians had united around Diefenbaker's call for a UN inspection, one the paper heartily endorsed. Kennedy's move to blockade Cuba, it added, was dangerous and "wrong."[70] Important to note, however, is that the images of the missile sites had not yet been made public, and so the world had to trust Kennedy's word. When the danger became apparent, the prime minister was on the outs with the public, the press, and his political opponents.

The contrast between the prime minister's statement on Cuba and his statements on Berlin is striking: unlike in 1961, Diefenbaker appeared to indicate doubts about Kennedy's plan of action, putting Canada gravely out of step with the United States. Cuban Ambassador Cruz remarked to Alfred Pick that "he had read and liked the Prime Minister's statement in the House" because the suggestion of an inspection "implied that Mr. Diefenbaker himself doubted President Kennedy's assertions." Pick was compelled to dissuade Cruz of this notion, but the damage was done. Speaking with David Ormsby-Gore, Britain's ambassador in Washington, Robert Kennedy, the US attorney general, reported that "the only half-hearted response" that his brother had received was from the Canadian prime minister.[71]

Indeed tepid, Diefenbaker's statement reflected his doubts about the American plan of action. It was also a misstep, which the prime minister recognized immediately. When Cabinet met the next morning, he mentioned that the press was pestering him over whether he doubted that there were missiles in Cuba. Highlighting the "political overtones in the American attitude," Diefenbaker averred that he, Green, and Harkness were "convinced" that nevertheless "there had been no exaggeration of the situation" by Kennedy. That afternoon he told the House of Commons that he had "not, of course, [been] casting any doubts on the facts of the situation as outlined by the President." Going on to explain that "there is ample evidence that bases and equipment for the launching of offensive weapons have been constructed in Cuba," Diefenbaker acknowledged that these missiles "exist in sufficient quantities to threaten the security of this hemisphere." Importantly, explaining that Kennedy's plan involved using a UN Security Council resolution to seek the missiles' removal, he sensed that this effort would likely fail due to the Soviet Union's veto. His purpose, then, was not to compete with an American resolution, but to put forward a proposal that could be used in the event that the Soviet veto was used.[72] Thus he was hoping to complement US initiatives, and given his claims that Kennedy had not exaggerated the evidence, one can conclude that Diefenbaker had blundered by emphasizing the role of the UN in a way that looked critical of Washington. A nonstarter, however, Green "played down" the prime minister's initiative to Ivan White by offering his assurance that Ottawa would go no further in this regard without Washington.[73]

Although not doubting that there were missiles in Cuba, the prime minister was doubtful about Kennedy's approach. On the quarantine, he told British diplomats that the "legal basis" for the president's actions was "weak." Questioning US policy further, Diefenbaker contended that it was unclear whether weapons could be classified as offensive or defensive, and he expressed fear at "the impulsiveness" of the United States military.[74] Still, he kept these concerns private. But worried that war was imminent, and also angered by the lack of consultation, Diefenbaker hedged when it came to approving military cooperation with US forces. As it went to heightened alert on October 22, the United States military requested that Canada match its level of readiness.[75] Harkness took this request to the prime minister, who referred the matter to the Cabinet where, on October 23, Canadian ministers fiercely debated whether or not to comply with the American entreaty. Even though Diefenbaker asserted that the facts presented by Kennedy in his address "were as cited," he spearheaded delaying the activation of Canadian forces, with several ministers citing the need to wait for Britain to respond before taking any action.[76] Soon after, a message arrived from Macmillan, who, privately, admitted his concern about Diefenbaker's "cold feet." Reporting that he had given Kennedy his full support, the British prime minister was careful to point out that it was vital not to "give the Russians an opportunity of exploiting differences of interest or at least of emphasis between the United States on the one hand and her American and European allies on the other. I feel certain that we must above all try to avoid any splits in the Alliance of this kind."[77]

At this point, an infamous incident apparently occurred. In his memoirs, Diefenbaker recounted a telephone exchange that took place between himself and the president, who wished to know why Canada had not put its air units on alert. The alleged chat then devolved into a shouting match between the two men over the issue of consultation: when the president "raised the question of a national alert in Canada, I asked, 'When were we consulted?' He brusquely replied, 'You weren't,' as if consultation in North American defence was of no importance to him." It is unlikely that such a phone call took place. No mention of it exists in the recordings taken during the Cuban missile crisis, nor is such a remarkable event—an argument between allied leaders in the midst of a major crisis—ever mentioned by anyone in the existing documentary record.[78] Pending the discovery of evidence that might prove otherwise, it seems far more accurate to support the conclusion of one historian—a critic of Kennedy no less—that this matter "may have been a case of confusing what should have happened with what did happen. Diefenbaker's pride would have made it difficult for him to admit that he was so poorly informed before the Merchant visit, or that the request for an alert was actually made through military channels."[79]

Given Diefenbaker's worries about American belligerency and pique that Kennedy had not consulted with him personally, a Cabinet-sanctioned alert was pending. Harkness pleaded his case to his fellow ministers on October 24, but deep divisions led to further delay. Learning afterward that the US military had moved to its highest state of readiness short of war, Harkness pressed Diefenbaker, who finally agreed to ready Canada's military. Unbeknownst to the prime minister, this move was a mere rubber stamp: on October 23 Harkness had authorized a secret alert. As Canadian ships patrolled for Soviet submarines in the North Atlantic, Royal Canadian Air Force pilots readied themselves to defend North American airspace; through the efforts of its minister of defense, Canada was the only American ally to take on an active military role during the crisis.[80] Furthermore, complying with a request made through the US Embassy, Ottawa closed its airspace to Soviet bloc aircraft en route to Cuba and put in place provisions to search aircraft from *Czechoslovak Airlines* and *Cubana Airlines*, whose flights could not be cut off because both Cuba and Czechoslovakia were members of the International Civil Aviation Organization.[81] Kennedy and his advisors were monitoring reports of the search of several planes and in instructions to the US NATO delegation to press for alliance-wide flight restrictions, Rusk noted that Ottawa had already adopted an "unequivocal stand."[82]

Equivocation shrouded Canada's overall position. On October 24, the *Winnipeg Free Press* was one of a number of newspapers to demand that "what is needed (and what has not thus far been forthcoming at Ottawa) is an outright declaration of wholehearted support for President Kennedy's stand." Decrying such press speculation about differences between Ottawa and Washington, Green told Ivan White that he wanted to be "helpful to the United States," adding that "as far as I can see, our policies on Cuba are the same as the UK."[83]

Asked that evening by reporters whether the Americans were being hypocritical in their reaction to the emplacement of missiles in Cuba given that they had ringed missiles around the USSR, Green defended Washington, averring that the current situation was "very different." "It is obvious," he stated, "that the Soviet Union has moved in secretly with these missiles, all the time proclaiming to the world that any missiles that the Cubans were getting were purely defensive . . . and now it turns out that that isn't the case." Also remarking that "I don't think the Americans have any doubt whatever that we're standing beside them," he glossed over any divergence between Ottawa and Washington. But at no point did Green outline what military actions his government had taken to support the United States, leading to press criticism of the minister for "sidestepping" this important issue.[84]

Raising this perception in Cabinet the next day, Green complained that the public unfortunately "did not appear to be sure whether Canada fully supported the U.S. action or whether it was neutral." With the Cabinet insistent that a statement be issued "clarifying" Canadian "support of the U.S. action," Diefenbaker informed the House of Commons that Canada was searching Cuba-bound aircraft and revealed that the Canadian military was on alert. Despite his own doubts about the legality of the quarantine, he dismissed arguments against it as "sterile and irrelevant." He then attacked the Soviet Union, which "by its actions has reached out across the Atlantic to challenge the right of free men to live in peace in this hemisphere." Offering his own support for Washington's blockade, Pearson explained that "we who are the closest neighbour and in some ways the closest friend of the United States at this time of grave emergency and threat to peace must support that action."[85]

These strong words of support went over well in Washington. Both Robert Kennedy and Dean Rusk voiced appreciation, and the CIA judged that the prime minister had placed Canada "solidly in support" of the United States, while Ivan White wrote that "although belated, [it] constituted a clear statement of Canada's association with the US in Cuban crisis." The American press was also pleased, with a *New York Times* reporter praising Diefenbaker for having "pledged his Government's full support to the United States," and the *Chicago Tribune* for doing their part in constructing "a wall of determined opposition reaching from Baffin Land to Tierra del Fuego." "Whatever the differences on Cuba policy between Canada and the United States in the past," gushed the *Washington Post*, "they have been swept aside by the Soviet's provocation."[86]

Diefenbaker's strong rhetoric masked his lingering doubts about US policy. To British diplomats he stated that he remained "suspicious of American methods and Electoral pressures," but had nevertheless found it necessary to speak in defense of the West.[87] In the midst of a dangerous situation, with a military alliance in place and domestic forces backing support for Washington, Diefenbaker was constrained in his response and so he tempered his own views. A contributing factor, too, must have been that hours before Diefenbaker launched his verbal tirade against the Soviet Union, Macmillan had defended Kennedy in Westminster.[88]

In the meantime, the Canadians were proving helpful in spite of their prime minister. Beyond restricting Canadian airspace and searching Cuba-bound flights, Ottawa boosted its intelligence-sharing. Responding to requests for information sent from Washington, Ambassador Kidd reported variously on the influence of US propaganda, Cuban public opinion, and government reactions to the crisis and its resolution.[89] These reports were evidently of some value to the Americans, who also found Canadian and British intelligence crucial in helping to monitor the withdrawal of Soviet technicians and missiles.[90] John Crimmins, the director of the State Department's Office of Caribbean and Mexican Affairs, spoke to Canadian diplomats "in the warmest and most complimentary terms" of the details received from Havana. Even President Kennedy was aware of this intelligence, later telling Diefenbaker of his appreciation of the helpful role played by the Canadian embassy staff in Cuba's capital.[91]

Aside from information, the Canadians also intervened with the Cubans to get them to back down. On October 25 Green took a hostile line with Ambassador Cruz, telling him that the missiles posed a "grave threat to the security of the Americas, including Canada," and that "one way or another, they had to go."[92] Havana's actions clearly alarmed the Canadian government and Green's statements here confirm where his loyalties lay. In the American capital, Charles Ritchie and Basil Robinson met with Rusk, giving him a message that Cruz had asked Green to rely to the Americans: Cuba was willing to negotiate its differences with the United States. Impressed by Green's firm stance, Rusk suggested that the Canadian minister probe Cruz further. He also requested that Ambassador Kidd seek out Castro with the "aim of implanting the view that Cuba cannot possibly win." With Rusk using Brazilian diplomats as a means of communicating with the Cuban government, it seems he wished to use Canadian officials as a backchannel as well.[93]

By this point there was only some vague possibility of a resolution, and on October 26 Ritchie ominously counseled Ottawa that it appeared that a "second and more critical phase of the crisis" was about to begin with Soviet ships approaching the US blockade.[94] The next day he was buoyed by a discussion with Britain's ambassador, who confided that there was secret and constructive communication going on between the Soviet premier and the US president. After confirming this news with William Tyler, Ritchie advised Ottawa that this development could herald a break in the crisis. White, meanwhile, had already briefed Robertson and Bryce on Kennedy's correspondence with Khrushchev. Next, meeting with Diefenbaker and Green—the latter "appeared to be in a state of euphoria"—White explained that a resolution could be at hand. Even so, he stressed, and the prime minister acknowledged, that the "time element" was of the utmost importance: an agreement had to be reached before the missiles became operational.[95] Then, on October 28, Khrushchev announced that the missiles in Cuba would be dismantled. From the Canadian Embassy in Moscow, Ambassador Arnold Smith reacted to this news by exulting that the West appeared to have won the ball game, "though not yet [the] World Series." A firm American response, which had elicited "unexpected solidarity" from Canada and other governments, had forced the failure of a "calculated and dangerous Khrushchev gambit" and so although the situation was still fluid, tempered celebration was in order.[96]

Pleased that a resolution was emerging, Green left Ottawa for New York on October 28, telling White that he hoped to be of use their to the United States. Reporting this comment to Washington, White counseled that Green could be helpful but, given his hope of coming up with new "Canadian initiatives," he could also be a problem.[97] The Canadian foreign minister was careful not to overstep. After deliberating with Canada's UN delegation, Green spoke with UN Secretary General U Thant, who had announced his intent to go to Havana to gain Castro's consent to the establishment of a mission to verify the dismantling of the missile sites. Green told Thant of his willingness to assist in any way possible. Later, after conferring with Adlai Stevenson, Green informed the secretary general that Canada would be willing to offer aircrew for a UN reconnaissance mission to confirm that the missiles were being removed. To speed up this process, Green also authorized the Washington Embassy to begin discussions with the Americans on the details of the mission. This move was merely preliminary, however, because there were no assurances that Thant, the Cubans, or the Soviets would agree to this mission and US officials, the president included, fully expected that the proposed mission would be rejected.[98]

Returning to Ottawa on October 30, Green met with the Cuban ambassador. In an effort to smooth the way for inspections, he urged Cruz to tell his government that "it was no less in Cuba's interests to cooperate" with the UN than it was to oppose a mission. Canada, he continued, would be willing to contribute toward the success of the mission and, hopeful of soliciting a positive response, he added that the Cuban government could rest assured of Canadian impartiality. But Green was not impartial, and as their discussion grew heated, with Cruz criticizing Kennedy, Stevenson, and Rusk, the Canadian minister defended these men as "voices of moderation in United States policies." This overture to Cruz, ending in an argument, had little effect: during meetings with Castro on October 30 and 31, Thant found the Cuban leader unwilling to permit inspections.[99] Castro's stance briefly hampered a resolution of the crisis. At American insistence Canada pressured the Cuban government, with Kidd stressing to Cuba's foreign minister that it was in Havana's "interest" to resolve the crisis.[100] In the end, the missiles were withdrawn. Relieved and impressed, Green telephoned Rusk and "congratulated" him on the American government's handling of the standoff.[101]

Other Canadians were less than impressed over the question of consultations. After the crisis abated, the *Toronto Star* asked: "Do we have no right to be consulted before being asked to support a decision on which the fate of every Canadian depends? Is our role to be simply that of sheep to be led unprotesting to the edge of disaster?" Similarly, the *Ottawa Citizen* complained that the Americans were "leading an alliance, not an empire" and that "we expect to play a part in the decision-making process at the top level of Cold War strategy." "If the United States has a bone to pick with Canada in regard to Ottawa's reaction to the Cuban emergency," added the *Edmonton Journal*, "it is equally true that Canada has reason to complain of the failure of Washington to notify and consult Ottawa in advance of President Kennedy's announcement."[102] Nor were complaints over the lack of consultation confined to the press. Having spoken with a number of administration officials and well-connected journalists, Charles Ritchie was worried that the administration's "successful essay in nuclear diplomacy, conducted as it was with speed, in secrecy and without consultation, has deeply impressed them with the conviction that this is the ideal pattern of effective action. It is not far from this state of mind to a feeling of impatience with what may seem an old-fashioned, cumbrous alliance machinery."[103] Diefenbaker was also upset that Washington had displayed little concern for its allies. In a public address he underlined that there had never been "any question as to where Canada stood on the Cuban situation," but added that "consultation is a prerequisite to joint and contemporaneous action being taken." Geared toward his domestic audience, this speech was meant to respond to critics who were clamoring for Diefenbaker to explain why it has not stood more forthrightly beside the United States. As Basil Robinson told State Department officials, the prime minister was "quite surprised" that Canadians were upset with the apparent lack of "energetic and forthright" support for Kennedy. Ottawa's position that Washington was obliged to consult with Canada had little traction with the public. A poll taken in early November showed that almost 80 percent of Canadians endorsed Kennedy's handling of the situation, while only 13 percent disapproved. "President Kennedy's wise and forceful handling of the Cuban crisis," one reporter wrote in *Saturday Night* magazine, "rallied the West more effectively than any American action since the breaking of the Berlin blockade." The prime minister's conduct, one Tory cabinet member later wrote, "led a great many staunch Conservatives to doubt Diefenbaker's ability to lead the nation in the event of an international crisis."[104]

In contrast to this domestic disapproval, there seems to have been little criticism of the Canadians by US officials. Certainly, none of them mention Canada's tardy response in memoirs or in postretirement interviews, nor did the subject come up in any of the Americans' deliberations throughout the crisis or in their discussions in early 1963 of their profound dislike for Diefenbaker. Analyzing the prime minister's October 22 speech, a State Department report noted that Diefenbaker "accepted without demurrer the facts as cited by the President but did not specifically approve of the course of action chosen," an omission chalked up to the fact that since the Canadians had no ships engaged in trade with Cuba, "the blockade would have little direct effect on Canada."[105] In the midst of the crisis Ivan White had observed that although Canada's government "in practice during [the] three days following President's speech was cooperative, e.g., control bloc aircraft, authorizing the equivalent alertness status with NORAD, [the] point had been reached where Canadian public was mystified as to where their government really stood." To White, it was evident that Diefenbaker's inherent indecisiveness and Green's "dislike for the hard realities of power situations" were both to blame. He was clear, however, that Canada, despite this fumbling, had been onside throughout the crisis, with Canadian officials working to assist the United States. White also went on to praise the Canadian public. Aside from some minor demonstrations against US brinksmanship at the Embassy and at the various US consulates along with some grumbling in some quarters about the lack of consultation or consideration of the crisis by the UN, on the whole most Canadians "publicly applauded US action" and criticized their own government's "hesitation and ambiguity." Ultimately, White concluded that in a crisis situation the bonds of friendship and of the bilateral alliance were stronger than the pull of neutralism or nationalism.[106] Given the high stakes, Diefenbaker's hesitation was understandable; as the White House tapes from the crisis indicate, Kennedy himself was hardly the decisive leader of myth.[107] But hesitancy aside, Diefenbaker had offered only grudging support and had made many of his doubts about US actions public.

On this point a more critical American voice was Merchant, who told Robinson of his disappointment over the prime minister's initial statement in the House of Commons as well as over Green's television interview. Turning to the PM's dissatisfaction with the lack of consultation, Robinson grudgingly agreed when the former ambassador argued that he "didn't think Canada had earned, by its actions and by certain non-actions, the right to an extreme intimacy of relations which had existed in years past."[108] How much the opinion of this retired diplomat mattered is unclear. Certainly his assessment of Canadian actions and inaction—on the EEC, nuclear weapons, the Rostow Memorandum—was fair. But despite anger at Diefenbaker in the White House, the Canadian prime minister was one of the few Western leaders who received a briefing in advance of Kennedy's televised address, as well as a personal message from the president. There was something still to be said for the close relationship between Ottawa and Washington. As for Merchant's negative view, he may have been unaware of the amount of assistance that Canada had given to the United States irrespective of the public blunders by Diefenbaker and Green. He was right to be disappointed, though, because such support had come from lower levels within the government and not from the prime minister, at least not at first. As Robert Kennedy is supposed to have remarked to Progressive Conservative Party organizer Dalton Camp, when the president heard Diefenbaker's statement on October 22, "he was just dumbfounded. That of all the nations in the world, the only one that gave him any trouble was Canada."[109] On that first day Diefenbaker had given only half-hearted support. No doubt his hesitancy only confirmed negative American views of prime minister, who remained persona non grata in Washington. On November 19, Kennedy offered a written update about the resolution of the crisis to Adenauer, de Gaulle, and Macmillan—not Diefenbaker.[110]

Two US presidents did evince kind words for the Canadian stance. Speaking with the press early in the crisis, former president Harry Truman had criticized Canada's position on Cuba: "We have supported them in former times and in crisis. They should stand behind us today." Worried by this criticism, Ritchie sent the retired president a copy of Diefenbaker's strong, supportive statement from October 25, as well as a rundown of Canadian efforts to back the US. "I am happy as can be," Truman soon replied, "that a complete understanding between your great country and ours is accomplished."[111] Sent a copy of this same speech by Diefenbaker, Dwight Eisenhower wrote back: "One advantage we gained from this sorry affair is the knowledge that when the chips are down, there is no question that your country and our stand firmly together to the end."[112] The problem, then, was the impression that Diefenbaker's initial stumble had given. In early November, Rufus Smith met with Canadian journalist Robert Reford to discuss Ottawa's actions during the crisis. After Reford asked about reports of American unhappiness with the Canadian response, Smith stressed "the difference in assessing the value of specific actions and assessing the significance of tone, style, and timing of the public statements that accompany them." Referring to an incident in 1960 when George Hees had called Cubans "fine businessmen," Smith said that "unfortunately" these types of statements tend "to be remembered by people, particularly editors, who may forget that in fact Canada has been more cooperative with [the US] trade embargo" than had other American allies.[113] Implicit, then, was that both the prime minister's October 22 statement and Green's television interview would be remembered more than Canadian efforts to support the United States throughout the crisis, a prediction that has proved accurate.

The Cuban missile crisis is commonly viewed as a crisis in Canada–US relations. A corollary to this view is that the Kennedy administration sought "to obtain vengeance for Diefenbaker's diplomatic cold shoulder" during the crisis by toppling Canada's government in early 1963.[114] Yet this viewpoint ignores Canada's helpful actions during those "thirteen days." With a major crisis unfolding, and despite their prime minister's hesitation, Canadian officials,

Green included, had responded by siding with the US and by playing a helpful role in providing the Americans with intelligence, by curtailing and monitoring flights heading toward Cuba, and by pressuring the Cuban government to withdraw the missiles. To observers in the British High Commission in Ottawa, Diefenbaker's "three day stutter" in withholding unequivocal support had looked bad even as there had been "no real doubt" that Canada would stand with the United States.[115] Moreover, although Diefenbaker did not authorize a military alert until October 24, the Canadian military, through the defense minister's initiative, played its part in keeping North America secure. Given Canada's support through NATO and NORAD, two historians have contended that "the Americans had few grounds for complaint."[116] But no complaints were forthcoming. Indeed, the fact that Ottawa offered its backing is an indication of why Canada appears little in American accounts of the crisis. During the standoff Canadians were not "invisible and inaudible," but were innocuous and, therefore, inconsequential.[117]

Still, Diefenbaker's early statement had been noted in the White House. If Ottawa was not inaudible in Washington, it was certainly invisible, at least in terms of the crisis resolution. The transcripts of Kennedy's deliberations with his advisors attest that these officials gave little thought to a role for the Canadian government, an omission not surprising given the mutual hostility between the president and the prime minister. As far as Washington was concerned, Canada, like virtually every other country, was irrelevant in the crisis. The Cuban missile crisis was largely a contest between the USSR and the United States, so much so that Cuba itself barely figured into the diplomatic picture and other Western allies, including the British, had very little impact on the events of those thirteen days.[118] Even so, what assistance Ottawa had given had pleased Washington. However, the optics of the situation— Diefenbaker's three-day stutter and his invocation of a UN mission—have led many Canadians to look back on the missile crisis as a moment when Ottawa stood up to Washington. In fact, the situation was marked by quiet cooperation between to the two governments to respond to mutual threat. Indeed, at the time, most Canadians applauded Kennedy's approach and looked askance as the actions of their own prime minister. Shortly after the crisis abated, one senior Canadian civil servant detected "a fairly well articulated public opinion in Canada that we should 'stand by the Americans'" both in response to Soviet provocation and because "quite simply that Canadians feel a fundamental alliance with the United States that is often covered over but never seriously threatened by noisy disagreements in normal times." Moreover, he added, Kennedy had "immense prestige" in Canada.[119] The same could not be said for Diefenbaker, whose popularity by late 1962 was slipping, in part because he had not stood stoutly beside the US president during the missile crisis.

Beyond Canada's assistance during the crisis itself, over the course of 1962, and despite both the nationalist bluster over trade with Cuba and US sniping on this issue, Canadians and Americans cooperated on Cuban policy, with Ottawa coming to share much of Washington's apprehension over Havana's foreign policy. Differences over Cuba had had little if nothing to do with the brief, disparate responses in the missile crisis. The Cuban issue—which Green had called the most serious problem in bilateral relations—with all its tough talk on both sides, had largely been resolved by October. Defending its independent Cuban policy and making clear that the American position was wrongheaded, the Canadian government had been able to portray itself as having stood up to United States pressure, all while quietly supporting elements of US policy and thus placating American officials. In turn, the Kennedy administration had avoided strong-arm measures that could have achieved a drop in Canada–Cuba trade but that would certainly have roused Canadian anger. Both sides agreed on a middle ground that partially accommodated the other government's position.

Canada's support for the United States over Cuba, both before and during the crisis did little to mask the fact that the relationship between the two governments was not warm. Diefenbaker's brief prevarication failed to improve Washington's long-term view of Ottawa, just as Kennedy's lack of consultation left a sour taste in the Canadian capital. Over the coming months relations were to become increasingly hostile, not because of Canadian actions or inactions on Cuba, but because of Diefenbaker's continued refusal to accept nuclear weapons. Indeed, in the wake of the Cuban crisis, Canada's defense relationship with the United States became the paramount issue in bilateral relations and a dominant issue in Canada's increasingly fractious domestic scene. Quiet diplomacy had soothed the differences between Ottawa and Washington over Cuban trade, but would prove unable to resolve the nuclear arms issue. Instead, distinctly unquiet diplomacy was used, pushing Canadian–American relations to their lowest point then or since. The result was Diefenbaker's fall from power and the rise of a more American-friendly but still nationalistic government under Lester Pearson.

# 6

# Troubled Endings

## From Diefenbaker to Pearson, 1963

Venting his frustration to senior State Department officials over Canada's reluctance to accept nuclear warheads, in March 1963 Dean Rusk affirmed that accommodating the Canadian government could not be done "without degrading unacceptably the capabilities of the delivery systems involved." In particular, he denounced as "fraudulent" Ottawa's suggestion of a missing part procedure, where an essential component for the warheads for Canadian BOMARC missiles and the missiles for CF-101 interceptors would be stored in the United States and transferred north in the midst of a crisis. Yet Rusk admitted that while the nuclear question was of vital importance for bilateral relations, "the real issues in this matter lay within Canada." A month earlier, the secretary of state had defended American efforts to supply the Canadian military with these warheads to the Soviet ambassador in Washington, who had lodged a protest with the White House over revelations that the two North American governments had been engaged in secret talks to share nuclear weaponry. Brushing away the ambassador's attack, Rusk affirmed that the "long-standing" arrangement between Ottawa and Washington was predicated on a need to respond to the Soviet threat to Western security.[1] His comments indicate the importance that American officials attached to Canada's acceptance of nuclear weapons. The issue had been ongoing since 1959, and while critics would charge that the US government failed "to understand the sensitive nature of the nuclear arms question in Canada," in fact the Eisenhower and Kennedy administrations had both appreciated John Diefenbaker's difficult balancing act on this issue and had shown patience over the Canadian premier's hemming and hawing over whether or not his government would accept the warheads.[2] By late 1962, their patience sapped, US policymakers pushed to resolve this question first through quiet negotiations and then, once Diefenbaker misrepresented the nature of these talks, in more aggressive tones.

In January 1963, the State Department issued a public statement seeking to clarify remarks that Diefenbaker had made in the House of Commons in which he both revealed the secret bilateral negotiations and stood simultaneously for and against the acceptance of nuclear warheads. The Canadian premier had also raised valid questions about the viability of Canada's nuclear-armed defenses in an era where the Americans and Soviets were developing ever more destructive missiles. The latest step in a long line of procrastination on the nuclear file, his comments forced Washington into action. The United States response added fuel to the political firestorm that was then raging over whether Canada should acquire the warheads; within days, the government collapsed. To many, it appeared that by interfering in Canadian domestic affairs, the US government had breached the bounds of propriety. To others, it looked as though Washington had spearheaded a coup. The Kennedy administration, Diefenbaker later charged, was guilty of "aiding and abetting the Liberal Party in its attempts to throw out my government," an accusation that has some truth to it.[3]

By 1963, the White House and State Department had come to favor the Liberals over the Progressive Conservatives. Moreover, the American press release rebutting the prime minister contributed to the nonconfidence vote that brought down Diefenbaker's government. In spite of worries that their actions would unleash a torrent of anti-Americanism, US officials, who had long deferred to Diefenbaker, felt compelled to act and threw quiet diplomacy by the wayside. Their intervention into Canadian domestic affairs is understandable—and, dare it be said, defensible—when one gets a sense of their intense frustration with four years of delay and broken promises. Furthermore, the question of nuclear weaponry was not simply a Canadian domestic issue; rather, it had direct connections to US national security. One need not buy into the mythmaking of the Kennedy presidency to empathize with American authorities who "had endured, once too often, what they judged to be Diefenbaker's erratic buffoonery."[4] But while the State Department's brazen act was entirely justifiable, Kennedy's support for the Liberals in the 1963 federal election, although minimal, bordered on being reprehensible.

Throughout the Kennedy era, US policymakers had recognized Canada's special importance to the United States and had displayed a pattern of restraint in dealings with Canadians. Conscious of the centrality of nationalism as a motivator for Canadian actions, they also acknowledged the resulting importance that Canadians placed upon the sanctity of sovereignty, just as they were also aware of the Diefenbaker's preoccupation with his electoral position. In this light, they had been careful to avoid heavy-handed actions on a host of issues, from trade with Cuba and China, to nuclear weaponry. The Canadian government's shifting position on the latter issue, a matter of mutual concern to both countries, provoked a well-deserved, sharp response. Diefenbaker was playing rough, and the Americans responded in kind. After the damage was done, these same officials were careful to hold back. During the ensuing election they chose a fatalistic policy, not an interventionist one, but were rewarded when Pearson emerged victorious.

With its roots in Diefenbaker's 1959 decision to acquire weapons that required nuclear warheads in order to be fully effective, the immediate cause of the prime minister's downfall was the Cuban missile crisis. It is simply not the case, however, that from the crisis onward "Kennedy made the defeat of the Diefenbaker government a prime objective of his foreign policy."[5] Diefenbaker had prevaricated during the missile crisis, but Canadian military and diplomatic officials had stepped into the breach, and so there were no grounds for US complaint. Instead of working to undermine Diefenbaker, throughout the remainder of 1962 the Americans sought to conclude a nuclear pact with the Canadians, for what the crisis served to do, was to bring the nuclear question to the fore. As Ivan White observed in early November, with Diefenbaker having never "adequately presented" the facts of the issue to the public, on defense issues Canadians were "confused and in many cases ashamed." Even before the events of that October, one of the government's sharpest journalistic critics had laid out two choices for the Tories: to accept the warheads or "scrap $685 million worth of military hardware and thereby renege on our obligations under NORAD and NATO ... Despite Prime Minister Diefenbaker's hints that there are other possibilities no other choice in fact exists."[6] The threat of nuclear war in the autumn only increased criticism of the government. During the crisis the *Edmonton Journal* complained that Canada was caught "with its armor down." Such criticism mounted in the wake of the standoff. The *Calgary Herald* dubbed Canada the "weak sister" of the NATO alliance, and CBC journalist Knowlton Nash warned that "the lack of nuclear defensive weaponry leaves a serious hole in North American defence." *Time* agreed that "across Ontario and Quebec, there is a 300-mile gap in NORAD's first line of air defense," as did retired Canadian Air Marshal W. A. Curtis, who told the *Montreal Gazette* that Ottawa's failure to equip its interceptors and Bomarc missiles with nuclear warheads had made Canada "the only gap in the entire North American defence system."[7]

Against the growing censure from the press, on October 30, with the emergency over Cuba still lingering, Douglas Harkness warned his Cabinet colleagues that without a firm position on nuclear weapons they occupied a "vulnerable position" in possessing no means of responding to criticism. Recognizing this danger, Diefenbaker stated that talks with the Americans should begin "but on the understanding that if there was any leak concerning the negotiations, they would stop forthwith." The Cabinet agreed, resolving that discussions with the US government should aim at concluding a package deal involving stockpiling the warheads destined for the Honest John rockets and CF-104 aircraft assigned to NATO in Europe, and securing US agreement to the "missing part" proposal calling for the provision of warheads to Canadian forces only during actual or threatened emergency.[8] Considering this plan in the summer, the Department of National Defence had rejected it on the grounds that it would be ineffective.[9] Government ministers, however, hoped that this maneuver would serve to meet defense commitments without actually having to store nuclear weapons on Canadian soil.[10] This compromise would help the Tories beat back criticism from all directions, an important point given the precarious position of Diefenbaker's minority government.

Armed with the Cabinet's instructions, Howard Green informed Ivan White of Ottawa's willingness to enter into negotiations. The news was welcomed in Washington, where officials were hopeful that a solution meeting their "vital" defense requirements could be balanced against the Canadians' domestic concerns.[11] Galvanized by the prospect of finally resolving this issue, the US Department of Defense dispatched a team of officials to work alongside White in negotiating with the Canadians. A series of meetings were soon arranged between the US team and Ross Campbell, Assistant Under-Secretary of State, and Air Chief Marshall Frank Miller, the Chairman of the Chiefs of Staff, who handled technical negotiations on the Canadian side, as well as with the three Canadian ministers spearheading the secret negotiations, Green, Harkness, and Gordon Churchill, minister of Veterans Affairs and a strong supporter of Diefenbaker. Debate centered on the "missing part" formula. Sensing that this proposal was viable, White recommended accepting it or a variation of it, particularly because within the Cabinet Harkness held the initiative, "with Green and his External Affairs Boy Scouts pushed into the corner for the moment."[12] Defence Secretary Robert McNamara had already seized on the momentum. Hoping to get "going forward as rapidly as possible," he had contacted Harkness. Aware that his presence in Ottawa or a visit by Harkness to Washington would create undue press speculation and possible political criticism, McNamara had suggested that the NATO ministerial summit in Paris in mid-December would be an opportune place to discuss nuclear weapons. Harkness agreed.[13] Learning of this meeting, Rusk decided to join in, inviting Green to participate as well. "Green's conversion," State Department officials advised, "is essential."[14]

Securing Green's support seemed to be working. Hinting to a State Department contact that a decision on nuclear weapons would soon be made at very high levels of the Canadian government, Basil Robinson added, in reference to Green, that his government was "casting about for some means which would enable it to accept such weapons on Canadian soil without seeming to abandon its present position."[15] Two weeks later, in advance of the NATO summit, White and the Pentagon officials met again with their Canadian counterparts. By now, the Americans had cooled somewhat to the "missing part" procedure and in these talks they emphasized the difficulties involved in quickly and safely transporting and installing the components in a crisis situation. Even so, the

Canadians indicated that they wished to "push forward to settle this problem as promptly as possible," with the talks at the NATO meeting offering a chance for a breakthrough.[16] The next day, before departing for Paris, Green told the House of Commons that there could be "no guarantee" that "there would never be nuclear weapons in Canada," a comment welcomed by American observers as a sign that the Canadian minister was shifting gears on defense policy.[17] Harkness was also busy. Protecting his domestic flank, he prepared a collection of briefing papers on Canada's nuclear commitment, which he then distributed to the Tory caucus.[18] But these developments amounted to little.

The talks in Paris proved fruitless. Although, as Canadian officials admitted, Rusk and McNamara had been "ready to accept any reasonable arrangement with which the Canadian Government felt it could live," Harkness and Green, reflecting Diefenbaker's caution, stuck to the missing part formula. Since the Canadian ministers were unready to part from this formula, the two Americans concluded that there was little "point in moving away from where we are to something so contrived or complicated as to merely make things more difficult." As "no satisfactory solution" had been found, Rusk recommended that talks continue in Ottawa.[19] Despite the disappointing results of the Paris meeting, Ross Campbell informed the Ottawa Embassy that his government was "anxious" to continue the secret negotiations.[20] The nuclear issue was left unresolved, when, on December 21, Canadian MPs began a month-long parliamentary recess.

With the Christmas holiday in full swing, Diefenbaker debated where to take his vacation. His thoughts turned to the Bahamas, where, from December 17 to 21, Kennedy and Harold Macmillan were meeting at Nassau. For several months, the British and Americans had been engaged in their own nuclear spat. Originally London had planned to take control of US-built, nuclear-tipped Skybolt missiles, meant to launch from British aircraft, but, with the missiles having failed a number of tests, the Americans signaled that they were unhappy with this arrangement. As Skybolt was meant to form the UK's independent nuclear deterrent, the cancellation of the missile program left Macmillan alarmed and angered. At Nassau, he and Kennedy concluded a special agreement—against the advice of the president's aides—whereby the United States would supply the Royal Navy with submarine-launched Polaris missiles. They also discussed the creation of a multilateral nuclear-armed submarine force within NATO that would preclude alliance members without nuclear weapons from acquiring them. The Polaris decision, recalled presidential speechwriter Ted Sorensen, was typical of Kennedy's "ability to look at things objectively and to do what was appropriate to the time and situation." With Canada, though, the president "did not like and did not respect Diefenbaker, and had no desire to see him continue in office."[21] After the Rostow Memorandum incident and the Canadian leader's evasiveness on atomic weaponry, Kennedy was unwilling to cut Diefenbaker a deal equivalent to the Nassau agreement, say by approving the "missing part" proposal. Had Canada's prime minister not burned up his diplomatic capital in Washington, he may have found a more helpful president.

As for Kennedy, his time in Nassau took a turn for the worse on the final day of talks when Diefenbaker arrived at Macmillan's behest. Learning of the Canadian premier's pending arrival, Kennedy sought to leave, but Macmillan persuaded him to stay.[22] Over a brief lunch, Diefenbaker reviewed several issues with Kennedy, including nuclear weapons, with the Canadian premier informing the president "that there were a number of matters [he] hoped [they] would have an opportunity to discuss soon in connection with the defence of North America and the provision of nuclear armed missiles for Canada." If this was an attempt to mollify Kennedy, it did not work. The president's distaste for Diefenbaker was palpable. At a press conference following the meal, Diefenbaker was asked whether it was true "that Kennedy doesn't like you," to which he scoffed: "I've never known relations between individuals or countries to be other than the closest since I became Prime Minister." Nothing could have been further from the truth. Reflecting later on this lunch, Kennedy said that he, Macmillan, and Diefenbaker had sat awkwardly "like three whores at a christening."[23]

With Kennedy quickly leaving the island, Diefenbaker was left with his British counterpart. Inquiring about the Nassau agreement's applicability to Canada, the Canadian premier emphasized that he wanted to avoid expanding the "nuclear family," especially in light of the disarmament talks in Geneva. If arms talks failed and if "the situation might require it," he admitted that his government would accept nuclear warheads. Macmillan's own notes record that Diefenbaker raised the opposition to such weaponry within Canada, which "remained as strong as ever." Still, the Canadian prime minister had pointed out that "it was clearly wasteful and unsatisfactory" that Canada's military "should be deprived of these weapons or have to rely on weapons which were stored so far away that it would take hours to arm them in a crisis." As for the Nassau agreement, Macmillan mentioned that "more effective missiles" signaled "the end of the era of the manned bomber." Asked by reporters about this agreement's relevance to Canada, Diefenbaker stated that it pertained only to arrangements between the United States and Britain.[24] Even so, Nassau raised doubts about the long-term viability of BOMARC and the CF-101 interceptors: in the missile age, what good were defenses aimed at protecting against airplanes? Indeed, as Canadian diplomats soon advised the prime minister, the Nassau agreement "heralds the gradual phasing out, over the next several years, of a major part of the U.S. Strategic Air Command's bomber fleets," and thus the end of the bomber age.[25]

Diefenbaker's talks in Nassau show that he was waffling over meeting Canadian defense commitments, though his indecision stemmed from a sense of the short-term viability of Canada's nuclear defenses. By the time he returned to Ottawa, he had come down opposed to accepting nuclear warheads. Briefing the Cabinet on January 3 about his meetings in the Bahamas, he made no mention of his comments to Kennedy or Macmillan about accepting nuclear weapons. Instead, referring to the Nassau agreement, he reported that it had become clear to him that "the day of the manned bomber had ended." Critically, he also indicated distaste for the president, who, he felt, had taken a generally anti-British approach during his talks with Macmillan.[26] At Nassau, the president had evinced obvious dislike of Diefenbaker and, having had his vacation to stew on this affront, it is unsurprising that the prime minister backed away from his pro-nuclear sentiments. Both his skepticism about Kennedy and his doubts about nuclear weapons were only worsened by an incident that occurred that same day.

While the Cabinet was meeting, American General Lauris Norstad, retiring from his post as NATO commander, arrived at a press conference. Having spent several weeks traveling to each NATO capital to bid farewell, Norstad landed in Ottawa on January 3. With the prime minister unable to greet him, he met with the governor general and then with members of the press alongside Air Marshall Miller and Pierre Sévigny, the associate defense minister. Opening the press conference with a prepared statement regarding general deficiencies in NATO and the steps taken to ameliorate them, Norstad singled out Canada's "tremendous progress" in strengthening the alliance, remarking that "Canada has been really quite outstanding in meeting its NATO commitments." Then queried as to whether the Canadian government had made a commitment to acquire tactical nuclear weapons for its fighter aircraft contingent in Europe, Norstad answered in the affirmative. When a reporter next asked "that if Canada does not accept nuclear weapons for these aeroplanes [does] that [mean] she is not actually fulfilling her NATO commitments?," Norstad responded, "I believe that's right."[27] Although cautious, Norstad had been unequivocal: Canada had made a commitment to take a nuclear role in Europe, one it had yet to live up to. The resulting reverberations in Canada were immense.

Diefenbaker would later come to view this press conference as one part of a "supra-governmental" plot between the Canadian and American militaries to defeat his government, while some historians have seen the incident as part of a US effort to "destabilize" the Canadian government. The charge has some truth in that the Canadian military had organized Norstad's program, and one of these organizers later admitted to a reporter that he had hoped that the press would raise the nuclear issue.[28] However, whether the Americans intended for the general to purposefully intervene with the aim of embarrassing the Canadian government on this issue is unclear given the lack of evidence to prove this contention. As Sévigny recalled, "the press was hellbent for leather in its efforts to destroy the Diefenbaker Government. Norstad knew that he was in a hot seat and did his best to be as evasive as possible."

Norstad, admitted the president of Canada's social democratic party, had been "under considerable pressure from Canadian newsmen." One British diplomat reported to London both that Norstad had spoken "honestly, and reluctantly" and that his colleagues in the Ottawa Embassy had remarked that they "were not putting on pressure over nuclear weapons." Indeed, US diplomats in Ottawa reported having not had notice of what Norstad was to say, while Willis Armstrong offered assurances that the retired general had not been acting in the capacity of a US spokesman and his statement "had come as a complete surprise to State Department." Moreover, given that McNamara had quietly fired Norstad, the general would have been an odd choice to be chosen as a cutthroat White House operative. Regardless, given the political climate, American officials must have expected that the general would be asked about Canada's nuclear weapons. Alternately, the State Department was also well aware that, as Delmar Carlson observed at this time, "there is always the hazard that something a high-ranking U.S. official would say could be misconstrued and viewed as interference in Canadian affairs."[29]

Innocent or not, Norstad's statement, which was confined only to the Canadian commitment to NATO, moved the whole nuclear issue to the forefront of Canada's political scene. Disagreeing with the general, the *Ottawa Citizen* acknowledged that the government had failed to meet its commitments. But, its editors argued, "this particular commitment can honourably be changed without reducing NATO's overall strength." The *Toronto Telegram*, criticizing the lack of a clear cut policy by both the Tories and the Liberals, and urging that nuclear weapons be accepted, argued that "the time for indecision and political evasion is past." In agreement with this view, the *Montreal Gazette* charged the government with pursuing a defense policy marked by "indecision and obscurity." The general's comments, it observed, had been neither unexpected nor unwarranted. Diefenbaker was therefore responsible for creating a "serious and embarrassing situation." Similarly, the *Globe and Mail* raised the worrying equivocations inherent in government policy: "We cannot have it both ways. We cannot be in NATO and not of it. We cannot accept the advantages of collective security without carrying our share of the burden." Stating that Norstad had given a healthy reminder in this regard, the *Globe*'s editors urged the acquisition of nuclear warheads. Their sole caveat was that Canada should ensure that it be fully consulted during a crisis for, as the *Globe*'s editors averred, Washington had failed to adequately consult with Ottawa over Cuba.[30]

With Parliament on break, there was no official reaction from the government until late that month, when Diefenbaker told the House of Commons that "some say you should take the advice of generals if they are eminent." However, he disagreed.[31] Many Canadians did agree, and Norstad's comments embarrassed them. For the Americans, the resulting criticism of the Tories was a godsend. In a report to Washington, Ambassador Butterworth sensed an increase in "public discussion" and "improved understanding" of the issue, which to-gether were increasing the pressure on Diefenbaker to escape his "present un-tenable position."[32] The pressure only mounted on January 12, when Pearson announced a drastic change in Liberal policy on nuclear weapons. After broach-ing Canada's obligations as a member of the Western alliance and as a partner with the United States in continental defense, the opposition leader blasted the government for failing to follow through on commitments made "in conti-nental and collective defence which can only be carried out by Canadian forces if nuclear warheads are available." The Tories' failure to meet Canada's obliga-tions left a gap in the defense of North America and Western Europe; a Liberal government would meet Canadian commitments, but would also work with the US eventually to remove the nuclear weapons from Canadian soil. Having long been a proponent of disarmament, Pearson was not only laying out a logical argument about the need to accept such weapons, he was also reacting to public opinion. Two days before his fateful announcement, party polling ranked nu-clear weapons and old age pensions as the winning issues in vote-rich Ontario and Quebec.[33] With good reason he reflected later that this "was the moment where I really became a politician." Yet because the move was blatantly politi-cal, and because it reversed Liberal policy on such a contentious issue, Pearson's claim to the moral high ground by restoring Canada's international reputation and meeting its commitments looked hollow. Angry at Pearson's volte-face, future prime minister Pierre Trudeau dubbed him the "defrocked priest of peace," while for similar reasons, Lloyd Axworthy, a future Liberal foreign min-ister, resigned, but briefly, from the Liberal Party.[34]

The Liberals' shift, praised by Butterworth as the "most significant and rational statement on defense" in recent years, did not greatly surprise the Americans, nor was it only the result of political expediency. On January 2, the day before Norstad's arrival in Ottawa, the Ottawa Embassy had been told that a change was coming, a development that had been expected for several months.[35] Paul Hellyer, the Liberal defense critic, had often discussed nuclear weapons with Charles Kiselyak, the Embassy's second secretary. In January 1962, for instance, the two had met for lunch, with Hellyer reviewing Liberal prospects in the expected election that year. Were the Liberals to form a gov-ernment, Hellyer stated that although he personally believed that BOMARCs were useless, he would be willing to press for the adoption of nuclear warheads. Meeting again with Kiselyak that November, Hellyer recounted a recent trip to Europe that he had taken with other MPs. In addition to glad-handing with other politicians from NATO countries, the parliamentary group had visited with Canadian forces stationed overseas. The low morale of these troops had worried Hellyer, as had talks with Norstad, who had been insistent that Ottawa was failing to meet its commitments. Taking these matters into account, the Liberal defense critic informed Kiselyak that "Canada has made a pledge and now must live up to it and accept nuclear weapons. Eighty percent of my colleagues agree." Hellyer was influential in prompting his party's change in defense policy that winter.[36]

Even though the Liberal defense critic's stance aligned with US interests, Kiselyak refused his request that the Embassy supply him with "whatever information propriety permits" regarding the commitments that Diefenbaker had made to the Americans. An internal State Department investigation confirmed that no classified information had been given to Hellyer, nor had anyone at the Ottawa Embassy urged Pearson to change his mind on nuclear weapons, evidence that the Americans were trying not to intervene in Canadian affairs.[37] Interestingly, Kiselyak had been party to an effort, coordinated by Livingston Merchant, to shape Canadian public opinion by briefing reporters on the American view of the nuclear weapons issue. Invited to Kiselyak's Rockcliffe Park home, members of the Ottawa press corps were plied with cocktails while Merchant and Kiselyak explained Canada's nuclear commitments. That this effort crossed the bounds of propriety seems doubtful, since briefing the press is a legitimate tool for diplomats. Charles Lynch, one of the reporters involved, waited until 1965 to break the story, and although remorseful for having waited so long to report the matter he recalled that at the time "it did not occur to me that Mr. Merchant was out of line in stating the American case since the Americans were our partners in the defence arrangements and had an important stake in their effectiveness."[38] Importantly, these briefings occurred before Merchant left Ottawa in May 1962, not in 1963, and so were quite divorced from the Norstad press conference and Pearson's policy reversal. Willing to brief reporters in a highly informal setting, Kiselyak was unwilling to cross a significant line by giving inside information to an opposition member of a foreign country's parliament. Nonetheless, the interplay between the US Embassy and the Liberal Party, combined with Norstad's remarks, has been fodder for those who believe that Diefenbaker's downfall was the result of collusion stemming from the prime minister's "refusal to jump when American power cracked its whip." The events that January seemed, as one Tory official recalled, "just as though someone had put together a great campaign, orchestrated it . . . I don't know whether this was inspired by American intelligence."[39] Evidence of a plot is highly circumstantial.

Representing good political judgment as well as a responsible decision vis-à-vis both defense policy and Canada's relationship with its key ally, Pearson's announcement shocked the Progressive Conservatives, who were reeling from poor polling numbers showing that since the June 1962 election, the Liberals had gained a fifteen point lead over the Tories, with the prime minister's personal popularity plummeting. "I have had a lot of worrying problems in the last week or so," Diefenbaker remarked to his brother on January 10, "and if I believed in Gallup polls the latest would be very disturbing."[40] Two days later came the Liberal announcement on nuclear weapons. Pearson's volte-face afforded the prime minister an opportunity to craft a cross-party consensus on nuclear weapons. As he had done with the question of Canadian membership in the OAS, championed by the Liberals, and, more contentiously, with supporting elements of the Grand Design, again supported by Pearson's party, Diefenbaker rejected an accord with his opponents. As Green informed his mother, the Liberal position "takes us off several hooks and I can't understand why [Pearson] didn't sit tight and let us stew!"[41] Yet the government was in a tough spot, and Canadian negotiators again took up the "missing part" procedure with their American counterparts. On January 15 the US Embassy delivered a definitive rejection of this proposal, effectively putting the nuclear talks on hold. Given the Pearson speech and the pro-nuclear statements made at a recent policy convention of the Progressive Conservative Party, Basil Robinson speculated that American officials were willing to "wait a little longer" in the hope that another Canadian election would lead to the possibility of a "palatable" solution.[42] Robinson was not far from the truth. On January 21, Kennedy accepted the advice of aides who emphasized that although Diefenbaker "probably feels that the US has been working with and for Lester Pearson" it was "best to stand fast. This course is easy to justify militarily . . . and it could materially enhance Diefenbaker's difficulties as the election approaches."[43] His credibility in Washington shredded, the Canadian prime minister found no sympathy from the United States. The result was a breathless display of equivocation in the House of Commons.

Still hoping to play both sides of the debate and to defend his position from both external and internal criticism, on January 25 Diefenbaker delivered a two-hour explanation of his defense policy to the House of Commons. Averring that no commitment by his government had been broken, he contended that the Nassau agreement necessitated a revision of Canadian policy because it cast doubt on the bomber threat and emphasized the primacy of nuclear missiles, thereby signaling "a tremendous step—a change in the philosophy of defence; a change in the views of NATO." Then mentioning several weapons systems that had been abandoned for being obsolete, Diefenbaker implied that BOMARC could be abandoned as well. "Every now and then," he inveighed, "some new white hope of rocketry goes into the scrap pile." Conceding, however, that Canada did have nuclear commitments, particularly in the context of NATO where one of the missions for Canadian air squadrons included "delivering nuclear weapons," Diefenbaker revealed that secret negotiations were being carried out with the United States and had "been going on quite forcibly for two months or more." His government, he concluded, would "negotiate with the United States so that, as I said earlier, in case of need nuclear warheads will be made readily available," but would also "have a policy that remains flexible so as to meet changing conditions. We will do nothing to extend the nuclear family.["]44 Diefenbaker's policy was flexible indeed. He had hinted that the weapons could be scrapped while also acknowledging that talks were ongoing with the Americans to pave the way for the acceptance of warheads. A better course would have been a firm statement either accepting or rejecting a nuclear role for Canada.

Predictably, Diefenbaker's equivocations failed to dampen criticism of the government. "Flexible confusion" was how the *Globe and Mail* characterized the statement. In comments typical of press reaction, its editors noted, as the prime minister had, that the circumstances surrounding defense procurement were quite fluid, but that fluidity "cannot be an excuse for doing nothing, for vacillating while our allies carry the burdens."[45] Having believed prior to the speech that he had finally secured the prime minister's agreement to accept nuclear weapons, Harkness was taken aback at the statement. Three days after Diefenbaker's speech he issued a statement declaring himself "surprised and disappointed" by the prime minister's comments and affirming that the government possessed "a definite policy for the acquisition of nuclear arms." This clarification and the effort at the Tories' policy convention favoring a pro-nuclear stance showcased growing fractures within the Progressive Conservative party, but the prime minister was unmoved. Defending his own speech, he told the House of Commons that his comments required no interpretation, as he had been "very clear, very direct and very comprehensive."[46] American policymakers disagreed.

US officials took offence with several aspects of Diefenbaker's speech. Only an hour afterward, Ivan White complained to Harkness, in a reference to the PM's disclosure of the ongoing negotiations, that it was unusual for a "top secret subject [to] move to classified in thirty-seconds." Diefenbaker's public revelation must have rankled those Americans who recalled the prime minister's own outrage at the September 1961 White House press leak, which had revealed negotiations between Washington and Ottawa and had scuttled momentum on nuclear negotiations.[47] Butterworth, meanwhile, swung into action. First, summoning the American consuls in Canada to Ottawa, he canvassed them about the potential results of a Canadian election. They concluded that the Liberals would likely form a minority government. As he later admitted to an interviewer, "with that at the back of one's mind, never to be brought out very openly, I recommended that we set the record straight." In an understandably caustic though hyperbolic cable to Washington, he characterized the prime minister's speech not simply as another attempt at procrastination, but as a "masterpiece [of] deception and persuasion" designed purposefully "to change Canada's defense relationship with us." If Diefenbaker were allowed to get away with his "shabby performance," the result would be the weakening of the bilateral alliance, leaving the United States to "face the critical years ahead with a half-hearted and irresponsible ally." Turning next to the effect of the speech within Canada, Butterworth attacked its misleading language, which was aimed at "destroying [the] clarity of national debate which was beginning to emerge in recent weeks." Added to this concern was a sense that the prime minister was determined to cast himself as the "defender of Canadian sovereignty" against the United States. Butterworth then came to the point of his message. Since the speech was "full of red herrings and nonsequiturs readily apparent to us but not likely to be recognized as such by most Canadians," he advocated that Washington challenge Diefenbaker's comments through a public statement. Knowing that it was highly undiplomatic for the United States to weigh in on a matter with strong domestic overtones, he pointed out that it was the prime minister who had "plunged the US into [the] Canadian political arena" on a question "vital" to American security.[48]

Butterworth's call for a tit-for-tat response was well-received in Washington. George Ball, serving as acting secretary of state while Rusk was away from Washington, discussed this recommendation with William Tyler, who, at Butterworth's insistence, had come down to Ottawa for the meeting of the consuls. Despite admitting that Kennedy would likely oppose the move, Tyler and Ball agreed on the need to publicly correct the record. At Ball's insistence, a working group was formed to draft a statement; its members were Rufus Smith, Willis Armstrong, and Colonel Lawrence Legere, a NSC official tasked with formulating policy toward a proposed NATO nuclear force.[49] These three men set about crafting a response to Diefenbaker's speech. Armstrong and Smith, both well-versed on the nuclear file and keen observers of Canadian affairs, were in no mood to take the prime minister's recent statement lightly. In reporting on their progress to McGeorge Bundy, Legere observed that Smith and Armstrong, "the experts in the premises," strongly favored publicly countering the prime minister and did "not feel that this will inflame Diefenbaker into an anti-American outburst or that it will benefit his cause." For Smith and Armstrong, the foremost authorities on Canada within the State Department, the prime minister had now become a problem, and no matter what action they took, he would continue to be an impediment. In their view, Diefenbaker would "pursue his own course regardless of what we say." The statement that they drew up aimed "to keep the record straight with a few facts, which will afford ammunition to Diefenbaker's opponents both within and without the Conservative Party."[50]

Armstrong and Smith's reactions give an indication of how frustrated US officials had become with Canada. In their reports and studies, in their cables and recommendations, and in their dealings with their Canadian counterparts these two diplomats had long emphasized the importance of not provoking Canadian nationalists; of giving due respect to Canada's sovereignty and Canadians' supposed inferiority complex; and of avoiding the use of Washington's preponderant power in dealings with Ottawa. In the wake of the prime minister's statement, they proposed a different approach, one that ignored the accepted practice of quiet diplomacy. As one scholar has recently argued, the press release was "a risky move" that was not supported by the "State Department's Canada specialists, who were given only a fleeting opportunity to comment on a draft of the release before it was made public, did not doubt that it was factually correct, but worried that it would be a diplomatic disaster." Yet neither Smith nor Armstrong seems to have opposed the plan and their involvement was more than fleeting. As Armstrong would boast to an interviewer years later: "I'm the guy who wrote the press release! I went back the other day and read it. I thought it was pretty good."[51] Through his conduct, Diefenbaker had shredded his credibility with even the most sympathetic members of the US diplomatic corps.

With tempers flaring, Basil Robinson learned from contacts in the State Department that a public response was being considered. At his urging, Charles Ritchie told Tyler not to give into the temptation of a public rebuke, which would have an "adverse effect" on Canada–US relations. But the Americans were not dissuaded.[52] By the evening of January 29, Armstrong, Smith, and Legere had completed a draft for Ball. In a covering memorandum approved by Tyler, Armstrong recorded that the statement had been designed to "clarify the record and sweep away the confusion" generated by Diefenbaker. He was careful to note the risks involved in moving forward with this plan: Canadian public opinion could be inflamed; there was "no assurance of an early election in Canada; and a Liberal victory in the next election is by no means certain." There was a distinct possibility, then, that Diefenbaker would remain in office. So while the statement could harm relations and was certainly no panacea to those outstanding problems "where we urgently need Canadian cooperation," it was seen to be a necessary step. Concluding with the prediction that the statement "will inspire respect," Armstrong urged Ball to approve the measure. "Diefenbaker," he concluded, "will or will not decide to use an anti-American line, almost regardless of what we do, and the statement should not push him into any new actions injurious to us."[53] The press release was a gamble, and Armstrong urged throwing the dice.

Signing off on the plan the next afternoon, Ball called Tyler, who reiterated his support: "Diefenbaker likes to play these things." Ball then secured Bundy's approval.[54] Half an hour later, and forty-five minutes before the press release was due to be issued, the Ottawa Embassy delivered copies of the statement to the Department of External Affairs, and, in Washington, Robinson was summoned to the State Department. Confronted by Armstrong and Delmar Carlson, he was given his own copy and was then treated to a lecture. The nuclear issue, Armstrong underscored, "had been discussed, considered and negotiated over a period of four years" and yet no resolution had been reached, the result of political concerns not technical issues. Reiterating both that the missing part procedure was unfeasible and that the Nassau agreement was not relevant to the matter at hand, he argued that while it would be excusable to scrap weapons that were obsolete, it was inexcusable to get rid of weapons that were obsolete only because they had not been provided with the necessary armaments. Washington's hand had been forced, Armstrong added, because Diefenbaker had disclosed the secret negotiations, a revelation that had sparked both considerable press speculation and concern about the Nassau agreement among other NATO members. The press release was aimed at clarifying these issues.[55]

As Robinson left the State Department, the fateful declaration was issued to the dozen Canadian correspondents in Washington and to a handful of American reporters. Judging it "a document phrased so bluntly that it might have been addressed by the Kremlin to a balky satellite," one of these Canadian journalists remarked that "it is, at times, difficult to appreciate how seriously Americans take the differences between their country and ours."[56] Beginning with a description of the commitments that Canada had made to requisition weaponry requiring nuclear weapons, the press release affirmed that while neglecting to arm these weapons, Ottawa had "not as yet proposed any arrangement sufficiently practical to contribute effectively to North American defense." The statement also took exception with Diefenbaker's comments about the Nassau agreement, offered an overview of the continued threat of Soviet nuclear bombers, and contended that "an effective continental defense against this common threat is necessary." Concluding that the acquisition of nuclear warheads by Canadian forces would not mean an expansion of the nuclear club as custody would remain with the United States, the final sentence reiterated that "joint control fully consistent with national sovereignty can be worked out."[57] With this point-by-point refutation of Diefenbaker's recent speech, the US government had called Canada's prime minister a liar.

Unsurprisingly, many Canadians were shocked and outraged. Attacking this "unfortunate intrusion," the Globe and Mail warned Kennedy not to "delude himself that he is talking to satellites," while the Toronto Star criticized the State Department for its "tactless" move. In contrast to the thrust of these editorials, the Winnipeg Free Press, a paper not fond of Diefenbaker, felt that the Americans were "justified" in attempting to clear away the "confusion and misrepresentation" inherent in the prime minister's speech. Offering a mixed review, the Montreal Gazette attacked the "blunt and rough treatment of an old friend and close neighbour." Even so, the Gazette's editors allowed that Canadian defense policy "has long been incoherent," and they implored the government to come to a decision. Similarly, the Ottawa Citizen's editors briefly chided the United States before explaining to readers that "the truth is that the government does not want to have a policy, which is to say that it has not the will to govern. The recourse for the Canadian people should be obvious."[58] The Liberals, meanwhile, declared that it was "surprising that the United States government found it necessary to issue a statement at all. It was prompted no doubt by a desire to help clear up the confusion produced and compounded by conflicting versions of our defence policy." As for Diefenbaker, in the House of Commons he railed against the State Department's "unprecedented" conduct. Acknowledging that his government "will, as always, honour its obligations," he vowed not to succumb to "external domination or interference" in making decisions. Turning to domestic critics, the prime minister drew a parallel between Pearson's recent statements on the nuclear issue and arguments contained in the press release. Insinuating that a plot was afoot, "Canada," he warned, "is determined to remain a firm ally but that does not mean that she should be a satellite." With the situation in the House of Commons inflamed, MPs engaged in a lengthy emergency debate throughout January 31, with the three opposition parties attacking the State Department and the government in equal measure.[59]

This parliamentary and press reaction was being closely monitored by US observers keen to elicit whether or not their gamble had been a success. From Ottawa, White reported to Rusk that there were no demonstrations in front of the Embassy and so there was no need to panic; instead, they should let the Canadians "debate it out." In a similar vein, Butterworth, who had left for New Orleans to address the American Bar Association, urged Rusk to "play it cool. We don't want to give the impression we are precipitating a government crisis."[60] Asking Ball for reports on the situation in Canada, Bundy wondered whether "Diefenbaker was going to crack back at us." Insistent that it would be hard for the prime minister to say much about US interference in Canadian affairs since he had revealed secret negotiations while distorting the record for political reasons, Ball reiterated: "We can't let these fellows get away with it." They turned then to the president's reaction: Bundy had neglected to notify Kennedy about the press release in advance, likely in the hope of shielding the president from blame. Perhaps he had also sensed that the president would not have approved of this measure, for when Kennedy found out what had been done he was upset, for, referring to de Gaulle's veto of British entry into the EEC, he warned against "getting in too many fights in one week." Diefenbaker, Kennedy worried, "might decide to call an election" and then stoke anti-Americanism in Canada during the resulting campaign. When Ball then informed the president that the prime minister had already told the House of Commons that he "wouldn't be pushed by America," Kennedy urged calm: with Rusk due to speak at a press conference the following day, he suggested taking the line that the press release was simply meant to clarify questions raised by Diefenbaker. Cognizant that Diefenbaker "has always been running against us," Kennedy reiterated the need for caution.[61] As for any animus that the president may have felt toward Ball, Bundy, and Butterworth for the press release, none of the men lost their positions.

Washington then moved into damage control. At his press conference on February 1, the secretary of state stuck to a statement prepared by Bundy, who had wanted to "turn away wrath from the fact that we made a statement, and draw attention to what we actually said in it." Beginning by evoking the "strong tradition of fair play" between Canada and the United States, Rusk expressed regret for any offence that may have been given. Nonetheless, he emphasized that "the need to make some clarifying statement arose from a situation not of our making" but out of a need to correct statements made in Ottawa. He concluded by stating, as he had in the past, that the decision to acquire nuclear weapons was both difficult and one for Canadians to choose of their own free will. No apology had been made. Reacting to these comments, Diefenbaker told reporters, "Canada is not part of the New Frontier and I think the State Department realizes it."[62] Concerned with this rhetoric, Kennedy asked Tyler to report on "whether Diefenbaker felt we had given him a sufficiently good issue for him to go to the country and run against the United States."[63] A roundup of public and press opinion quickly compiled by the Ottawa Embassy concluded that initial anger at Washington was subsiding in the face of a "strong swing" toward a view that the US action had been justified in order to clarify the facts. The United States, the Canadian press was acknowledging, "had long been patient and forbearing."[64] In an expanded appraisal, Butterworth took a long view. Since Diefenbaker's election in 1957, he argued, "we have—doubtless correctly—tolerated" a "neurotic" Canadian outlook on the world. However, hopes that Canada would adopt a "more realistic understanding" of global affairs had been dashed. A "sudden dose of cold water" had been necessary, and negative reaction would be short-lived. Consequently, he wrote, the "traditional psychopathic accusations of unwarranted US interference in domestic Canadian affairs" would subside, leaving Canadians to confront several "hard realities." Believing that Diefenbaker was content to live in a "dream world," the ambassador predicted that the Canadian people would no longer tolerate the PM's "irresponsible nonsense."[65] A reflection of his bellicose approach to diplomacy and his sense of US superiority, Butterworth's analysis also proved perceptive.

True to Butterworth's prediction, a backlash against the prime minister set in. Since issuing his own clarification of the prime minister's speech, Harkness had been mulling over his future. At a Cabinet meeting on February 3 he urged Diefenbaker to resign by noting that the "people of the nation, party, cabinet, and he have lost confidence in the prime minister."[66] His comments sparked a Cabinet revolt, which Diefenbaker defeated. Afterward, Harkness resigned, becoming the first Canadian minister to step down on a matter of principle since the Second World War. Looking upon Harkness's move with evident satisfaction, Butterworth believed that the reasoning behind the defense minister's departure would not be lost upon either other Cabinet members or Canadian voters. Prompted in part by a failed effort by government ministers to force the prime minister's ouster, Harkness was followed six days later by Pierre Sévigny and George Hees. In stepping down, both ministers cited Diefenbaker's anti-Americanism and indecision as the reasons for their move.[67] Most importantly, a motion of nonconfidence in the government had been passed in the House of Commons on February 5. An election was called the following day. Diefenbaker's government had collapsed, and American actions had seemingly brought about this turn of events.

While the intention of forcing Diefenbaker's downfall was not explicitly discussed or alluded to in the run up to the press release, mention had been made of using the press statement as a means of aiding Diefenbaker's opponents, and recognizing the Tories' growing unpopularity, US policymakers had seized the moment. The statement, Butterworth enthused, had "set in motion" the Tories' collapse.[68] Nevertheless, the press release could have backfired by rallying outraged Canadians to the Progressive Conservatives. That it helped bring down Diefenbaker's government seems to have surprised Bundy who remarked to Ball soon after that "we didn't know how big a bomb we were setting off."[69] Given his bewilderment, it seems only prudent to view as boasting Bundy's comment to President Lyndon Johnson a year later: "I might add that I myself have been sensitive to the need for being extra polite to Canadians ever since George Ball and I knocked over the Diefenbaker government by one incautious press release."[70] Far from knocking over the Tories, the Americans were simply one of many contributing factors.

Throughout 1962 Diefenbaker had stumbled on a number of fronts. In the June election the Tories had gone from a massive majority to a minority government, an undoubted reflection of public dissatisfaction. Since then, the government had been fumbling with an economic crisis as well as with several foreign policy issues, hardly to the benefit of its popularity. Even before the train of events begun by Norstad, *Maclean's*, citing Canada's sluggish economy, ongoing high levels of unemployment, and the "unsettled" international situation that gave added impetus to the need for a decision on defense, called for an election.[71] In a front-page editorial on the day following the government's collapse, the *Globe and Mail* attacked the prime minister and urged him not to run in the campaign. Blaming his mishandling of the economy, it also criticized his "indecision" and "paralysis" when it came to external affairs. Still upset about the State Department press release, the *Globe's* editors nevertheless noted that this statement, at least, had "told the truth." Adopting a similar approach, the *Ottawa Citizen* asked voters to elect a "government that can help accelerate the country's retarded economic growth, that can help repair the damage done to the country's relations with its allies, that can help promote broader free trading concepts than we have now." Only "competent" politicians could accomplish these necessary tasks, and "in six years, the Diefenbaker government has proved itself incapable of such action."[72] There was discontent with Diefenbaker in Canada, and nuclear weaponry was simply the issue that sparked a political firestorm.

The Kennedy administration was facing its own domestic critics. The American press panned the press release. Pointing to Canada's small size and to Canadians' worry "about the danger of being swallowed up," the *Washington Post* emphasized: "We can afford some distemper in Ottawa; we cannot afford to respond in kind." Eminent columnist Walter Lippmann contended that the differences with Canada should "have been handled by quiet diplomacy," Arthur Krock, the dean of Washington correspondents, characterized the press release as "one of the most ham-handed, ill-conceived and undiplomatic employments in the record of American diplomacy," while the *New York Times* attacked the statement for having further damaged the Western alliance and for having "naturally aroused deep resentment among Canadians of all parties." Through "inept diplomacy," the White House, complained the *Chicago Tribune*, had "invited the Canadian allegation that the United States was attempting to push Canada around and was seeking to impose external domination over Canadian affairs."[73] If the press release had a silver lining for Canadians, it was that it focused American press attention northward and prompted sympathetic comment.

Beyond the press corps, the White House also received criticism from political foes, with Republican congressmen denouncing the statement and Arizona senator and presumptive GOP presidential candidate Barry Goldwater complaining that Kennedy had left "our neighbor and staunch ally, Canada, seething with anger and anti-American sentiment."[74] Moreover, on February 4 Rusk was called before the Senate Foreign Relations Subcommittee on Canadian Affairs, a body that seldom met. Highly critical of the State Department, subcommittee chairman George Aiken, a Vermont Republican with a long established interest in bilateral relations, questioned why such a "clumsy" approach had been adopted when past experience with Canada indicated that "overt" pressure seldom did more than injure Canadian "national pride." Picking up on this theme, Senate Foreign Relations Committee Chairman William Fulbright grilled Rusk on why this action had been taken when it was clearly "liable to re-elect Diefenbaker." Another heavyweight, Democratic Majority Leader Mike Mansfield, complained that whatever the possible merits of issuing the press release, it had angered "our closest friends" and was bound to have dire long-term effects on bilateral relations. Defending his department, the secretary outlined the history of the nuclear issue and the reasoning behind the press release. Here Rusk made it clear that he, his staff, and the administration were acting to defend US interests. Insisting that the Canadians had "agreed to accept certain weapons systems which are totally or partially ineffective without nuclear armament," he explained that Diefenbaker, "largely for political reasons," had procrastinated on the nuclear issue for almost four years. The administration had been patient, that is, until the prime minister had made it clear that he wanted to prevaricate further and had "brought into the debate U.S. policies, programs, and relation-ships" outside of the realm of bilateral relations. The senators did not challenge this view of a reluctant administration forced to act. Moreover, it was a view-point that was entirely accurate. As the *New York Times* soon opined: "It is un-fortunate that a clumsy and ill-considered release by the State Department trig-gered the crisis, but the issue does involve the security of the United States and the American people obviously have a direct and vital interest in it."[75]

Throughout the Diefenbaker years, in a host of intelligence summaries, po-sition papers, and diplomatic briefings, US officials had noted that both the Canadian prime minister and Canadian nationalism could frustrate American goals and policies, but ultimately they acknowledged that Canada's actions were not inimical to the United States. In early 1963 this assessment had changed, as did US tactics, which ignored quiet diplomacy. Taking this line in a report on the incident for Kennedy, Bundy first apologized to the president for having made "an obvious error" by clearing the statement over the phone with Ball "with-out giving you a whack at it." However, he defended the press release. Offering Kennedy a lengthy timeline of Ottawa's procrastination on the nuclear issue since 1961—and making no mention of Canada's actions or inactions during the Cuban missile crisis—this report contended that there was nothing in Diefenbaker's "record to lead anyone to believe that he would not have pursued a crooked course in his own self-interest right through to re-election . . . pluck-ing the Eagle's tail feathers all along the way." A strong reaction had been neces-sary and correct, because, after all, "the prime fact to be evaluated is that the Diefenbaker government has fallen and three of his ministers have resigned."[76] Such *ex post facto* logic showcased the administration's arrogance, which had seldom come into play in dealings with Canada to that point. But the report was also a sound assessment of the situation. Privately, Basil Robinson admit-ted that the State Department's action had been "an outburst of long pent-up exasperation," and while not defending the press release, he did acknowledge the need to put "this deplorable fortnight" into "the long perspective."[77]

Accustomed to a serious yet friendly rapport with their American col-leagues, Canadian diplomats were concerned by what seemed to be a new US approach to foreign policy. An official in Green's office prepared a study for the minister in which he traced evidence of "Kennedy's 'tougher' attitude" toward US allies. No less disturbed by this "clumsy and ill-advised violation of normal diplomatic procedures," Ed Ritchie and Harry Carter, head of the US Division, agreed that the press release could not be justified no matter how frustrated Washington had felt. Carter, in particular, was concerned that American poli-cymakers would come to see their move as setting a precedent, especially be-cause the collapse of Diefenbaker's government appeared to vindicate their approach. He and Ritchie decided, therefore, that in private discussions with their US counterparts, Canadian diplomats should ensure that they in no way indicated approval of a "government by press release" method to resolving differences. From Washington, Robinson chimed in to note that the Embassy was seeking to "maintain correct and pleasant official and personal relations" with the State Department, but the "melancholy fact" was that "the conduct of business is seriously prejudiced by the lack of trust" between Ottawa and Washington.[78] Even the diplomatic relationship appeared to be frayed.

Diefenbaker and Green, meanwhile, had already issued a protest, recalling Ambassador Ritchie for consultations, a move unprecedented and, as yet, unparalleled in the Canada–US relationship. Arriving in the Canadian capital "in the hope of repairing the damage" to bilateral relations, Ritchie confided to his diary that he "soon realized that the government was not interested in patching things up and hoped to win an election on the issue of United States interference in our affairs." His thoughts on this campaign strategy were mixed. Disapproving "of the manufactured anti-Americanism of the government . . . deep down I feel satisfaction at hearing the Canadian government finally lash out at the omniscience and unconscious arrogance of Washington." Believing that the White House had not noticed his recall, he convinced Diefenbaker and Green to allow him to return to his post.[79] Upon returning to Washington, Ritchie observed what seemed to him to be a concerted goodwill campaign by the White House and State Department to offer "many expressions of friendship toward Canada," along "with a certain apologetic nervousness of manner." Encountering Ritchie at a dinner party, Rusk proposed a toast to Canadians and Americans "getting together and settling their troubles." At another soirée several weeks later, Ball went "out of his way to express friendship for Canada." After similar encounters with Tyler and Bundy, Ritchie reported to Ottawa these "indications of an apologetic attitude," which fell short of an actual apology.[80]

With no regrets about having intervened, American officials sought to ensure that no further damage was done to relations with the Canadians. Concurring with advice from the Ottawa Embassy that all elements of the government refrain from making any comments concerning Canada, Tyler noted: "We have little to gain and lots to lose in making statements in an election period when some elements will be seeking to use almost any statement emanating from a United States Government source against our interests."[81] Kennedy supported this stance. Fielding questions at a press conference in early February, he refrained from any mention of Canada, despite a rather pointed question about Diefenbaker and the skepticism expressed by some allies regarding what had been agreed to at Nassau.[82] As his enquiries about Canadian reaction to the press release indicate, Kennedy was concerned with public sentiment north of the border and he wanted to keep things quiet. Asked about relations with Canada by reporters in March, he indicated only a desire that "having been joined together by nature" the two North American countries would again work closely together.[83]

Sharing some of the president's concern over the extent to which the campaign could be an anti-American one, US diplomats actually had fairly bright expectations for the election. In early February Ivan White learned from separate conversations with three senior Tory MPs that many of their caucus members had concerns about anti-American rhetoric being used in their party's campaign. Reflecting on this information, and with reference to an historically anti-American election campaign, White made a bold prediction: "The ghost of 1911 will be laid; we will have a workable relationship in defense matters; the Conservative party will be out of power, and US–Canadian relationships will be on a much sounder basis than during the past four years." He was quite sure that despite the worried of some within the State Department, who believed that the Ottawa Embassy's advice had led them "down an uncomfortable garden path," the election appeared to be proceeding "in the U.S. national interest."[84] A report jointly authored by the Canada Desk and the State Department's Bureau of Intelligence and Research arrived at similar conclusions, "that though anti-Americanism will certainly be present, and could become very dirty, especially if Prime Minister Diefenbaker senses he is definitely losing the election, it will probably not be the dominant theme."[85] Written only five days into the campaign, these were rosy predictions, and, over the following two months, US officials tried to ensure that these forecasts came true.

Unfortunately for the Americans, the prime minister was performing spectacularly. The Tories' campaign dealt with a host of issues, with nuclear weapons and relations with the United States looming large. Playing up the need to protect Canada's independence and to safeguard the country against American interference to a crowd in Lindsay, Ontario, for instance, Diefenbaker criticized Pearson for taking advice from "American Generals." To an audience in Winnipeg he defended his government's record on military matters, arguing that no commitments had been broken. Then, decrying BOMARC as being inadequate to defend against intercontinental ballistic missiles, he derided the Liberals' changed defense policy telling his listeners that the choice was between a prime minister prone to "political gyrations" or one who would discharge Canada's responsibilities "in co-operation" with other countries "but never from coercion."[86] Diefenbaker's position on nuclear weapons had gyrated too. But his rhetoric of resistance to outside pressure resonated with many Canadians. Analyzing the prime minister's campaign tactics in a report for the president, the NSC's William Brubeck characterized Diefenbaker as a strong and vigorous candidate. "The campaigning," he pointed out, "has acted upon Diefenbaker like a powerful shot of adrenalin. He is not pursing any openly anti-American line but his 'Made in Canada' policy often has anti-American overtones." Rufus Smith was equally impressed. In a report to which he attached both a transcript and a recording of a speech by the Tory leader, Smith advised that notes be made of Diefenbaker's "efforts to justify his defense policy, his readiness to adduce, out of context official American statements or positions in support of his arguments, and his efforts to portray himself as the defender of Canadian sovereignty under attack from powerful forces." No admirer of Diefenbaker, Butterworth struck a similar chord, admitting that the Tory leader, beginning in a "nearly hopeless position," had, "by sheer frenetic activity," made himself a serious contender.[87]

On Pearson, the Americans offered mixed reviews. In contrast to Diefenbaker's performance, the Ottawa Embassy found the Liberal leader dull. Failing "to generate much warmth," the Liberal campaign was overly reliant on "gimmicks," which tarnished the "carefully built-up image of Pearson as sober and responsible if uninspired." There were other factors that explained the lackluster performance of the Liberal campaign: Canadian memories of two decades of Liberal rule; the Liberals' mixed record as an opposition party; and Pearson's current position as the forerunner in the election, making him the prime target for the other parties. To American officials, these elements worked against an easy Liberal victory and it seemed doubtful that Pearson, "dry and undramatic" and "already a two-time loser," could reverse this situation by winning more than a minority government. Regardless, a victory for Pearson was the only desired result. Throughout the campaign, he expounded on his argument that the Progressive Conservative government had "demoralized our defence services, betrayed our allies and it jeopardized" Canada's reputation. Canada, Pearson reiterated, was "part of an alliance to keep the free world strong enough so it will not be attacked. If we do not do our share in that alliance, we will have little influence among our friends."[88] The Americans applauded these types of statements and approved of the way in which Pearson was "courageously" pursuing the nuclear weapons issue in the face of criticism about being too close to the United States. Indeed, at one rally, the Liberal leader was denounced by hecklers as "an American slave" and a "Yankee lover," and he spoke stoically as protestors burned a US flag.[89]

That the Americans favored Pearson is clear; that Washington intervened in the election to help the Liberals is likely; that this assistance proved vital in the Tories' defeat is murky. In 1961—well before the Kennedy–Diefenbaker relationship soured—senior Liberal officials Walter Gordon and Keith Davey had hired Lou Harris, a pollster affiliated with the Democratic Party. His polling proved helpful to the Liberals during the 1962 federal election, even if Pearson refused to follow all of Harris's advice—he retained his trademark bowtie, though it did not sit well with voters.[90] Harris, owner of a private firm, was well within his rights to work for whomever he wished. But the situation in 1963 was far more divisive; no doubt aware that his presence might be misconstrued, he allegedly he sought and received Kennedy's "unofficial blessing" to return to Canada to help the Liberals, apparently traveling north under an assumed name and with a fake passport. He stayed briefly, meeting with Liberal Party officials, but left the polling to an American associate, Oliver Quayle, and only "occasionally" spoke with Walter Gordon. During the campaign, meanwhile, Kennedy seems to have contacted Harris about poll numbers on a handful of occasions.[91] Assisting Pearson, and working against Diefenbaker, Harris later recalled, was "one of the highlights of my life." Yet to what extent this state of the art polling affected the election is unclear. "I think it was helpful," admitted Richard O'Hagan, an assistant to Pearson, "but not a determinant."[92]

Was this assistance given by Kennedy to the Liberals an inexcusable intervention in Canadian affairs? Perhaps. Harris ran a private business and had been hired by the Liberals well in advance of the 1963 election. However, if he was indeed in Canada at Kennedy's behest—with a fake passport to boot—then this intervention was beyond the pale. In contrast, the State Department press release—a more important act of intervention—was perfectly justifiable: Diefenbaker had prevaricated and lied on an issue of US national security and seemed to call into question the future of NATO, and so the Americans responded in kind by calling him to task. Still, it is hard to get too excited about polling, a method of gauging opinion that, at best, is of questionable credibility. In any event, Harris's work for the Liberals was the extent of American involvement in the election, for US officials were guided by the directive to avoid provoking the Tories or stoking nationalist anger. Their maxim, joked Legere, was "Remember January 30."[93] Both the need for silence and the raw emotions created by the campaign were vividly displayed at several points in March.

First, when Richard King, the US vice consul in Vancouver, attended a local rally for Green, the Canadian foreign minister accused him of "improper" conduct by "checking up" on him. Informed by his staff that King's actions were an accepted part of diplomatic practice, Green ordered that instructions be sent to all Canadian posts abroad barring Canada's diplomats from attending political gatherings. Butterworth's response, meanwhile, was to send a cautionary message to all US diplomats in Canada, warning them that given the "exposed nerves" of various Canadian politicians it was advisable to keep a low profile.[94] Next, with a week to go before election day, the Pentagon released testimony that McNamara had given before the House Appropriations Committee in February in which he admitted that the BOMARC installations were largely meant to "draw fire" away from important sites rather than provide protection. The missiles, one of the congressmen questioning the defense secretary then remarked, were simply "expensive targets." Indeed. McNamara's testimony provided evidence that BOMARC was hardly an effective means of protecting Canadian cities. *Time* noted, then, that his comments were "an unexpected present" for the Canadian prime minister, who, seizing on this testimony, was quick to denounce the Liberals and the Americans for seeking to turn Canada into a "burnt sacrifice."[95]

McNamara's statement brought nuclear weapons back to the forefront of the campaign. The Ottawa Embassy judged that not only had the testimony "bolstered" the Progressive Conservatives' position during the final days of electioneering, but also that it would make it hard for any future government to justify BOMARC. Reassuring Kennedy that McNamara's testimony "isn't coming through at all," Lou Harris advised that if the issue went unmentioned by the White House, then the Liberals could refocus attention back on their platform.[96] Upset by the Defense Department's indiscretion, Kennedy chastised McNamara for having "strengthened Diefenbaker's hand considerably and increased our difficulties." He therefore advised Pentagon officials to "be on alert for our political, as well as military, security." During a NSC meeting that same day, Kennedy expressed further discomfort by commenting that Diefenbaker now might win and that anti-Americanism might be adopted as a popular political tool in Britain and France. Problems with Canada, the president felt, reflected growing divides within the Western alliance.[97] With Diefenbaker and Charles de Gaulle both expressing hostility toward Washington, Kennedy was right to be fearful.

Given the president's concerns, it seems odd, then, that he would have contacted Pearson to offer the Liberal leader his help. Yet Kennedy is alleged to have "phoned Pearson himself several times with campaign advice—an intervention that, had it been known at the time, would have won the election for Diefenbaker."[98] Others have pointed to a single call on March 28, when the president arranged for journalist Max Freedman, a confidante who happened to be a Liberal supporter, to call Pearson on his behalf. Reaching the Liberal leader via a payphone in a hotel lobby, Freedman apparently asked Pearson whether there was anything that the White House could do on his behalf. Sensibly, Pearson is said to have responded: "For God's sake, tell the president to keep his mouth shut."[99] A curious incident, upon which contemporaneous documents shed no light but considerable doubt, given Kennedy's worry over statements by US officials being seized upon by the Tories. Pearson later admitted that Freedman indeed rang him, but that the reporter simply wanted "to see how we were doing" on the campaign and that his own concern was that the call could be traced back to the White House Press Room. Richard O'Hagan recalled that Pearson and Freedman spoke but was unsure if the president spoke as well, while Freedman, interviewed later, could not recall the phone call itself, though his memory had suffered as a result of a heart attack in April 1963.[100] Perhaps this story was conflated with another event, which occurred in early February, when Bundy used Freedman as a conduit through which to assure the Canadian government that Kennedy had had nothing to do with the press release. Freedman's overture on behalf of the Americans produced what one Canadian diplomat described as "a bit of an explosion in our Minister's office. It is most usual for the White House to choose an active Canadian Liberal as a diplomatic instrument in dealing with our country."[101] On the question of Kennedy's personal involvement, we might turn to Walter Gordon, who in May, following the election, asked Pearson to tell the president "how grateful I was to him for being silent on certain occasions when any comment of any kind would have been most damaging."[102]

Freedman's call on Bundy's behalf was not the only questionable journalistic incident to occur in the campaign. In February, *Newsweek*—a magazine with close links to Kennedy—splashed an unflattering picture of the prime minister across its cover. Inside, the magazine opined that "in full oratorical flight" Diefenbaker was "a sight not soon to be forgotten: the India-rubber features twist and contort in grotesque and gargoyle-like grimaces; beneath the electric gray V of the hairline, the eyebrows beat up and down like bats' wings; the agate-blue eyes blaze forth cold fire. Elderly female Tory supporters find Diefenbaker's face rugged, kind, pleasant, and even soothing; his enemies insist that it is sufficient for barring Tory rallies to children under sixteen."[103] It is certainly plausible that Kennedy may, as some have suggested, asked *Newsweek* to print this devastating critique. As Diefenbaker wrote in his memoirs, "Who, among those who voted in 1963, will ever forget the Kennedy-conceived message conveyed to the Canadian electors by the cover and contents of the 18 February issue of Newsweek – its editor was President Kennedy's close friend."[104] It remains highly debatable as to what influence, if any, this report had on the election; certainly it assigns immense agency to *Newsweek* to think that it may have swayed the Canadian electorate. Moreover, negative portrayals of the prime minister abounded during the campaign. The same week that *Newsweek* attacked the prime minister, *Time* printed a similar critique of Diefenbaker over his "inability to make a firm decision." Two weeks before the election, unflattering images of a doughty Diefenbaker accompanied a *Maclean's* cover story by Peter Newman, who crafted a portrait of a man gifted with the ability to inspire his listeners but who suffered "from an almost morbid inability to make up his mind."[105] In contrast, *Maclean's* showcased images of a smiling Pearson on its front cover, although the accompanying story emphasized his chameleon-like views on issues: "He almost completely lacks ideology, and he possesses nothing that could be called an obsession."[106]

Alongside their concern over unwittingly aiding the Tories, American authorities grew uneasy at the thought that the prime minister would employ the Rostow memorandum in the final, desperate moments of the campaign. Lunching with various newspaper editors at the Rideau Club in Ottawa in the lead-up to the nonconfidence vote in early February, Butterworth had been warned that Diefenbaker's possession of the document was an open secret.[107] Then, in late March, Charles Lynch reported in the *Ottawa Citizen* that the prime minister held a secret, damning document, which urged Kennedy to "push"

Canada into accepting nuclear weapons. The *New York Times* and *Washington Post* quickly picked up his story. Reporting further on April 1, Lynch wrote that the prime minister denied having the paper but that sources in Ottawa and Washington confirmed the story to be true. The Americans were livid. When Lynch hinted to Embassy officials that Diefenbaker had leaked the story to him, one NSC official decried that this was a "pretty clever use of the 'push' document with 'using' it!"[108] Caution remained paramount in the White House. Hearing about the news story, Kennedy inquired with Tyler about a contingency plan in the event that Lynch's story began to have a major impact on the campaign, stating, "if it is helping Diefenbaker, we ought to think about knocking it down." He suggested leaking both an actual copy of the memorandum and the story of how the prime minister had threatened Merchant with the document. But prudence prevailed. Keeping quiet, Legere advised, would create uncertainty, hopefully causing the prime minister's "turgid act" to "backfire." As Legere put it, "I just have the feeling that Diefenbaker's dirty pool works better for him when he has a foil than when he doesn't." The subsequent appearance of a story about the document in the *Globe and Mail* two days before the election was not enough to stir the Americans to action.[109]

In the wake of the rumors about the Rostow paper and McNamara's damning testimony, Bundy advised senior administration officials that with the president wishing "to avoid any appearance of interference, even by responding to what may appear to be untruthful, distorted, or unethical statements or actions," the "shut-up policy" in effect since the beginning of the campaign was to be even more strongly enforced.[110] This order came just as a new incident threatened to spark a messy row between Diefenbaker and the Ottawa Embassy. Copies of a letter began appearing in the mailboxes of Canadian MPs and reporters. Bearing Butterworth's signature as well as the State Department seal, these letters extended the ambassador's "congratulations" to Pearson for his "excellent and logical" change in Liberal defense policy, a move that was deeply "appreciated" by the White House. The US government, the letter continued, would like to assist the Liberals and seek out ways to "be useful to you in the future." One of many recipients of this damning document, Diefenbaker immediately sought the advice of those closest to him, who pressed the prime minister not to act. The problem was not that the Americans had been caught red-handed, but that the letter was a clumsy forgery.[111] Hearing of the letter on April 5 from Ross Munro, editor of *The Winnipeg Tribune*, Butterworth immediately called Robert Bryce to report that the document was counterfeit. Bryce tried his best to soothe the ambassador, promising that he would contact the prime minister, who was campaigning outside of Ottawa.[112] Although Munro had refused to print the story in his paper, on April 6 a Vancouver *Province* article referred to a document that was "so hot" even the Tories were "afraid to use it." His reputation maligned, Butterworth learned of Diefenbaker's involved in this story, and he asked the State Department for permission to strike back. His request was denied, and so another confrontation between the United States and the prime minister was avoided.[113]

With the election entering its last days, there was anxiety among American observers over the likely results. "We were watching the election fairly carefully," remembered Bundy, "and it would been very poor if old Dief had won."[114] Two days before the vote, Butterworth examined the prime minister's last-minute "whistle-stop demagogic" campaigning in which he was underlining the theme of "sovereignty not subservience for Canada particularly with regard to defense policy." Reaffirming his grudging admiration for the Tory leader, Butterworth argued that a major point of interest in this extraordinary campaign had been Diefenbaker's vigorous effort at turning in one of the "most remarkable performances in Canadian history."[115] Alarmed by this performance, Kennedy took a fatalistic position, telling Ben Bradlee, *Newsweek*'s Washington bureau chief, that should Diefenbaker win, "well, then we'll just have to live with him." The president was no doubt relieved at the election of a Liberal minority government. In his diary, Charles Ritchie likely reflected the views of many observers on both sides of the border: "The government is out. Diefenbaker is gone ... I consider his disappearance a deliverance; there should be prayers of thanksgiving in the churches. And these sentiments do not come from a Liberal."[116]

After five years as opposition leader and two electoral defeats, Lester Pearson was now prime minister. His face graced the cover of *Time*, which contended that the election had been a catharsis of sorts. Among Canadians there was hope that the new government would deal with genuine issues that needed attention—from a faltering economy to relations between Quebec and the rest of Canada—rather than bicker with Washington in a "sham debate" over nuclear weapons. Making a similar argument in *Foreign Affairs*, John Holmes admitted that there had been anti-Americanism throughout the election, but that this force had not been decisive, nor had the issue of US interference been of paramount importance. Instead, Canadian voters focused on far more important issues—namely, the economic and cultural foundations of their country—and, due to the threat of Quebec nationalism, Canada's very future, had opted for a "fresh start" under Pearson.[117] In his own assessment, Butterworth judged that "anti-Americanism, even when labeled pro-Canadianism," was no longer a "magic formula" for electoral success. Looking to the results in specific ridings, he was also satisfied that Harkness had been re-elected with an increased number of votes, while Green, that "sanctimonious Beelzebub," had lost his seat. His conclusion was that the results indicated "not triumph but certainly victory for forces compatible with our interests." Canada would henceforth "be more stable, responsible, sophisticated and generally cooperative than at any time since 1958." He cautioned, however, that although the Diefenbaker era appeared to have come to an end, "this does not mean that fundamental problems of economics and geography which underline our relations with Canada have disappeared." In truth, Butterworth felt, these factors meant that nationalism would remain a potent force.[118] Butterworth's observation was important. Whatever the results of the election, Canadians, while important allies and trading partners, remained jealous of their independence. The election showed that while nationalist rhetoric could be important in drumming up support, it was not all-powerful. Despite the State Department's heavy-handedness, there had been no major backlash toward the United States.

So ended the troubled Kennedy–Diefenbaker relationship. Speaking to Harold Macmillan soon after the election, the president mused that the result in Canada "was helpful."[119] American officials had little love for Diefenbaker, and some had helped to precipitate his downfall. Rather than being guilty of premeditated murder, the Americans had, at worst, committed manslaughter, but had done so out of self-defense. The nuclear weapons issue was not simply important to Canada, but was important to the United States, too. Regardless of their concerns with Canadian nationalism, which had led them, more often than not, to concede to Ottawa's viewpoints, in the wake of Diefenbaker's dishonest House of Commons speech US policymakers had felt compelled to act. The press release— and Norstad's press conference, should one wish to see conspiracy here—was a risky gamble that could just as easily have backfired on the administration, as the comments made by American officials during the election campaign seemed to do. Asked by Kennedy whether the State Department's press release had helped the Liberal campaign, Pearson retorted "it probably cost me fifty seats."[120]

An act of retaliation over the Diefenbaker's double-dealing on defense, the press release first aimed to force a settlement of the nuclear weapons issue, a pressing matter for the Kennedy administration, particularly after the nuclear standoff with Moscow over Cuba. Commenting publicly on defense issues in November 1962, Willis Armstrong avoided BOMARC but mentioned the missile crisis, noting that "the recent events in the western hemisphere have shown that we too are now, or easily can be, in front line danger."[121] Such fears had led Washington to seek to resolve the issue with Ottawa through the dispatch of negotiators to the Canadian capital, and talks between cabinet members from both countries. These discussions bogged down over the missing part procedure, championed by the Canadians as a way of saving face, but rejected by the Americans for being ineffective. Perhaps a deal could have been struck, but with little faith in Diefenbaker after incidents such as that over the Rostow memorandum, Kennedy had no willingness to overrule his advisors and cut a deal for Canada's prime minister as he had done for Macmillan on Skybolt. Thus, the secondary aim of the press release, as Butterworth had admitted, was to stir up the domestic situation in Canada. That this move was so successful in doing so—despite general revulsion among Canadians over American intrusion—is not testament to the ability of US officials to manipulate events in Canada but rather to the complete shambles of Diefenbaker's governing style, which led to ministerial resignations, his government's collapse following a successful nonconfidence vote, and the refusal of several senior Tories—Donald Fleming, David Fulton—to run alongside him in the ensuing election.

Ultimately, Diefenbaker bore responsibility for his own fall from power. In two elections held in less than a year the Tories had gone from a massive majority to banishment on the opposition benches. The prime minister was brought down not by enemies in the White House scheming to seek revenge for his actions during the missile crisis, but by his own inability to handle a range of domestic and foreign policy issues. The view that Diefenbaker was prone to incessant vacillation on the nuclear question has some validity: the matter had been under review since February 1959 and showed little sign a resolution in January 1963. It is tempting, then, simply to point to the old aphorism "to govern is to choose." But there were reasons beyond divisions in Cabinet why a final decision proved difficult. Growing domestic support for disarmament—an important factor for a politician—and a changing strategic emphasis away from manned bombers toward nuclear missiles were factors that emerged strongly in 1962. In particular, the altered strategic reality threatened to invalidate the need for BOMARC missiles and nuclear-armed interceptors, a consideration important to Diefenbaker, who had faced immense criticism over the AVRO Arrow, a boondoggle that demonstrated the economic waste surrounding defense procurement. Yet if he was changing course on defense, as seems to have been the case, this move was poorly communicated to the Americans, with the result that his actions appeared to be another instance of disingenuous prevarication. With diplomatic relations strained, Diefenbaker's actions could not but provoke the Americans. It is important to note, though, that the Americans, exasperated by Diefenbaker's wavering, were oblivious to the strategic confusion that they had created with the Nassau agreement.

The prime minister's handling of the nuclear file precipitated a crisis with the United States as well as a crisis of confidence among his ministers, within Parliament, and, ultimately, among the populace. The American action succeeded only because enough Canadian politicians agreed that the government was failing to govern, an opinion confirmed by Canadian voters in the subsequent election. Nuclear weapons were simply a catalyst for wider dissatisfaction with Diefenbaker, but they were the reason why Washington was angered in January 1963, why many Tories were outraged with their leader that February, and why Canadians voted in a Liberal minority government that April. "I can't imagine," Rusk later stated, "that the United States has the slightest capacity to tell the people in Canada how to vote."[122] And most of those who did vote in 1963 did not pick Diefenbaker's party.

Washington was certainly not responsible for the increasing unpopularity of Diefenbaker and his government; rather, the Tories' indecision on the nuclear weapons issue, ongoing unemployment, fraying Anglo Canadian–French Canadian relations, obstinacy on Britain's entry into the EEC, and poor handling of the 1962 economic crisis made the Liberals a more attractive choice. Loaning Lou Harris to the Liberals proved to be the sum of American involvement in the election, a foolhardy move that was uncharacteristic of Kennedy's handling of Canadian affairs. Throughout his time in the White House the president had shown himself, as Rusk put it at the time, to be "quite concerned about our being drawn into internal politics up there."[123] In the wake of the 1963 election, historian Kenneth McNaught had contended that given "the nature of the nuclear alliance system the United States is bound to take an ever more intimate interest in our politics just at the time when her indirect influence through mass-media and investment reaches almost the saturation point. Conversely, to retain any real control over either our domestic or foreign policies, Canadians will *have* to be anti-American."[124] It was this sense of nationalism that had seemed to frustrate the smooth conduct of Canada–US relations under Diefenbaker and that appeared set to pose future problems.

# Epilogue

## *The Spirit of Hyannis Port and the End of Camelot*

In April 1963, the advent of a new government gave US policymakers hope that Canadian nationalism, embodied by John Diefenbaker, had been defeated at the polls and that bilateral relations could be improved. Guidelines prepared by the Canada Desk for McGeorge Bundy predicted that Lester Pearson "would want and work for cordial relations" with Washington, though he would cautiously avoid "any implication or image of being a U.S. pawn." In light of the climate created by months of sniping between the Canadian and American governments, the State Department contended that it was important that the White House temper any expectation that simply because Diefenbaker was gone there would be "automatic solutions" to outstanding bilateral problems. Furthermore, the Kennedy administration should avoid embracing Pearson's government too closely "and thereby embarrass it by providing ammunition" to opponent who would seek to label the new prime minister "a U.S. stooge." Taking these points into account, Kennedy informed his Cabinet that although the Liberal victory had "naturally stirred" hope that progress could be made on a host of issues, it was vital that any negotiations with the new government be "carefully coordinated" under his "personal direction" through the State Department.[1] The move to consolidate policymaking toward Canada under his watch reflected the president's anxiety with the state of bilateral affairs.

In Pearson, Kennedy found an affable partner also committed to rebuilding the bonds between the two countries. But the new prime minister had to contend with nationalists within his own party as well as with nationalism within his country. Moreover, US policy posed problems for the new government, especially on economic matters, a key concern for Walter Gordon, the Liberal finance minister, the architect of Pearson's victory, and a leading nationalist. As a result, relations between Ottawa and Washington remained rocky. Unsettled by this state of affairs, the Kennedy administration turned to a variety of methods through which it hoped to ameliorate these issues and place the Canada–US relationship on an even keel. Confronted by nationalist forces, they found this task a difficult one, because, despite Diefenbaker's fall from power, Canadian nationalism was in the ascendant.

Just as the State Department and the White House each recognized that the rancor of the first few months of 1963 meant that there could be no quick resolution of outstanding issues, Canadians officials, invested in the smooth functioning of the bilateral relationship, were also cognizant that it would be slow-going in the wake of the election. The Liberal Party's nationalist wing, led by Walter Gordon—given the finance portfolio as his reward for spearheading the Liberal election effort—posed difficulties for any quick settlement with the Americans on certain points, leading one senior diplomat to hope that Ottawa and Washington would "be able to get through the immediate future without too much antagonism." Echoing this sentiment, Ed Ritchie nevertheless recommended getting the Pearson-Kennedy relationship "off to the right kind of start" by pushing the speedy resolution of items such as nuclear weaponry. However, he was not advocating that the new government capitulate as a means of displaying its good faith. Rather, on matters of principle, as with trade to Cuba, Pearson should reiterate Canada's distinct viewpoint and defend legitimate Canadian interests.[2] Pearson, too, gave thought to breaking the deadlock. Only days after assuming the premiership, he told Walton Butterworth that he would be pleased to meet Kennedy, preferably not in Washington—he wished to avoid the "paraphernalia" of a visit to the American capital—but somewhere such as a point on the Canada–US border.[3] Springing into action, the president invited Pearson to his family's seaside retreat at Hyannis Port, a relaxed setting befitting a low-key summit.

Highlighting the importance that he attached both to the summit and to good relations with Canada, Kennedy chaired a lengthy meeting with senior officials to review and establish policies for the meeting with Pearson, a step he had not taken in advance of his talks with Diefenbaker. The Canadian prime minister was apprehensive too. Prior to leaving for Massachusetts, Pearson reviewed with his Cabinet the many issues to be dealt with, and confided that because of the tremendous interest shown in his impending visit by the American press, "he had never approached an international discussion with deeper concern." Pearson was pleasantly surprised by his visit. Arriving by helicopter, he and Kennedy re-established their easy rapport, discussing baseball and joking about Diefenbaker. As Charles Ritchie recorded, the meeting "was tinged with euphoria. The atmosphere was that of clearing skies after a storm—the clouds of suspicion covering Canada–U.S. relations had parted, the sunshine of friendship shone."[4] As for their substantive discussions, Kennedy left the initiative to Pearson. Moving through the mass of agenda items, the prime minister affirmed that he would honor the previous government's nuclear commitments.

Other issues, from shipping disputes to water rights, were discussed and then referred to officials for further study, with neither side willing to disturb the friendly atmosphere through lengthy debate. Perhaps the most important point came when Pearson raised American ownership of Canadian industry and pointed out that his government "was going to take steps which would not penalize US investments, but would encourage Canadians to buy in, so as to have a real sense of participation" in their own economy.[5] Pearson's nationalism was soft, doing little to upset the affable summit.

The experience in Hyannis Port was a refreshing one. At a postmeeting press conference, Bundy remarked that although there had been a "relative breakdown" in Washington's relations with Ottawa over the past year, with existing differences likely to remain, there was now a desire to "put oil in the various pieces of machinery available for discussion" of bilateral issues.[6] Kennedy reported to several aides that Pearson had impressed him, and years later Butterworth reflected that the meeting was akin to "a new page being turned in Canadian–American relations." As for the prime minister, briefing his ministers on the outcome of these talks, he praised the president's "quick mind," "great capacity," and "forward-looking attitude." The summit, he sensed, had "laid a good foundation for further discussions on particular subjects," a sentiment he repeated to Dean Rusk when the two met at a NATO ministerial meeting held in Ottawa at the end of May. Indeed, Pearson told Rusk that while "anxieties" existed over certain issues like trade and defense, "there was a country-wide feeling of relief at the end of the intense bickering" between the two governments.[7]

The Kennedy–Pearson honeymoon was widely applauded. Walter Lippmann likened it to "a good scrubbing and a cool shower after a muddy brawl," while the *Atlantic* was pleased that with the "pipeline between Ottawa and Washington" now thawed, it could "be filled with meaningful communications."[8] Canada's consul in New York reported that normally unfriendly Manhattanites were exultant, with the election and the Hyannis Port meeting having "brought undisguised relief in all circles" alongside an "instinctive feeling among Americans that 'our side' had won in Canada." In its own show of naked delight, the *Calgary Herald* proclaimed: "Good Relations Are Restored." The *Ottawa Citizen* was equally succinct, praising "the return to sanity" in bilateral relations. In a more sober editorial, the *Globe and Mail* commented on the advent of this good feeling, advising that Canadians "have to be frank without being acrimonious. We have to get rid of suspicions that when we disagree it is because Canadians are anti-American or Americans are anti-Canadian. We have to accept that although one nation is large and the other relatively small, we are mutually interdependent." As for concrete results coming out of the seaside summit, the *Montreal Gazette* wrote: "Pearson has acted wisely in taking immediate steps to fulfill Canada's military commitments. For a Canada that does not fulfill its commitments cannot deserve to receive from others the co-operation so necessary for its protection and progress."[9]

Ottawa did move to resolve the nuclear issue. As Paul Martin, now secretary of state for external affairs, emphasized to Pearson, a speedy resolution was important to Washington not simply "from a military point of view but was of the first psychological importance in relation to Canada–U.S. relations."[10] Signaling the new temperament in the bilateral relationship, on May 20, Martin presented Butterworth with a draft treaty. At a meeting with Bundy, McNamara, and other top-level officials prior to the Hyannis Port meeting, Kennedy had remarked that he was unsure whether Pearson would be able to commit so soon to taking possession of warheads for the BOMARCs—no such hesitation was expected for the warheads destined for Canadian weapons platforms in Europe—so the White House welcomed the presentation of this draft.[11] Negotiators from both countries met throughout the summer months to hammer out an agreement, which was reached in August. So ended an issue that had bedeviled bilateral affairs for over four years, though not all was well on the nuclear front. Concerned both about nuclear proliferation and about the anti-nuclear sentiment of several of his ministers, Pearson tiptoed around a suggestion that Kennedy had made at Hyannis Port involving the use of nuclear weaponry by Canadian naval forces for anti-submarine warfare. The president had also suggested that the United States Air Force disperse nuclear-armed interceptor aircraft throughout northern Canada. Sensibly, when Pearson pointed out that these requests did not constitute part of the "existing commitments" that Diefenbaker had made and that the Liberals had pledged to meet, Kennedy reversed himself, ordering that US officials refrain from discussing these matters further with their Canadian counterparts.[12] Having resolved the main nuclear weapons issue, Kennedy was not averse to helping Pearson, who, after all, was instrumental in putting this matter to rest.

Cuba was also effectively shelved. Within days of the Liberal election victory Robertson had written Ed Ritchie to highlight that while in opposition, Martin and Pearson had been somewhat critical of Diefenbaker's position on this issue. "While no one can be entirely happy with our past relationship with Cuba," mused Robertson, "I think it would be a mistake for the Government to make any quick or substantial change in policy on this matter. We do recognize, however, that even the same old policies might be presented in a better light than we have managed to bring to bear on them in the past."[13] Pearson did more than present Canada's careful support in a new light. At Hyannis Port he expressed approval of US handling of Cuba, which used "economic pressure without provocation." Affirming that Canada would maintain its diplomatic ties with Havana, he promised that his government "would do nothing to indicate support or sympathy for the Castro regime." Moreover, since the events of October 1962 had alarmed him greatly, he agreed to step up intelligence sharing with the United

States, a move that Kennedy appreciated.[14] Still, Canada–Cuba trade continued, as did American frustration at Ottawa's overall position. As Butterworth soon complained following a meeting with Martin, the Canadian foreign minister "by no means saw the Castro government as clearly communist as we do."[15] Yet in the face of continued and increasingly vociferous Congressional pressure to secure allied support for the embargo, when the White House put in place additional economic sanctions in July it refrained from targeting Canada over its Cuban policy. As for the OAS, although the Liberals had supported membership while in Opposition, in government a combination of concern over both the US–Cuba confrontation and the appearance of succumbing to US pressure stayed any positive movement by the Pearson government.

It turned out that dealing with nuclear warheads and Cuba were simple matters. Balancing friendly bilateral relations with Canadian economic nationalism proved more difficult. In late May, the White House counsel had remarked to Canadian diplomats that "the new atmosphere" in bilateral relations was making a "great difference ... in the way the White House approaches Canadian problems."[16] But the atmosphere quickly changed. That same week, Pearson professed to Butterworth his preoccupation with economic matters, adding that he had been working with Walter Gordon on the budget, which "would be tough."[17] Just how tough was made clear on June 13, when Gordon, economic nationalism's standard-bearer, presented this budget to the House of Commons. The bill, he declared, would ensure that Canadian industry operated "with due regard to the over-all interest of Canadians and the Canadian economy." To this end, it included a 30 percent tax to be applied on foreign purchases of Canadian stock as well as increases to a withholding tax paid on dividends for companies where the shares were not at least a quarter Canadian-owned.[18] Quite rightly, Americans viewed this measure as an attack on US investment. "Such drastic measures," the *Los Angeles Times* lamented, "come as a shock to Americans who hoped Pearson's recent election victory over ultra-nationalist John Diefenbaker meant the anti-American sentiment in Canada had been exaggerated." In highly condescending tones, the *New York Times* chided Canada, "the most economically advanced and political sophisticated of all of the developing nations," for abandoning its "responsibility to act in a manner that promotes the free flow of capital to speed its own growth rate."[19] Such angry comments reflected American surprise that nationalism was not the preserve of Canada's Tories.

Regardless of any frustration on the part of US government officials with the budget measures, in keeping with the general thrust of US policy toward Canada during this period, the Americans responded calmly without retribution. At Pearson's behest, Basil Robinson asked Willis Armstrong whether the US government would decline public comment. The administration complied with this request; it helped, though, that a hue and cry came from the Canadian press and from investors. In a stunning reversal, Gordon withdrew the measures.[20] His decision by no means decreased the tensions that had been caused by the budget. In late June, Griffith Johnson, the assistant secretary of state for economic affairs, lectured Robinson and Maurice Schwarzmann on the danger that the investment measures had posed to the American standpoint that foreign investment should be treated the same as domestic investment. Were Canada, a close and friendly country, to violate this principle, the results could be disastrous for US investment in other countries where the American presence was even less welcome. Johnson indicated also a concern that "much of the net drain" on United States balance of payments was to Canada, a comment indicating that anti-investment taxes were not the sole area of financial trouble that summer.[21]

Indeed, as a means to prevent money flowing out of the United States and thus contributing to balance of payments problems, in July, Kennedy introduced to Congress an Interest Equalization Tax. Reducing the return on foreign investment, the tax aimed to diminish US investment abroad, thereby keeping American dollars at home. The result in Canada—beyond a plummeting stock exchange—was a fear that the government would be incapable of covering its current account deficit, which was offset by American investment. Incensed that Ottawa had not been informed or consulted on the tax measure, and mindful that the move could be retaliation for Gordon's budget, Canadian officials protested the proposed tax, insisting that Canada be granted an exemption and that the US government publicly state that the bill was not a retaliatory attack.[22] The State Department and the Treasury were forthcoming on this latter point, with Ball emphasizing to Bundy: "We should make it plain that this is totally unrelated to the Canadian budget." As for an exemption, it took time for the White House to come around. When Ambassador Ritchie appealed to Ball to have Canada exempted, the American pointed to his government's "restraint in reacting to the Canadian budget measures," despite their harm to US interests. Referring to the previous year's financial crisis, he added that even though Canada had imposed surcharges and other measures targeting the United States, Washington had been very helpful to Ottawa. Cheekily, he pointed out that the investment tax was entirely "consistent" with the measures in Gordon's budget meant to increase Canadian ownership in Canada's economy.[23] Ball was playing rough.

With the State Department unsympathetic, Canadian officials turned to lobbying the Treasury for an exemption. Led by Louis Rasminsky, the governor of the Bank of Canada, a Canadian delegation traveled to Washington "simply raising hell." In a series of lengthy meetings, they pressed Douglas Dillon for an exemption. Charles Ritchie reflected in his diary on how he "watched with silent admiration" Rasminsky's "superb and sustained diplomatic performance," which convinced the US side "much against their previous stand, that the interests of the United States would best be served by granting us an exemption." As

Rasminsky contended, since Canadians paid for US goods and services through the money invested into their economy, less investment would mean fewer American exports to Canada.[24] After two difficult days of discussions, during which time Dillon remained in close contact with the president, the Canadians convinced the administration that Canada should not suffer for US balance of payments woes. James Reed, an assistant secretary at the Treasury, was with Kennedy when Dillon called to request that an exemption for Canada be placed in the legislation. He later recalled that Kennedy "was entirely familiar with the bill. He was entirely familiar with what the prospects were going to be to our balance of payments if this bill was passed. He was entirely familiar with our relationship with Canada.... He had confidence in Secretary Dillon, so when the Secretary put the question to him, he said 'Mr Secretary, if you think that's what is best under all the circumstances, that's alright with me.'"[25]

As with a host of issues, the Kennedy administration conceded to the Canadian position, continuing the American practice of "exemptionalism" that girded the bilateral special relationship. Indeed, if the tax was meant as retribution for Gordon's budget, the fact that the White House granted an exemption indicates that a strong commitment to punishing the Pearson government was lacking. In some respects US officials even sympathized with Canada's stance. As Ball remarked to Bundy that summer, "if I were in Walter Gordon's place with the position the Government has to take—that it must defend the integrity of Canada as a state—I would be doing what he is doing." Still, Ball complained that Gordon's plan violated "traditional liberal commercial policies" and was not "a rational thing to do."[26] The exemption granted for Canada was important not just in its own right. Throughout his presidency, the American balance of payments situation proved to be "one of Kennedy's biggest obsessions."[27] Action on the issue had been contemplated in April, well before the Canadian budget, only days after Pearson's government took office. Ball had even speculated to the president and senior administration officials that since Gordon favored "buying back Canada" he might in fact "be sympathetic" to the US move. Dillon, however, had criticized applying the tax to Canada, emphasizing, as Rasminsky later would, that the measure would damage US exports to that country. Interdependence cut both ways. "When the U.S gets hay fever, Canada gets asthma," Kennedy's top economic advisor had put it in 1962, and "our fiscal anti-histamines are probably the best cure for their economic allergies."[28] The investment tax proved to be unwanted medicine.

Given the immense level of US investment in the Canadian economy, that the tax would target Canada was entirely understandable. That the Kennedy administration backed down on such an important matter indicates again both the degree to which it valued smooth relations with Ottawa and Canadian diplomats' ability to use their close relationship with their American counterparts for profit. However, that an exemption was not included in the original bill also shows the US government's frustrations with Canada. As Butterworth later reflected, he, Ball, and Dillon had resolved "in the interest of more serious debate that we would start off the legislation without an exemption for Canada and let them have their flurry. Maybe this would give them a pause for thought as to how two people could play games."[29] A long-considered policy with global ramifications—it applied to some twenty-two countries—the tax was not simply a retaliatory move implemented with the specific aim of demonstrating "very effectively that Canada—and its Minister of Finance—needed the United States."[30] It could serve this purpose, true, but as Dillon had assured Rusk, the tax "has no bearing whatsoever on their earlier actions—nor was it motivated by them."[31]

This summer of economic discontent worried many observers in both countries. The financial squabbling, Ambassador Ritchie lamented in August, was evidence that "the Hyannisport honeymoon is already over," while to Peter Newman the events of the summer had removed "any lingering doubts that Canada has become an economic dependency (if not a satellite) of the United States."[32] Discussing this unrest with Bundy, Ball sought approval to conduct a study examining Canada–US finance, which he felt was the "central issue to our long-term relations with Canada." Bundy granted his request, agreeing that something had to be done to address this "permanent political issue up there." What Ball wanted was to avoid ongoing "mutual harassment" by seeking mutually beneficial policies.[33] He enlisted the aid of Harvard economist Raymond Vernon. Reviewing the bilateral economic relationship, Vernon cast a critical eye on both Canadian concerns with "alleged U.S. domination" of Canada's economy and American preoccupation with management of the global economy. Having in mind a focus on the bilateral relationship over the long run, his idea was for the creation of guiding principles that, while recognizing both countries' own "distinct national goals," would call for Ottawa and Washington to pursue opportunities "for profiting from the proximity of the two economies" such as jointly setting up procedures to permit the "easy flow of people, capital and goods" across the border. With this aim, he recommended setting up four working groups to explore specific problem areas: energy, the operation of US subsidiaries in Canada, balance of payments, and the extraterritorial application of American law.[34]

The document arrived just in time for the joint Canada–US committee on trade and economic affairs. Prone to championing grand projects, Ball proceeded with caution and mentioned only a notion of issuing with the Canadians a joint declaration of principles to guide bilateral relations, particularly in the economic sphere. Canada's side, reluctant to engage in such lofty talk, deferred discussion on the grounds that such a momentous proposal should be made at the highest level. The summit then moved from Ball's grandiose idea to acrimonious debate about Gordon's budget, labor strife, and the Canadian desire to encourage domestic ownership, particularly in the automotive industry.[35] The latter issue had been a point of contention for some time. Canada had a small domestic market, leaving little room for Canadian manufacturers to expand sales, a situation worsened by high US tariffs, which made Canadian-produced vehicles expensive for export to the United States as well as for domestic consumers. The result was increased imports of foreign vehicles, in turn generating a decline in domestic production, a large trade deficit, and growing unemployment in the automotive sector. Important, then, were moves capable of lowering the cost of vehicles produced in Canada. Diefenbaker's government had pursued a limited scheme affecting automatic transmissions, allowing manufacturers to claim a rebate on duties paid, provided the firm importing the transmissions then increased exports. Gordon, with the support of his brother-in-law, Charles Drury, the industry minister, sought to expand the Tories' rebate scheme to include most parts and vehicles. The Kennedy administration had acquiesced to Diefenbaker's modest program, but the Liberals' plan was too much. At the joint committee meeting, the US side stressed that the automotive issue was a bilateral question and so Canada could not impose unilateral measures that seemed to subsidize exports to the United States. If Ottawa went ahead, they warned, Washington might impose countervailing duties.[36]

Undeterred, Gordon and Drury pushed ahead, with the industry minister introducing the planned duties in late October in the House of Commons. They were to come into effect on November 1.[37] Ball thought that the auto issue could be handled "in a way which does not look as if we are harassing the Canadians too much." Yet he feared that this dispute could lead to "a greater crisis than we've had at any time in Canadian relations." The US Trade Representative's office agreed, cautioning against hasty action that could lead Ottawa and Washington into instituting a series of recriminating tariffs and thus creating "a sharp deteriorating in political relations between the two Governments and a rise in anti-Americanism in Canada." Aiming to negotiate with the Canadian government, members of the administration were concerned that US automotive manufacturers might protest and thereby force the United States into action.[38] Talks were arranged but the results were limited and the issue would drag on with the potential of provoking a trade war, though US officials were careful to avoid aggressive action.

These continuing economic squabbles caught Kennedy's attention. Through Pierre Salinger, the president established plans to visit Toronto in December, a trip that would involve several public appearances as well as substantive talks with Pearson.[39] Kennedy also moved to take tighter control of policymaking toward his country's northern ally. In a memorandum to senior administration officials in mid-November, Bundy wrote that "all aspects of Canadian–American relations are of intense interest and concern to the President," who therefore "desires that the White House be fully informed of all significant negotiations or plans for negotiations with the Government of Canada." To assist him in coordinating policy toward Canada, the president appointed the NSC's William Brubeck to be his personal assistant on Canadian affairs. Brubeck immediately began planning to address economic problems and at his insistence, Kennedy broached Canadian nationalism at a meeting with senior advisors. There it was decided that Ball would chair a special committee to examine bilateral relations and to suggest ways to improve Washington's stance toward Ottawa.[40] Having put in place these new mechanisms for controlling Canadian policy, and viewing the relationship with Canada—and continuing nationalism—in a serious light, Kennedy was preparing to mount a major effort to deal with trouble spots with Ottawa. His handling of Canadian relations reflected a growing maturity and an education in power and in policymaking, characteristic of Kennedy at the end of his presidency.[41]

Days after the formation of Ball's committee, the president was gunned down in Dallas. Reflecting in his diary on the "horror" of this event, Charles Ritchie wrote: "The adventure is over, brightness falls from the air; that probing mind, that restlessness of spirit, are snapped off as if by a camera shutter. We shall no more see that style of his, varying from gay to grim and then to eloquent, but always with a cutting edge."[42] 1963 had been a fractious year for Canada–US relations. Beginning with the unquiet diplomacy over nuclear weapons, followed by the tense election, the honeymoon at Hyannis Port, and then the squabbling over economic questions, the relationship between Ottawa and Washington showed signs of strain. Of course, throughout the Kennedy years tension had marked bilateral affairs, as had been the case since the year before Diefenbaker won power in 1957. Even so, the special relationship between the two countries had continued to function, with quiet, candid discussion taking place to resolve issues, particularly those dealing with economic questions. In this climate, quiet diplomacy seemed even more important to those interested in the smooth functioning of the Canada–US relationship.

Given this feeling, Kennedy had welcomed Lester Pearson's victory. Commenting on the postelection "wave of good will on both sides of the border," Paul Martin noted only two weeks before Kennedy's death that the notion of "the spirit of Hyannis Port" was too superficial, for it failed to grasp "the complexity of the relationship between our two countries—or even the purpose of the meeting," which had been meant not to solve problems but to lay the groundwork for the future by reviving dialogue "which regrettably had been allowed to lapse" under Diefenbaker.[43] This renewed dialogue proved to be important during the brief Kennedy–Pearson period. The change in administration may have removed some points of friction, but it created others. Walter Gordon had entered the finance ministry hoping to succeed where Diefenbaker had failed to act on his desire to inhibit Canadian economic reliance on the United States. So began a summer of economic discontent in Canada–US relations, though the summer soon stretched into a long decade during which economic nationalism soured the bilateral partnership.

As a result of the simmering tension with the Liberals, and the recognition that nationalism was not the preserve of the Progressive Conservatives, John Kennedy sought to centralize Canadian policy in the White House, a trend apparent since the 1963 election, while his advisors, George Ball in particular, similarly weighed means of ameliorating relations over the long term. Kennedy never got the chance to pursue such an approach. Three weeks after taking office, his successor, Lyndon Johnson, was advised by Rusk that the Pearson government, while "in spirit, friendly to us and, in principle, much more sympathetic with US objectives" than Diefenbaker, nevertheless "felt compelled to take a series of measures that have kept our relations on the edge of tension— measures that can, if carried too far, result in serious economic and political problems between our two countries." In recognition of this Canadian outlook the Johnson administration pursued a tolerant course, one in line with Kennedy's own approach to Canada. As the young president had put it in the Canadian Parliament in 1961, "the unity of equal and independent nations, co-tenants of the same continent, heirs of the same legacy, and fully sovereign associates in the same historic endeavor: to preserve freedom for ourselves and all who wish it."[44] Giving a nod to nationalist concerns, such soaring rhetoric was premised on the assumption that Canada would work alongside the United States in the pursuit of common interests. A mixture of nationalism, domestic calculations, and genuine policy differences had prevented easy, smooth, or automatic cooperation between Canada and Camelot.

"Americans," McGeorge Bundy once remarked, "at once too close and too far removed, may not be the best qualified of people to render accurate perceptions of Canada." Recalling his own familiarity with Canadians prior to joining the Kennedy administration, he confessed to "distance from the kind of understanding of Canada one ought to have before engaging in so challenging a subject."[45] Bundy's admission indicates that Canadians are right to complain about American ignorance of their country: here, a senior member of the Kennedy and Johnson administrations, a man who at times had taken important policy decisions toward Canada, acknowledged that he had not been the most competent person to handle Canadian affairs. However, Bundy was being too contrite. Members of the Kennedy White House may have shared his inexperience with Canada, but there was a substantial amount of understanding amongst those officials tasked with dealing with Canadian matters on a day-to-day basis. The diplomats at the Ottawa Embassy and at the Canada Desk recognized the importance of their northern ally economically, politically, and militarily. They were keen observers of Canadian politics and were mindful of the influence of what they identified as the psychological factor in Canada–US relations. With these thoughts in mind, the guiding maxim for these professional Canadianists was patient understanding. Furthermore, those who were inexperienced in Canadian matters, President Kennedy amongst them, were quick learners who adapted to this style of diplomacy.

Its rhetoric about pursuing a vigorous foreign policy aside, when it came to Canada the Kennedy team adjusted rapidly to the less vibrant style of Canadian–American relations. Vigor gave way to pragmatism, sometimes grudgingly as in the case of OAS membership, with the White House preferring a conciliatory and constructive stance to a confrontational one. Apart from concerns with setting a precedent that would damage its sanctions regime against China, the administration permitted an American-owned Canadian subsidiary to sell oil to a shipping company engaged in transporting grain to the Communist Chinese. Similar American care over impinging on Canadian sovereignty was shown on Cuba. Fixated on removing Fidel Castro from power through a host of unsavory methods, nevertheless the Kennedy White House stopped short of coercing Canada into participating in its embargo. In early 1962 tensions flared over this question, but American threats were toothless, lacking coercive action, such as the use of provisions in the Trading with the Enemy Act. Indeed, a White House decision in May 1961—upheld in 1963—accorded Canada special status by exempting Canadian firms and the Red Cross from such measures. Canada's special place in economic matters was reaffirmed in 1962. In the midst of the Canadian economic crisis that June, US policymakers came to Ottawa's aid. Even with Canadian ingratitude over this assistance—the import surcharges that Diefenbaker's government slapped in place—Washington, to its credit, avoided using its economic power as leverage to force a prostrate Ottawa to toe the line on the multitude of divisive points. When "Canadian policies have in fact collided with those of the United States," observed political scientist Denis Stairs in 1968, "they apparently have *not* produced serious or permanent ruptures in the important Washington connection."[46] For US officials, retaliation and linkage were off the table.

Given the many outstanding issues with Canada, it is surprising that leveraging American power was ruled out as a serious option especially for an administration characterized as active and aggressive. Like its predecessors, the Kennedy White House wagered that coercion would do little to secure Canadian cooperation on the acceptance of nuclear weapons, or a change in Ottawa's position in disarmament talks, or the abandonment of Diefenbaker's hesitancy to support the Grand Design. On the latter, London's plan to join the EEC and the Kennedy administration's hope of building a transatlantic nexus both seemed to strike at the Commonwealth and at Canada's British connection, two historic factors prized deeply by Diefenbaker and other conservative nationalists as sentimental symbols that also offset economic and cultural dependence on the United States. American and Canadian officials never saw eye to eye on this issue. Ultimately, the contretemps over the EEC was not the result of a malicious policy emanating from Washington, but of a decision made in London. For their part, American policymakers believed that their own policies, particularly the Trade Expansion Act, would offset any losses for Canada, and they were baffled by Canadian reluctance to take a constructive stance by supporting freer trade. And Ottawa's position on this question was not constructive: spurning US overtures to enter into joint talks with the Australians and New Zealanders, instead Diefenbaker sought to obstruct British plans. Referring to Canada's place alongside Britain and the United States, Charles Ritchie, who valued a counterweight to the Americans as much as Diefenbaker, admitted: "We are the odd man out and it is we who have put ourselves in this position, not only by the content of our policy but by the manner of it."[47]

The manner of Canadian policy over nuclear weapons issues was equally destructive. Ottawa's approach led to the brief rupture in bilateral relations, including both the press release and Ambassador Ritchie's subsequent, unprecedented recall from Washington. On disarmament, the division between Canada and the United States was over tactics, not strategy. Provided that genuine verification could be implemented, Kennedy and his team were hopeful of pursuing arms limitation, and in August 1963 the American, British, and Soviet foreign ministers signed the Partial Test Ban Treaty. Tragically, by then Howard Green, the great champion of disarmament, was out of office. Although his approach was a principled one, Green, who more often than not was just as much of a problem for the Americans as was Diefenbaker, had handled talks over arms control in a way that upset Washington and London, for he appeared to put more trust in the Soviets than in his country's allies. But to those in the American capital his stance was evidence of a trend where, far too often, Ottawa adopted an independent position. American concern about Canada's lack of support on disarmament issues paled next to worry over the unremitting saga of nuclear warheads. Diefenbaker's strategy of delay was initially accepted, but soon it perplexed and angered US policymakers, who for four years refrained from pressing matters—until they felt that they could do so no longer. In light of the long stretch of American patience with Diefenbaker, Washington's response to his January 25 speech in the House of Commons, rather than demonstrating the domineering and aggressive nature of US foreign policy, was instead uncharacteristic of the US attitude toward Canada. Moreover, Washington's outburst is entirely understandable. Diefenbaker was playing rough, and the Americans responded in kind. Had the prime minister not made misleading comments in the House of Commons—following years of prevarication—then Washington would have had neither cause nor justification to strike back with a press release. Afterward, despite a worrying row over investment issues with the new Liberal government, the Kennedy administration reverted to a policy of conciliation.

Apart from the flare up over nuclear weapons, American treatment of Canada during the Kennedy years was unexceptional with regard to the general thrust of postwar Canada–US relations. Regardless of the massive disparity in power between the two North American neighbors, Kennedy did not use American might to pressure Canada. On the nuclear file, and in spite of Diefenbaker's continual inaction, he demonstrated considerable patience. On more minor issues, such as oil bunkering, Canada's fiscal health, and trade with Cuba, Kennedy was "very helpful," as Howard Green readily conceded years later, because "considering how powerful they are and what they could do," the Americans opted not to retaliate in response to independent Canadian positions.[48] The president treated Canada as a sovereign, independent country, one free to disagree with the United States; he did not, as nationalists feared, view Canada as a satellite. Indeed, in 1961 he even sought concrete help from Ottawa in Latin America and Southeast Asia and, like every president since Franklin Roosevelt, he recognized Canada's importance as a partner in both North American and transatlantic defense. Basil Robinson would complain that "with Kennedy in office, the supply of understanding and goodwill in the White House had quickly dwindled. And with Diefenbaker, so much was personal."[49] True, Diefenbaker was the sole foreign leader whom Kennedy found "genuinely uninteresting," a view that "began as a sense of what a footless character this was and turned into just plain disgust."[50] Nonetheless, Kennedy pursued a patient course, according Canada special status on some points and allowing his officials to defer to the Canadians on a range of bilateral issues from trade with communist countries to financial management.

As for Canadian nationalism, American policymakers, Kennedy included, realized that it was best not to upset their northern allies unless doing so was unavoidable. A case in point is the Grand Design, a policy in which Canada was of secondary importance. The sole instance where US policymakers dealt with Ottawa in an unremittingly aggressive manner was in January 1963. When US officials overstepped by accident, as they did on the OAS—thanks to advice offered by Arnold Heeney—or with the press leak on nuclear weaponry in September 1961, they found their interests damaged. Such missteps reinforced the need for caution, as did effective negotiating and lobbying by Canadian diplomats, who used a mixture of quiet diplomacy and nationalist bluster to press back against US encroachment. In turn, conscious of nationalism and hopeful of not upsetting Canada–United States relations, American officials seldom overstepped. By recognizing the reality of this nationalist feeling, US policy affirmed Canada's independence, which nationalists feared was a mere figment, undermined by quiet diplomacy. For the White House and the State Department, Canadian independence was all too real. The State Department's official policy guidelines paper for Canada emphasized that the "ever present nationalist sensitivity requires that we should not take Canada for granted but treat it as a major and independent associate of the U.S."[51] And American officials were well aware, as a May 1961 National Intelligence Estimate put it, of "Canadian sensitivity to the increasing Canadian dependence—cultural, economic, and military—upon the US and by a determination to pursue a more distinctly Canadian line in foreign policy."[52] Accepting such assessments, officials in Washington and in the Ottawa Embassy tempered their actions accordingly. Retaliation and linkage were ruled out not simply because they would violate the accepted diplomatic relationship between Canadians and Americans, but because they would rile nationalists.

The fracas over nuclear weapons is a case where the Americans—justifiably— did exceed the bounds of propriety, but, oddly, faced no serious repercussions for their transgression. Offering an apologia of sorts for this episode years later, Bundy explained that he and other administration officials had "found Canadians good people to bargain with. They lack the insecurity which so often breeds misunderstanding and deception. Indeed, that is precisely why Diefenbaker was exceptional. It was our failure to understand how exceptional he was that led us to overreact. The fact that he was exceptional also led the Canadian democratic process in the end to disown him."[53] It may have been an overreaction on Washington's part to fire off the infamous press release, but this action was not done out of ignorance. Those instrumental in crafting the document, Willis Armstrong and Rufus Smith, had a deep mastery of Canadian affairs and had often, as Canadian diplomats recognized, "vigorously taken up the cudgels" on Canada's behalf with their colleagues throughout the US government.[54] By 1963, their stores of patience were gone. Having spent years opposing strong-arm tactics against Canada, they now advocated an assertive line. Armstrong and Smith's willingness to repudiate Diefenbaker publicly is even more remarkable given their appreciation of the power of Canadian nationalism. Nor were these two State Department veterans alone. By the time he left the Ottawa Embassy in May 1962, Livingston Merchant had become thoroughly worried both by the nationalist undercurrent and by the actions of the prime minister. George Ball, who pushed the infamous press release out through the bureaucracy, had less long-term knowledge of Canada. However, he had dealt with Ottawa for over two years on a range of issues from Canadian trade with communist countries to thorny economic matters in which Ottawa's obstinate position on the EEC, lack of support for the Trade Expansion Act, and deception over import surcharges had caused anger and outrage in Washington. Other US diplomats, notably Dean Rusk, William Tyler, and Walt Rostow, had each seen American plans ruined and goals frustrated by the actions and inactions of their ally to the north. These officials had no doubts that Canada followed an independent foreign policy.

Washington's inability to affect Canadian positions, or its unwillingness to do so through coercive means, reflected an oddity of US foreign relations throughout the 1960s when "the United States, at the zenith of its power and influence, often found itself at the mercy of decisions made by other nations and other leaders."[55] Having been at Canada's mercy for two years, it is no wonder that Kennedy administration officials favored a tough approach in January 1963. The wonder is that it took so long for Washington to respond to Canadian provocations. Frustrations aside, US policymakers took the view that Canada was an important ally and market, and so it would be disastrous to take precipitate actions that might harm a vital relationship. They certainly regretted independent Canadian positions and the lack of total cooperation on the range of issues from the Cuban embargo to the Grand Design. Even in the face of growing Canadian nationalism and mounting disagreements as the 1960s progressed, it was these American policymakers—notably Smith, Ball, and Bundy—who continued to counsel a conciliatory course. These men, having learned their craft under Kennedy, became the "tolerant allies" of Lyndon Johnson's White House.

The messy disagreements that plagued Canada–US relations during the final months of Diefenbaker's government worried officials on both sides of the border. As a result, on Ball's initiative, and with the blessing of Johnson and Lester Pearson, Merchant and Arnold Heeney prepared a report setting out guidelines to rebuild the "sound and sane relationship" that they each valued and to keep it in good repair.[56] Drawing on their vast experience at managing bilateral relations, Heeney and Merchant devised their guidebook by tracing the nature of the Canada–US dyad, examining areas where problems commonly arose, and offering suggestions toward building a more successful partnership. They advised that Canadian policymakers, while of course entitled to their own views and judgments, should acknowledge the unique role of the United States in the world and, within this context and "in the absences of special Canadian interests or obligations, avoid so far as possible, public disagreement especially upon critical issues." Going on to note that it was in the interest of both countries to avoid situations where "divergent views" were "expressed" openly, they counseled that conflicting views should be "if possible resolved in private, through diplomatic channels." When their report, *Canada and the United States: Principles for Partnership*, was published in 1965, this passage was highly criticized, with many Canadians upset at what they believed was a call for them to shut up. Such criticisms ignored Merchant and Heeney's observation that "there are bound to arise cases of genuine conflict of national interest which by their nature are, at the time at least, incapable of mutually acceptable solutions In such matters there may indeed be no immediate alternative to an agreement to disagree." The aim of the Merchant-Heeney report was not to keep Canadians quiet, but to avoid the open trauma of the Kennedy–Diefenbaker years and to seek ways of managing what was becoming a more interdependent relationship in an era of bilateral tension.[57] Disagreement was to be expected; sound and fury was to be avoided.

Coming on the heels of the escalation of the American war in Vietnam, which prompted many Canadians to demand their government engage in a louder, more forthright diplomacy meant to showcase Canada's opposition to the conflict and bring pressure to bear so that the fighting would end, *Principles for Partnership* was quietly shelved. But its recommendations remained the accepted approach to bilateral relations. A policy paper on Canada–US relations approved by Paul Martin only days prior to the report's release made clear: "As a matter of normal practice we should as far as possible make use of a private type of diplomacy in our dealings with the United States."[58] With immense criticism leveled at the former ambassadors' study, Canadian officials found it impolitic to preach what they practiced. Furthermore, with quiet diplomacy increasingly derided, the diplomatic culture in which Heeney and Merchant had operated was beginning to change, with the Canada–US relationship changing alongside it. Still, in the Kennedy years specialness remained a hallmark of bilateral relations. Even if disagreements grew louder, from issues such as Laos and Cuba to crises over the Canadian dollar and Berlin, forbearance and quiet assistance were the norm.

The clash over nuclear weaponry aside, Canada had cooperated with the United States on numerous issues, often in spite of doubts about American policy or disagreements relating to bilateral affairs. Take China, a country with which Canada was willing to trade, but not officially recognize. Or Cuba, where Canadian trade and diplomatic ties were maintained alongside both an effort by Canadian diplomats in Havana to gather intelligence on Washington's behalf and actions taken in Ottawa to limit the sale of strategic goods. During the missile crisis, and throughout the standoff over Berlin, Canada stood resolutely beside the United States, while in Vietnam, Canadians turned a blind eye to American efforts to arm Saigon in contravention of the Geneva Accords. After all, Canada and the United States were allies in the Cold War. Even so, the two countries did not march in lockstep. Partly, the differences between these two allies were the result of the vast gulf between Canadian and American power and the resulting sense of responsibility. Of importance too was the influence of Canadian nationalism and the way in which this sensibility influenced Canadian thinking, particularly the outlook of Diefenbaker, Walter Gordon, and other conservative nationalists who were much more preoccupied with Canada's cultural and economic existence than they were with the direction of US foreign policy abroad, a much more galvanizing issue for the New Nationalists, of a far more left-wing bent, who became increasingly more prominent in the mid-1960s. Vietnam, and Canada's complicity in the US war effort, became a cause célèbre for the Canadian New Left, which was concerned too with issues of cultural and economic domination from the south.[59]

What of Diefenbaker, then? As Basil Robinson recalled, the prime minister "had very little inclination or talent for negotiation in the substance of foreign policy. He did not appreciate the environment in which others were operating, and was not willing to give in search of compromise." Thus, for "those who wanted a creative, resourceful role for Canada in the world, Diefenbaker was not the answer."[60] On the one hand, the prime minister *was* a deft foreign policymaker, standing up for the Canadian position on trade with communist countries, supporting NATO during the standoff over Berlin, seeking an independent position in Latin America, and aiding his US allies in Southeast Asia. On the other hand, with the Grand Design he had shown no appreciation for the British or American positions nor had he adopted the more constructive stance urged by the Liberals, by Australia and New Zealand, or by a range of economists, including his own finance minister. And his handling of the nuclear file was inept. His concern with domestic opinion was understandable; citing this factor as an insurmountable stumbling block was indefensible, both in light of his huge majority in the House of Commons from 1958 to 1962 and his responsibility as an ally of the United States who had committed to acquiring weapons systems that appeared vital for the defense of the nuclear deterrent. Of course, a more justifiable concern was the uselessness of the weaponry itself: in the age of the ICBM, the BOMARC was redundant. Had he wished to back away from a nuclear role, as he hinted at in the autumn of 1961 and in early 1962, he could and should have done so; instead, he continued to string along the Americans. His efforts at evasion in 1962 and in 1963 were irresponsible.

Among American authorities, there was a sense that Diefenbaker alone determined Canada's position on issues, with Green playing a supporting role. Beyond the prime minister's idiosyncrasies—his penchant for delay above all—they recognized that he was a politician motivated by a desire to stay in power, and that to do so he was willing to play to the darker emotions of his electorate. In this regard, they saw a distinct Diefenbaker-style of foreign leader. British Labour Prime Minister Harold Wilson, Bundy wrote in 1965, was one who might "be mortally tempted to begin to make critical noises about us, thus appealing both to his own party and to the natural nationalism of many independent Englishmen. This would not be helpful to Wilson in the long run, but it would not be helpful to us either, as the history of Diefenbaker proves." "When we fall out with Prime Ministers," he added, "it's usually painted as our fault."[61] The White House and State Department bore blame for taking actions that made nationalists bristle—Kennedy's regrettable public appeal on the OAS—but Diefenbaker was also at fault for the deterioration of bilateral relations through his tantrum over the Rostow memorandum and his drawing out of the nuclear issue. The Americans could not stand having their defensive efforts undermined for political reasons, at least not after four years of broken promises and a near nuclear war over Cuba. What they could stomach was his populist rhetoric and, indeed, they expected it.

Nationalism—the manifestation of the psychological factor in Canada–US relations—had distinct and powerful political uses. Canadians, always insecure about their place in North America, have had a need to prove their independence, a mood from which politicians like Diefenbaker have drawn support. As the US ambassador to Ottawa in the mid-1990s reflected: "If we didn't have the difference over Cuba, the Canadian government would probably have to invent something else. . . . From time to time, Canadian politicians have to show their people that they're overseeing a sovereign nation, not just rubber-stamping the policies made in Washington."[62] Either Livingston Merchant or Walton Butterworth could have written this comment, except that US diplomats in the 1960s also felt that nationalism possessed actual causal power. They were not wrong. While differing viewpoints and calculations of interest divided Canada and the United States on Cuba, China, the Common Market, and nuclear weapons, notable too was the Diefenbaker government's desire to pursue policies at actual variance from the Kennedy administration out of a belief that Canadian sovereignty was truly threatened. And many Canadians applauded them for it. Nationalism was not simply a figment of US imagination, nor was it meaningless rhetoric.

In light of the nationalist impulse in Canada, too much blame for the weakening of Canadian–American ties should not be leveled at Diefenbaker. However much he and some of his ministers may have dithered and deceived, their actions were reflective of two larger trends. First, many of the issues that clouded this period in bilateral relations brought into question Canada's place in an increasingly smaller world. On the Common Market, for instance, one of the root causes of Diefenbaker's discontent was over where Canada stood in the face of efforts to unite Western Europe. Some Canadians, the prime minister included, feared that the answer was North America. The issue of OAS membership raised a similar concern, for joining the organization would draw Canada more firmly into the Western hemisphere and into the US sphere of influence. Further—as its very name suggests—continental defense, and the issues surrounding it, boiled down to this problem of place. In turn, the question "whither Canada?" raised doubts about Canadian economic, military, and diplomatic autonomy, the very issues of concern to Canadian nationalists.

Second, slowly but surely Canada and the United States were moving apart, not in terms of economics or culture—here, the opposite trend was true—but in terms of foreign policy and Cold War outlook. Reflecting on this movement years later, Bundy observed that "Canada is also naturally perceived as a fast friend and ally of America's, although the bilateral relationship has seen a marked shift over the long term toward a greater degree of distancing and the exercise of independent judgment on Canada's part."[63] In the 1960s Canadians, like other American allies, viewed a lessening of Cold War tension as a favorable course, while US officials initially took a differing view at least in terms of mounting a more militant effort in the Third World. This development, shown most starkly with Vietnam, in turn strained the bonds that had united Canada, Western Europe, and the United States from the dark days of the late 1940s through to the crisis years of Kennedy's presidency. Beginning on Kennedy's watch, this process was part of a global trend in the 1960s toward a weakening of the Cold War consensus on both sides of the iron curtain.[64]

Differences over global policies and changing perceptions of the Cold War world developed alongside concerns amongst Canadians over their economic and cultural growth as well as the unity of their country in the face of nationalism emanating from Quebec. Hence, "as the United States turned outward, Canada increasingly turned inward."[65] A prelude to the development of the New Nationalism that took hold in Canada in the mid-1960s, the Kennedy period bridged the relative bilateral harmony of the 1950s and the antagonism of later years when conservative, Anglo-centric nationalism fed into New Left critiques, with Canadian philosopher George Grant and his 1965 *Lament for a Nation* an important linchpin in the process. A revulsion against the conflict in Vietnam, the violence and chaos surrounding both the opposition to that war and the black freedom struggle, and a trend—personified by Walter Gordon— against US investment in Canada all fed this new pro-Canadian, anti-American outlook. Economic integration with the United States seemed to threaten Canada's identity and its survival as a country, and so there existed a "sense of vulnerability to the United States, one made all the more worrisome given the crumbling of John F. Kennedy's Camelot among internal civil protests and external militarism." But this trend was more an "ideological happening" than a "political revolution."[66] Like the New Nationalists who followed him, Diefenbaker certainly made provocative statements about the United States yet failed to provide fundamental policy changes. The Canadian–American alliance endured the 1960s tumult.

A change did come, though, under Richard Nixon, who, as president, abandoned economic exemptions for Canada. Under his watch, the two joint ministerial committees—on trade and economic matters, and on defense—were left to wither. And in 1972 he told the Canadian House of Commons that it was necessary to "move beyond the sentimental rhetoric of the past." What amounted to an elegy for the special relationship prompted the Canadian government to look, in earnest, for new foci abroad. Thus both Ottawa and Washington opted to go their separate ways, with Pearson's successor, Pierre Trudeau, pursuing policies to diversify trade and restrict US investment. One scholar would soon declare—too soon as it turned out—that the Canada–US relationship was a "forgotten partnership."[67] Diefenbaker had preferred Nixon to Kennedy in 1960. But one wonders whether a Nixon White House in 1963 would have been any more charitable to the Canadian prime minister's deceptions and delays than the New Frontiersmen.

In the end, the Kennedy administration and the core of Canadianists in the State Department saw Canada as an ally, albeit an increasingly difficult one. On this theme Ambassador Butterworth offered a prophetic assessment only days after Diefenbaker's electoral defeat in 1963. Comparing the Progressive Conservatives and Liberals, he cautioned that Washington should remember that the latter, although seen to be more pro-American, were "none the less Canadians and their relative sophistication does not mean they do not suffer from a familiar national compulsion to demonstrate to themselves and others that they are not Americans." Despite the change in governments, the ambassador still expected Canadian psychology to remain a factor in bilateral relations. The difference now, Butterworth remarked, was that neither Pearson nor Paul Martin would evince the "same ignorance and mistrust of us" as displayed by Diefenbaker and Green. Drawing upon the experiences of his embassy staff over the past few years, Butterworth concluded with a frank observation of the need to question the "premise which has so long been implicit in our concept of Canada's role, namely that she would automatically, accurately, and effectively represent essentially our own view." The United States "experience" with Canada of late had proven a need "for less encouragement of separate Canadian roles and pretentions, more of a down to earth approach from us, and more of a turning to other allies such as the Australians when a strong and unembarrassed Western presence is needed as a counterbalance to a Soviet satellite."[68] Still viewed as allies, Canadians, thanks to nationalism, had, in the American mind, become a little less special and a little more independent.

# Abbreviations

| | |
|---|---|
| ANF | Alpha-Numeric Files Relating to Canadian Affairs, 1957–1963 |
| ARA-CCA-SF | Bureau of Inter-American Affairs, Office of the Coordinator of Cuban Affairs, US State Department |
| *ARCS* | *American Review of Canadian Studies* |
| AWF | Ann Whitman File |
| EUR-BNA | Bureau of European Affairs, Office of British Commonwealth and Northern European Affairs, US State Department |
| Ball | Executive Secretariat, Records for Under Secretary of State George W. Ball, 1961–1966 |
| CC | Cabinet Conclusions |
| CDF | Central Decimal File, 1950–1963 |
| CGR | Classified General Records, Ottawa Embassy, 1959–1961 |
| CRO | Commonwealth Relations Office |
| *CT* | *Chicago Tribune* |
| CVA | City of Vancouver Archives |
| *D&S* | *Diplomacy and Statecraft* |
| DCER | *Documents on Canadian External Relations* |
| DDEL | Dwight D. Eisenhower Library, Abilene, Kansas |
| *DH* | *Diplomatic History* |
| EUR-CDC | Bureau of European Affairs, Country Director for Canada, US State Department |
| EUR-RPE | Bureau of European Affairs, Office of Atlantic Political and Economic Affairs, US State Department |
| *FA* | *Foreign Affairs* |
| FAOHC | Foreign Affairs Oral History Collection of the Association for Diplomatic Studies and Training, Library of Congress |
| *FRUS* | *Foreign Relations of the United States* |
| *G&M* | *Globe and Mail* |
| GCM | General Correspondence and Memo Series |

GWB        George Ball Papers
HOC        House of Commons *Debates*, Parliament of Canada
IJ         *International Journal*
JFD        John Foster Dulles Papers
JFKL       John F. Kennedy Presidential Library, Boston, Massachusetts
LAC        Library and Archives Canada
LAT        *Los Angeles Times*
LBJL       Lyndon B. Johnson Library, Austin, Texas
MG         *Montreal Gazette*
MHS        Massachusetts Historical Society
NARA       United States National Archives and Records Administration II,
           College Park, Maryland
NSAM       National Security Action Memorandum
NSF        National Security Files
NYHT       *New York Herald Tribune*
NYT        *New York Times*
OC         *Ottawa Citizen*
POF        President's Office Files
PP         Pre-Presidential Files
PPP        *Public Papers of the President*
QUA        Queen's University Archives
RBW        Richard B. Wigglesworth Papers
RREM       Records Relating to Economic Matters
RRMM       Records Relating to Military Matters
RRPM       Records Relating to Political Matters
RRTEA      Records Relating to the Joint US–Canada Committee on Trade and
           Economic Affairs
RRUK       Records Relating to United Kingdom Negotiations for Membership
           in the European Economic Community, 1961–1962
Rusk TTC   Records of Dean Rusk, Transcripts of Telephone Calls
S&S        *Statements and Speeches*, Canada, Department of External Affairs
SMML       Seeley G. Mudd Manuscript Library, Princeton University
TNA        The National Archives of the United Kingdom, Kew
TS         *Toronto Star*
WHCSF      White House Central Subject Files
WP         *Washington Post*
WSJ        *Wall Street Journal*

# Notes

## Introduction

1. Diary, Jan. 22, 1961, LAC/MG 30 E144/vol. 2; "Inaugural Address," Jan. 20, 1961, *PPP*.
2. "Wisdom in Washington," *G&M*, Jan. 20, 1961; "President Kennedy's Inauguration," *OC*, Jan. 20, 1961; "A President Speaks," *MG*, Jan. 21, 1961.
3. "Students Pick Kennedy To Be Next President," *The Varsity*, Nov. 7, 1960; Ottawa to State, no. 923, May 19, 1961, JFKL/NSF/box 18/folder Canada, General 4/61-5/14/61; L. Baldridge Hollensteiner Oral History, Apr. 24, 1964, JFKL.
4. Ottawa to State, no. A-572, Dec. 23, 1962, JFKL/NSF/box 18/folder Canada, General 10/62-1/63.
5. L. Axworthy, *Navigating a New World: Canada's Global Future* (Toronto: Vintage, 2004), 33; Mulroney to O'Brien, Jul. 20, 1962, JFKL/WHCSF/box 43/folder CO 438/ 1/62; Vanier to Kennedy, May 31, 1961, JFKL/WHCSF/box 43/folder Canada 1/1/ 61-6/30/61; E. Drake, *A Stubble-Jumper in Striped Pants: Memoirs of a Prairie Diplomat* (Toronto: University of Toronto Press, 1999), 24; H. B. Robinson, *Diefenbaker's World: A Populist In Foreign Affairs* (Toronto: University of Toronto Press, 1989), 207.
6. R. Bothwell, *Your Country, My Country: A Unified History of the United States and Canada* (New York: Oxford University Press, 2015), 234.
7. There is no book-length study of Canada–US relations in the Eisenhower years.
8. Z. Steiner, "On Writing International History: Chaps, Maps and Much More," *International Affairs* 73, no. 3 (1997), 531.
9. R. Touhey, *Canada and India in the Cold War World, 1946–76* (Vancouver: UBC Press, 2015); D. Meren, *With Friends Like These: Entangled Nationalisms and the Canada-Quebec-France Triangle* (Vancouver: UBC Press, 2012); K. Spooner, *Canada, the Congo Crisis, and UN Peacekeeping* (Vancouver: UBC Press, 2009); D. Webster, *Fire and the Full Moon: Canada and Indonesia in a Decolonizing World* (Vancouver: UBC Press 2009); M. Carroll, *Pearson's Peacekeepers: Canada and the United Nations Emergency Force, 1956–67* (Vancouver: UBC Press, 2009); R. Bothwell, *Alliance and Illusion: Canada and the World, 1945–1984* (Vancouver: UBC Press, 2007); R. Gendron, *Towards a Francophone Community: Canada's Relations with France and French Africa, 1945–1968* (Montréal and Kingston: McGill–Queen's University Press, 2006); A. Chapnick, *The Middle Power Project: Canada and the Founding of the United Nations* (Vancouver: UBC Press, 2005); and G. Donaghy, *Tolerant Allies: Canada and the United States, 1963–1968* (Montréal and Kingston: McGill–Queen's University Press, 2002).
10. S. Azzi, "The Nationalist Moment in English Canada," in *Debating Dissent: Canada and the 1960s*, eds. L. A. Campbell, D. Clément, and G. Kealey (Toronto: University of Toronto Press, 2012), 213–28.
11. D. Kunz, *The Diplomacy of the Crucial Decade: American Foreign Relations During the 1960s* (New York: Columbia University Press, 1994).

12. M. Beschloss, *The Crisis Years: Kennedy and Khrushchev, 1960–1963* (New York: Edward Burlingame Books, 1991); and J. G. Hershberg, "The Crisis Years, 1958–1963," in *Reviewing the Cold War: Approaches, Interpretations, Theory*, ed. O. A. Westad (London: Frank Cass, 2000), 303–25.

13. M. J. Selverstone, "Introduction," in *A Companion to John F. Kennedy*, ed. M. J. Selverstone (Chichester: Wiley, 2014), 1.

14. "Prairie Lawyer," *Time*, Aug. 5, 1957; Briefing memo, "Diefenbaker, John George," May 1961, JFKL/POF/box 113/folder JFK Trip to Ottawa, 5/61; Diary, Jun. 5, 1960, LAC/ MG 31 E144/vol. 2.

15. P. C. Newman, *Renegade in Power: The Diefenbaker Years* (Toronto: McClelland and Stewart, 1963); D. Smith, *Rogue Tory: The Life and Legend of John G Diefenbaker* (Toronto: MacFarlane, Walter and Roass, 1995); and R. Gwyn, *The 49th Paradox: Canada in North America* (Toronto: McClelland and Stewart, 1985), 66.

16. P. Lyon, *Canada in World Affairs, 1961–1963* (Toronto: University of Toronto Press, 1968), 492.

17. Smith, *Rogue Tory*, 378; Robinson, *Diefenbaker's World*, 165; J. H. Thompson and S. J. Randall, *Canada and the United States: Ambivalent Allies*, Fourth Edition (Montréal and Kingston: McGill–Queen's University Press, 2008), 200.

18. Smith, *Rogue Tory*, xiii. See also: P. McMahon, *Essence of Indecision: Diefenbaker's Nuclear Policy, 1957–1963* (Montréal and Kingston: McGill–Queen's University Press, 2009), x. McMahon's work is part of a welcome trend offering a nuanced look at aspects of Diefenbaker's foreign policy. See also: D. C. Story and R. B. Shepard, eds., *The Diefenbaker Legacy: Politics, Law and Society Since 1957* (Regina: Canadian Plains Research Centre, 1998); Spooner, *Canada, the Congo Crisis, and UN*; M. D. Stevenson, "'A Very Careful Balance': The 1961 Triangular Agreement and the Conduct of Canadian–American Relations," *Diplomacy & Statecraft* 24, no. 2 (2013), 291–311; M. D. Stevenson, "'Tossing a Match into Dry Hay': Nuclear Weapons and the Crisis in U.S.–Canadian Relations, 1962–1963," *Journal of Cold War Studies* 16, no. 4 (2014), 5–34; and A. McKercher, "Southern Exposure: Diefenbaker, Latin America, and the Organization of American States," *Canadian Historical Review* 93, no. 1 (2012), 57–80.

19. Robinson, *Diefenbaker's World*, 314.

20. L. B. Pearson, *Words & Occasions* (Toronto: University of Toronto Press, 1970), 68.

21. K. Nash, *Kennedy and Diefenbaker: Fear and Loathing Across the Undefended Border* (Toronto: McClelland and Stewart, 1990), 12; M. Potter, "JFK and Why Camelot Was a Living Nightmare for Canada," *Star Dispatches* (Toronto: Toronto Star, 2013); N. Hillmer and J. L. Granatstein, *For Better of For Worse: Canada and the United States into the Twenty-First Century* (Toronto: HarperCollins, 2007), 210; Smith, *Rogue Tory*, 457. For a recent, largely derivative take on Kennedy and Canada, see J. Boyko, *Cold Fire: Kennedy's Northern Front* (Toronto: Knopf, 2016).

22. L. Freedman, *Kennedy's Wars: Berlin, Cuba, Laos, and Vietnam* (Oxford: Oxford University Press, 2000), 7; T. White, "The Action Intellectuals," *Life* (June 1967).

23. J. F. Kennedy, "Review," *Saturday Review* (Aug. 1, 1959). And see A. Chapnick, "The Canadian Middle Power Myth," *IJ* 55, no. 2 (2000): 188–206; H. MacKenzie, "Golden Decade(s)? Reappraising Canada's International Relations in the 1940s and 1950s," *British Journal of Canadian Studies* 23, no. 2 (2010): 179–206; G. Donaghy, "Coming off the Gold Standard: Re-assessing the 'Golden Age' of Canadian Diplomacy," paper presented to the symposium A Very Modern Ministry: Foreign Affairs and International Trade Canada, University of Saskatchewan, Sep. 28, 2009.

24. L. B. Pearson, "Where is North American Going?," *Fourth Seminar on Canadian–American Relations at Assumption University of Windsor* (Windsor: Assumption University, 1962), 8.

25. Quoted in J. English, *The Worldly Years: The Life of Lester Pearson 1949–1972* (Toronto: Alfred A. Knopf, 1992), 59.

26. Granatstein and Hillmer, *Better or Worse*, vii. And see D. Stairs, *The Diplomacy of Constraint: Canada, the Korean War and the United States* (Toronto: University of Toronto

Press, 1974); T. A. Sayle, "A Pattern of Constraint: Canadian–American Relations in the Early Cold War," *IJ* 62, no. 3 (2007), 689–705.

27. Thompson and Randall, *Ambivalent Allies*, 1.

28. D. Reynolds, "A Special Relationship? America, Britain and the International Order Since the Second World War," *International Affairs* 62, no. 1 (1985–86), 2, 3; W. F. Kimball, "The 'Special' Anglo-American Special Relationship: 'A Fatter, Larger Underwater Cable,'" *Journal of Transatlantic Studies* 3, no. 1 (2005), 2.

29. R. Bothwell, *Canada and the United States: The Politics of Partnership* (New York: Twayne, 1992), 39, 42.

30. C. F. Doran, *Forgotten Partnership: U.S.–Canada Relations Today* (Baltimore: Johns Hopkins University Press, 1984), 21. And: L. Aronsen, *American National Security and Economic Relations with Canada, 1945–1954* (Westport: Praegar, 1997); G. R. Perras, *Franklin Roosevelt and the Origins of the Canadian–American Security Alliance, 1933–1945: Necessary But Not Necessary Enough* (Westport: Praegar, 1998); D. Haglund, "The US-Canada Relationship: How 'Special' Is America's Longest Unbroken Alliance?," in *America's Special Relationships*, eds. J. Dumbrell and A. Schäfer (London: Routledge, 2009), 60–75.

31. B. Bow, *The Politics of Linkage: Power, Interdependence, and Ideas in Canada–US Relations* (Vancouver: UBC Press, 2009), 2, 3. Emphasis original.

32. B. Muirhead, *Dancing Around the Elephant: Creating a Prosperous Canada in an Era of American Dominance, 1957–1973* (Toronto: University of Toronto Press, 2007), 8. Muirhead's outstanding study is focused largely on economic questions, whereas this study focuses on other issues and so offers a complementary look at bilateral relations.

33. R. O. Keohane and J. S. Nye Jr., *Power and Interdependence: World Politics in Transition*, Second Edition (Boston: Little, Brown, 1989), 165–209; B. Bow, "Rethinking 'Retaliation' in Canada–US Relations," in *An Independent Foreign Policy for Canada? Challenges and Choices for the Future*, eds. B. Bow and P. Lennox (Toronto: University of Toronto Press, 2008), 63–82.

34. R. Smith, "Defence and North American Solidarity," *Fifth Seminar on Canadian–American Relations at Assumption University of Windsor* (Windsor: Assumption University, 1963) 117.

35. P. Lyon, "Problems of Canadian Independence," *IJ* 16, no. 3 (1960–61), 251–2. And see P. Lyon, "Quiet Diplomacy Revisited," in *An Independent Foreign Policy for Canada?*, ed. S. Clarkson (Toronto: McClelland and Stewart, 1968), 29–41.

36. Lyon, *Canada in World Affairs*, 529.

37. J. F. Hilliker, "The Politicians and the 'Pearsonalities': The Diefenbaker Government and the Conduct of Canadian External Relations," *Historical Papers* 19, no. 1 (1984), 151–67.

38. E. Mahant and G. S. Mount, *Invisible and Inaudible in Washington: American Policies toward Canada* (Vancouver: UBC Press, 1999).

39. B. Anderson, *Imagined Communities: Reflections on the Origin and Spread of Nationalism*, Revised Edition (London: Verso, 1991), 5–7.

40. F. Underhill, "The Image of Confederation," *1963 Massey Lecture* (Toronto: Canadian Broadcasting Corporation, 1964), 4.

41. S. Brooks, *As Others See Us: The Causes and Consequences of Foreign Perceptions of America* (Toronto: University of Toronto Press, 2006), 140. See also: C. Berger, *The Sense of Power: Studies in the Ideas of Canadian Imperialism 1867–1944* (Toronto: University of Toronto Press, 1970), 265; D-C. Bélanger, *Prejudice and Pride: Canadian Intellectuals Confront the United States, 1891–1945* (Toronto: University of Toronto Press, 2011); J. Igartua, *The Other Quiet Revolution: National Identities in English Canada, 1945–71* (Vancouver: UBC Press, 2006), 89–136; and R. Edwardson, *Canadian Content: Culture and the Quest for Nationhood* (Toronto: University of Toronto Press, 2008), 8–22 and 135–59.

42. A. McPherson, *Yankee No! Anti-Americanism in U.S.-Latin American Relations* (Cambridge, MA: Harvard University Press, 2003), 5; P. Hollander, *Anti-Americanism: Critiques at Home and Abroad 1965–1990* (Oxford: Oxford University Press, 1992), viii, 411–6; D. Fulton, "Opening Address," *Second Seminar on Canadian–American Relations at Assumption University of Windsor* (Windsor: Assumption University, 1960), 3–4. And see

J. MacLennan, "Dancing with Our Neighbours: English Canadians and the Discourse of 'Anti-Americanism,'" in *Transnationalism: Canada–United States History into the 21st Century*, eds. M. D. Behiels and R. C. Stuart (Montréal and Kingston: McGill–Queen's University Press, 2010), 69–85; B. Bow, "Anti-Americanism in Canada, Before and After Iraq," *ARCS* 38, no. 3 (2008), 341–59.

43. S. Azzi, "Foreign Investment and the Paradox of Economic Nationalism," in *Canadas of the Mind: The Making and Unmaking of Canadian Nationalisms in the Twentieth Century*, eds. A. Chapnick and N. Hillmer (Montréal and Kingston: McGill–Queen's University Press, 2007), 68; R. Cook, *Canada, Quebec, and the Uses of Nationalism*, Second Edition (Toronto: McClelland and Stewart, 1986), 211. And see L. Aronsen, "An Open Door to the North: The Liberal Government and the Expansion of American Foreign Investment, 1945–1953," *ARCS* 22, no. 2 (1992): 167–97; and R. D. Cuff and J. L. Granatstein, *American Dollars, Canadian Prosperity: Canadian–American Economic Relations, 1945–50* (Toronto: Samuel Stevens, 1978).

44. G. Grant, *Lament for a Nation: The Defeat of Canadian Nationalism* (Montréal and Kingston: McGill–Queen's University Press, 2000 [1965]); L. Kuffert, "'Stabbing our Spirits Broad Awake': Reconstructing Canadian Culture, 1940–1948," in *Cultures of Citizenship in Post-war Canada, 1940–1955*, eds. N. Christie and M. Gauvreau (Montréal and Kingston: McGill–Queen's University Press, 2003), 27–62; P. Massolin, *Canadian Intellectuals, the Tory Tradition and the Challenge of Modernity, 1939–1970* (Toronto: University of Toronto Press, 2001); and R. D. Francis, *The Technological Imperative in Canada: An Intellectual History* (Vancouver: UBC Press, 2009). And see R. Latham, *The Liberal Moment: Modernity, Security and the Making of Postwar International Order* (New York: Columbia University Press, 1997); N. Cullather, "Modernization Theory," in *Explaining the History of American Foreign Relations*, ed. M. J. Hogan (Cambridge: Cambridge University Press, 2003), 212–20.

45. J. L. Granatstein, *Canada 1957–1967: Years of Uncertainty and Innovation* (Toronto: McClelland and Stewart, 1986), 1. And see C. Spittal, "The Diefenbaker Moment" (PhD diss., University of Toronto, 2011).

46. Igartua, *Quiet Revolution*; P. Buckner, "The Long Goodbye: English Canadians and the British World," in *Rediscovering the British World*, eds. P. Buckner and R. D. Francis (Calgary: University of Calgary Press, 2005), 181–207.

47. Quoted in P. C. Newman, "Who Really Owns Canada?," *Maclean's*, Jun. 9, 1956.

48. R.A. Preston, "Introduction: National Imagery—The Canadian Image of the United States Today," in *Canada Views the United States: Nineteenth Century Political Attitudes*, eds. S. F. Wise and R. C. Brown (Toronto: Macmillan, 1967), 9.

49. A. Chapnick, "Running in Circles: The Canadian Independence Debate in History," in *An Independent Foreign Policy for Canada? Challenges and Choices for the Future*, eds. B. Bow and P. Lennox (Toronto: University of Toronto Press, 2008), 25–40.

50. S. Clarkson, "The Choice to be Made," in *An Independent Foreign Policy for Canada?*, 260–63. And see A. Purdy, ed., *The New Romans: Candid Canadian Opinions of the US* (Edmonton: Hurtig, 1968); J. Warnock, *Partner to Behemoth: The Military Policy of a Satellite Canada* (Toronto: New Press, 1970); and I. Lumsden, ed., *Close the 49th Parallel Etc.: The Americanization of Canada* (Toronto: University of Toronto, 1970).

51. A. Chapnick, "Peace, Order and Good Government: The 'Conservative' Tradition in Canadian Foreign Policy," *IJ* 60, no. 3 (2005), 635–50.

52. Muirhead, *Dancing*, 30; Bothwell, *Alliance and Illusion*, 177, 157.

53. M. P. Friedman, "Anti-Americanism and U.S. Foreign Relations," *DH* 32, no. 4 (2008), 499.

54. "Department of State Guidelines for Policy and Operations—Canada," Mar. 1962, JFKL/NSF/box 18/folder Canada, General, 2–62-3/62.

55. Armstrong to White, Nov. 9, 1960 and Armstrong to Consul Generals, Sept. 23, 1960, NARA/RG 59/EUR-BNA/ANF/Box 1/folder Nationalism, Neutralism and Anti-Americanism, 1960–1962.

56. "The Roots of Canadian–American Problems," Dec. 1960, NARA/RG 84/CGR/box 224/ folder international political rel classified 1959–61 Canada–US; NIE 99–61, "Trends in Canadian Foreign Policy," May 2, 1961, JFKL/POF/box 113/folder JFK Trip to Ottawa, 5/61.

57. Ottawa to State, no. A-369, Apr. 3, 1962, NARA/RG 59/CDF/611.42/4–362.

58. Doran, *Forgotten Partnership*, 41.

59. F. Underhill, "Canada and the North Atlantic Triangle," in *In Search of Canadian Liberalism*, ed. F. Underhill (Don Mills: Oxford University Press, 2013 [1960]), 255; Memcon, "Visit of Canadian Prime Minister Diefenbaker," Feb. 20, 1961, JFKL/NSF/ box 18/folder Canada, General 1/61-3/61.

60. J. L. Granatstein, "When Push Came to Shove: Canada and the United States," in *Kennedy's Quest for Victory: American Foreign Policy, 1961–1963*, ed. T. G. Paterson (New York: Oxford University Press, 1989), 103; S. J. Randall, "Great Expectations: America's Approach to Canada," in *Transnationalism*, 286.

61. Thompson and Randall, *Canada and the United States*, 203, 201; G. T. Stewart, *The American Response to Canada since 1776* (East Lansing: Michigan State University Press, 1992), 167; R. Bothwell and J. Kirton, "A Sweet Little Country," in *Partners Nevertheless: Canadian–American Relations in the Twentieth Century*, ed. N. Hillmer (Toronto: Copp Clark Pitman, 1989), 63.

62. J. Zorbas, *Diefenbaker and Latin America: The Pursuit of Canadian Autonomy* (Newcastle: Cambridge Scholars Publishers, 2011), 137.

63. United States Senate, 87th Congress, *Executive Sessions*, Foreign Relations Committee together with the Armed Services Committee (Washington, DC, 1962); News Conference, Jun. 24, 1963, JFKL/POF/box 60.

64. K. J. Gloin, "Canada–US Relations in the Diefenbaker Era: Another Look," in *The Diefenbaker Legacy*, eds. Story and Shepard, 8–9.

65. Donaghy, *Tolerant Allies*.

66. Letter, Armstrong to Butterworth, Nov. 30, 1962, NARA/RG 59/EUR-CDC/box 3/ folder New US Ambassador, 1962; Merchant to Seymour, Jul. 26, 1961, NARA/RG 59/ EUR-BNA/AFN/box 4/folder Speeches 1961–1963.

67. M. Hunt, *Ideology and U.S. Foreign Policy* (New Haven: Yale University Press, 1987).

68. C. Ritchie, *Storm Signals: More Undiplomatic Diaries, 1962–1971* (Toronto: Macmillan, 1983), 52.

69. "Let's Stop Yapping at the United States," *United Church Observer*, Dec. 15, 1960; H. MacLennan, "After 300 Years, Our Neurosis is Relevant," in *Canada: A Guide to the Peaceable Kingdom*, ed. William Kilbourn (Toronto: Macmillan, 1970), 8; P. V. Lyon, "Problems of Canadian Independence," *IJ* 16, no. 3 (1960–61), 251; F. Underhill, "Foreword," in *Nationalism in Canada*, ed. P. Russell (Toronto: McGraw-Hill, 1966), xix.

70. C. W. Mills, *White Collar: The American Middle Classes* (New York: Oxford University Press, 1951), xx. And see E. Herman, *The Romance of American Psychology: Political Culture in the Age of Experts* (Berkeley: University of California Press, 1995). On emotions in international affairs, see F. Costigliola, "'I Had Come as a Friend': Emotion, Culture, and Ambiguity in the Formation of the Cold War," *Cold War History* 1, no. 1 (2000), 103–28; Costigliola, "Culture, Emotion, and the Creation of Atlantic Identity, 1948–52," in *No End to Alliance*, ed. G. Lundestad (London: St. Martin's Press, 1998), 21–36; and B. Keys, "Henry Kissinger: The Emotional Statesman," *DH* 35, no. 4 (2011), 587–609.

71. S. G. Rabe, "John F. Kennedy and the World," in *Debating the Kennedy Presidency*, eds. J. N. Giglio and S. G. Rabe (Lanham: Rowman & Littlefield, 2003), 6, 7.

72. R. B. Rakove, *Kennedy, Johnson, and the Nonaligned World* (Cambridge: Cambridge University Press, 2012), xxii; P. Muehlenbeck, *Betting on the Africans: John F. Kennedy's Courting of African Nationalist Leaders* (New York: Oxford University Press, 2012).

73. N. Ashton, *Kennedy, Macmillan and the Cold War: The Irony of Interdependence* (Basingstoke: Palgrave Macmillan, 2002).

Chapter 1

1. Remarks at the University of Montréal, Dec. 4, 1953, Address at the Convocation of the University of New Brunswick, Oct. 8, 1957, JFKL/PP/box 898.
2. J. Barber, *Good Fences Make Good Neighbors: Why the United States Provokes Canadians* (Indianapolis: Bobbs-Merrill Company, 1958), 21, 16.
3. J. Diefenbaker, *One Canada*, II (Toronto: Macmillan, 1975.), 172; D. Molinaro, "'Calculated Diplomacy'; John Diefenbaker and the Origins of Canada's Cuba Policy," in *Our Place in the Sun: Canada and Cuba in the Castro Era*, eds. R. Wright and L. Wylie (Toronto: University of Toronto Press, 2009), 89; L. Martin, *The Presidents and the Prime Ministers: Washington and Ottawa Face to Face: The Myth of Bilateral Bliss, 1867–1982* (Toronto: Doubleday, 1982), 19. Diefenbaker's memoirs have served as the basis for much erroneous information about Canada–US relations. The ghostwriter of these memoirs has explained how the prime minister played fast and loose with facts: J. Munro, "Trials and Tribulations: The Making of the Diefenbaker and Pearson Memoirs," in *Political Memoir: Essays on the Politics of Memory*, ed. G. Egerton (London: Frank Cass, 1994), 242–56. And see A. McKercher, "Diefenbaker's World: *One Canada* and the History of Canadian–American Relations, 1961–63," *The Historian* 75, no. 1 (2013): 94–120.
4. Memcon, "Visit of Canadian Prime Minister Diefenbaker," Feb. 20, 1961, JFKL/NSF/box 18/folder Canada, General 1/61–3/61. Bizarrely, despite Diefenbaker's praise, John Boyko interprets the speech in a highly negative light: Boyko, *Cold Fire*, 51.
5. B. Hutchinson, *Canada: Tomorrow's Giant* (Toronto: Oxford University Press, 2012 [1957]), 11. In 1945, Hutchison had authored *The Unknown Country: Canada and Her People* (Toronto: Oxford University Press, 2011 [1942]).
6. W. Gordon, *Troubled Canada: The Need for New Domestic Policies* (Toronto, 1961), 84; R. F. Parke, "Canada Bulwarks Defense in Output," *NYT*, Feb. 15; T. Kent, "The Changing Place of Canada," *FA* 35 (July 1957), 592.
7. HOC, Nov. 27, 1956, 51. The comment was made by Howard Green, soon to be Diefenbaker's influential foreign minister.
8. On the consensus, see R. Teigrob, *Warming Up to the Cold War: Canada and the United States' Coalition of the Willing, from Hiroshima to Korea* (Toronto: University of Toronto Press, 2009).
9. Underhill, "Canada and the North Atlantic Triangle," 258.
10. Granatstein, "When Push Came to Shove," 90; Hillmer and Granatstein, *Better or Worse*, 211.
11. Halla to Lay, "U.S.–Canadian Relations," Jul. 18, 1960, DDEL/White House/NSC Staff/Special Staff Files/box 2/folder Canada.
12. Telegram From The Embassy in Canada to the Department of State, Jun. 11, 1957, *FRUS*, 1955–1957, XXVII, 893–4; Memcon attached to Ottawa to State, no. 678, Jun. 22, 1957, DDEL/AWF/International Series/box 6/folder Canada (7); and Dulles to Eisenhower, Jul. 29, 1957, DDEL/AWF/Dulles-Herter Series/box 9/folder Dulles, John Foster July 1957.
13. Despatch From the Embassy in the United Kingdom to the Department of State, Sep. 9, 1957, *FRUS*, 1955–1957, XXVII, 910–3. See T. Rooth, "Britain, Europe, and Diefenbaker's Trade Diversion Proposals, 1957–58," in *Canada and the End of Empire*, ed. P. Buckner (Vancouver: UBC Press, 2005), 117–32.
14. Northern European Chiefs of Mission Conference, London, Sep. 19–21, 1957: Summary of Proceedings, *FRUS* 1955–1957, vol. IV, 617–9.
15. *S&S* 57/30, Oct. 28, 1957.
16. Quoted in J. Eayrs, *Canada in World Affairs, 1955–57* (Toronto: Oxford University Press, 1959), 125; Gordon, *Troubled Canada*; "New Leader for Canada, New Problems for U.S.," *U.S. News & World Report*, Jun. 21, 1957; "Canada," *Time*, Aug. 5, 1957.
17. Extract from Minutes of Third Meeting of Joint Canada–United States Committee on Trade and Economic Affairs, 7-8/10/57, *DCER*, 1957–1958, II, 341.

18. Memorandum of Conversation with Mr. Clarence B. Randall, Aug. 8, 1957, DDEL/JFD/GCM/Memcons, General, N Through R (1).
19. D. Acheson, *Power and Diplomacy* (New York: Atheneum, 1966 [1958]),73; M. Bundy, "Diplomatic Strategy in a Nuclear Age," in *National Values in a Changing World* (Toronto: Canadian Institute of Public Affairs, 1957), 68.
20. M. Barkway, "Canada Rediscovers Its History," *FA* 36 (1958): 409–17.
21. E. Griffin, "Bolder Canada Will Speak Up in Parleys with Washington," *CT*, Apr. 6, 1958; R. Daniell, "Nationalism Backed by Canadian Voters," *NYT*, Apr. 6, 1958; "Tidal Wave in Canada," *WP*, Apr. 2, 1958;
22. "Working with Canada," *NYT*, May 18, 1958; Bill Henry, "By the Way . . . ," *LAT*, 13 July 1958; "Canadian Nationalism," *WSJ*, May 15, 1958.
23. CC, Oct. 19, 1957, LAC/RG 2/vol. 1893; Diefenbaker, *One Canada*, II (Toronto, 1976), 152.
24. D. Macfarlane, *Negotiating a River: Canada, the US, and the Creation of the St. Lawrence Seaway* (Vancouver: UBC Press, 2014); and "Caught Between Two Fires: The St. Lawrence Seaway and Power Project, Canadian–American Relations, and Linkage," *IJ* 67, no. 2 (2012): 465–82.
25. A. W. G. Herd, "A 'Common Appreciation': Eisenhower, Canada, and Continental Air Defense," *Journal of Cold War Studies* 13, no. 3 (2011): 4–26.
26. Robinson, *Diefenbaker's World*, 18–20.
27. "Meeting at the White House," Oct. 17, 1957, DDEL/JFD/GCM/Memcons, General, A Through D (4); J. Jockel, *Canada in NORAD 1957–2007: A History* (Montréal and Kingston: McGill-Queen's University Press, 2007), 9–41.
28. Memcon, Jul. 8, 1958, DDEL/AWF/International Series/box 6/folder Canada (6).
29. C. Bright, *Continental Defense in the Eisenhower Era* (Basingstoke: Palgrave Macmillan, 2010), 1.
30. HOC, Feb. 20, 1959, 1221–4.
31. Heeney to file, "Conversation with the Minister (Mr. Green), June 30; Relations with the United States," Jun. 30, 1959; Heeney to file, "Conversation with the Prime Minister, June 30; Relations with the United States," Jun. 30, 1959, LAC/MG 30 E144/vol. 1.14.
32. D. Heidt, "'I Think That Would Be the End of Canada': Howard Green, the Nuclear Test Ban, and Interest-Based Foreign Policy, 1946–1963," *ARCS* 42, no. 3 (2012): 343–69.
33. Discussion at the 451st Meeting of the National Security Council, Jul. 15, 1960, DDEL/AWF/NSC/box 12/folder 451st Meeting; Briefing memo, "Green, Howard (Charles)," May 1961, JFKL/POF/box 113/folder JFK Trip to Ottawa, 5/61; "Talk with Under Secretary of State George Ball," Apr. 4, 1962. JFKL/Robert Eastabrook papers, box 1/folder George Ball, London, 4/4/62.
34. T. Casgrain, *A Woman in a Man's World* (Toronto: McClelland and Stewart, 1972), 157. And see T. Brookfield, *Cold War Comforts: Canadian Women, Child Safety, and Global Insecurity* (Waterloo: WLU Press, 2012), chapter 3.
35. J. Minifie, *Peacemaker or Powdermonkey: Canada's Role in a Revolutionary World* (Toronto: McClelland and Stewart, 1960), 3; Heeney to file, "Memorandum of Conversations with the Prime Minister in Ottawa, Tuesday, August 30, 1960, and Wednesday, August 31, 1960," n.d, LAC/MG 30 E144/vol. 1.15.
36. Diary, May 29, 1959, LAC/MG 30 E144/vol. 2.
37. Butterworth to Merchant, Jun. 20, 1964, NARA/RG 59/EUR-CDC/RRMM/box 11/folder Canadian–US Economic Relations. And see F. McKenzie, "A.D.P. Heeney: The Orderly Undersecretary," in *Architects and Innovators: Building the Department of Foreign Affairs and International Trade, 1909–2009*, eds. G. Donaghy and K. R. Nossal (Montréal and Kingston: McGill-Queen's University Press, 2009), 151–68.
38. Léger to Smith, "Speech by Livingston T. Merchant," 20/1/58, and attached Address to the Women's Canadian Club of Hamilton, Jan. 22, 1958, LAC/RG 25/vol. 6786/file 1415-40-pt. 6.1; US Senate, *Review of Foreign Policy, 1958—Hearings Before the Committee on Foreign Relations*, May 16, 1958.

39. Dulles to Eisenhower, "Your Visit to Ottawa," Jul. 3, 1958, DDEL/AWF/International Series/box 6/folder Canada (7).

40. "Address to the Members of the Canadian House of Parliament," Jul. 9, 1958, James Hagerty Papers/box 17/folder Canada Conference—Press Conferences and Statements; Memcon, Jul. 9, 1958, DDEL/AWF/International Series/box 6/folder Canada (6).

41. 376th Meeting of the National Security Council, Aug. 14, 1958, DDEL/AWF/NSC Series/box 10/folder 376th Meeting; and NSC 5822/1, "Certain Aspects of US Relations with Canada," Dec. 30, 1958, DDEL/White House Office/Office of the Special Assistant for National Security Affairs/NSC Series/Policy Papers Subseries/box 26/folder NSC 5822/1.

42. Address to the National War College, Jan. 30, 1959, SMML/MC 095/box 18/folder Speeches, Statements, Testimony, 1959.

43. Merchant to Wigglesworth, Sep. 30, 1958, MHS/RBW.

44. Address to the Canadian Club of Ottawa, Feb. 4, 1959, MHS/RBW; Muirhead, *Dancing Around the Elephant*, 25.

45. Bright, *Continental Defense*, 148.

46. CC, Aug. 26, 1959, CC, Aug. 27, 1959, LAC/RG 2/vol. 2745.

47. Ottawa to State, no. 144, Aug. 29, 1959, NARA/RG 59/CDF/711.5442/8-2959.

48. Robinson to Robertson, "Operation Skyhawk," Aug. 31, 1959, LAC/MG 31 E83/vol. 2.12; CC, Sep. 1, 1959, LAC/RG 2/vol. 2745.

49. Eisenhower to Diefenbaker, Sep. 1, 1959, Diefenbaker to Eisenhower, Sep. 6, 1959, DDEL/AWF/International Series; CC, Sep. 2, 1959, LAC/RG 2/vol. 2745,

50. K. Nash, "Christian Herter: New Face at the Summit," *Maclean's*, May 21, 1960; Memcon, "Joint US-Canadian Cabinet Defense Committee Meeting; Operation SKYHAWK," Sep. 21, 1959, NARA/RG 59/Executive Secretariat/The Secretary's and Undersecretary's Memoranda of Conversation/box 17/folder Secy's M. of Con. Sep. 11–23, 1959.

51. Wigglesworth to Merchant, Oct. 14, 1959, NARA/RG 59/box 2/folder SKYHAWK 1959.

52. CC, Nov. 6, 1959, LAC/RG 2/vol. 2745.

53. Canada–United States Ministerial Committee on Joint Defence, Record of Meeting, Nov. 8–9, 1959, LAC/MG 31 E83/vol. 8.10; Summary Record of the Meeting of the United States-Canada Ministerial Committee on Joint Defence, Nov. 8–9, 1959, DNSA/Doc. NH01179; CC, Nov. 10, 1959, LAC/RG 2/vol. 2745.

54. Heeney to Rae, "Operation Skyhawk," Mar. 21, 1960, Nutt to Heeney, "Operation Sky Hawk," Mar. 24, 1960, Rae to Heeney, "Operation Sky Hawk," Apr. 1, 1960, and Washington to External, tel. 892, Apr. 5, 1960, LAC/RG 25/vol. 3094/file 3-2-2-7-pt. 4.

55. Washington to External, tel. 1062, Apr. 22, 1960, Nutt to file, "Briefing on Air Defence Exercise Sky Shield," Apr. 21, 1960, LAC/RG 25/vol. 3094/file 3-2-2-7-pt. 4; CC, Apr. 20, 1960, LAC/RG 2/vol. 2746.

56. Washington to External, tel. 1237, May 11, 1960, LAC/RG 25/vol. 5028/file 1415-40-pt. 8.

57. CC, May 16, 1960, CC, May 19, 1960, LAC/RG 2/vol. 2746.

58. *S&S* 60/22, May 19, 1960.

59. Robinson to file, "President Eisenhower's Letter of May 27 to the Prime Minister," May 31, 1960, LAC/MG 31 E83/vol. 3.5; Memorandum of Discussion at the 446th Meeting of the National Security Council, May 31, 1960, DDEL/AWF/NSC Series/box 10/folder 446th Meeting.

60. Bryce, "Notes on the Discussion in President Eisenhower's Office, June 3rd, 1960," Jun. 17, 1960, LAC/RG 25/vol. 5032/file 1415-K-40-pt. 1; CC, Jun. 14, 1960, and CC, Jun. 15, 1960, LAC/RG 2/vol. 2746.

61. Memcon, "U.S.–Canadian Relations," Sep. 20, 1960, NARA/RG 84/CGR/box 224/folder international political rel classified 1959–61 Canada–US.

62. Minutes of Cabinet Meeting, Mar. 6, 1959, DDEL/AWF/Cabinet Series/box 13/folder Meeting of March 6, 1959.

63. J. Kirton, "The Consequences of Integration: The Case of the Defence Production Sharing Agreements," in *Continental Community? Independence and Integration in North America*, W. Andrew Axline (Toronto: McClelland and Stewart, 1974), 116–35.

64. CC, Feb. 4, 1960, LAC/RG 2/vol. 2746.
65. A.E. Ritchie to Robertson, Mar. 24, 1960, LAC/RG 25/vol. 5935/file 50210-H-40-pt. 2.1.
66. Chappell to Heeney, May 26, 1960, LAC/RG 25/vol. 3175/file Canada–US Defence Relations, 1958–1960. And see M. D. Stevenson, "'A Very Careful Balance': The 1961 Triangular Agreement and the Conduct of Canadian–American Relations," *D&S* 24, no. 2 (2013): 291–311.
67. Discussion at the 440th Meeting of the National Security Council, Apr. 7, 1960/DDEL/AWF/NSC/box 12/folder 440th Meeting.
68. Memorandum of Conference with the President, May 9, 1960, 11:30 a.m., May 10, 1960, DDEL/White House/Office of the Staff Secretary/International/box 2/folder Canada (2) [September 1959–May 1960].
69. Telephone Conversation with the President, Apr. 8, 1960, DDEL/Christian Herter Papers/box 10/folder Presidential Telephone Calls 1-6/60 (2).
70. 446th Meeting of the National Security Council, May 31, 1960, DDEL/AWF/NSC Series/box 12/folder 446th Meeting.
71. Memorandum of Conference with the President, June 3, 1960, Jun. 4, 1960/DDEL/White House/Office of the Staff Secretary/Subject Series/Department of State Subseries/box 3/folder State Department-1960 (June–July) (1).
72. Bryce, "Notes on the Discussion in President Eisenhower's Office, June 3rd, 1960," Jun. 17, 1960, LAC/MG 31 E83/vol. 3.8.
73. Meeting between Canada–United States Committee on Joint Defence, Jul. 12, 1960, LAC/MG 31 E83/vol. 9.
74. "The Real Threat of the Bomarc Bungle," *Maclean's*, Mar. 12, 1960; Diefenbaker, "Re: Disarmament," Dec. 3, 1960, LAC/MG 31 E83/vol. 9.1.
75. 450th Meeting of the National Security Council, Jul. 7, 1960, DDEL/AWF/NSC Series/box 12/folder 450th Meeting.
76. Kohler to Rusk, "Courtesy Call by Mr. Norman A. Robertson," Mar. 10, 1961, NARA/RG 59/EUR-BNA/ANF/box 2/folder US-Canadian Committee on Trade and Economic Affairs, 1961.
77. Briefing memo, "Robertson, Norman Alexander," May 1961, JFKL/POF/box 113/folder JFK Trip to Ottawa, 5/61; Louise Armstrong Oral History, FAOHC.
78. External to Washington, tel. G-87, Jul. 16, 1960, LAC/MG 31 E44/vol. 1.4; Robertson, "The Cuban Situation," Jul. 13, 1960; and Bryce to Robertson, "re. Your remarks on Cuba at Seigniory Club," Jul. 15, 1960, LAC/MG 30 E163/vol. 18/file Personal Correspondence 1960 Part 2.
79. 451st Meeting of the National Security Council, Jul. 15, 1960, DDEL/AWF/NSC Series/box 12/folder 451st Meeting.
80. I. Sclanders, "Is the U.S. talking itself into hot war?," *Maclean's*, Jul. 30, 1960. Similar views would soon be voiced by Eisenhower in his valedictory speech criticizing the military-industrial complex.
81. CC, Jul. 16, 1960, LAC/RG 2/vol. 2747.
82. CC, Aug. 9, 1960 and Aug. 12, 1960, LAC/RG 2/vol. 2747.
83. Memcon, Sep. 1, 1960, NARA/RG 59/EUR-CDC/RRMM/box 9/folder Defense Policy-Press & Miscellaneous.
84. Memcon, Aug. 29, 1960, NARA/RG 59/EUR-BNA/ANF/box 1/folder Basic Policy-Canada.
85. Heeney to file, "Memorandum of Conversations with the Prime Minister in Ottawa, Tuesday, August 30, 1960, and Wednesday, August 31, 1960," n.d, LAC/MG 30 E144/vol. 1.15.
86. "Let's Not Let Politics Distort the Issue of Nuclear Weapons," *Maclean's*, Sep. 10, 1960; P.C. Newman, "The PM's Election Role: The Paul Revere of Canada," *Maclean's*, Sep. 10, 1960.
87. Heeney to file, "Memorandum of Conversation with the Under-Secretary of State for Political Affairs in Washington, Tuesday, September 13, 1960," Sep. 14, 1960, LAC/MG 30 E144/vol. 1.15.

88. Memcon, "September 19, 1960," Sep. 23, 1960, LAC/MG 30 E144/vol. 1.15.
89. Memcon, "The Minister's Talk with the Secretary of State," Sep. 23, 1960, LAC/MG 30 E144/vol. 1.15; Memcon, Sep. 20, 1960, NARA/RG 84/CGR/box 224/folder international political rel classified 1959–61 Canada–US.
90. Heeney to Diefenbaker, Sep. 27, 1960, LAC/MG 30 E144/vol. 1.15.
91. CC, Sep. 6, 1960, LAC/RG 2/vol. 2747; Heeney to Green, "Proposal for USA Purchase of CL-44 Aircraft," Sep. 19, 1960, LAC/MG 32 B13/vol. 11.8.
92. CC, Sep. 21, 1960, LAC/RG 2/vol. 2747; Memorandum of Conference with the President, Sep. 30, 1960, DDEL/AWF/International Series/box 6/folder 2.
93. Memcon, "Canadian 101B/CL-44/Pinetree Proposal," Oct. 6, 1960 and Kohler to Merchant, Oct. 4, 1960, NARA/RG 59/CDF/742.5612/10-460.
94. Washington to External, tel. 2979, Dec. 1, 1960, LAC/MG 32 B13/vol. 11.8; Memcon, "Triangular Exchange with Canada Involving United States Purchase of Canadian Cargo Aircraft," Dec. 5, 1960, NARA/RG 59/CDF/742.5612/12-560.
95. Herter to Eisenhower, Dec. 8, 1960, DDEL/White House Office/Office of the Staff Secretary: Records of Paul T. Carroll, Andrew Goodpaster, L. Arthur Minnich, and Christopher H. Russell, 1952–1961/International Series/box 2/folder Canada (4).
96. Kohler to Dillon, "Possible Effect on U.S.-Canadian Relations of Proposed U.S. Export Controls re Cuba," Oct. 5, 1960, NARA/RG 59/EUR-BNA/ANF/box 5/folder Cuba 1960–1961.
97. Heeney to file, "Memorandum of Conversations with the Prime Minister in Ottawa, Tuesday, August 30, 1960, and Wednesday, August 31, 1960," n.d., LAC/MG 30 E144/vol. 1.15; Robinson to Robertson, "Cuba," Oct. 19, 1960, and Robinson to file, "Cuba," Oct. 20, 1960, LAC/MG 31 E83/vol. 3.10; and CC, Oct. 20, 1960, LAC/RG 2/vol. 2747.
98. Memcon, "United States Embargo on Cuba," Oct. 20, 1960, NARA/RG 59/ARA-CCA-SF/box 10/folder Relations Canada-Cuba 1960. For negative views of Ritchie as a tough defender of Canadian interests, see Willis Armstrong Oral History, FAOHC.
99. 464th Meeting of the National Security Council, Oct. 20, 1960, DDEL/AWF/NSC Series/box 13/folder 464th Meeting.
100. HOC, Dec. 12, 1960, 700–1; Davis to Mann, "Visit of Canadian Ambassador Heeney," Dec. 14, 1960, NARA/RG 59/EUR-BNA/ANF/box 5/folder Cuban Export Ban 1960–1962; and CC, Dec. 14, 1960, LAC/RG 2/vol. 2747.
101. Heeney to file, "Memorandum of Conversations with the Prime Minister in Ottawa, Tuesday, August 30, 1960, and Wednesday, August 31, 1960," n.d., LAC/MG 30 E144/vol. 1.15.
102. Robinson to file, "Cuba," Nov. 9, 1960, Robinson to Heeney, Nov. 10, 1960, Diefenbaker to Kennedy, Nov. 9, 1960, and Robinson to diary file, "Exchange of Messages with Senator Kennedy," Nov. 22, 1960, LAC/MG 31 E83/vol. 3.13.
103. Washington to External, tel. 2807, Nov. 11, 1960, Washington to External, D-1615, Nov. 2, 1960, and Washington to External, D-1634, Nov. 4, 1960, LAC/RG 25/vol. 6751/file 340-40-pt. 11.2.
104. Robertson to Green, "President-elect Kennedy," Oct. 10, 1960, LAC/MG 31 E83/vol. 3.13.
105. Hillmer and Granatstein, *For Better or For Worse*, 201.
106. Speech, Jan. 14, 1954. JFKL, PPP, box 654, folder St. Lawrence Seaway, 1/25/1953-1/8/1954. Kennedy had also visited Canada in November 1957, taking part in a debate at the University of Toronto on the resolution "Has the United States Failed in its Responsibilities As World Leader?." Admitting to certain failures in US foreign policy, nevertheless Kennedy had defended his country's role in the world. The audience agreed with him by a slim margin of 204–194. See "U.S Senator Sees Mideast Strife," *G&M*, Nov. 15, 1957; Mark Nichols, "Confidence Vote For U.S. After Kennedy's Defence," *The Varsity*, Nov. 15, 1957.
107. "Mr. Kennedy's Victory," *OC*, Nov. 9, 1960; "The U.S. Makes Its Choice," *MG*, Nov. 9, 1960; "One Half of a Nation," *G&M*, Nov. 10, 1960.

108. Diefenbaker, *One Canada,* II. 166. Similarly, one historian has maintained that "severe difficulties" in bilateral affairs "only began to emerge after John F. Kennedy came to the presidency": Gloin, "Canada–US Relations," 14.

109. R. Evans, "Time of Vast, Varied Change in U.S. Dawns," *LAT,* Jan. 1, 1961; "The Atlantic Report: Canada," *Atlantic Monthly,* May 1961; Max Freedman, "Kennedy Faces U.S.–Canadian Rifts," *WP,* Dec. 4, 1960; "Kennedy Facing Canada Problem," *Chicago Sun Times,* Dec. 29, 1960; "The Eisenhower Era," *G&M,* Jan. 21, 1961.

110. Heeney to Robertson, Nov. 22, 1960, LAC/MG 31 E44/vol. 2.9.

111. *S&S* 60/41, Nov. 24, 1960.

112. CC, Dec. 6, 1960, LAC/RG 2/vol. 2747.

113. McMahon, *Essence of Indecision,* x.

114. Ottawa to State, no. 620, Feb. 27, 1961, JFKL/NSF/box 18/folder Canada, General 1/61–3/61.

115. See E. Simpson, *NATO and the Bomb: Canadian Defenders Confront Critics* (Montréal and Kingston: McGill–Queen's University Press, 2001); A. Richter, *Avoiding Armageddon: Canadian Military Strategy and Nuclear Weapons, 1950–63* (Vancouver: UBC Press, 2002); and S. Maloney, *Learning to Love the Bomb: Canada's Nuclear Weapons During the Cold War* (Washington, DC: Potomac Books, 2007).

116. C. Rowan, "Ominous Rumbles Heard in Canada," *WP,* Apr. 21, 1960; Garner to Sandys, "Canada: Relations with the United States," Feb. 13, 1961, TNA/DO 182/1; H. Martin, "Are the Canadians Still Our Friends?," *Saturday Evening Post,* Jun. 17, 1961; "Why Don't Canadians Like Us?," *Cleveland Plain Dealer,* Jan. 22–30, 1961; "Dilemma in Canada . . . ," *Milwaukee Journal,* Apr. 2–12, 1961; P. Deane, "Danger of U.S. Engulfment Looms Large," *G&M,* Oct. 26, 1960.

117. Armstrong to White, Nov. 9, 1960, NARA/RG 59/EUR/BNA/ANF/box 1/folder Nationalism, Neutralism and Anti-Americanism, 1960–1962.

118. Heeney to Green, Nov. 2, 1960, LAC/MG 30 E144/vol. 2.6.

119. Ottawa Embassy, "The Roots of Canadian–American Problems," Dec. 1960, NARA/RG 84/CGR/box 224/folder international political rel classified 1959–61 Canada–US. Canadian officials in both the Washington Embassy and the Prime Minister's Office were aware of the report's conclusions regarding both Canadian nationalism and the sense that the US should seek to cooperate with Canada: Farquharson to Heeney, "Memorandum for the Ambassador," Dec. 1, 1960, LAC/MG 31 E83/vol. 3.13.

120. Armstrong to Rewinkel, Dec. 30, 1960, NARA/RG 84/CGR/box 224/folder international political rel classified 1959–61 Canada–US.

121. "The Roots of Canadian–American Problems," attached to Tyler to McGhee, Mar. 9, 1962, NARA/RG 59/EUR-BNA/ANF/box 1/folder Nationalism, Neutralism and Anti-Americanism, 1960–1962.

122. Officer in Charge of Canadian Affairs, "Approach to Canadian-United States Relations," Jan. 9, 1961, and covering letter Rewinkel to Armstrong, Jan. 11, 1961, NARA/RG 84/CGR/box 224/folder international political rel classified 1959–61 Canada–US.

123. Memcon, Dec. 16, 1960, NARA/RG 84/CGR/box 224/folder international political rel classified 1959–61 Canada–US.

124. "Our American Alliance; A Washington Viewpoint," Address to the Toronto and Montreal Branches of the CIIA, Nov. 14 and 17, 1960, LAC/MG 30 E144/vol. 11.8; and Armstrong to Merchant, Nov. 21, 1960, NARA/RG 84/CGR/box 224/folder international political rel classified 1959–61 Canada–US.

125. Washington to External, numbered letter 1856, Dec. 30, 1960, and Washington to External, tel. 316, Jan. 31, 1961, LAC/RG 25/vol. 8521/file 6605-T-40-pt. 3.2. Heeney was correct in his assessment of the role played by Kennedy's ambassadors: D. Mayers, "JFK's Ambassadors and the Cold War," *D&S* 11, no. 3 (2000): 183–211.

126. A.E. Ritchie to Rae, Jan. 30, 1961, and Rae to A.E. Ritchie, Jan. 26, 1961, LAC/RG 25/vol. 5087/file 4901-40-pt. 13; A.E. Ritchie to Cleveland, Feb. 3, 1961, JFKL/Cleveland Papers/box 102/folder Trips—Ottawa 6/4/61.

127. "Canada and the United States Must Not Let Fundamental Solidarity Disintegrate," Address to the Primrose Club, Dec. 3, 1960, LAC/RG 25/vol. 5089/file 4901-40-pt. 13; and "Equality Comes First," *G&M*, Dec. 6, 1960.

128. Briefing book: "Africa, Air Pollution, Airlift, Arab States and US Policy, B-70 Bomber, Belgian Congo, Budget Policies, Canada, Child Welfare, Civil Defense, Communist China and Formosa, Conflict of Interest, Conventional Weapons and Non-Nuclear Deterrence," n.d. JFKL, PPP, Presidential Campaign Files, 1960, box 993.

129. Heeney to Rusk, Dec. 14, 1960, LAC/MG 30 E144/vol. 1.15.

130. Heeney to Diefenbaker, Jan. 9, 1961, and attached letter Heeney to Green, Jan. 9, 1961, LAC/MG 30 E144/vol. 1.16.

131. Diefenbaker to file, "Re: Conversation with Arnold Heeney," Jan. 17, 1961, LAC/MG 31 E83/vol. 4.2; A. Heeney, *The Things that are Caesar's* (Toronto: University of Toronto Press, 1972), 172; and Willis Armstrong Oral History, FAOHC.

132. Robinson to file, "Prime Minister's Visit to Washington," Jan. 19, 1961, LAC/MG 31 E83/vol. 4.2.

133. Robinson to USA Division, "Prime Minister's Visit to Washington for Signing of Columbia River Treaty," Jan. 18, 1961, and Robinson to Heeney, Jan. 18, 1961, LAC/MG 31 E83/vol. 4.3.

134. Robinson to Heeney, Jan. 18, 1961, LAC/MG 30 E144/vol. 1.16; "Canada and the U.S.A.," *NYT*, Jan. 17, 1961.

135. Howard Green Oral History, DDEL.

136. Bow, *Linkage*, 3.

137. Memorandum of Meeting with the President, Jul. 19, 1960, 5:30 p.m., DDEL/White House/NSA/Special Assistant Series/Presidential Subseries/box 5/folder 1960-Meetings with the President-Volume 2 (9).

138. Freedman, *Kennedy's Wars*, 277.

## Chapter 2

1. "Close-Up," Transcript, Mar. 14, 1961, and Address to the Canadian Club of Ottawa, Apr. 25, 1961, SMML/MC 095/box 19/folder Speeches, Statements, Testimony, 1961.

2. Merchant to White, Apr. 4, 1961, NARA/RG 59/EUR-BNA/ANF/box 1/folder Nationalism, Neutralism and Anti-Americanism, 1960–1962.

3. Merchant to Kennedy, Apr. 4, 1961, JFKL/NSF/box 18/folder Canada, General, 4/61–5/14/61. On Kennedy and the American image abroad, see M. Hafele, "John F. Kennedy, USIA, and World Public Opinion," *DH* 25, no. 1 (2001): 63–84.

4. Remarks of the President at the American Embassy Chancery, May 17, 1961, JFKL/WHCSF/box 970/folder TR3 5-17-61.

5. Robinson to Robertson, "Possible Visit to Washington by Prime Minister," Feb. 3, 1961; and Robinson to Robertson, "Prime Minister's Visit to Washington," Feb. 5, 1961, LAC/MG 31 E83/vol. 4.3; and Robinson, *Diefenbaker's World*, 169; Rusk to O'Donnell, 11:35 am, Feb. 3, 1961, NARA/RG 59/Rusk TTC/box 44.

6. News Conference, Feb. 8, 1961, JFKL/POF/box 54.

7. Nash, *Kennedy & Diefenbaker*, 63–64; Rusk from Salinger, 2:33 pm, Feb. 10, 1961, NARA/RG 59/Rusk/TTC/box 44; Robinson downplays how seriously the prime miniser was allegedly upset; indeed, he fails to mention the incident: Robinson, *Diefenbaker's World*, 169.

8. Rusk to Kennedy, "Prime Minister Diefenbaker's Visit, February 20, 1961," Feb. 17, 1961, JFKL/POF/box 113/folder Canada, Security, 1961.

9. Tovell note, "Proposed Aircraft 'Swap' Deal," Feb. 17, 1961, LAC/MG 31 E83/vol. 4.3.

10. Gilpatric to Kennedy, "Defense Production Sharing with Canada," Feb. 18, 1961, JFKL/NSF/box 18/folder Canada, General 1/61–3/61.

11. HOC, Feb. 15, 1961, 2061; and G. Bain, "Canada Should be Flattered by Mr. Merchant's Return," *G&M*, 10/2/1961.

12. Schlesinger to Merchant, Feb. 4, 1961, NARA/RG 59/CDF/611.42/2-461; and S. Alsop to M. Sommers, Feb. 2, 1961, Library of Congress/Alsop Papers/box 30/folder 5.

13. K. McNaught, "On Understanding Mr. Kennedy," *Saturday Night*, Mar. 18, 1961.

14. Rusk to Kennedy, "Memorandum for Meeting with Prime Minister Diefenbaker— Status and Atmosphere of U.S.–Canadian Relations," and attached "Prime Minister Diefenbaker's Visit, February 20, 1961," Feb. 17, 1961, JFKL/POF/box 113/folder Canada, Security, 1961.

15. A. Duke Oral History Interview, JFKL.

16. Memcon, "Visit of Canadian Prime Minister Diefenbaker," Feb. 20, 1961, JFKL/ NSF/box 18/folder Canada, General 1/61–3/61; Memo, "Conversations between the President of the United States and the Prime Minister of Canada, the White House, Washington, February 20, 1961," Feb. 21, 1961, LAC/MG 31 E83/vol. 4.4.

17. Memcon, "Visit of Canadian Prime Minister Diefenbaker," Feb. 20, 1961, JFKL/NSF/box 18/folder Canada, General 1/61–3/61; Memo, "Conversations between the President of the United States and the Prime Minister of Canada, the White House, Washington, February 20, 1961," Feb. 21, 1961, LAC/MG 31 E83/vol. 4.4. And see P. Kyba, "Alvin Hamilton and Sino-Canadian Relations," in *Reluctant Adversaries: Canada and the People's Republic of China, 1949–1970*, eds. P. M. Evans and B. M. Frolic (Toronto: University of Toronto Press, 1991), 168–86; and G. Donaghy and M. D. Stevenson, "The Limits of Alliance: Cold War Solidarity and Canadian Wheat Exports to China, 1950–1963," *Agricultural History* 83, no. 1 (2009): 29–50.

18. CC, Feb. 14, 1961, and CC, Feb. 17, 1961, LAC/RG2/vol. 6176.

19. "Visit to Washington, PM's Notes," n.d., LAC/MG 31 E83/vol. 4; and Dutton to Kennedy, Feb. 20, 1961, JFKL/POF/box 113/folder Canada, General, 1961.

20. Thompson and Randall, *Canada and the United States*, 200. After returning to Ottawa, Diefenbaker ordered Canada's national librarian to seek out paintings depicting British naval victories in the conflict and he brushed off his staff's objections by noting, "we must teach him history. History must be taught." A painting was found and hung in Diefenbaker's office for Kennedy's visit in May. Perhaps this desire to educate the president was a sign of distaste, or, given that the prime minister had voiced considerable praise for Kennedy, perhaps it was good natured ribbing. See P. Stursberg, *Diefenbaker: Leadership Gained, 1956–62* (Toronto: University of Toronto Press, 1975), 171.

21. Robinson to Rae, Feb. 21, 1961, LAC/MG 31 E83/vol. 4.3; HOC, Feb. 20, 1961, 2220.

22. CC, Feb. 21, 1961, LAC/RG 2/vol. 6176; Heeney to Diefenbaker, Feb. 20, 1961, LAC/ MG 30 E144/vol. 1.16; Robinson to Robertson, Feb. 21, 1961 and "PM's Notes, Feb. 21, following visit to Wash.," n.d., LAC/MG 31 E83/vol. 4.3; and Garner to Caccia, Mar. 2, 1961, TNA/DO 182/1.

23. A. Schlesinger Jr, *A Thousand Days: John F. Kennedy in the White House* (Boston: Houghton Mifflin, 1965), 343; Nash, *Kennedy and Diefenbaker*, 99.

24. Call on the President prior to departure for post, Mar. 8, 1961, *FRUS*, 1961–1963, XIII, 1150.

25. "A Warm Trip South," *Time*, Mar. 3, 1961.

26. Gerald Waring, "Back of Diefenbaker's Visit," *NYHT*, Feb. 19, 1961; Carroll Kilpatrick, "U.S., Canada Reaffirm Resolve on Joint Aims," *WP*, Feb. 21, 1961; "The Canadian Visitor," *NYT*, Feb. 22, 1961.

27. Robertson to Green, "Proposed Aircraft Swap Deal," Mar. 1, 1961, LAC/MG 32 B13/vol. 11.8; CC, Mar. 2, 1961, LAC/RG 2/vol. 6176.

28. Ottawa to State, no. 893, May 11, 1961, JFKL/POF/box 113/folder JFK Trip to Ottawa, 5/61.

29. This divergence existed between the United States and most of its Western allies: J. A. Engel, "Of Fat and Thin Communists: Diplomacy and Philosophy in Western Economic Warfare Strategies toward China (and Tyrants, Broadly)," *DH* 29, no. 3 (2005): 445–74.

30. Green to Diefenbaker, "Oil Bunkers for Vessels Carrying Canadian Grain to China," Feb. 23, 1961, LAC/RG 25/vol. 7607/file 11280-1-40-pt. 2.1.

31. Washington to External, tel. 587, Feb. 24, 1961, LAC/RG 25/vol. 7607/file 11280-1-40-pt. 2.1.

32. Memcon, "Joint United States–Canadian Committee on Trade and Economic Affairs, Washington, March 13–14, 1961," May 22, 1961, JFKL/NSF/box 19/folder Canada, Subject, Joint US–Canadian Committee on Trade and Economic Affairs Meeting, 3/13/61–3/14/61.

33. CC, Mar. 16, 1961, LAC/RG 2/vol. 6176.

34. Green to Diefenbaker, "United States Foreign Assets Control Regulations—Oil Bunkers for Grain Ships to China," Mar. 24, 1961; External to Ottawa, tel. E-806, Apr. 20, 1961, LAC/RG 25/vol. 7607/file 11280-1-40-pt. 2.2.

35. Memcon, "Bunkering in Canadian Ports of Ship Transporting Canadian Grain to Communist China," Apr. 28, 1961, JFKL/NSF/box 18/folder Canada, General, 4/61–5/14/61; Washington to External, tel. 1377, Apr. 28, 1961, LAC/RG 25/vol. 7607/file 11280-1-40-pt. 2.2. Washington's acquiescence to Ottawa's view on bunker oil reflected a general American failure to secure support from its allies on trade with the Sino-Soviet bloc; see A. P. Dobson, *US Economic Statecraft for Survival, 1933–1991: Of Sanctions, Embargoes and Economic Warfare* (London: Routledge, 2002).

36. Diefenbaker, *One Canada*, II, 181. Citations of this suspect phone can be found in Muirhead, *Dancing*, 34–5; Donaghy and Stevenson, "The Limits of Alliance," 42; Martin, *The Presidents and the Prime Ministers*, 193; and F. Edwards, "Chinese Shadows," in *Canadian Among Nations 2008: 100 Years of Canadian Foreign Policy*, eds. R. Bothwell and J. Daudelin (Montréal and Kingston: McGill–Queen's University Press, 2009), 301. On Diefenbaker's suspect story, see McKercher, "Diefenbaker's World," 101–2.

37. Washington to External, tel. 1816, Jun. 7, 1961, and Washington to External, tel. 1820, Jun. 7, 1961, LAC/RG 25/vol. 5280/file 9030-40-pt. 7; A.E. Ritchie to Holmes, Jun. 23, 1961, LAC/RG 25/vol. 5030/file 1415-40-pt. 9.

38. CC, Jun. 8, 1961, LAC/RG 2/vol. 6176.

39. Granatstein, "When Push Came to Shove," 92.

40. Rae to Robertson, May 8, 1961, LAC/MG 31 E44/vol. 2.14.

41. See Robinson to Diefenbaker, Feb. 5, 1962, LAC/RG 25/vol. 7607/file 11280-1-40-pt. 2.2; J. Grasso, "The Politics of Food Aid: John F. Kennedy and Famine in China," *D&S* 14, no. 4 (2003): 153–78; and J. Fetzer, "Clinging to Containment: China Policy," in *Kennedy's Quest for Victory*, 178–97.

42. Telcon: Bundy, Ball. 4:50 p.m., May 7, 1962, SMML/MC 031/box 103/folder 1.

43. Memcon, "Visit of Canadian Prime Minister Diefenbaker," Feb. 20, 1961, JFKL/NSF/box 18/folder Canada, General 1/61–3/61.

44. Ottawa to State, no. 693, Mar. 20, 1961, NARA/RG 84/CGR/box 62/folder Cuba 1961.

45. Kohler to Rusk, "Further Economic Measures with Respect to Cuba," Feb. 24, 1961, NARA/RG 59/EUR-BNA/ANF/box 5/folder Cuban Export Ban, 1960–1962; Rusk, Memorandum for the President, Feb. 24, 1961, JFKL/POF/box 115/folder Cuba: Security, 1961.

46. Campbell to Green, "Cuba—Foreign Assets Control (USA)," Mar. 10, 1961, and Washington to External, tel. 806, Mar. 14, 1961, LAC/RG 25/vol. 7607/file 11280-1-40-pt. 2.2; and Diary, Mar. 12, 1961, LAC/MG 30 E144/vol. 2.

47. Washington to External, tel. 806, Mar. 14, 1961, LAC/RG 25/vol. 7607/file 11280-1-40-pt. 2.2; Washington to External, tel. 820, Mar. 15, 1961, LAC/RG 25/vol. 7607/file 11280-1-40-pt. 2.2; CC, May 16, 1961, LAC/RG 2/vol. 6176; Telcon: Dillon—Ball. 2:40 p.m., Apr. 26, 1961, and Telcon: Kohler—Ball. Apr. 27, 1961, SSML/MC 031/box 103/folder 1.

48. Ball to Rusk, Mar. 18, 1961, SSML/MC 031/box 103/folder 1.

49. Notes on the 479th Meeting of the National Security Council, Apr. 27, 1961, Sterling Memorial Library/Chester Bowles Papers/box 392/folder 154.

50. 478th Meeting of the NSC, Apr. 22, 1961, JFKL/NSF/box 313/folder NSC Meetings 1961; Telcon: Dillon—Ball. 2:40 p.m., Apr. 26, 1961, SMML/MC 031/box 103/folder 1.
51. 483rd Meeting of the NSC, May 5, 1961, JFKL/NSF/box 313/folder NSC Meetings 1961.
52. Washington to External, tel. 1480, May 8, 1961, Washington to External, tel. 1483, May 9, 1961, and Washington to External, tel. 1489, May 9, 1961, LAC/RG 20/vol. 939/file 7-544-2; CC, May 9, 1961, LAC/RG 2/vol. 6176; Telcon: Dillon—Ball. May 8, 1961, and Telcon: Heeney—Ball. May 8, 1961, SMML/MC 031/box 103/folder 1.
53. Zorbas, *Diefenbaker and Latin America*, 138; Bothwell, *Alliance and Illusion*, 166.
54. Diary, Apr. 19, 1961, LAC/MG 31 E83/vol. 35. See E. Griffin, "Voices Canada Alarm at Red Hold on Cuba," *CT*, Apr. 20, 1961; "Canada Sees Danger," *NYT*, Apr. 20, 1961; "A Canadian Looks at Cuban Crisis," *WP*, Apr. 22, 1961.
55. HOC, Apr. 19, 1961, 3795; Hilsman to Rusk, "Intelligence Note: World Reactions to Events in Cuba," Apr. 26, 1961, NARA/RG 59/ARA-Office of the Special Assistant on Communism-Subject Files/box 8/folder Cuba—Misc., March–April 1961; Ottawa to State, no. 821, Apr. 20, 1961, and State to Ottawa, no. 691, Apr. 21, 1961, NARA/RG 84/CGR/box 224/folder Cuba 1961.
56. Ottawa to State, G-253, Apr. 26, 1961, NARA/RG 59/CDF/611.42/4-2661.
57. Robinson to Robertson. Apr. 27, 1961, LAC/MG 31 E83/vol. 5.4.
58. Washington to External, tel. 1401, May 2, 1961, LAC/RG 25/vol. 5040/file 2002-40-pt. 6.
59. Memcon, May 8, 1961, NARA/RG 84/CGR/box 224/folder Cuba 1961.
60. Ottawa to State, no. G-252, Apr. 25, 1961, NARA/RG 84/CGR/box 224/folder Cuba Limited Distribution, 1959–1961.
61. Green to Diefenbaker, "Proposed Interview with the United States Ambassador," Apr. 28, 1961, and Robertson to Green, "Proposed representations to the United States regarding the Cuban Invitation to Talk," Apr. 28, 1961, LAC/MG 31 E44/vol. 1.6; Robinson to Robertson, "Cuba," May 4, 1961, LAC/MG 31 E83/vol. 5.5; Ottawa to State, no. 863, May 3, 1961, NARA/RG 84/CGR/box 224/folder Cuba 1961.
62. Geneva to External, tel. 529, May 11, 1961, LAC/RG 25/vol. 5050/file 2444-A-40-pt. 1; and Remarks on Cuba by the Secretary of State for External Affairs at the North Atlantic Council, Oslo, 8/5/61, NARA/RG 59/ARA-CCA-SF/box 34/folder Relations–Canada–Cuba, 1961.
63. Oslo to External, tel. 528, May 11, 1961, LAC/RG 25/vol. 5075/file 4568-40-pt. 5; Rusk to Ottawa, Oslo 6, May 10, 1961, NARA/RG84/CGR/box 224/folder Cuba Limited Distribution, 1959–1961; Rusk to Kennedy, secto. 113, May 14, 1961, JFKL/NSF/box 18/folder Canada, General 5/15/61–5/30/61.
64. Heeney, *The Things That Are Caesar's*, 178.
65. "Canada Set to Mediate Cuba Dispute," *WP*, May 12, 1961; Washington to External, tel. 1551, May 13, 1961, LAC/MG 31 E83/vol. 5.5; Bowles to Rusk, May 12, 1961, JFKL/POF/box 113/folder JFK Trip to Ottawa, 5/61; State to Ottawa, no. 781, May 13, 1961, NARA/RG 84/CGR/box 224/folder Cuba 1961; Memcon, May 12, 1961, NARA/RG 59/EUR-CDC/RRPM/box 3/folder OAS—1960-63.
66. "Let's Give the New President Some Time to Show His Mettle," *Maclean's*, Jan. 28, 1961; K. McNaught, "On Understanding Mr. Kennedy," *Saturday Night*, Mar. 18, 1961.
67. "The Invasion That Failed," *MG*, Apr. 24, 1961; "For Cubans To Decide," *OC*, Apr. 20, 1961; "The United States' Dilemma," *OC*, Apr. 22, 1961; "The Cuban Tragedy," *G&M*, Apr. 21, 1961.
68. Robinson to Robertson. Apr. 27, 1961, LAC/MG 31 E83/vol. 5.4.
69. Diefenbaker to Green, "Organization of American States," Apr. 24, 1960, and Diefenbaker to Green, Apr. 24, 1960. LAC/RG 25/vol. 7760/file 12426-40-pt. 2. On Diefenbaker and Latin America, see McKercher, "Southern Exposure," 57–80.
70. Kennedy quoted in J. Taffet, *Foreign Aid as Foreign Policy: The Alliance for Progress in Latin America* (London: Routledge, 2007), 12–3.
71. Rostow to Kennedy, "Draft of Crucial Portion of Foreign Aid Message," Mar. 13, 1961, JFKL/POF/box 64a/folder Rostow, Walt W., 3/61–5/61.

72. "The New Dimensions of American Foreign Policy," Nov. 1, 1957, JFKL/PP/Senate Speech Files; Remarks of Senator Kennedy at Young Democrats State Convention Banquet, Racine, Wisconsin, Mar. 9, 1960, and Remarks of Senator Kennedy at Howard County Court House, Indiana, Apr. 29, 1960, JFKL/PP/1960 Campaign Files.

73. HOC, Apr. 26, 1961, 4026–33; and HOC, Mar. 14, 1961, 2955.

74. Memo, "President's Trip to Ottawa, May 16–18, 1961—Canadian Relations with Latin America," May 2, 1961, JFKL/POF/box 113/folder JFK Trip to Ottawa, 5/61. Washington had not always been so welcoming: D. Anglin, "United States Opposition to Canadian Membership in the Pan American Union: A Canadian View," *International Organization* 15, no. 1 (1961): 1–20.

75. Goodwin to Kennedy, Apr. 24, 1961, and Clifton to Kennedy, May 8, 1961, JFKL/NSF/ box 18/folder Canada, General 4/61–5/14/61.

76. Rostow to Kennedy, May 13, 1961, JFKL/POF/box 113/folder JFK Trip to Ottawa, 5/61.

77. Ottawa to State 908, May 15, 1961, JFKL/NSF/box 18/folder Canada, General 4/61– 5/14/61; Rostow to Kennedy, "What We Want from the Ottawa Trip," May 16, 1961, JFKL/NSF/box 18/folder Canada, General, Rostow Memorandum and Related Material 5/61–5/63.

78. Bryce to Diefenbaker, "Suggested Points for Discussion with President Kennedy," May 15, 1961, LAC/MG 31 E83/vol. 5.8.

79. The West Indies were another matter, but, even here, Diefenbaker's government showed considerable hesitancy: G. Donaghy and B. Muirhead, "'Interests but No Foreign Policy': Canada and the Commonwealth Caribbean, 1951–1966," *ARCS* 38, no. 3 (2008), 282–5; CC, Sep. 7, 1961, LAC/RG 2/vol. 6177.

80. M. Latham, *Modernization as Ideology: American Social Science and "Nation Building" in the Kennedy Era* (Chapel Hill: UNC Press, 2000); A. Chapnick, "Peace, Order and Good Government: The 'Conservative' Tradition in Canadian Foreign Policy," *International Journal* 60, no. 3 (2005), 635–50.

81. Quoted in Robinson, *Diefenbaker's World*, 196

82. NIE 99–61, "Trends in Canadian Foreign Policy," May 2, 1961, JFKL/POF/box 113/ folder JFK Trip to Ottawa, 5/61. This analysis would remain in effect until the Nixon administration.

83. Ottawa to State, no. 780, Apr. 12, 1961, JFKL/NSF/box 18/folder Canada, General 4/ 61–5/14/61.

84. Memo, "President's Trip to Ottawa, May 16–18, 1961—Scope Paper," May 2, 1961, JFKL/POF/box 113/folder JFK Trip to Ottawa, 5/61.

85. Memo, "President's Trip to Ottawa, May 16–18, 1961—Points for the President to make," May 12, 1961, JFKL/POF/box 113/folder JFK Trip to Ottawa, 5/61.

86. "Kennedy at Ottawa," *NYT*, May 16, 1961; G. Waring, "Canada Has Lot to Talk About With Mr. Kennedy," *NYHT*, May 14, 1961; "Welcome For Kennedy," *Baltimore Sun*, May 14, 1961.

87. P. C. Newman, "Why Kennedy Will Try to Enlist John Diefenbaker as His Next New Frontiersman," *Maclean's*, May 20, 1961.

88. Tania Long: "Canada's Spring Fever," *NYT*, May 20, 1961; E. Griffin, "Ottawa Is in Full Bloom for Visit of Kennedy, Wife," *CT*, May 16, 1961; Recording, "Remarks upon Arrival at the RCAF Uplands Airport in Ottawa," May 16, 1961, JFKL/Accession WH-030-003/JFKWHA-030-003; C. Roberts, "Kennedy and Canadian Minister Trade Pledges of Friendship," *WP*, May 17, 1961. On the comments about French, see Diary, May 16, 1961, LAC/MG 31 E83/vol. 35; Drake, *Stubble-Jumper in Striped Pants*, 24; and Nash, *Kennedy and Diefenbaker*, 107–8. Nash alleges that Kennedy again mispronounced Diefenbaker's name during this ceremony, but the recording of the event reveals this contention to be false.

89. R. Dallek, *An Unfinished Life: John F. Kennedy, 1917–1963* (New York: Back Bay Books, 2003), 397–8.

90. Robinson, *Diefenbaker's World*, 199.

91. Memcon, "Conversation between President Kennedy and Prime Minister Diefenbaker—Cuba and Latin America," May 17, 1961, JFKL/NSF/box 18/folder Canada, General, Ottawa Trip 5/17/61 Memoranda of Conversation; Memo, "Visit of President Kennedy to Ottawa, May 16–18, 1961. Meeting with the Prime Minister, May 17," LAC/MG 31 E83/vol. 5.7.

92. Memcon, "Conversation between President Kennedy and Prime Minister Diefenbaker—Canada, the OAS and IA-ECOSOC," and Memcon, "Conversation between President Kennedy and Prime Minister Diefenbaker—Common Market and Aid to Underdeveloped Areas," May 17, 1961, JFKL/NSF/box 18/folder Canada, General, Ottawa Trip 5/17/61 Memoranda of Conversation.

93. Memcon, "Conversation between President Kennedy and Prime Minister Diefenbaker—Disarmament," and Memcon, "Conversation between President Kennedy and Prime Minister Diefenbaker—NATO and Nuclear Weapons," May 17, 1961, JFKL/NSF/box 18/folder Canada, General, Ottawa Trip 5/17/61 Memoranda of Conversation.

94. Rostow to Sorensen, May 3, 1961, and EUR to Rostow and Sorensen, undated, JFKL/NSF/box 18/folder Canada, General 4/61–5/14/61.

95. Rostow to Kennedy, May 13, 1961, JFKL/POF/box 113/folder JFK Trip to Ottawa, 5/61.

96. "Address before the Canadian Parliament in Ottawa," May 17, 1961, *PPP.*

97. Robinson, *Diefenbaker's World,* 208; and Livingston Merchant Oral History, JFKL.

98. Holborn to Kennedy, May 16, 1961, JFKL/WHCSF/box 970/folder TR 3, Ottawa, Ontario, Canada, Spring 1961, 1/20/61–5/16/61.

99. Rostow to Kennedy, May 17, 1961, JFKL/POF/box 113/folder Canada, General 1961; "Kennedy's Charm Wows Canadians," *NYHT,* May 21, 1961; J. Diefenbaker to E. Diefenbaker, May 18, 1961, in *Personal Letters of a Public Man: The Family Letters of John G. Diefenbaker,* ed. T. McIlroy (Toronto: Doubleday, 1985), 106; Ottawa to State, no. 930, May 23, 1961, JFKL/NSF/box 18/folder Canada, General 5/15/61–5/30/61.

100. O. Diefenbaker to Jacqueline Kennedy, May 22, 1961, SMML/MC 095/box 8/folder Re Kennedy, John F., 1961–Includes visit to Canada, May 16, 1961.

101. Kennedy to Diefenbaker, May 25, 1961, JFKL/WHCSF/box 970/folder TR 3 5/17/61. And see Diefenbaker to Kennedy, May 28, 1961; Kennedy to Diefenbaker, Jun. 15, 1961, POF, box 113, folder Canada, Security 1961, as well as the correspondence cited in chapter 3.

102. Granatstein, "When Push Came to Shove," 93; Glazov, J. *Canadian Policy toward Khrushchev's Soviet Union* (Montréal and Kingston: McGill-Queen's University Press, 2002), 116.

103. "Presidential Party," *Maclean's,* Jul. 1, 1961; "Kennedys Hailed by 50,000; Enthusiasm Astounds Officialdom," *G&M,* May 17, 1961; "Must Stand Together, PM, President Pledge," *MG,* May 17, 1961; "Fond Farewells At Airport As Kennedys Wind Up Visit," *OC,* May 18, 1961; "Foreign Relations: Melting the Canadian Ice," *Time,* May 26, 1961; *Life,* May 25, 1961; and ConGen NY to External, NL-343, May 24, 1961, LAC/RG 25/vol. 4130/file 1415-N-40-pt. 1.

104. Ottawa to State, no. 923, May 19, 1961, JFKL/NSF/box 18/folder Canada, General 4/61–5/14/61.

105. Amory to CRO, "Canada: Visit of the President of the United States of America," Jun. 14, 1961, TNA/DO 182/1.

106. Schlesinger, *A Thousand Days,* 343; Heeney to Diefenbaker, May 18, 1961, LAC/MG 31 E44/vol. 2.9; Gloin, "Another Look," 10.

107. Rostow to Kennedy, "Follow-On From Canada," May 22, 1961 and Ottawa to State, 930, May 23, 1961, JFKL/NSF/box 18/folder Canada, General 5/15/61–5/30/61; CC, June 9, 1961, LAC/RG 2/vol. 6176.

108. Heeney to Diefenbaker, May 18, 1961, LAC/MG 31 E44/vol. 2.9.

109. Diefenbaker to file, "Heeney," May 22, 1961, LAC/MG 31 E44/vol. 2.9; CC, May 23, 1961, LAC/RG 2/vol. 6176.

110. Robinson, *Diefenbaker's World*, 206–7.
111. Fowler to Hampshire, Jul. 27, 1961, TNA/DO 182/1.
112. Heeney, *The Things*, 175; C. Ritchie to Robertson, "Views of Walt Rostow," Dec. 4, 1962, LAC/MG 31 E83/vol. 6.13.
113. White to Rostow, n.d, and attached speech draft, JFKL/POF/box 113/folder Address to Canadian Parliament, Ottawa, May 17, 1961; Walton Butterworth Oral History, JFKL.
114. Memcon, May 26, 1961, NARA/RG 59/EUR-BNA/ANF/box 1/folder Nationalism, Neutralism and Anti-Americanism, 1960–1962. The academic to whom Ignatieff referred may have been his brother-in-law, George Grant, who would later write *Lament for A Nation*, both a critical look at American influence in Canada and a spirited defence of Diefenbaker; Ottawa to State, no. G-309, Jun. 7, 1961, JFKL/NSF/box 18/folder Canada, General, 6/61–9/61.
115. Campbell to Latin American Division, "Public Opinion Concerning Membership in O.A.S.," May 26, 1961, Robertson to Green, "Survey of Public Correspondence Regarding Canadian Participation in the Organization of American States," Jun. 6, 1961, and Robertson to Green, "Press reaction to President Kennedy's appeal that Canada join the O.A.S.," May 29, 1961, LAC/RG 25/vol. 5069/file 4035-C-40-pt. 2.
116. Robertson to Green, "Canadian Editorial Opinion Regarding Canadian Membership in the Organization of American States," Jul. 10, 1961, LAC/RG 25/vol. 5068/file 4035-C-40-pt. 3; A.E. Ritchie to Green, "Survey of Public Correspondence Regarding Canadian Participation in the Organization of American States," Jul. 6, 1961, and Robinson to Latin American Division, Jul. 8, 1961, LAC/RG 25/vol. 5043/file 2226-40-pt. 12.
117. HOC, 7 Sep. 1961, 8081.
118. HOC, 11 Sep. 1961, 8203.
119. Molinaro, "Calculated Diplomacy," 76.
120. J. C. M. Ogelsby, "Canada and the Pan American Union: Twenty Years On," *IJ* 24, no. 3 (1969): 576.
121. Freedman, *Kennedy's Wars*, 293–313.
122. M. Jones, "The Diplomacy of Restraint: Britain and the Laos Crisis, 1961–1962," in *The Failure of Peace in Indochina, 1954–1962*, eds. C. Goscha and K. Laplante (Paris: Les Indes Savantes, 2010), 159–77.
123. Memorandum of Conference with the President, Mar. 9, 1961, JFK/NSF/box 130/folder Laos, General, 3/25/61–3/31/61.
124. CC, Jan. 11, 1961, LAC/RG 2/vol. 6176.
125. Memcon, "Visit of Canadian Prime Minister Diefenbaker," Feb. 20, 1961, JFKL/NSF/box 18/folder Canada, General 1/61–3/61; CC, Apr. 25, 1961, LAC/RG 2/vol. 6176.
126. Rostow to White, "The International Control of Frontiers Against Guerrilla War," May 15, 1961, JFKL/NSF/box 18/folder Canada, General 5/15/61–5/30/61.
127. Rostow to Kennedy, "What We Want from the Ottawa Trip."
128. Rusk to Kennedy, secto. 113, May 14, 1961, JFKL/NSF/box 18/folder Canada, General 5/15/61–5/30/61.
129. Laos Del. Geneva to External, tel. 653, May 25, 1961, LAC/RG 25/vol. 4695/file 50052-B-11-40-pt. 2.
130. Washington to External, tel. 1722, May 29, 1961, LAC/RG 25/vol. 4675/file 50052-B-40-pt. 37.
131. Ottawa to State, G-300, May 31, 1961, JKFL/NSF/box 18/folder Canada, General, 5/15/61–5/30/61.
132. Laos Del. Geneva to External, tel. 495, May 13, 1961, LAC/RG 25/vol. 4675/file 50052-B-40-pt. 37.
133. Laos Del. Geneva to External, tel. 944, Jun. 19, 1961 and Laos Del. Geneva to External, tel. 950, Jun. 20, 1961, LAC/RG 25/vol. 4676/file 50052-B-40-pt. 40.
134. Rostow to Kennedy, Jul. 21, 1961, JFKL/NSF/box 231/folder Southeast Asia, General, Rostow Memo, 7/21/61.
135. Washington to External, tel. 3533, Nov. 20, 1961, LAC/RG 25/vol. 4638/file 50052-A-40-pt. 38.

136. J. Hilliker and D. Barry, "Uncomfortably in the Middle: The Department of External Affairs and Canada's Involvement in the International Control Commissions in Vietnam, 1954–73," in V. Howard, ed., *Creating the Peaceable Kingdom* (East Lansing: Michigan State University Press, 1998), 167–95.

137. Memcon, "Conversation between President Kennedy and Prime Minister Diefenbaker—Southeast Asia," May 17, 1961, JFKL/NSF/box 18/folder Canada, General, Ottawa Trip 5/17/61 Memoranda of Conversation.

138. Robertson to Green, "South Vietnam—USA Proposal to Increase Strength of Military Assistance Advisory Group," May 31, 1961, LAC/RG 25/vol. 4668/file 50052-A-13-40-pt. 2.

139. Can. Del. NATO to Washington, tel. 2877, Nov. 23, 1961, LAC/RG 25/vol. 4638/file 50052-A-40-pt. 38.

140. Rae to Robertson, Nov. 13, 1961, LAC, MG 31 E44/vol. 2.14.

141. Washington to External, tel. 3790, Dec. 15, 1961, Washington to External, tel. 3804, Dec. 16, 1961, LAC/RG 25/vol. 4638/file 50052-A-40-pt. 39.

142. State to Saigon, no. 974, Feb. 9, 1962, NARA/RG 59/CDF/751G.00/2-962.

143. Memcon, "ICC and Vietnam," Mar. 2, 1962, NARA/RG 59/CDF/751G.00/3-262.

144. HOC, Mar. 8, 1962, 1602.

145. Ottawa to State, no. 780, Feb. 16, 1962, JFKL/NSF/box 18/folder Canada, General 2/62–3/62;

146. Washington to External, tel. 1439, May 10, 1962, LAC/RG 25/vol. 4638/file 50052-A-40-pt. 40.

147. ICC, "Special Report to the Co-Chairmen of the Geneva Conference on Indo-China," Jun. 2, 1962, LAC/RG 25/vol. 3072/file 9.

148. Memorandum for the Record, Aug. 29, 1962, JFKL/NSF/box 132/folder Laos, General, 8/28/62–8/31/62; Ottawa to State, no. 1229, May 31, 1962, JFKL/NSF/box 18/folder Canada, General 5/16/62–6/62.

149. Memcon, "Vietnam and the ICC," Mar. 15, 1962, NARA/RG 59/CDF/751G.00/3-1562.

150. A. Preston, "Balancing War and Peace: Canadian Foreign Policy and the Vietnam War, 1961–1965," *DH* 27, no. 1 (2003): 73–111; and R. Bothwell, "The Further Shore: Canada and Vietnam," *IJ* 56, no. 1 (2000/2001): 89–114.

151. J. Holmes, "Canada and the United States in World Politics," *FA* 40 (1961): 105–17.

## Chapter 3

1. Address to the Annual Meeting of the RCAF Association, Winnipeg, May 19, 1961, LAC/MG 32 B9/vol. 68/file Defence Policy—Notes on, by Mr. Harkness, December 1962; "The Nuclear Weapons Muddle," *G&M*, May 22, 1961.

2. McMahon, *Essence of Indecision*; and Simpson, *NATO and the Bomb*.

3. Bright, *Continental Defense*, 151.

4. "Address before the Canadian Parliament in Ottawa," May 17, 1961, *PPP*; Freedman, *Kennedy's Wars*, 18–26, 45–111. But see F. J. Gavin, *Nuclear Statecraft: History and Strategy in America's Atomic Age* (Ithaca: Cornell University Press, 2012), 30–56.

5. Willis Armstrong Oral History, FAOHC; Robertson to Green, "Visit of Mr. Rusk—August 24," Aug. 29, 1962, LAC/RG 25/vol. 5030/file 1415–40-pt. 12; Memcon, "NATO-Present State of Solidarity; Degree of Consultation; Relations to UN Problems; Effect of European Unity," Aug. 24, 1962, JFKL/NSF/box 18/folder Canada, General, 7/62–9/62; and BNA to Tyler, Sep. 5, 1962, NARA/RG 59/EUR-BNA/ANF/box 6/folder Secretary's Trip to Canada, August 24, 1962.

6. Merchant to Hutton, Jun. 8, 1961, NARA/RG 84/CGR/box 224/folder Cuba 1961.

7. Ottawa to State, no. 893, May 11, 1961, JFKL/POF/box 113/folder JFK Trip to Ottawa, 5/61; Heeney to Diefenbaker, May 18, 1961, LAC/MG 31 E44/vol. 2.9. The comment about JFK's inability comes from Granatstein, "When Push Came to Shove," 92.

8. Rostow to Kennedy, "Follow-On From Canada," May 22, 1961, JFKL/NSF/box 18/folder Canada, General 5/15/61–5/30/61.

9. Ottawa to State, G-329, Jun. 27, 1961, JFKL/NSF/box 18/folder Canada, General 6/61–9/61.

10. Memcon, "Acquisition of Nuclear Weapons by Canada," Jul. 7, 1961, NARA/RG 84/CGR/box 224/folder Canada–US Limit Distribution 1959–1961.

11. J. Glazov, *Canadian Policy toward Khrushchev's Soviet Union* (Montréal and Kingston: McGill–Queen's University Press, 2002), 123–4; P. T. Haydon, *The 1962 Cuban Missile Crisis: Canadian Involvement Reconsidered* (Toronto: Canadian Institute of Strategic Studies, 1993), 179.

12. A. Fursenko and T. Naftali, *Khrushchev's Cold War: The Inside Story of an American Adversary* (New York W. W. Norton, 2007), 371; R. D. Williamson, *First Steps toward Détente: American Diplomacy in the Berlin Crisis, 1958–1963* (Lanham: Rowman & Littlefield, 2012); and G. Schild, "The Berlin Crisis," in *Kennedy: The New Frontier Revisited*, ed. M. J. White (New York: NYU Press, 1998), 91–131.

13. T. A. Sayle, "Canada, NATO, and the Berlin Crisis, 1961–1962: 'Slow-Boil' or 'Pressure Cooker?'," *IJ* 68, no. 2 (2013): 255–68.

14. D. Macfarlane, "Courting War Over a Rubber Stamp," *IJ* 63, no. 3 (2008): 751–68; Granatstein, "When Push Came to Shove," 93.

15. M. Trachtenberg, *A Constructed Peace: The Making of the European Settlement, 1945–1963* (Princeton: Princeton University Press, 1999), 251–82.

16. Diefenbaker to Kennedy, May 28, 1961, JFKL/POF/box 113/folder Canada, Security 1961; Memo, "Visit of President Kennedy to Ottawa, May 16–18, 1961. Meeting with the Prime Minister, May 17," LAC/MG 31 E83/vol. 5.7; Memcon, "Conversation between President Kennedy and Prime Minister Diefenbaker—Kennedy-Khrushchev Meeting," May 17, 1961, JFKL/NSF/box 18/folder Canada, General, Ottawa Trip 5/17/61 Memoranda of Conversation.

17. Memcon, Kennedy-Khrushchev, Jun. 4, 1961, *FRUS*, 1961–1963, XIV, 89–98; Kennedy to Diefenbaker, Jun. 15, 1961, JFKL/POF/box 113/folder Canada, Security 1961.

18. Green to Diefenbaker, "Soviet Aide-Memoire on Germany and Berlin," Jun. 8, 1961, LAC/RG 25/vol. 6075/file 50341-40-pt. 14.1.

19. Washington to External, tel. 2083, Jun. 29, 1961, LAC/RG 25/vol. 6075/file 50341-40-pt. 14.2.

20. *S&S* 61/7, Jul. 3, 1961.

21. Cadieux to Robertson, "Berlin," Jul. 11, 1961; Green to Diefenbaker, "Germany and Berlin: Replies to the Soviet Aide-Memoire," Jul. 17, 1961, and Green to Diefenbaker, "Germany and Berlin," Jul. 17, 1961, LAC/RG 25/vol. 6075/file 50341-40-pt. 15.1; and "U.S. Note of 17 July," *Department of State Bulletin* 45 (1961): 224–33.

22. Telephone conversation with the Prime Minister of Canada, Jul. 22, 1961, JFKL/Accession WH-044-005/JFKWHA-044-055.

23. CC, Jul. 24, 1961, LAC/RG 2/vol. 6177; Garner to Clutterbuck, Jul. 20, 1961, TNA/FO 371/156450.

24. National Security Council Minutes, Jul. 19, 1961, *FRUS*, 1961–1963, XIV, 220.

25. Radio and Television Report to the American People on the Berlin Crisis, Jul. 25, 1961, *PPP*; Diefenbaker to Kennedy, Aug. 11, 1961, JFKL/POF/folder Canada, Security 1961.

26. Robertson to Diefenbaker, "Berlin," Aug. 14, 1961, LAC/RG 25/vol. 6075/file 50341-40-pt. 16.2.

27. Speech to the Canadian Weekly Newspapers Association Annual Convention, Halifax, Aug. 15, 1961, LAC/MG 31 E83/vol. 7.11.

28. Reid to Diefenbaker, "Berlin," Aug. 16, 1961, LAC/RG 25/vol. 6075/file 50341-40-pt. 17.1.

29. CC, Aug. 17, 1961; and CC, Aug. 22, 1961, LAC/RG 2/vol. 6177.

30. Washington to External, tel. 2588, Aug. 18, 1961, LAC/RG 25/vol. 6076/file 50341-40-pt. 17.2; Kohler to Rusk, "Canadian Government's Views on Berlin Problem," Aug. 22, 1961, NARA/RG 59/EUR-BNA/ANF/box 5/folder Germany.

31. E. Reid, *Radical Mandarin: The Memoirs of Escott Reid* (Toronto: University of Toronto Press, 1989), 312.

32. Reid to Heeney, "Germany and Berlin," Aug. 22, 1961, LAC/RG 25/vol. 6076/file 50341-40-pt. 17.3.

33. Green to Diefenbaker, "Senatorial Opinion on Berlin," Aug. 25, 1961, LAC/RG 25/vol. 6076/file 50341-40-pt. 18.1.

34. Memcon, "Germany and Berlin," Aug. 24, 1961, Washington to External, tel. 2645, Aug. 24, 1961, LAC/MG 31 E46/vol. 10.32; Memcon, "Canadian Views on Berlin Problem," Aug. 24, 1961, NARA/RG 59/EUR-BNA/ANF/box 5/folder Germany.

35. Reid, "Impressions of the Washington Approach to the Berlin Problem," Aug. 24, 1961, Reid, "Notes on conversation August 23 after dinner at the Canadian Embassy residence," Aug. 24, 1961, LAC/MG 31 E46/vol. 10.32; and Reid, *Radical Mandarin*, 313.

36. Heeney to Robertson, Aug. 25, 1961, LAC/MG 30 E144/vol. 1.16. Reid meanwhile felt that while Bundy might be willing to negotiate, Rusk, Bohlen and Kohler did not want to be guilty of what they saw to be appeasement: Reid, *Radical Mandarin*, 317.

37. Bundy's emphasis. Bundy to Heeney, Aug. 24, 1961, and Heeney to Robertson, Aug. 28, 1961, LAC/MG 30 E144/vol. 1.16.

38. Reid, "Berlin and Germany: Current U.S. Thinking," Aug. 29, 1961, LAC/RG 25/vol. 6076/file 50341-40-pt. 18.2. Reid's interpretation aside, Rusk put great emphasis on negotiating with the Soviets: T. Aono, "'It Is Not Easy for the United States to Carry the Whole Load': Anglo-American Relations during the Berlin Crisis, 1961–1962," *DH* 34, no. 2 (2010): 325–56.

39. Robinson to Robertson, "The Prime Minister's Address to the Canadian Bar Association," Aug. 22, 1961, LAC/RG 25/vol. 6075/file 50341-40-pt. 17.3.

40. Reid to Robertson, Aug. 25, 1961, LAC/RG 25/vol. 6076/file 50341-40-pt. 18.1; Robinson to Robertson, "Berlin—The Prime Minister's Speech to the Canadian Bar Association," Aug. 29, 1961, and Robinson to Robertson, Aug. 30, 1961, LAC/RG 25/vol. 6089/file 50346-3-40-pt. 3.2.

41. Address to the Canadian Bar Association, Winnipeg, Sep. 1, 1961, LAC/MG 31 E83/vol. 7.10.

42. "Don't Deny Hope," *MG*, Sep. 4, 1961; "Canada and Berlin," *G&M*, Sep. 4, 1961.

43. Heeney to file, "Germany and Berlin: Conversation with the Prime Minister," Sep. 5, 1961, LAC/RG 25/vol. 6089/file 50346-3-40-pt. 3.3.

44. External to Washington, tel. N64, Aug. 31, 1961, and memo, "Call on Secretary of State for External Affairs by U.S.A. Ambassador, August 31," Sep. 1, 1961, LAC/RG 25/vol. 6076/file 50341-40-pt. 18.3; Ottawa to State, no. 226, Aug. 31, 1961, JFKL/NSF/box 18, folder Canada, General, 9/1/61–9/30/61; Arthur Schlesinger Jr., *Journals, 1952–2000* (New York: Penguin, 2007), 122. See also: Beschloss, *Crisis Years*, 292, 307; G. T. Seaborg, *Kennedy, Khrushchev, and the Test Ban* (Berkeley: University of California Press, 1981); and K. Oliver, *Kennedy, Macmillan, and the Nuclear Test Ban Debate, 1961–63* (New York: St. Martin's Press, 1998).

45. Robinson to Robertson, "United States Decision to Resume Nuclear Testing," Sep. 6, 1961, RG 25/vol. 6011/file 50271-M-40; CC, Sep. 6, 1961, LAC/RG 2/vol. 6177; HOC, Sep. 7, 1961, 8061–2; *S&S* 61/12, Sep. 11, 1961; CC, Oct. 26, 1961, LAC/RG 2/vol. 6177.

46. HOC, Sep. 7, 1961, 8053–4.

47. Ottawa to State 291, Sep. 14, 1961, JFKL/NSF/box 18/folder Canada, General 6/61–9/61; Rusk to Heeney, 11:19 am, Sep. 11, 1961, NARA/RG 59/Records of Dean Rusk/Transcripts of Telephone Calls/box 45; Washington to External, tel. 2828, Sep. 11, 1961 and NATO Del. Paris to External, tel. 2210, Sep. 8, 1961, LAC/RG 25/vol. 4532/file 5030-V-4-40-pt. 4.

48. Rusk to Heeney, Sep. 13, 1961, and Tyler to Rusk, Sep. 11, 1961, NARA/RG 59/EUR-CDC/RRPM/box 3/folder External Affairs Minister, 1961–1962.

49. Heeney to Robertson, Sep. 18, 1961, LAC/MG 31 E44/vol. 2.9; Telegram From the Mission to the North Atlantic Treaty Organization and European Regional Organizations to the Department of State, Sep. 22, 1961, *FRUS*, 1961–1963, XIV, 434–5.

50. Campbell to file, "Germany and Berlin: Negotiating Positions," Sep. 7, 1961, and Campbell to Robertson, "Germany and Berlin," Sep. 7, 1961, LAC/RG 25/vol. 6076/file 50341-40-pt. 19.2; CC, Dec. 18, 1961, LAC/RG 2/vol. 6177.

51. Washington to External, tel. 3013, Sep. 26, 1961, LAC/RG 25/vol. 4532/file 5030-V-4-40-pt. 4.

52. See Sayle, "Canada, NATO, and the Berlin Crisis".

53. Ottawa to State, no. 523, Nov. 28, 1961, JFKL/NSF/box 18/folder Canada, General 10/ 61–1/62.

54. CC, Jul. 24, 1961, LAC/RG 2/vol. 6177.

55. Kennedy to Diefenbaker, Aug. 3, 1961, JFKL/NSF/box 20/folder Canada, Subjects, Diefenbaker, Correspondence 1/20/61–8/10/61; Diefenbaker to Kennedy, Aug. 11, 1961, JFKL/POF/box 113/folder Canada, Security, 1961.

56. Speech to the Canadian Weekly Newspapers Association Annual Convention, Halifax, 15 Aug 1961, LAC/MG 31 E83/vol. 7.11.

57. CC, Aug. 17, 1961, LAC/RG 2/vol. 6177.

58. CC, Aug. 22, 1961, CC, Aug. 23, 1961, and CC, Aug. 25, 1961, LAC/RG 2/vol. 6177.

59. Merchant to Lincoln, Aug. 22, 1961, JFKL/POF/box 113/folder Canada, General, 1961.

60. Memcon, "U.S.-Canadian Negotiations on Nuclear Weapons," Aug. 15, 1961, and Memcon, "Pending Negotiations on Nuclear Weapons," Aug. 21, 1961, NARA/RG 59/ EUR-CDC/RRMM/box 2/folder US & Canadian Policy re. Acquisition & Control of Nuclear Weapons, 1961.

61. HOC, Sep. 12, 1961, 8222–3, 8230–1.

62. Ottawa to State, no. 290, Sep. 14, 1961, NARA/RG 59/EUR-CDC/RRM/box 2/folder US & Canadian Policy re. Acquisition & Control of Nuclear Weapons, 1961; and Ottawa to State, no. 291, Sep. 15, 1961, JFKL/NSF/box 18/folder Canada, General, 6/61–9/61.

63. Heeney to file, "Germany and Berlin: Conversation with the Prime Minister," Sep. 5, 1961, LAC/RG 25/vol. 6089/file 50346-3-40-pt. 3.3; CC, Sep. 14, 1961, LAC/RG 2/vol. 6177; J. Diefenbaker to E. Diefenbaker, Sep. 14, 1961, in McIlroy, *Personal Letters of a Public Man*, 107.

64. "The Periscope," *Newsweek*, Sep. 25, 1961; "JFK Presses Canada on Nuclear Warheads," *MG*, Sep. 20, 1961.

65. Handwritten transcript of telephone conversation, Sep. 19, 1961, NARA/RG 59/EUR-CDC/RRMM/box 2/folder US & Canadian Policy re. Acquisition & Control of Nuclear Weapons, 1961.

66. HOC, Sep. 20, 1961, 8596; Notes of Speech on The Nation's Business, Sep. 20, 1962, LAC/MG 31 E83/vol. 7.10.

67. Ottawa to State, no. 317, Sep. 20, 1961, NARA/RG 59/EUR-CDC/RRMM/box 2/folder US & Canadian Policy re. Acquisition & Control of Nuclear Weapons, 1961.

68. Butterworth Oral History, JFKL; CC, Nov. 30, 1961, and CC, Nov. 21, 1961, LAC/RG 2/ vol. 6177; Address to the Air Industries and Transport Association, Quebec City, Nov. 1, 1961, LAC/MG 32 B9/vol. 68/file Defence Policy—Notes on, by Mr. Harkness, Dec/62.

69. J. Gellner, "Wanted: Hard Facts on National Defence," *Saturday Night*, Nov. 25, 1961.

70. Address to the Association of Canadian Universities and Colleges, Ottawa, Nov. 14, 1961, LAC/MG 31 E83/vol. 7.9.

71. Ottawa to State, no. 519, Nov. 27, 1961, NARA/RG 59/CDF/711.5611/11-2761.

72. Memcon, "Recent Developments in Canada," Nov. 10, 1961, JFKL/NSF/box 18/folder Canada, General, 10/61–1/62.

73. Memcon, Nov. 21, 1961 and covering letter, Armstrong to Schaetzel, Nov. 27, 1961, NARA/RG 59/EUR-BNA/ANF/box 4/folder Briefing Papers 1959–1962.

74. A. Burtch, *Give Me Shelter: The Failure of Canada's Cold War Civil Defence* (Vancouver: UBC Press, 2012), 175.

75. "Statesman-President," *Saturday Night*, Oct. 14, 1961.

76. Robinson to Robertson, "Nuclear Weapons Policy," Oct. 6, 1961; Robinson, "Record of Conversation with the Prime Minister," Oct. 6, 1961, LAC/MG 31 E83/vol. 9.1.

Diefenbaker reiterated these points to Bryce the next day: Robinson to Robertson, "Nuclear Weapons Policy," Oct. 7, 1961, LAC/MG 31 E83/vol. 9.1.

77. Robinson, *Diefenbaker's World*, 231–2.
78. Heeney to Diefenbaker, Nov. 3, 1961; and Diefenbaker to Heeney, Nov. 9, 1961, LAC/ MG 30 E144/vol. 1.16.
79. Gloin, "Another Look," 2.
80. Memo, "Canadian-United States Relations Background," Dec. 18, 1961, NARA/RG 59/ EUR-BNA/ANF/box 4/folder Briefing Papers 1959–1962.
81. Merchant to Rewinkel, Dec. 5, 1961, and Rewinkel to Merchant, Nov. 17, 1961 and attached draft, "Canada—Department of State Guidelines for Policy and Operations," Oct. 1961, NARA/RG 84/CGR/box 224/folder international political rel classified 1959–61 Canada–US.
82. *Department of State Guidelines for Policy and Operations—Canada*, Mar. 1962 and attached memo, Battle to Bundy, "Department of State Guidelines for Policy and Operations Concerning Canada," Mar. 16, 1962, JFKL/NSF/box 18/folder Canada, General, 2/ 62–3/62. This document replaced the Eisenhower-era report, NSC 5822/1, discussed in chapter 1.
83. HOC, Jan. 22, 1962, 42.
84. *Macleans*, Jan. 17, 1962.
85. Robinson to Robertson, "Prime Minister's Request for Information on Defence Matters," Jan. 10, 1962, LAC/MG 31 E83/vol. 9.2.
86. Robinson to Diefenbaker, Jan. 16, 1962, Robinson to Ignatieff, Jan. 19, 1962 and draft speech "Nuclear Weapons," LAC/MG 31 E83/vol. 9.2.
87. Robinson, "Nuclear Weapons Policy," Feb. 27, 1962, LAC/MG 31 E83/vol. 9.2; Diefenbaker to Robinson, Feb. 25, 1962, LAC/MG 31 E83/vol. 9.2.
88. Transcript, "Press Conference," Feb. 24, 1962, LAC/MG 31 E83/vol. 7.16.
89. HOC, Feb. 26, 1962, 1250–1.
90. Robinson, "Nuclear Weapons Policy," Feb. 27, 1962, LAC/MG 31 E83/vol. 9.2.
91. "Not Necessarily ... But ... ," *MG*, Mar. 1, 1962; "Questions on Defence," *G&M*, Feb. 26, 1962.
92. Ottawa to State, no. 807, Feb. 26, 1962, JFKL/NSF/box 20/folder Canada, Subjects, Diefenbaker, Correspondence, 8/11/61–10/10/62.
93. Ottawa to State, no. 823, Feb. 27, 1962, JFKL/NSF/box 18/folder Canada, General 2/ 62–3/62.
94. Tyler to Rusk, "Suggested Statement for Your Press Conference Today," Mar. 1, 1962; Transcript, "The Secretary's Press Conference," Mar. 1, 1962, NARA/RG 59/EUR-CDC/ RRMM/box 2/folder Canada–US & Canadian Policy Acquisition & Control of Nuclear Weapons, 1962.
95. Tyler to Rusk, "Prime Minister Diefenbaker's Reaction to the Secretary's Statement on Nuclear Weapons," Mar. 2, 1962, NARA/RG 59/EUR-CDC/RRMM/box 2/folder Canada–US & Canadian Policy Acquisition & Control of Nuclear Weapons, 1962; Robinson, *Diefenbaker's World*, 253; ECS to Rusk, Mar. 2, 1962, NARA/RG 59/Rusk/ TTC/box 45.
96. Ottawa to State, no. 873, Mar. 8, 1962, NARA/RG 59/CDF/742.5611/3-862; Ottawa to State, no. 871, Mar. 8, 1962, JFKL/NSF/box 18/folder Canada, General 2/62–3/62.
97. E. Bergbusch and M. D. Stevenson, "Howard Green, Public Opinion, and the Politics of Disarmament," in *Architects and Innovators: Building the Department of Foreign Affairs and International Trade, 1909–2009*, eds. G. Donaghy and K. R. Nossal (Montréal and Kingston: McGill–Queen's University Press, 2010), 196. See Green to Diefenbaker, Feb. 5, 1962, and Robertson to Green, "Disarmament and Nuclear Weapons Tests—Review of Events," Feb. 5, 1962, LAC/RG 25/vol. 6015/file 50271-T-40-pt. 1. Two scholars of Canada's role in disarmament negotiations have advanced a more critical view, arguing that Green was motivated by a "simplistic idealism," making him determined to "pursue negotiations at all costs": A. Legault and M. Fortmann, *A Diplomacy of Hope: Canada and*

*Disarmament, 1945–1988* (Montréal and Kingston: McGill–Queen's University Press, 1992), 203.

98. Memorandum of Conversation with the President and the Congressional Leadership, Jun. 6, 1961, *FRUS*, 1961–1963, VII, 93.

99. NIE 4-2-61, "Attitudes of Key World Powers on Disarmament Issues," Apr. 6, 1961, *FRUS*, 1961–1963, VII, 37.

100. Disarmament Del. Geneva to External, tel. 193, Mar. 13, 1962, LAC/RG 25/vol. 6016/ file 50271-T-40-pt. 3.2.

101. *S&S* 62/6, Mar. 19, 1962.

102. Disarmament Del. Geneva to External, tel. 458, Mar. 21, 1962, LAC/RG 25/vol. 50271- 40-pt. 4.2. For a discussion of the Eighteen-Nation Disarmament Committee, see Legault and Fortmann, *Diplomacy of Hope*, 195–228; Oliver, *Nuclear Test Ban Debate,* 73–134; and Seaborg, *Kennedy, Khrushchev, and the Test Ban*, 142–9. On the impor- tance of verification for the United States, see P. F. Ilsaas Pharo, "A Precondition for Peace: Transparency and the Test-Ban Negotiations, 1958–1963," *International History Review* 22, no. 3 (2000): 557–82. On Canada's inability to affect the ultimate outcome of disarmament negotiations see C. Ungerer, "Influence Without Power: Middle Power and Arms Control Diplomacy during the Cold War," *D&S* 18, no. 2 (2007): 393–414.

103. A.E. Ritchie to file, "Disarmament Negotiations," Apr. 3, 1962, LAC/RG 25/vol. 6016/ file 50271-T-40-pt. 5.1.

104. Rusk to Heeney, 1:35 pm, Apr. 1, 1961, NARA/RG 59/Rusk/TTC/box 46.

105. Washington to External, tel. 1122, Apr. 11, 1962, LAC/RG 25/vol. 6016/file 50271-T-40-pt. 5.2.

106. Rusk with Bundy, 1:05 pm, Apr. 12, 1961, NARA/RG 59/Rusk/TTC/box 46; Kennedy to Diefenbaker, Apr. 13, 1962, JFKL/POF/box 113/folder Canada, General, 1962.

107. HOC, Apr. 17, 1962, 3035; and HOC, Apr. 13, 1962, 2970; and HOC, Apr. 14, 1962, 2997.

108. Ottawa to State, A-311, Feb. 21, 1962, JFKL/NSF/box 18/folder Canada, General 2/ 62–3/62.

109. Diary, Mar. 18, 1962, LAC/MG 30 E144/vol. 2.30.

110. Editorial Note, *FRUS*, 1961–1963, VII, 209–10.

111. Washington to External, tel. 1122, Apr. 11, 1962, LAC/RG 25/vol. 6016/file 50271-T-40-pt. 5.2.

112. Rewinkel to Duke, "Photograph of President Kennedy for Ambassador Heeney," Apr. 2, 1962, Tyler to Duke, "Farewell Lunch for Departing Canadian Ambassador," Mar. 19, 1962, and Memcon, "Canadian Ambassador's Farewell Call," Apr. 17, 1962, NARA/RG 59/EUR- CDC/RRPM/box 3/folder Canadian Embassy in Washington, 1961–1962; and Washington to External, tel. 1199, Apr. 17, 1962, LAC/RG 25/vol. 5030/file 1415-40-pt. 10.

113. Ottawa to State, A-416, May 8, 1962, JFKL/NSF/box 18/folder Canada, General, 4/62– 5/16/61.

114. R. A. Bell quoted in P. Stursberg, *Diefenbaker: Leadership Lost, 1962–1967* (Toronto: University of Toronto Press, 1976), 5; P. Sévigny, *This Game of Politics* (Toronto: McClelland and Stewart, 1965), 225.

115. Rewinkel to Tyler, "Canadian Election Results," Jun. 19, 1962, NARA/RG 59/EUR-BNA/ ANF/box 6/folder Visits to US, 1962.

116. Robinson, *Diefenbaker's World*, 271.

117. D. Anderson, "A Gesture of Sanity and Faith," *Chatelaine*, Feb. 1962; C. McCall, "Can You Protect Your Family from the Bomb?," *Chatelaine*, Apr. 1962. And see V. Korinek, "'It's a Tough Time to be in Love': The Darker Side of *Chatelaine* during the Cold War," in *Love, Hate, and Fear in Canada's Cold War*, ed. Richard Cavell (Toronto, 2004).

118. A. Hailey, *In High Places* (New York: Doubleday, 1962), 89.

119. Comments of the Chairman Joint Chiefs of Staff to the National Defence College, 8/2/ 1961, LAC/MG 31 E83/vol. 9.1.

120. R.J. Sutherland, "Canada's Long Term Strategic Situation," *IJ* 17, no. 3 (1962): 199–223. And see D. Barry and D. Bratt, "Defense Against Help: Explaining Canada–U.S. Security Relations," *ARCS* 38, no. 1 (2008): 63–89.

121. M. Conant, "Canada's Role in Western Defense," *FA* 40 (1962): 431–42; and M. Conant, *The Long Polar Watch* (New York: Harper, 1962).

122. Ottawa to State, no. 78, Jul. 16, 1962, NARA/RG 59/CDF/611.42/7-1662.

123. Amory to Sandys, "Canadian Defence Policy," May 16, 1962, TNA/DO 182/84.

## Chapter 4

1. "State of the Union Address," Jan. 11, 1962. *PPP.*

2. Rusk quoted in F. Costigliola, "The Pursuit of an Atlantic Community: Nuclear Arms, Dollars, and Berlin," in *Kennedy's Quest for Victory*, ed. T. G. Paterson (New York: Oxford University Press, 1989), 29. See also F. Costigliola, "The Failed Design: Kennedy, de Gaulle, and the Struggle for Europe," *DH* 8, no. 3 (1984): 227–51; T. Zeiler, *American Trade & Power in 1960s* (New York: Columbia University Press, 1992), 1–130; and J. G. Giauque, *Grand Designs and Visions of Unity: The Atlantic Powers and the Reorganization of Western Europe, 1955–1963* (Chapel Hill: UNC Press, 2002).

3. H. MacKenzie, "The ABCs of Canada's International Economic Relations, 1945–1951," in *Canada and the Early Cold War, 1943–1957*, ed. G. Donaghy (Ottawa: Department of Foreign Affairs and International Trade, 1998), 215–50.

4. "Canada, the United States and Developing Trading Blocs," Speech to the Third Annual Seminar on Canadian–American Relations, Assumption University, Windsor, Nov. 9, 1961, LAC/MG 32 B39/vol. 109/file Speech—Canada, the United States and Developing Trading Blocs. And see B. Muirhead, "The Development of Canada's Foreign Economic Policy in the 1960s: The Case of the European Union," *Canadian Historical Review* 82, no. 4 (2001): 690–719.

5. R. Rodgers, "Nationalism and Canadian Parties," *Saturday Night*, Aug. 19, 1961; Newman, "The PM's election role."

6. 'The Nation's Business," Nov. 29, 1961, LAC/MG 31 E83/vol. 7.9; A. Benvenuti and S. Ward, "Britain, Europe, and the 'Other Quiet Revolution' in Canada," in *Canada and the End of Empire*, ed. P. Buckner (Vancouver: UBC Press, 2005); Igartua, *The Other Quiet Revolution*, 115–92; P. Robertson and J. Singleton, "The Old Commonwealth and Britain's First Application to Join the EEC, 1961–3," *Australian Economic History Review* 40, no. 2 (2000): 153–77.

7. Ball to Kennedy, "U.K. Adherence to the European Common Market," Aug. 23, 1961, JFKL/NSF/box 170/folder UK General, 8/21/61–9/10/61.

8. For this narrow view, see G. Stewart, "'An Objective of US Foreign Policy since the Founding of the Republic': The United States and the End of Empire in Canada," in *Canada and the End of Empire*, ed. P. Buckner (Vancouver: UBC Press, 2005), 94–116.

9. Diary Entry Aug. 9, 1961, *Ambassador to Sixties London: The Diaries of David Bruce, 1961–1969*, eds. J. W. Young and R. Roy (Dordrecht: Republic of Letters, 2009), 27.

10. Memo, "Minute of Meeting between Prime Minister Macmillan and Prime Minister Diefenbaker, April 10, 1961," n.d., LAC/RG 25/vol. 6151/file 50412-40-pt. 3; CC, Apr. 11, 1961, LAC/RG 2/vol. 6176; and "Prime Minister's Visit to Ottawa, April 1961," C. (61) 55, Apr. 18, 1961, TNA/CAB 129/105.

11. Memo, "Visit of President Kennedy to Ottawa, May 16–18, 1961. Meeting with the Prime Minister, May 17," LAC/MG 31 E83/vol. 5.7.

12. Record of a Meeting Held at the White House, Apr. 5, 1961, PM (W)(61) 1st Meeting, C (61) 54, TNA/CAB 129/105.

13. Meeting of Canadian Ministers with the Right Honourable Duncan Sandys, July 13, 1961, LAC/MG 32 B39/vol. 158.1; CC, Jul. 15, 1961, LAC/RG 2/vol. 6177.

14. Sandys, "Europe: Talks with the New Zealand, Australian and Canadian Governments," C. (61) 111, Jul. 21, 1961, TNA/CAB 129/106.

15. CC, Aug. 29, 1961, LAC/RG 2/vol. 6177; Benvenuti and Ward, "'Other Quiet Revolution'," 171; "Must Pick Commonwealth or Inner 6, Hees Tells U.K.," *G&M*, Sep. 14, 1961.

16. "Lamentations at Accra," *G&M*, Sep. 15, 1961; HOC, Sep. 15, 1961, 8407.

17. CC, Sep. 26, 1961, LAC/RG 2/vol. 6177.
18. J. Bill, *George Ball: Behind the Scenes in U.S. Foreign Policy* (New Haven: Yale University Press, 1997), 130.
19. G. Ball, *The Discipline of Power: Essentials of a Modern World Structure* (Boston: Little, Brown, 1968), 113.
20. A.E. Ritchie to Rae, Jan. 30, 1961, LAC/RG 25/vol. 5087/file 4901-40-pt. 1; Willis Armstrong Oral History, FAOHC.
21. Vienna to External, tel. 492, Sep. 19, 1961, LAC/RG 19/vol. 4461/file 8625-04-8-pt. 1.
22. Washington to External, tel. 3048, Sep. 28, 1961, LAC/RG 19/vol. 4461/file 8625-04-8-pt. 1.
23. Komer to Rostow, Oct. 7, 1961, JFKL/NSF/box 322/folder Staff Memoranda, Robert Komer, 10/61.
24. Memo, "UK Negotiations with the EEC: The Role of the United States," Oct. 18, 1961, attached to Fleming to Diefenbaker, Oct. 19, 1961, LAC/MG 32 B39/vol. 158.1.
25. CC, Oct. 10, 1961 and CC, Oct. 26, 1961, LAC/RG 2/vol. 6177; Schwarzmann to Grandy, Oct. 24, 1961, LAC/RG 19/vol. 4461/file 8625-04-8-pt. 1; Schaetzel to Warren, Oct. 25, 1961 and Warren to Ritchie, Nov. 6, 1961, LAC/RG 25/vol. 5060/file 3300-40-pt. 19
26. "Canada, the United States and Developing Trading Blocs," Nov. 9, 1961, LAC/MG 32 B39/vol. 109/file Speech—Canada, the United States and Developing Trading Blocs.
27. F. Coffin, "Opportunities for North American Economic Statesmanship," *Third Seminar on Canadian–American Relations at Assumption University of Windsor* (Windsor: Assumption University, 1961), 31–2.
28. Memcon, Nov. 11, 1961, NARA/RG 59/EUR-BNA/ANF/box 3/folder UK-Common Market; Washington to External, tel. 3477, Nov. 11, 1961, LAC/RG 19/vol. 4215/file 8780/U58-01-pt. 4.
29. "Notes on Conference with the Honourable George Ball, U.S. Under-Secretary of State on Wednesday, November 15, 1961, at Paris," LAC/MG 32 B39/vol. 158/file Memoirs, European Common Market, 1962—notes, memos, telegrams, file 2.
30. "Notes on Conference with President Charles de Gaulle, on Saturday, November 18, 1961, at Paris" and "Notes on Conference with the Right Honourable Harold Macmillan, Prime Minister, on Monday, November 20, 1961, at London," LAC/MG 32 B39/vol. 158/file Memoirs, European Common Market, 1962—notes, memos, telegrams, 2.
31. Rewinkel to Koren, Nov. 2, 1961, NARA/RG 59/EUR-BNA/ANF/box 3/folder US-Japan-Canada Pacific Community.
32. Schaetzel to Ball, Nov. 2, 1961, NARA/RG 59/EUR-BNA/ANF/box 3/folder US-Japan-Canada Pacific Community.
33. Washington to External, tel. 3477, Nov. 11, 1961, LAC/RG 19/vol. 4215/file 8780/U58-01-pt. 4.; Ottawa to State, no. 631, Jan. 4, 1962, JFKL/NSF/box 18/folder Canada, General, 10/61–1/62. And see T. P. Maga, *John F. Kennedy and the New Pacific Community, 1961–63* (Basingstoke: Palgrave, 1990).
34. Memcon, Nov. 21, 1961 and covering letter Armstrong to Schaetzel, Nov. 27, 1961, NARA/RG 59/EUR-BNA/ANF/box 4/file Briefing Papers 1959–1962; Department of State Press Release 833, Dec. 2, 1961, LAC/RG 19/vol. 4215/file 8780/U58-01-pt. 4.
35. Washington to External, tel. 3589, Nov. 25, 1961, LAC/RG 19/vol. 4215/file 8780/U58-01-pt. 4; Ottawa to State, no. A-206, Dec. 4, 1961, JFKL/NSF/box 18/folder Canada, General 10/61–1/62.
36. *S&S* 62/2, Dec 1961; Green quoted in "U.K. Foreign Policy Change Feared with Europe Link," *G&M*, Dec. 4, 1961.
37. Telegram From the Department of State to Embassy in Germany, Jan. 15, 1962, *FRUS*, 1961–1963, XIII, 1165; J. Minifie, "Washington Newsletter," *The Business Quarterly*, Apr. 1962. Fleming recalled that this group was "the strongest" US delegation to yet attend a joint economic meeting: D. Fleming, *So Very Near*, Volume II (Toronto: McClelland and Stewart, 1985), 443.
38. Memo, "Canada—Basic Information," Jan. 5, 1962; Memo, "Scope and Objectives," Dec. 28, 1961, NARA/RG 59/EUR-BNA/RRTEA/box 2/folder 1962 Meeting.

39. Memcon, "Joint US—Canada Committee on Trade and Economic Affairs—U.S. Record of Meeting, 12–13 January, 1962," NARA/RG 59/EUR-BNA/RRTEA/box 2/folder 1962 Meeting.

40. Ibid.

41. Telegram From the Department of State to Embassy in Germany, Jan. 15, 1962, *FRUS*, 1961–1963, XIII, 1165.

42. Fleming, *So Very Near*, II, 444–5. Muirhead disputes Fleming's version, yet ignores that the minster had spoken out in favor of Kennedy's approach and coninuted to do so after the summit: *Dancing*, 45. Robinson, however, corroborates the finance minister's claim: *Diefenbaker's World*, 242.

43. "Canada's Trade in a Changing World," Speech to the Canadian Club of Winnipeg, Jan. 19, 1962, LAC/MG 30 E144/vol. 10.11; HOC, Jan. 24, 1962, 114.

44. B. Hutchinson, "Our Risky Place in the Grand Design for the Atlantic," *Maclean's*, Dec. 16, 1961. And see H. E. English, "Solution—Cooperation with U.S. to Broaden ECM," *Canadian Commentator*, Dec. 1961; J. Deutsch, "Selective Free Trade in the North American Bloc as a Defensive Concept," *Third Seminar on Canadian–American Relations at Assumption University of Windsor* (Windsor: Assumption University, 1961), 93; and H. G. Johnson, "Canada in a Changing World Economy," in *Visions of Canada: Alan B. Plaunt Memorial Lectures 1958–1992*, eds. B. Osty and J. Yalden (Montréal and Kingston: McGill–Queen's University Press, 2004), 116.

45. Ball to JFK, "The Macmillan Visit—The Problem of Commonwealth Preferences in the UK-EEC Negotiations," Apr. 24, 1962, JFKL/NSF/box 175/folder UK, Subjects,.

46. HOC, Jan. 22, 1962, 44–9, 57.

47. "Speech to the Royal Commonwealth Society of Toronto," Mar. 30, 1962, LAC/MG 30 E144/vol. 10.11.

48. Ottawa to State, A-291, Feb. 8, 1962, JFKL/NSF/box 18/folder Canada, General, 2/62–3/62.

49. "Challenge and Response," Address to the Canadian Club of Montreal, Feb. 12, 1962, attached to Merchant to Robertson, Feb. 15, 1962, LAC/MG 31 E44/vol. 4.1; "Canada and the United States in a World of Change," Address to the Guelph Canadian Club, Apr. 19, 1962, and "Canada–U.S. Relations in a Revolutionary World," Address to the Peterborough Kiwanis Club, Apr. 26, 1962, SMML/MC 095/box 19/folder Speeches, Statements, Testimony, 1962.

50. Heeney, "Factors in Canada's External Relations," Jan. 31, 1962, LAC/MG 30 E144/vol. 21/file "Speeches 1962–1964 General."

51. CC, Mar. 13, 1962, LAC/RG 2/vol. 6192.

52. Robinson to Stoner, "Telegram 1434 from London—Mr. Ball's Visit," Apr. 18, 1962, LAC/MG 31 E83/vol. 6.1; London to External, tel. 1434, Apr. 17, 1962, LAC/RG 19/vol. 4461/file 8625-04-8-pt. 1.

53. Quoted in "PC Views on Inner Six Sterile, Pearson Says," *G&M*, Apr. 27, 1962; "Notes for Address by Pearson, Calgary," May 2, 1962, QUA/Kent Papers/box 7/folder Election Speeches, May–June 1962.

54. Ottawa to State, no. 1030, Apr. 11, 1962, JFKL/NSF/box 18/folder Canada, General, 4/62–5/16/61. Merchant later recalled having cleared the invitation with Diefenbaker, who had not objected to Pearson's visit to the White House: Livingston Merchant Oral History, JFKL. Robinson recalled learning of the invitation on April 4 and then record-ing in his diary: "He [Diefenbaker] will not enjoy the news": Robinson, *Diefenbaker's World*, 262.

55. Memcon, "Canadian Ambassador's Farewell Call," Apr. 17, 1962, NARA/RG 59/EUR-CDC/RRPM/box 3/folder Canadian Embassy in Washington, 1961–1962; Washington to External, tel. 1199, Apr. 17, 1962, LAC/RG 25/vol. 5030/file 1415-40-pt. 10.

56. Rusk to Tyler, 10:45 am, Apr. 14, 1961, NARA/RG 59/Rusk/TTC/box 46.

57. L. B. Pearson, *Mike: The Memoirs of the Right Honourable Lester B. Pearson*, Vol. III (Toronto: University of Toronto Press, 1975), 100. In an interview, Liberal MP John Matheson later placed this meeting in Boston, noting that Kennedy arranged for

Pearson to receive an honorary degree from Boston University so that he could pick his brain about Khrushchev. Pearson was indeed awarded an honorary doctorate from BU in June 1961, but he himself placed his meeting with Kennedy in Washington and made no mention of the degree: See P. Stursberg, *Lester Pearson and the American Dilemma* (Toronto: Doubleday, 1980), 181. On Pearson's remarks at BU, see "Pearson Asks U.S. Understand Canada," *NYT* June 5, 1961. Boyko errs by stating that the degree was from Boston College and that Kennedy arranged for it to be awarded in 1962 in the midst of Canada's federal election: Boyko, *Cold Fire*, 156.

58. Pearson quoted in Nash, *Kennedy & Diefenbaker*, 157; and "Remarks at Dinner Honoring Nobel Prize Winners of the Western Hemisphere," Apr. 29, 1962, *PPP*; Dorothy McCardle, "49 Nobel Guests at Notable Evening," *WP*, May 1, 1962.

59. T. Creery, "Political Benefits In Visit to Kennedy," *OC*, Apr. 30, 1962; "A Chat Before Dinner," *G&M*, Apr. 30, 1962.

60. Meeting between Prime Minister Macmillan and Prime Minister Diefenbaker in the Privy Council Chamber, Ottawa, April 30, 1962, LAC/RG 25/vol. 6151/file 50412-40-pt. 4.

61. Robinson to file, "Prime Minister's Meeting with Prime Minister Macmillan, April 30, 1962, 10.00 a.m.," Apr. 30, 1962, LAC/MG 31 E83/vol. 6.1; Cabinet Conclusion, May 3, 1962, C.C. 31 (62). TNA/CAB 128/36.

62. Diary, Mar. 18, 1962, LAC/MG 30 E144/vol. 2.30. The Rostow Memorandum made no mention of nuclear weapons, but it is telling that Diefenbaker included the warheads with issues on which he felt pushed.

63. Contrary to what was speculated at the time, the memo did not contain any notation referring to the Canadian prime minister as an "S.O.B."; supposedly, this comment was to have been written by the president himself. In his memoirs Diefenbaker himself called this a "Liberal invention" designed to make him the butt of jokes. During a dinner conversation in May 1963 at Hyannis Port, with both Kennedy and Lester Pearson in attendance, Basil Robinson was asked whether he had seen the Rostow Memorandum. He replied that he had and that it did not have any handwritten notations upon it. Robinson also wrote that in his career he had seen two copies of the memo; on one of these the word "push," appearing four times, had been underlined. "This I am sure, reflected [Diefenbaker's] irritation with the assumption on the part of the writer of the memorandum that Canada could be 'pushed' around." See Diefenbaker, *One Canada*, II, 183; Memcon, "Memorandum prepared by Mr. Rostow," May 10, 1963. JFKL/POF/box 113/file Canada, Security, 1963; Robinson to file, "General Colour of Hyannisport Meeting," May 15, 1963, LAC/MG 31 E83/vol. 12.1; and Note, "Rostow," May 31, 1983, LAC/MG 31 E83/vol. 5.7.

64. Robinson, *Diefenbaker's World*, 267.

65. Merchant to Ball, May 5, 1962, JFKL/NSF/box 18/folder Canada, General, Rostow Memorandum and Related Materials 5/61–5/63.

66. Ibid.

67. Telcon: Bundy, Ball. 6:30 p.m., May 7, 1962, Telcon: Bundy, Ball. 6:40 p.m., May 7, 1962, and Telcon: Bundy, Ball. 7:40 p.m., May 7, 1962, SMML/MC 031/box 103/folder 1.

68. Bundy to Ball, May 8, 1962, JFKL/NSF/box 18/folder Canada, General, 4/62–5/16/61.

69. Robinson, "Conversations with Ambassador Merchant and Mr. Armstrong of the United States Embassy," May 9, 1962, LAC/MG 31 E83/vol. 6.2.

70. Ottawa to State, no. 1164, May 13, 1962, JFKL/NSF/box 18/folder Canada, General, Rostow Memorandum and Related Materials 5/61–5/63.

71. Kennedy quoted in Nash, *Kennedy and Diefenbaker*, 160. On the Kennedy administration's *machismo*, see: R. D. Dean, *Imperial Brotherhood: Gender and the Making of Cold War Foreign Policy* (Amherst: University of Massachusetts Press, 2001).

72. News Conference, May 17, 1962, JFKL/POF/box 56.

73. Memcon, "Ambassador Merchant's Farewell Call on the President," May 25, 1962, NARA/RG 59/EUR-BNA/ANF/box 4/folder Briefing Papers 1959–1962; and Livingston Merchant Oral History, JFKL.

74. Merchant to Ball, Jul. 11, 1962, JFKL/NSF/box 18/folder Canada, General, Rostow Memorandum and Related Materials 5/61–5/63.
75. "Ambassador Merchant," *G&M*, Apr. 11, 1962; E. Griffin, "Canada Hails U.S. Envoy on Retirement," *CT*, May 13, 1962.
76. Armstrong to Carlson, Jun. 11, 1962, and attached memoranda, NARA/RG 59/EUR-BNA/ANF/box 6/folder Vice President 1962.
77. Willis Armstrong Oral History, FAOHC; Robertson to Green, "Visit of Mr. Rusk—August 24," Aug. 29, 1962, LAC/RG 25/vol. 5030/file 1415-40-pt. 12; Memcon, "NATO-Present State of Solidarity; Degree of Consultation; Relations to UN Problems; Effect of European Unity," Aug. 24, 1962, JFKL/NSF/box 18/folder Canada, General, 7/62–9/62; BNA to Tyler, Sep. 5, 1962, NARA/RG 59/EUR-BNA/ANF/box 6/folder Secretary's Trip to Canada, August 24, 1962; and Howard Green Oral History, DDEL.
78. Griswold to Kennedy, Aug. 1, 1962, JFKL/POF/box 113/folder Canada, General, 1962; Schlesinger to Kennedy, "Ambassador to Canada," Aug. 27, 1962, JFKL/POF/box 65a/folder Schlesinger, Arthur M, 3/62; Telcon: Stevenson, Ball. 10:10 a.m. Aug. 22, 1962, JFKL/GWB/box 2/folder Canada, 4/26/61–11/8/63 and Meeting on Europe and General Diplomatic Matters, Jul. 30, 1962, *The Presidential Recordings—John F. Kennedy: The Great Crises, Volume One*, ed. T. Naftali (New York: W. W. Norton, 2001), 47–9.
79. Macy to LBJ, "Canada," Aug. 24, 1966, LBJL/WHCF/Subject Files/box 19/folder CO 43 7/20/66–6/19/67.
80. Diefenbaker, "Bahamas Meetings—December 21–22, 1962. Specific points discussed with President Kennedy at Luncheon Meeting, December 21," n.d., LAC/RG 25/file 50391-A-40; Ottawa to State, no. 797, Dec. 17, 1962, JFKL/NSF/box 18/folder Canada, General 10/62–1/63; Dier to Robertson, "Call by Ambassador Butterworth on the Prime Minister," Dec. 18, 1962, LAC/RG 25/vol. 5030/file 1415-40-pt. 12.
81. Read to Rostow, "Farewell Call on President by Canadian Ambassador," Jun. 13, 1966 and Ottawa to State, no. 50, July 11, 1966, LBJL/NSF/Country Files/box 166/folder Canada, Memos.
82. Washington to External, tel. 1219, Apr. 19, 1962, LAC/RG 19/vol. 4461/file 8625-04-8-pt. 1.
83. Quoted in Stursberg, *Lester Pearson*, 181–2.
84. C. Ritchie, *Storm Signals: More Undiplomatic Diaries, 1962–1971* (Toronto: Macmillan, 1983), 4–6, 17.
85. Ibid., 12–13.
86. Memcon, "UK-Six Matters," Jul. 27, 1962, NARA/RG 59/EUR-RPE/RRUK/box 3/folder L.1.c(3) UK-EEC Negotiations—Canadian Attitude, 1962.
87. Robinson to file, "Lunch with Mr. R. Schaetzel of the State Department on August 31, 1962," Aug. 31, 1962, LAC/MG 31 E83/vol. 6.5.
88. Hart, *A Trading Nation*, 209.
89. Ottawa to State, no. 571, Dec. 8, 1961, JFKL/NSF/box 18/folder Canada, General, 10/61–1/62.
90. Ottawa to State, no. 213, Aug. 18, 1962, JFKL/NSF/box 18/folder Canada, General, 7/62–9/62; Memcon, "Meeting with Canadian Officials," Aug. 24, 1962, and Memcon, "Various Canadian Matters," Aug. 11, 1962, NARA/RG 59/EUR-RPE/RRUK/box 3/folder L.1.c(3) UK-EEC Negotiations—Canadian Attitude, 1962.
91. CC, Aug. 30, 1962, LAC/RG 2/vol. 6193.
92. *S&S* 62/10, Aug. 1962.
93. Benvenuti and Ward, "Other Quiet Revolution," 176–79.
94. Armstrong to Butterworth, Jul. 27, 1962, NARA/RG 59/EUR-RPE/RRUK/folder L.1.c(3) UK-EEC Negotiations—Canadian Attitude, 1962.
95. Rasminsky to Gordon, May 9, 1963, LAC/MG 32 B44/vol. 22.10.
96. Ottawa to State, no. 1364, Jun. 28, 1962, JFKL/NSF/box 18/folder Canada, General 5/16/62–6/62. On Rasminsky and the economic crisis, see B. Muirhead, *Against the Odds: The Public Life and Times of Louis Rasminsky* (Toronto: University of Toronto Press,

1999), 183–208. The use of economic leverage, or rather its nonuse, during this period is covered by Bow, *Politics of Linkage*.

97. Dillon to JFK, "Gold and the Canadian Situation," Jun. 19, 1962, JFKL/POF/Treasury Records/box 89/folder June 1962; Robinson, *Diefenbaker's World*, 276.

98. Statement reprinted in "Need of 'Immediate Emergent Action' Stressed by Diefenbaker," *MG*, Jun. 25, 1962; Lyon has erroneously argued that the surcharges were met with "understanding and tolerance in Washington": Lyon, *Canada in World Affairs*, 362. For a different view, approximating the one made here, see Muirhead, *Dancing Around the Elephant*, 43–5.

99. Telcon: Dillon, Ball. 10:00 a.m., Jun. 21, 1962, Telcon: Dillon, Ball. 5:30 p.m., Jun. 22, 1962, and Telcon: Bundy, Ball. 11:05 a.m., Jun. 24, 1962, SMML/MC 031/box 103/folder 1; and State to London, Tosec 55, Jun. 24, 1962, JFKL/NSF/box 246/folder Secretary of State's European Trip, 6/62

100. "Text of PM's Talk on Economy," *G&M*, Jun. 26, 1962.

101. Ball to Dillon, Jul. 5, 1962, attached to Kaysen to Kennedy, Jul. 6, 1962, and Kaysen to Bundy, Jul. 6, 1962, JFKL/NSF/box 18/folder Canada, General, 7/62–9/62.

102. Ball to Kennedy, "GATT Waiver for Canadian Import Surcharges," Jul. 8, 1962, NARA/RG 59/Ball/box 20/folder Under Secretary Ball—1962.

103. Telcon: Bundy, Ball. 12:50 p.m., Jul. 9, 1962, SMML/MC 031/box 103/folder 1; and Kennedy to Dillon, Jul. 9, 1962, JFKL/NSF/box 18/folder Canada, General, 7/62–9/62.

104. Ball and Dillon to Kennedy, "Understanding with Canada on Emergency Financial Program," Jul. 17, 1962, NARA/RG 59/Ball/box 20/folder Under Secretary Ball—1962; Washington to External, tel. 2041, Jul. 10, 1962, LAC/RG 25/vol. 5450/file 11389-A-40-pt. 2.2; and "Europeans Deplore New Ottawa Tariff," *G&M*, Jul. 13, 1962.

105. "They Don't Like Us Much," *Financial Post*, Aug. 4, 1962.

106. Kennedy to Diefenbaker, Oct. 18, 1962; Diefenbaker to Kennedy, Oct. 11, 1962, JFKL/POF/box 113/folder Canada, General, 1962. And see Diefenbaker to file "Interview with Basil Robinson—July 27, 1962," Jul. 28, 1962, LAC/MG 31 E83/vol. 6.2; and Washington to External, tel. 2072, Jul. 1, 1962, LAC/RG 25/vol. 4215/file 8780/U58-01-pt. 5.

107. Canadian–American Committee, *The Perspective of Canadian–American Relations* (New York: Canadian–American Committee, 1962).

108. Ottawa to State, no.75, Jul. 17, 1962, JFKL/NSF/box 18/folder Canada, General, 7/62–9/62.

109. Kiselyak, "Canada 1962: What is it and Where is it Going?," attached to Ottawa to State, A-272, Sep. 18, 1962, JFKL/NSF/box 18/folde Canada, General, 7/62–9/62.

110. Smith to Carlson, Jun. 26, 1961, NARA/RG 84/CGR/box 224/folder international political rel classified 1959–61 Canada–US.

111. "Address at Independence Hall, Philadelphia," July 4, 1962, PPP 1962, 537–9.

112. Memcon, Aug. 24, 1962, *FRUS* 1961–1963, X, 958–9.

## Chapter 5

1. Washington to External, tel. 2987, Oct. 15, 1962, LAC/MG31 E83/vol. 6.11.

2. J. M. Ghent, "Canada, the United States, and the Cuban Missile Crisis," *Pacific Historical Review* 48, no. 2 (1979), 160. The same point is made in Granatstein, "When Push Came to Shove," 96–7. As the authors of the authoritative study of Canadian–Cuban relations have noted, "the official Canadian position on Cuba, contrary to the popular image projected in both Havana and Washington, revealed major differences of opinion with the Cuban government": J. Kirk and P. McKenna, *Canada–Cuba Relations: The Other Good Neighbor Policy* (Gainesville: University Press of Florida, 1997), 52. And see A. McKercher, "'The Most Serious Problem'?: Canada–US Relations and Cuba, 1962," *Cold War History* 12, no. 1 (2012): 69–88.

3. Donaghy, *Tolerant Allies*, 7.

4. W.H. Pope, "NATO After Nassau," Jan. 9, 1963, LAC/MG 32 C28/vol. 125/file External Affairs and National Defence; Moscow to External, tel. 661, Nov. 28, 1962, LAC/MG 31 E47/vol. 80.21.

5. Y. Engler, *Pearson's Peacekeeping: The Truth May Hurt* (Vancouver: Fernwood, 2012), 96.

6. Robertson to Green, "The Cuban Question," Jan. 11, 1962, LAC/MG 32 B13/vol. 7.10.

7. CIA, Current Intelligence Memorandum, "Cuban Trade with Non-bloc Countries, 1958–1961, with Special Reference to Canada," Jan. 13, 1962, JFKL/NSF/box 51/folder Cuba, Subjects, Intelligence 1/62–9/62; "Canada's Exports to Cuba Up," *NYT*, Apr. 28, 1962.

8. R Hilsman, *To Move a Nation: The Politics of Foreign Policy in the Administration of John F. Kennedy* (Garden City: Doubleday, 1967), 177; M. Bundy, *Danger and Survival: Choices about the Bomb in the First Fifty Years* (New York: Vintage, 1988), 410–13; NIE 85–62, "The Situation and Prospects in Cuba," Mar. 21, 1962, JFKL/POF/box 115/folder Cuba: Security, 1962.

9. Review of Operation Mongoose by Chief of Operations Lansdale, Jan. 18, 1962, *The Kennedys and Cuba: The Declassified Documentary History*, Revised Edition, ed. M. J. White (Chicago: Ivan R. Dee, 2001), 93. On Mongoose see A. Fursenko and T. Naftali, *"One Hell of a Gamble": Khurshchev, Castro, and Kennedy, 1958–1964* (New York: W. W. Norton, 1997), chapters 6, 7, and 8; T. G. Paterson, "Fixation with Cuba: The Bay of Pigs, Missile Crisis, and Covert War Against Fidel Castro," in *Kennedy's Quest for Victory*, ed. T. G. Paterson (New York: Oxford University Press, 1989), 123–55.

10. On the Punta del Este conference, see L. Schoultz, *That Infernal Little Cuban Republic* (Chapel Hill: UNC Press, 2009), 173–5.

11. Washington to External, tel. 398, Feb. 9, 1962, LAC/RG 25/vol. 5228/file 6660–40-pt. 4.

12. Ottawa to State, no. 708, Jan. 29, 1962, JFKL/Schlesinger Collection/White House Files/box 3a/folder Canada; HOC, Jan. 29, 1962, 301–2.

13. Rusk quoted in "Rusk Hopeful Canada Will Join Boycott of Cuba," *G&M*, Feb. 2, 1962.

14. HOC, Feb. 2, 1962, 479–80. The following day these remarks were repeated in a press release by Canada's embassy in Washington. This was meant to explain to Americans that Canada possessed stiff export regulations: Press Release, "Canadian Trade with Cuba," Feb. 3, 1962, LAC/RG25/vol. 5077/file 4568-40-pt. 10,

15. "Fiasco at Punta del Este," *G&M*, Jan. 31, 1962; "Trade with Cuba," *G&M*, Feb. 3, 1962; "Canada's Trade with Cuba," *OC*, Feb. 3, 1962; "Anti-Cuba Embargo Unlikely," *MG*, Feb. 5, 1962.

16. Ottawa to State, no. 728, Feb. 2, 1962, and Ottawa to State, A-291, Feb. 8, 1962, JFKL/NSF/box 18/folder Canada, General, 2/62–3/62.

17. Telcon: Bundy-Ball. Feb. 2, 1962, SMML/MC 031/box 103/folder 1.

18. NATO Delegation, Paris to External, tel. 466, Feb. 21, 1962, LAC/RG25/vol. 5352/file 10224-40-pt. 12.1.

19. Ottawa to State, no. 772, Feb. 15, 1962, NARA/RG 59/CDF/637.44/2-1562.

20. Tyler to Rusk, Feb. 13, 1962, NARA/RG 59/EUR-BNA/ANF/box 5/folder Cuban Export Ban, 1960–1962.

21. Feldman to Kennedy, "Embargo upon imports from Cuba," Feb. 16, 1962, JFKL/WHCSF/box 240/folder FO 3-3-1/CO 55 Cuba (Executive & General).

22. Memcon, "The Problem of Cuba in Relation to Canada," Feb. 16, 1962, NARA/RG 59/EUR-CDC/RRPM/box 3/folder Cuba 1962–63; and Washington to External, tel. 515, Feb. 19, 1962, LAC/RG25/vol. 5030/file 1415-40-pt. 10.

23. Diefenbaker quoted in Robinson, *Diefenbaker's World*, 250; CC, Feb. 20, 1962, LAC/RG 2/vol. 6192. HOC, Feb. 6, 1962, 575; HOC, Feb. 15, 1962, 910.

24. "Canada to Buy More from Cuba Soon, Castro Envoy Declares," *MG*, Feb. 15, 1962; HOC Feb. 16, 1962, 930; CC, Feb. 26, 1962, LAC/RG 2/vol. 6192.

25. Campbell to Robertson, "Cuba—Trade Policy," Feb. 23, 1962, LAC/MG 31 E83/vol. 5.18. Robinson recorded that Green urged Diefenbaker to make "a somewhat less aggressive defence of existing government line" on Cuban policy: Diary, Feb. 21, 1962, LAC/MG 31 E83/vol. 35.

26. Havana to External, tel. 28, Mar. 6, 1962; Montevideo to External, tel. 24, Mar. 2, 1962, Quito to External, tel. 15, Mar. 2, 1962, Rio de Janeiro to External, tel. 33, Mar. 9, 1962, Bogota to External, tel. 16, Mar. 5, 1962, and Santiago to External, tel. 30, Mar. 6, 1962, LAC/RG 25/vol. 5030/file 1415-40-pt. 10.

27. Washington to External, tel. 627, Mar. 1, 1962, LAC/RG 25/vol. 5030/file 1415-40-pt. 10.

28. "How Canada Helps Keep Castro Going," *US News & World Report,* Feb. 26, 1962.

29. "Only the First Step," *Dallas Morning News,* Feb. 6, 1962; Text of Statement by United States Senator Kenneth Keating as broadcast on CBC Newsmagazine, Feb. 7, 1962, Interview with J. N. Minifie of Canadian Broadcasting Corporation, Mar. 8, 1962, folder KBK on Trade with Cuba & Canada, University of Rochester, Rush Rhees Library, Kenneth Keating Papers, 10:5:17; G. Sokolsky, "These Days," *WP,* Mar. 12, 1962.

30. Heeney to Green, "U.S.A. Press Criticism of Canada," Mar. 22, 1962, LAC/RG 25/vol. 5030/file 1415-40-pt. 10.

31. Ottawa to State, A-323, Mar. 1, 1962, NARA/RG 59/CDF/637.42/3-162.

32. Robertson to Green, "Relations with Cuba," Mar. 8, 1962, LAC/MG 31 E83/vol. 5.19.

33. Memcon, "Canadian Trade with Cuba," Mar. 2, 1962, NARA/RG 59/CDF/437.429/3-262.

34. CC, Apr. 10, 1962, LAC/RG 2/vol. 6192.

35. *Congressional Record,* Mar. 16, 1961, 4229.

36. USA Division to file, "Canada–US Interparliamentary Group, Sixth Meeting, Ottawa, February 29–March 3, 1962, Economic Committee," n.d., LAC/RG 25/vol. 5031/file 1415-F-40-pt. 8. See also: "Talks With U.S. Flowery, Thorny," *G&M,* Mar. 2, 1962; and "Legislators of Canada and U.S. Hold Talk," *CT,* Mar. 2, 1962.

37. See Robinson, *Diefenbaker's World,* 252–3; and Draft, "Notes for Prime Minister's use at dinner in honour of members of the Canada–United State Inter-parliamentary Group, Ottawa, March 1, 1962," LAC/MG 31 E83/vol. 5.19.

38. Summary of Conversation, May 1, 1962, LAC/RG 25/vol. 6151/file 50412-40-pt. 4.

39. Diefenbaker to file, "Telegram Received from Confederation of Cuban Professionals, Washington," Mar. 24, 1962, and Robinson to Robertson, Mar. 24, 1962, LAC/RG 25/vol. 5076/file 4568-40-pt. 9; HOC, Mar. 26, 1962, 2160.

40. Ottawa to State, no. 971, Apr. 1, 1962, JFKL/NSF/box 18/folder Canada, General, 4/62–5/16/62.

41. "Statement by the Prime Minister Regarding the Trials of Cuban Prisoners," Apr. 1, 1962, LAC/RG 25/vol. 5076/file 4568-40-pt. 9; and State to Ottawa, no. 960, Apr. 1, 1962, JFKL/POF/box 113/folder Canada, Security, 1962.

42. Memcon, "NATO Policy toward Cuba," May 3, 1962, NARA/RG 59/EUR-CDC/RRPM/box 3/folder Cuba 1962–63; and Ignatieff to Robertson, "Minister's Conversation with Mr. Rusk at NATO Ministerial Meeting at Athens," May 11, 1962, LAC/RG 25/vol. 5077/file 4568-40-pt. 10.

43. "Conversations with Ambassador Merchant and Mr. Armstrong of the United States Embassy," May 9, 1962, LAC/MG 31 E83/vol. 6.2.

44. NATO Del. Paris to External, tel. 1314, May 29, 1962, and NATO Delegation, Paris to External, tel. 1646, Jun. 21, 1962, LAC/RG 25/vol. 5077/file 4568-40-pt. 10.

45. Telegram from the Department of State to the Embassy in the United Kingdom, Aug. 30, 1962, *FRUS,* 1961–1963, X, document 396; Lansdale, "Review of Operation Mongoose," Jul. 25, 1962, JFKL/NSF/box 319/folder Special Group (Augmented), General 7/62.

46. United States Senate, 87th Congress, Committee on Foreign Relations and Committee on Armed Services, "The World Situation," Sep. 5, 1962; House of Representatives, 87th Congress, Hearings before Select Committee on Export Control, Oct. 3, 1962; "U.S.–Canada Rift Now a Dead Issue," *OC,* Sep. 22, 1962.

47. Robertson to Green, "Relations with Cuba," Sep. 26, 1962, LAC/RG 25/vol. 5077/file 4568-40-pt. 10.

48. Battle to Bundy, "Canadian Reporting From Havana," Dec. 1, 1961, JFKL/NSF/box 35/folder Cuba, General.

49. Havana to External, tel. 401, Aug. 16, 1962, LAC/RG 25/vol. 5352/file 10224-40-pt. 12.2; Cruz quoted in Kirk and McKenna, *Canada–Cuba Relations*, 62.

50. Robertson to Green, "Policy on Cuba," Oct. 5, 1962, LAC/RG 25/vol. vol. 5077/file 4568-40-pt.10.

51. Havana to External, tel. 172, Sep. 13, 1962, and Washington to External, tel. 2672, Sep. 14, 1962, LAC/RG 25/vol. 5352/file 10224-40-pt. 12.2.

52. Washington to External, NL-1579, Oct. 16, 1962, LAC/RG 25/vol. 4184/file 2444-40-pt. 9.

53. D. R. Gibson, *Talk at the Brink: Deliberation and Decision During the Cuban Missile Crisis* (Princeton: Princeton University Press, 2012).

54. "Meeting at 6:30 p.m. on 16 Oct. 1962," in *The Kennedy Tapes: Inside the White House during the Cuban Missile Crisis*, eds. E. May and P. Zelikow (Cambridge, MA: Harvard Belknap, 1997), 114.

55. "Meeting on the Cuban Missile Crisis, Tuesday 16 October 1962, 11:50 A.M.–1:00 P.M.," in *The Presidential Recordings: John F Kennedy—The Great Crises, Volume Two*, eds. T. Naftali and P. Zelikow (New York: W. W. Norton, 2001), 405–6, 413; and J. G. Hershberg, "The United States, Brazil, and the Cuban Missile Crisis (Part II)," *Journal of Cold War Studies* 6, no. 3 (2004): 9–10.

56. "Meeting on the Cuban Missile Crisis, Tuesday 16 October 1962, 6:30–8:00 P.M.," in *Kennedy—The Great Crises, Volume Two*, 434, 443.

57. Ottawa to State, no. 573, Oct. 28, 1962, JFKL/NSF/box 41/folder Cuba Cables 10/28/62.

58. Ghent, "Cuban Missile Crisis," 182; Jockel, *Canada in NORAD*, 55.

59. Costigliola, "Kennedy and the Failure to Consult"; D. Munton and D. A. Welch, *The Cuban Missile Crisis* (New York: Oxford University Press, 2007), 65–6; and P. Lennox, *At Home and Abroad: The Canada–US Relationship and Canada's Place in the World* (Vancouver: UBC Press, 2009), 39–55.

60. Glazov, *Canadian Policy*, 147.

61. Kennedy to Diefenbaker, Oct. 18, 1962, and Diefenbaker to Kennedy, Oct. 11, 1962, JFKL/POF/box 113/folder Canada, General, 1962. Willis Armstrong had discussed a draft of Kennedy's message with Basil Robinson a few days before, and Robinson had urged him to leave any mention of the surcharges out. That the Americans left it in says something about their view of the prime minister: Robinson to file, "U.S. Draft Reply to Prime Minister's Message to President Kennedy," Oct. 16, 1962, LAC/MG 31 E83/vol. 6.13.

62. New York to State, no. 1316, Oct. 17, 1962, JFKL/NSF/box 18/folder Canada, General 10/62–1/63; Kennedy to Diefenbaker, Oct. 20, 1962, LAC/MG 32 B13/vol. 11.2.

63. Ghent, "Cuban Missile Crisis," 183. On Kennedy and Macmillan, see L. V. Scott, *Macmillan, Kennedy and the Cuban Missile Crisis* (Basingstoke: Palgrave Macmillan, 1999).

64. NATO Del. Paris to External, tel. 2454, Oct. 22, 1962, and Washington to External, tel. 3075, Oct. 22, 1962, LAC/RG 25/vol. 4181/file 2444-40-pt. 9.

65. Memcon, "Meeting with Prime Minister Diefenbaker to Deliver Copy of President Kennedy's Letter of October 22 on Cuban Situation," Oct. 22, 1962, JFKL/NSF/box 18/folder Canada, General 10/62–1/63. After hearing Merchant read the president's speech, the prime minister urged the removal of a reference in the speech to the Soviet foreign minister as being "dishonest and dishonourable." Merchant relayed this to Rusk and the advice was accepted.

66. Haydon, *1962 Cuban Missile Crisis*, 189; Green to Diefenbaker, "Cuba," Oct. 22, 1962, LAC/RG 25/vol. 4184/file 2444-40-pt. 9; and Smith, *Rogue Tory*, 455. And see A. McKercher, "A 'Half-Hearted Response'?: Canada and the Cuban Missile Crisis, 1962," *International History Review* 33, no. 2 (2011): 335–52.

67. State to Ottawa, no. 496, Oct. 22, 1962, JFKL/POF/box 113/folder Canada, Security, 1962.

68. "Radio and Television Report to the American People on the Soviet Arms Buildup in Cuba," Oct. 22, 1962, *PPP*.

69. HOC, Oct. 22, 1962, 805–6.
70. "Canada and the Crisis," *G&M*, Oct. 24, 1962; "The Commons United," and "The Blockade of Cuba," *OC*, Oct. 23, 1962.
71. Pick to Robertson, "Views of the Cuban Ambassador on the Crisis," Oct. 23, 1962, LAC/RG 25/vol. 4184/file 2444-40-pt. 9; Washington to Foreign Office, tel. 2650, Oct. 23, 1962, TNA/PREM 11/3689.
72. CC, Oct. 23, 1962, LAC/RG 2/vol. 6193; HOC, Oct. 23, 1962, 821.
73. Campbell to Robertson, "Cuba," Oct. 24, 1962, LAC, RG 25, vol. 4184, file 2444-40-pt. 10; Ottawa to State, no. 537, Oct. 24, 1962, JFKL/NSF/box 41/folder Cuba Cables October 24, 1962.
74. Ottawa to CRO, 979, Oct. 24, 1962, TNA/DO 200/113.
75. Jockel, *Canada in NORAD*, 57.
76. CC, Oct. 213, 1962, LAC/RG 2/vol. 6193. See Jockel, *Canada in NORAD*, 58, where he asserts that Diefenbaker was "firmly supported by Green." It is doubtful how much support Green may have given Diefenbaker, however. In his pseudo-memoir, Harkness recalled that Green in fact supported a military alert, and the Cabinet minutes contain no statement attributed to Green to challenge this argument; see Harkness's recollections in "The Nuclear Arms Question and the Political Crisis which Arose from it in January and February 1963": LAC/MG 32 B19/vol. 57.
77. *Macmillan Diaries*, 511; Macmillan to Diefenbaker, Oct. 23, 1962, TNA/PREM 11/3689.
78. Diefenbaker, *One Canada*, III, 82–3. Since Kennedy recorded his conversations with Macmillan during the crisis, it is odd that he would not have recorded a discussion with Diefenbaker. Robinson, though, has written that Diefenbaker's secretary took notes of his side of the conversation but failed to cite from them: see *Diefenbaker's World*, 288. Interestingly, Diefenbaker's memoirs placed the telephone call on October 22, while Robinson wrote that it took place on October 23. As mentioned previously, the ghostwriter of Diefenbaker's memoirs has pointed out that much of the work, despite his own efforts, was fiction. Scholars citing Diefenbaker's recollection of the telephone call include: Jockel, *Canada in NORAD*, 57; Glazov, *Canadian Policy*, 143; Lennox, *At Home and Abroad*, 48; Smith, *Rogue Tory*, 459; Hillmer and Granatstein, *For Better or For Worse*, 204; and Boyko, *Cold Fire*, 190.
79. Ghent, "Cuban Missile Crisis," 166.
80. CC, Oct. 24, 1962, LAC/RG 2/vol. 6193; Smith, *Rogue Tory*, 459; Haydon, *Missile Crisis*, 211; and Ghent, "Cuban Missile Crisis," 180. The question of whether or not Harkness was legally allowed to put Canadian forces on alert is open to debate as the Department of National Defence War Book had been under revision, causing confusion over who within the government could authorise an alert: see B. W. Gladman and P. M. Archambault, *Confronting the "Essence of Decision": Canada and the Cuban Missile Crisis–Centre for Operational Research and Analysis Technical Memorandum 2010–250* (Ottawa: Department of National Defence, 2010), 39–45.
81. White to A.E. Ritchie, Oct. 23, 1962, LAC/RG 25/vol. 4184/file 2444-40-pt. 9; External to Havana, XL90, Oct. 23, 1962, LAC/RG 25/vol. 5077/file 4568-40-pt. 10.
82. Robertson to Green, "Cubana Aircraft Landing at Goose Bay," Oct. 24, 1962, LAC/RG 25/vol. 5077/file 4568-40-pt. 10; CC, Oct. 23, 1962, LAC/RG2/vol. 6193; McCone, "Memorandum for the Files," Oct. 25, 1962, *FRUS 1961–1963*, XI: 200; State to Paris, circular 741, Oct. 24, 1962, JFKL/RFK/Attorney General Papers/Classified Files/folder 71-4-16-26.
83. "Firm Support," *Winnipeg Free Press*, Oct. 24, 1962; Ottawa to State, no. 537, 24 Oct. 1962, JFKL/NSF/box 41/folder Cuba, Cables, 10/24/62.
84. Transcript, "Text of a Television Interview with the Secretary of State for External Affairs on the CBC, October 22, 1962," LAC/MG 32 B13/vol. 12.45—note that the transcript bears the wrong date; "Green Sidesteps Answer on Blockade Endorsation," *Edmonton Journal*, Oct. 25, 1962. Green repeated his sentiments about consultation both in a December 1962 address in the House of Commons and in a 1969 interview with Jack Granatstein: *S&S* 62/17, Dec. 17, 1962; and Transcript "Interview with J. L.

Granatstein, York University Oral History Programme," 35–8, CVA/Add. MSS 903/605-D-1/file 2.

85. CC, Oct. 25, 1962, LAC/RG 2/vol. 6193; HOC, Oct. 25, 1962, 911–3.

86. Washington to External, tel. 3166, Oct. 27, 1962, LAC/RG 25/vol. 4184/file 2444-40-pt. 11; CIA Memorandum, "The Crisis USSR/CUBA," Oct. 26, 1962, JFKL/NSF/box 46/folder Cuba Subjects, CIA Memoranda; Ottawa to State, no. 565, Oct. 26, 1962, JFKL/NSF/box 41/folder Cuba, Cables; Raymond Daniell, "Canada Supports U.S. Views on Cuba," *NYT*, Oct. 26, 1962; "Support from Canada," *CT*, Oct. 27, 1962; and "Support From Ottawa," *WP*, Oct. 27, 1962.

87. Ottawa to CRO, no. 991, Oct. 26, 1962, TNA/DO 200/113.

88. *Hansard*, Oct. 25, 1952, vol. 664: cc1053-64.

89. Havana to External, tel. 21, Oct. 27, 1962, LAC/RG 25/vol. 5352/file 10224-40-pt. 12.2; and Havana to External, tel. 229, Nov. 5, 1962, LAC/RG 25/vol. 4184/file 2444-40-pt. 12. For citations of Kidd's reportage, see, for example: CIA Memorandum, "The Crisis USSR/CUBA," Oct. 27, 1962, JFKL/NSF/box 46/folder Cuba Subjects, CIA Memoranda.

90. CIA memo, "Evidence of Soviet Withdrawals from Cuba," Mar. 6, 1963, JFKL/NSF/box 51.

91. Washington to External, tel. 3502, Nov. 29, 1962, LAC/MG 31 E83/vol. 6.13; Diefenbaker to file, "Bahamas Meetings—Dec. 21–22, 1962. Specific points discussed with President Kennedy at Luncheon Meeting, Dec. 21," n.d., LAC/MG 31 E83/vol. 6.12.

92. External to Permanent Mission, NY and Washington, XL-106, Oct. 25, 1962, LAC/RG 25/vol. 4184/file 2444-40-pt. 10.

93. Memcon, "Cuban Situation," Oct. 26, 1962, NARA/RG 59/EUR-CDC/RRPM/box 3/folder Cuba Quarantine, 1962; Washington to External, tel. 3166, Oct. 27, 1962, LAC/RG 25/vol. 4184/file 2444-40-pt. 11; Hershberg, "Brazil, and the Cuban Missile Crisis," 30–1.

94. Washington to External, tel. 3163, Oct. 26, 1962, LAC/RG 25/vol. 4184/file 2444-40-pt. 10.

95. Washington to External, tel. 3171, Oct. 27, 1962 and Washington to External, tel. 3173, Oct. 28, 1962, LAC/RG25/vol. 4184/file 2444-40-pt. 11; Ottawa to State, no. 569, Oct. 27, 1962, JFKL, NSF, box 41, folder Cuba Cables Oct. 27, 1962; Ottawa to State, no. 573, Oct. 28, 1962, JFKL/NSF/box 41/folder Cuba Cables.

96. Moscow to External, tel. 777, Oct. 28, 1962, LAC/RG25/vol. 4184/file 2444-40-pt. 11.

97. Ottawa to State, no. 573, Oct. 28, 1962, JFKL/NSF/box 41/folder Cuba Cables.

98. UN Division to Robertson, "Cuba and the United Nations," Oct. 30, 1962, Permanent Mission, NY to External, tel. 1983, Oct. 29, 1962, LAC/RG 25/vol. 4184/file 2444-40-pt. 11; and Campbell to Robertson, Oct. 29, 1962, LAC/RG 25/vol. 5077/file 4568-40-pt. 10; Telegram From the Department of State to the Mission to the United Nations, Oct. 29, 1962, and Telegram From the Department of State to the Mission to the United Nations, Oct. 31, 1962, *FRUS*, 1961–1963, XI, 302 and 325–331; and Transcript of the Ex-Comm Meeting, Oct. 29, 1962 at 10:10 a.m. in *The Kennedy Tapes*, 630–61.

99. Campbell to Robertson, "Cuba," Oct. 30, 1962, LAC/RG 25/vol. 4181/file 2444-40-pt. 11; and Robinson to Ritchie, "Cuba," Nov. 1, 1962, LAC/MG 31 E83/vol. 6.13; W. Dorn and R. Pauk, "Unsung Mediator: U Thant and the Cuban Missile Crisis," *DH* 33, no. 2 (2009): 261–92.

100. External to Havana, M-102, Oct. 31, 1962, LAC, RG 25, vol. 4184, file 2444-40-pt. 11.

101. Rusk from Green, 1:25 pm, Nov. 2, 1962, NARA/RG 59/Rusk/TTC/box 47.

102. "Bloody, but Unbowed," *TS*, Nov. 1, 1962; "A lesson from the crisis," *OC*, Nov. 7, 1962; "Cause of Complaint," *Edmonton Journal*, Oct. 31, 1962.

103. Ritchie to Robertson, Nov. 13, 1962, LAC/MG 31 E44/vol. 2.14.

104. Excerpt, "Address by the Prime Minister at the Diamond Jubilee Banquet of the Zionist Organization of Canada, Beth Tzedec Synagogue, Toronto," Nov. 5, 1962, LAC/RG 25/vol. 4184/file 2444-40-pt. 12; Kriebel to Carlson, "Luncheon Conversation with Basil Robinson, Deputy Chief of Mission, Canadian Embassy, 23 November 1962," Nov. 30, 1962, NARA/RG 59/EUR-CDC/RRPM/box 3/folder Canadian Government, 1961–1962;

"Poll Finds Canadians Back U.S. Cuban Stand," *G&M*, Nov. 23, 1962; J. Gellner, "World Affairs: The Story of 1962," *Saturday Night*, Jan. 1963; Sévigny, *This Game of Politics*, 253.

105. Hilsman to Rusk, "Western European Reactions to the Cuban Situation (Through October 27, 1962)," Oct. 28, 1962, JFKL/NSF/box 46/folder Cuba Subjects, Intelligence, INR

106. Ottawa to State, no. 565, Oct. 26, 1962, and Ottawa to State, no. 621, Nov. 2, 1962, JFKL/NSF/box 41/folder Cuba, Cables.

107. Gibson, *Talk at the Brink*.

108. Merchant to Rusk and Ball, undated, attached to Brubeck to Ball, Dec. 10, 1962, JFKL/NSF/box 18/folder Canada, General, Rostow Memorandum and Related Materials, 5/61–5/63.

109. Pick to Robertson, "Views of the Cuban Ambassador on the Crisis," Oct. 23, 1962, LAC/RG 25/vol. 4184/file 2444-40-pt. 9; Washington to Foreign Office, tel. 2650, Oct. 23, 1962, TNA/PREM 11/3689; Camp quoted in Stursberg, *Diefenbaker: Leadership Lost*, 19.

110. State to Paris, no. 2645, Nov. 19, 1962, JFKL/NSF/box 173/folder Macmillan Correspondence 10/22/62–12/28/62.

111. "Canada's Stand on Cuba Criticized by Truman," *G&M*, Oct. 26, 1962; Washington to External, tel. 3261, Nov. 5, 1962, LAC/RG 25/vol. 4184/file 2444-40-pt. 12.

112. Eisenhower to Diefenbaker, Nov. 9, 1962, DDEL/Post-Presidential Papers, 1962/Principal File/box 32/folder Di.

113. Smith to file, "Canadian Attitude Toward Cuban Crisis," Nov. 2, 1962, NARA/RG 59/EUR-CDC/RRPM/folder "Cuba Quarantine, 1962." Reford left this conversation out of his own account of Canada's role in the missile crisis; see R. Reford, *Canada and Three Crises* (Toronto: Canadian Institute of International Affairs, 1968), 149–217. Two other US diplomats with dealings with Canada, Willis Armstrong and Del Carlson, would also tell Basil Robinson that in US government circles there was no criticism of Canadian conduct during the crisis: Robinson to Campbell, Nov. 20, 1962, LAC/MG 31 E83/vol. 9.2.

114. Kirk and McKenna, *Canada–Cuba Relations*, 62.

115. Greenhill to Cleary, Nov. 9, 1962, and Ottawa to CRO, Nov. 7, 1962, TNA/DO 200/113.

116. J. Ghent-Mallet and D. Munton, "Confronting Kennedy and the Missiles in Cuba, 1962," In *Canadian Foreign Policy: Selected Cases*, ed. D. Munton and J. Kirton (Scarborough: Prentice-Hall, 1992), 92.

117. Mahant and Mount, *Invisible and Inaudible*, 63. Here, the authors also fault Kennedy for not despatching to Ottawa a special envoy as he did to De Gaulle. What, then, was Merchant doing in Ottawa on October 22?

118. See J. I. Domínguez, "The @#$%& Missile Crisis (Or What Was 'Cuban' about U.S. Decisions during the Cuban Missile Crisis?)," *DH* 24, no. 2 (2000): 305–15.

119. D.B.D. to Bryce, "Lessons of the Cuban Crisis," Nov. 20, 1962, LAC/RG 2/box 76/file F-2-8 (a).


Chapter 6

1. Memcon, "NATO Nuclear Problems," Mar. 8, 1963, NARA/RG 59/EUR-CDC/RRMM/box 2/folder US-Canada, Policy re. Acquisition Nuclear Weapons, 1963; Memornadum of Conversation on Non-Proliferation of Nuclear Weapons, Feb. 7, 1963, *FRUS*, 1961–1963, VII, 640

2. Warnock, *Partner to Behemoth*, 197.

3. Diefenbaker, *One Canada*, III, 2. Although my interpretation differs considerably, see Michael Stevenson's excellent article reviving this view: "'Tossing a Match into Dry Hay': Nuclear Weapons and the Crisis in U.S.–Canadian Relations, 1962–1963," *Journal of Cold War Studies* 16, no. 4 (2014): 5–34. For an analysis imitative of 1960s anti-US scaremongering, see: Boyko, *Cold Fire*.

4. Bothwell, *Alliance and Illusion*, 173.

5. Gwyn, *49th Paradox*, 112–13, and Engler, *Lester Pearson's Peacekeeping*, 96.

6. Ottawa to State, no. 621, Nov. 2, 1962, JFKL/NSF/box 41/folder Cuba, Cables 2/11/62; P.C. Newman, "Backstage in Ottawa," *Maclean's*, Oct. 20, 1962.

7. "Canada and NORAD," *Edmonton Journal*, Oct. 25, 1962; "The Weak Sister," *Calgary Herald*, Nov. 13, 1962; Knowlton Nash, "Cuban Crisis Poses Question: Canada's Future in NORAD," *Halifax Chronicle Herald*, Nov. 8, 1962; "Canada: Defensive Gap," *Time*, Nov. 9, 1962; and "Lack of A-Arms Only Gap in Defence, Says Curtis," *MG*, Nov. 30, 1962.

8. CC, Oct. 30, 1962, LAC/RG 2/vol. 6193.

9. Miller to Harkness, Aug. 17, 1962, and Harkness to Diefenbaker, Aug. 17, 1962, LAC/MG 32 B19/vol. 57/file The Nuclear Arms Question.

10. Robinson, "Nuclear Weapons Policy," Oct. 16, 1962, LAC/MG 31 E83/vol. 9.4.

11. Tyler to Rusk, "Nuclear Weapons Negotiations with Canada," Nov. 3, 1962, NARA/RG 59/EUR-CDC/RRMM/box 2/folder Canada—U.S. & Canadian Policy Acquisition & Control of Nuclear Weapons, 1962.

12. Ottawa to State, no. 709, Nov. 24, 1962, NARA/RG 59/CDF/box 1679/file 742.551/2-460.

13. Harkness to McNamara, Nov. 15, 1962, and McNamara to Harkness, Nov. 8, 1962, LAC/MG 32 B19/vol. 57/file Nuclear Arms Crisis—Reference, 1961–1963.

14. Memo, "Bilateral Meeting in Paris December 14, 1962 with Canadian Ministers Green and Harkness," Nov. 29, 1962, NARA/RG 59/EUR-CDC/RRMM/box 2/folder Canada—U.S. & Canadian Policy Acquisition & Control of Nuclear Weapons, 1962.

15. Kriebel to Carlson, "Luncheon Conversation with Basil Robinson, Deputy Chief of Mission, Canadian Embassy, 23 November, 1962," Nov. 30, 1962, NARA/RG 59/EUR-CDC/RRPM/box 3/folder Canadian Government, 1961–1962.

16. Ottawa to State, no. 761, Dec. 5, 1962, JFKL/NSF/box 18/folder Canada, General 10/62–1/63.

17. HOC, Dec. 5, 1962, 2345; Vancouver to Ottawa, "Green on Nuclear Weapons for Canada; Berlin; Cuba," Dec. 5, 1962, NARA/RG 59/EUR-CDC/RRMM//box 2/folder Canada—U.S. & Canadian Policy Acquisition & Control of Nuclear Weapons, 1962.

18. Harkness to Progressive Conservative MPs, Dec. 14, 1962, LAC/MG 32 B9/vol. 68/file Defence Policy—Notes on, by Mr. Harkness, Dec/62.

19. Campbell to Robinson, Jan. 15, 1963, LAC/MG 31 E83/vol. 31.10; Paris to State, no. Secto 23, Dec. 15, 1962, JFKL/NSF/box 225/file NATO, Weapons, Cables, Canada 12/61–11/63 [1 of 4].

20. Ottawa to State, no. 832, Dec. 26, 1962, JFKL/NSF/box 18/folder Canada, General 10/62–1/63.

21. T. Sorensen Oral History #3 and #4, JFKL. On Nassau, see D. Murray, *Kennedy, Macmillan and Nuclear Weapons* (Basingstoke: Macmillan, 2000).

22. H. Macmillan, *At the End of the Day, 1961–1963* (London: Macmillan, 1973), 360–1. When Kennedy and Macmillan had met in Bermuda the previous December, Diefenbaker had been upset at having not been invited: Robinson, *Diefenbaker's World*, 217.

23. Diefenbaker to file, "Discussion with President Kennedy, Nassau, Bahamas—December 21, 1962," Dec. 23, 1962, and Diefenbaker to file, "Bahamas Meetings—December 21–22, 1962. Specific Points Discussed with President Kennedy at Luncheon Meeting, December 21," n.d., LAC/MG 31 E83/vol. 6.12; Robinson to file, "General Colour of Hyannis Port Meeting," May 15, 1963, LAC/MG 31 E83/vol. 12.1; "PM Says Canada Excluded," *G&M*, Dec. 22, 1962.

24. Diefenbaker to file, "Bahamas Meetings—December 21–22, 1962. Conversations with Prime Minister Macmillan P.M. Friday, December 21, 1962," n.d., LAC/MG 31 E83/vol. 6.12; "Meeting Between the Prime Minister of Canada and the Prime Minister at Nassau on December 22, 1962, at 12:30 p.m.," TNA/PREM 11/4229; "PM Says Canada Excluded," *G&M*, Dec. 22, 1962.

25. Robertson to Diefenbaker, "NATO Nuclear Weapons Policy: Some Preliminary Comments on the Nassau Agreement," Jan. 2, 1963, LAC/RG 25/vol. 5959/file 50219-AL-2-40-pt. 6.1.

26. CC, Jan. 3, 1963, LAC/RG 2/vol. 6253. Given that at Nassau Kennedy gave Macmillan everything that the British prime minister asked for—doing so against the advice of his aides—Diefenbaker's sense that Kennedy had taken an anti-British line is odd.

27. Transcript, "Press Conference by General Lauris Norstad, Retiring Supreme Commander, Europe, Held in Ottawa," Jan. 3, 1963, LAC/MG 32 B19/vol. 70/file Nuclear Weapons Question—Part 2, 1959–1963.

28. Diefenbaker, *One Canada,* III, 3; Thompson and Randall, *Canada and the United States,* 211; Nash, *Kennedy and Diefenbaker,* 223.

29. Sévigny, *This Game,* 258; M. Oliver, "Canadian Defence Policy," Jan. 19, 1963, MG 32 C28/vol. 125/file External Affairs and National Defence; McCarthy to Chisholm, Jan. 4, 1963, TNA/DO 182/99; Robinson to C. Ritchie, "General Norstad's Remarks in Ottawa," Jan. 4, 1963, LAC/MG 31 E83/vol. 9.2; Washington to External, tel. 38, Jan. 5, 1963, LAC/RG 25/vol. 4534/file 50030-AB-40-pt. 6; Robert S. Jordon, *Norstad, Cold War NATO Supreme Command, Airman, Strategist, Diplomat* (New York: St. Martin's Press, 2000), 3–11; Carlson to Butterworth, "Montreal Canadian Club Invitation to Ambassador Bowles," Dec. 31, 1962, NARA/RG 59/EUR-BNA/ANF/box 4/folder Speeches, 1961–1963. Originally, Norstad had planned his trip for November, but the Cuban missile crisis had forced a delay: Norstad to Frank Miller, Sep. 19, 1962, DDEL/Norstad Papers/box 117/folder Tentative trips (1).

30. "Canada's Defence Commitment," *OC,* Jan. 5, 1963; "Decision," *Toronto Telegram,* Jan. 5, 1963; "Canada's Defence: A Role Accepted," *MG,* Jan. 7, 1963; and "General Norstad's Reminder," *G&M,* Jan. 5, 1963. For coverage of further press comment, see M. A. Eaton, "Canadian Editorial Opinion and the 1963 Nuclear Weapon Acquisition Debate," *ARCS* 35, no. 4 (2005): 641–66.

31. HOC, Jan. 25, 1963, 3127.

32. Ottawa to State, no. 882, Jan. 9, 1963, Ottawa to State, no. 890, Jan. 11, 1963, JFKL/NSF/box 18/folder Canada, General 10/62–1/63.

33. Address to the York-Scarborough Liberal Association, Toronto, Jan. 12, 1963, LAC/MG 26 N6/vol. 32/file Defence—Liberal Policy Statements 1959–1963; Penetration Research Ltd., "A Survey of the Political Climate of Ontario and Quebec," QUA/Kent Papers/box 2/folder Correspondence Jan.–Feb. 1963.

34. Trudeau quoted in D. Smith, *Gentle Patriot: A Political Biography of Walter Gordon* (Edmonton: Hurtig, 1973), 119; Axworthy, *Navigating a New World,* 32.

35. Ottawa to State, no. 909, Jan. 16, 1963, JFKL/NSF/box 225/folder NATO, Weapons, Cables, Canada, 12/61–11/63; Ottawa to State, no. 857, Jan. 2, 1963, JFKL/NSF/box 18/folder Canada, General 10/62–1/63.

36. Memcon, Jan. 23, 1962, and Memcon, Nov. 23, 1962, NARA/RG 59/EUR-CDC/RRMM/box 2/folder Canada—U.S. & Canadian Policy Acquisition & Control of Nuclear Weapons, 1962. See also: English, *The Worldly Years,* 248–50; and McMahon, *Essence of Indecision,* 156–61.

37. Memcon, Nov. 23, 1962 . . .; Rusk to Carlson, 10:00 am, Feb. 4, 1963, NARA/RG 59/Rusk TTC/box 48.

38. C. Lynch, "Reflections on Patriotism," *OC,* Feb. 9, 1966 and "Conspiracy of Silence," *OC,* Jul. 14, 1965. When Merchant learned of the story, he complained not that it was untrue, but that Lynch had mistakenly reported that the briefings had been conducted in 1963, when they occurred the previous year. Note, he wrote Butterworth, "the fact that (contrary to Lynch's assertion) I was not U.S. Ambassador to Canada in 1963": Merchant to Butterworth, Feb. 28, 1966, NARA/RG 59/EUR-CDC/RRPM/box 8/folder POL 12 Conservative Party.

39. B. Palmer, *Canada's 1960s: The Ironies of Identity in a Rebellious Era* (Toronto: University of Toronto Press, 2009), 63; Ghent, "Did He Fall or Was He Pushed?," 256; Dalton Camp quoted in Stursberg, *Diefenbaker,* 97.

40. "Storm of Spears," *Time,* Jan. 25, 1963; J. Diefenbaker to E. Diefenbaker, Jan. 10, 1963, in *Personal Letters of a Public Man,* 118.

41. Green quoted in Stevenson, "Tossing a Match."

42. Robinson to Campbell, Jan. 23, 1963 and Robinson, "Nuclear Weapons Policy," Jan. 28, 1963, LAC/MG 31 E83/vol. 9.2.
43. Legere to Kennedy, Jan. 21, 1963, and Bundy minute, JFKL/NSF/box 225/folder NATO, Weapons, Cables, Canada, 12/61–11/63.
44. HOC, Jan. 25, 1963, 3127–3136.
45. "Flexible Confusion in Defence," *G&M*, Jan. 28, 1963; "Mr. Diefenbaker's Confusion," *OC*, Jan. 26, 1963; "Indecision by Decision," *MG*, Jan. 31, 1963.
46. Harkness statement printed in *G&M*, Jan. 31, 1963; HOC, Jan. 28, 1963, 3157.
47. Ottawa to State, no. 946, Jan. 26, 1963, JFKL/NSF/box 225/folder NATO, Weapons, Cables, Canada 12/61–11/63.
48. Ottawa to State, no. 949, Jan. 27, 1963, JFKL/NSF/box 18/folder Canada, General 10/62–1/63; and Walton Butterworth Oral History, JFKL.
49. Telcon: Tyler, Ball. 1:00 p.m., Jan. 28, 1963, SMML/MC 031/box 103/folder 2.
50. Legere to Bundy, "Proposed Press Statement on Canadian Nuclears," Jan. 29, 1963, JFKL/NSF/box 225/folder NATO, Weapons, Cables, Canada 12/61–11/63 [1 of 4].
51. Bow, *Politics of Linkage*, 71; Willis Armstrong Oral History, FAOHC.
52. Robinson to file, Jan. 28, 1963, LAC/MG 31 E83/vol. 9.2; Armstrong to Tyler, "Post-Nassau Developments in Summary," Jan. 29, 1963, NARA/RG 59/EUR-CDC/RRPM/box 3/folder External Affairs Minister, 1961–1962; Telcon: Tyler, Ball. 3:55 p.m., Jan. 29, 1963, JFKL/GWB/box 2/folder Canada, 4/26/61–11/8/63.
53. Tyler to Ball, "Proposed Press Statement on United States-Canadian Negotiations Regarding Nuclear Weapons," Jan. 29, 1963, NARA/RG 59/CDF/742.5611/1-2963.
54. Telcon: Tyler, Ball. 4:30 p.m., Jan. 30, 1963, and Telcon: Bundy, Ball. 4:55 p.m., Jan. 30, 1963, SMML/MC 031/box 103/folder 2; and Bundy to Kennedy, "Canadian Chronology," Feb. 14, 1963, JFKL/POF/box 113/folder Canada, Security, 1963.
55. Memcon, "Press Statement on U.S. and Canadian Negotiations Regarding Nuclear Weapons," Jan. 30, 1963, NARA/RG 59/EUR-CDC/RRMM/box 2/folder Canadian Nuclear Weapons Problem.
56. I. Sclanders, "The Washington Guessing Game: Who Told State to Tell Canada Off?," *Maclean's*, Mar. 9, 1963.
57. State Department Press Release 59, "United States and Canadian Negotiations Regarding Nuclear Weapons," Jan. 30, 1963.
58. "An Unfortunate Intrusion," *G&M*, Feb. 1, 1963; "This is Not 1911," *Toronto Star*, Feb. 1, 1963; "Justified and Necessary," *Winnipeg Free Press*, Jan. 31, 1963; "No Time for Quarrels," *MG*, Feb. 1, 1963; "Still No Nuclear Policy," *OC*, Feb. 1, 1963.
59. Office of the Leader of the Opposition Press Release, Jan. 30, 1963, QUA/Kent Papers/box 2/folder Correspondence Jan.–Feb. 1963; HOC, Jan. 31, 1963, 3289.
60. Rusk from White, 8:13 pm, Jan. 31, 1963 and Rusk to Butterworth, 9:15 pm, Jan. 31, 1963, NARA/RG 59/Rusk TTC/box 47.
61. Telcon: Bundy, Ball. 10:00 a.m., Jan. 31, 1963; Telcon: President, Ball. 7:30 p.m., Jan. 31, 1963, and Telcon: President, Ball. 9:00 p.m., Jan. 31, 1963, SMML/MC 031/box 103/folder 2.
62. Bundy to Rusk, Feb. 1, 1963, JFKL/NSF/box 402/folder Chronological File, February 1963; Transcript, "Press Conference of Secretary of State Dean Rusk," Feb. 1, 1963, NARA/RG 59/EUR-CDC/RRMM/box 2/folder Canadian Nuclear Weapons Problem; and Ottawa to State, no. 983, Feb. 1, 1963, JFKL/NSF/box 225/folder NATO, Weapons, Cables, Canada 3/61–3/63.
63. Tyler, "Canadian Situation," Feb. 2, 1963, NARA/RG 59/EUR-CDC/RRMM/box 2/folder Canadian Nuclear Weapons Problem.
64. Ottawa to State, no. 987, Feb. 2, 1963, JFKL/NSF/box 18/folder Canada, General 2/63; and Bundy to Kennedy, "Additional Miscellaneous Weekend Reading," Feb. 2, 1963, JFKL/NSF/box 402/folder Chronological File, February 1963.
65. Ottawa to State, no. 990, Feb. 3, 1963, JFKL/NSF/box 18/folder Canada, General 2/1/63–2/14/63.
66. Diary, Feb. 3, 1963, LAC/MG 32 B 29/vol. 1.

67. Ottawa to State, no. 991, Feb. 4, 1963, and Ottawa to State, no. 996, Feb. 4, 1963, JFKL/ NSF/box 18/folder Canada, General 2/63; Nash, *Kennedy and Diefenbaker*, 270–1.

68. Ottawa to State, no. 1039, Feb. 11, 1963, JFKL/NSF/box 18/folder Canada, General 2/ 1/63–2/14/63.

69. Telcon: Bundy, Ball. 12:20 p.m., Feb. 7, 1963, JFKL/GWB/box 2/folder Canada, 4/26/ 61–11/8/63.

70. Bundy to Johnson, May 1, 1964, LBJL/NSF/Memos to the President/box 1/folder McGeorge Bundy 5/1–27/64. Others have seen this comment as an admission of guilt regarding US conspiracies against Canada: G. Mount, *Canada's Enemies: Spies and Spying in the Peaceable Kingdom* (Toronto: Dundurn Press, 1993), 106–18.

71. "If What Was True in '58 Is True in '63 (and It Is), We Need an Election Now," *Maclean's*, Jan. 5, 1963.

72. "Now Is the Time," *G&M*, Feb. 6, 1963; "It Is Time for Change," *OC*, Feb. 7, 1963.

73. "The Canadian Tempest," *WP*, Feb. 2, 1963; W. Lippmann, "The Mess with Canada," *WP*, Feb. 7, 1963; A. Krock, "In The Nation," *NYT*, Feb. 5, 1963; "USA and Canada," *NYT*, Feb. 7, 1963; "Losing Friends Fast," *CT*, Feb. 2, 1963.

74. "G.O.P. Assails 'Inept Foreign Affairs Moves,'" *CT*, Feb. 12, 1963; B. Goldwater, "Rosy Glow Fades From Kennedy's Picture of International Affairs," *LAT*, Feb. 21, 1963.

75. US Senate, Subcommittee on Canadian Affairs, "Supplying of Nuclear Arms to the Canadian Forces," Feb. 4, 1963, *Executive Sessions of the Senate Foreign Relations Committee, 1963*; "Canada's Election Issue," *NYT*, Feb. 15, 1963.

76. Bundy to Kennedy, "Canadian Chronology," Feb. 14, 1963, JFKL/POF/box 113/folder Canada, Security, 1963.

77. Robinson to Carter, Feb. 12, 1963, LAC/MG 31 E83/vol. 9.2.

78. Bow to Green, Feb. 13, 1963, LAC/MG 32 B13/vol. 7.12; Carter to A.E. Ritchie, Feb. 6, 1963, and Carter to Robinson, Feb. 8, 1963, LAC/RG 25/vol. 5030/file 1415-40-pt. 12; Robinson to Carter, Feb. 12, 1963, LAC/MG 31 E83/vol. 9.2.

79. Ritchie, *Storm Signals*, 33–4.

80. Ritchie to Robertson, 21 Feb 1963, LAC/MG 31 E44/vol. 2.14.

81. Tyler to Manning, "Desirability of U.S. Government Refraining from Statements Regarding Canada During Canadian Election," Feb. 8, 1963, NARA/RG 59/EUR-CDC/ RRMM/box 2/folder Canadian Nuclear Weapons Problem.

82. News Conference, Feb. 7, 1963, JFKL/POF/box 58.

83. News Conference, Mar. 6, 1963, JFKL/POF/box 59.

84. White to Carlson, Feb. 11, 1963, and attached report "Conservative Party Policy Towards Anti-Americanism," NARA/RG 59/EUR-CDC/RRMM/box 2/folder Canadian Nuclear Weapons Problem. The three MPs were Donald Fleming, Davie Fulton and Arthur Smith.

85. Hilsman to Rusk, "Canadian General Election," Feb. 11, 1963, and covering letter, Klein to Bundy, Feb. 12, 1963, JFKL/NSF/box 18/folder Canada, General 2/1/63–2/14/63.

86. Excerpts from an Address by the Rt. Hon. John G. Diefenbaker, Winnipeg, Mar. 4, 1963, and Progressive Conservative Party, *News Digest* 21, Mar. 20, 1963, LAC/MG 32 B39/ vol. 48/file 1963 Election, National Campaign Headquarters—memos to candidates, 1.

87. Brubeck to Bundy, "Assessment for the President of Canadian Election Campaign," Mar. 14, 1963, and Ottawa to State, A-822, Mar. 13, 1963, JFKL/NSF/box 18/folder Canada, General 2/15/63–3/15/63; Ottawa to State, no. 1241, Mar. 28, 1963, JFKL/NSF/box 18/folder Canada, General, 3/16/63–3/31/63.

88. Ottawa to State, no. 1196, Mar. 20, 1963, and Ottawa to State, A-808, Mar. 11, 1963, JFKL/NSF/box 18/folder Canada, General 3/16/63–3/31/63; Address by Pearson to National Liberal Federation in Ottawa, "A Time for Action," Feb. 11, 1963, QUA/Kent Papers/box 2/folder Correspondence Jan.–Feb. 1963; and Liberal Party Press Release, "Statement by Hon. Lester B. Pearson on Nuclear Policy for Canada," Feb. 20, 1963, LAC/MG 26 N6/vol. 42/file Nuclear—Defence.

89. Brubeck to Bundy, "Canadian Election Assessment," Apr. 5, 1963, JFKL/NSF/box 18/ folder Canada, General 4/1/63–4/10/63; English, *Worldly Years*, 264.

90. English, *Worldly Years*, 234–5, 239.
91. Gordon to Pearson, "Re: Conversations with President Kennedy," May 7, 1963, LAC, MG 32 B44, vol. 22.10; Newman, *Renegade in Power*, 267; English, *Worldly Years*, 261; Telephone Conversation, Kennedy and Harris, Apr. 2, 1963, JFKL/POF/Dictabelt 17B.
92. A. Panetta, "JFK's Old Pollster Speaks on Role in Canadian Elections: 'Highlight of My Life'," *Winnipeg Free Press*, Nov. 20, 2013; A. Panetta, "What Did Kennedy Do for the History of This Country? Plenty, Experts Say," *G&M*, Nov. 20, 2013.
93. Legere to Bundy, "Canadian Developments," Mar. 1, 1963, and Legere to Bundy, "Canada," Mar. 13, 1963, JFKL/NSF/box 18/folder Canada, General 2/15/63–3/15/63.
94. Consulate, Vancouver to State, A-91, Mar. 4, 1963, and Ottawa to State, no. 1140, Mar. 7, 1963, JFKL/NSF/box 18/folder Canada, General 2/15/63–3/15/63; Bow to Robertson, "Vigil of the U.S. Vice Consul in Vancouver," Mar. 6, 1963, LAC/RG 25/vol. 5030/file 1415-40-pt. 12; Rusk to Tyler, 4:04 pm, Mar. 6, 1963, NARA/RG 59/Rusk TTC/box 48.
95. "McNamara Gives Testimony on Bomarc," *G&M*, Mar. 30, 1963; "Gift from Washington," *Time*, Apr. 5, 1963; Television Address by the Rt. Hon. John G. Diefenbaker, Mar. 29, 1963, and Progressive Conservative Party, *News Digest* 32, Apr. 3, 1963, LAC/MG 32 B39/vol. 48/file 1963 Election, National Campaign Headquarters—memos to candidates, 2.
96. Telephone Conversation, Kennedy and Harris, Apr. 2, 1963, JFKL/POF/Dictabelt 17B
97. Ottawa to State, no. 1293, Apr. 6, 1963, Ottawa to State, no. 1285, Apr. 4, 1963, and Kennedy to McNamara, Apr. 2, 1963, JFKL/NSF/box 18/folder Canada, General 4/1/63–4/10/63; Summary Record of the National Security Council Meeting, Apr. 2, 1963, JFKL/NSF/box 317/folder NSC Meetings, no. 510.
98. Gwyn, *49th Paradox*, 110.
99. See Nash, *Kennedy and Diefenbaker*, 278–9; English, *Worldly Years*, 264.
100. Pearson, *Mike* III, 81; Stursberg, *Pearson*, 186.
101. Farquharson to Irwin, Mar. 1, 1963, LAC/MG 31 E97/vol. 29.3; Robinson to Robertson, Feb. 4, 1963, LAC/MG 31 E44/vol. 2.14.
102. Gordon to Pearson, "Re: Conversations with President Kennedy," May 7, 1963, LAC/MG 32 B44/vol. 22.10.
103. Dwight Martin, "Canada's Diefenbaker: Decline and Fall," *Newsweek*, Feb. 18, 1963.
104. Diefenbaker, *One Canada* III, 107; Warnock, *Partner to Behemoth*, 194.
105. "Diefenbaker's Shambles," *Time*, Feb. 15, 1963; P.C. Newman, "The powerful gifts and glaring flaws of John Diefenbaker," *Maclean's*, Mar. 23, 1963.
106. R. Fulford, "The Puzzling—to Almost Everybody—Personality of Lester B. Pearson," *Maclean's*, Apr. 6, 1963.
107. Butterworth to Tyler, Feb. 2, 1963, JFKL/NSF/box 18/folder Rostow Memorandum and Related Materials 5/61–5/63.
108. Klein minute on Ottawa to State, no. 1267, Apr. 1, 1963, Ottawa to State, no. 1236, May 27, 1963, Ottawa to State, no. 1271, Apr. 2, 1963, and Noffe to Bundy, "Diefenbaker's 'Secret Document,'" Apr. 3, 1963, JFKL/NSF/box 18/folder Rostow Memorandum and Related Materials 5/61–5/63. See "Story of Secret Paper Denied by Diefenbaker," *WP*, Mar. 29, 1963; T. Long, "Diefenbaker's Threat to Use U.S. Memo Disturbs Canada," *NYT*, Mar. 30, 1963.
109. Telephone Recording, Dictation Belt 16A.5, 28/3/63, JFKL; Legere to Bundy, "Ottawa 1244 of March 28," Mar. 29, 1963, JFKL/NSF/box 18/folder Canada, General 3/16/63–3/31/63; G. Bain, "Lost Kennedy Note Reported Damaging U.S.–Canadian Ties," *G&M*, Apr. 6, 1963.
110. Bundy to Rusk and McNamara, "Canadian Election Campaign," Apr. 1, 1963, JFKL/NSF/box 18/folder Canada, General 4/1/63–4/10/63.
111. See a copy of the letter attached to Diefenbaker to Fleming, Mar. 26, 1963, LAC/MG 32 B39/vol. 158/file Memoirs, Nuclear Arms Issue—notes, correspondence, miscellaneous—1963; and Smith, *Rogue Tory*, 508–9.
112. Ottawa to State, no. 1295, Apr. 7, 1963, JFKL/NSF/box 18/folder Canada, General 4/1/63–4/10/63; and Bryce to Pearson, May 28, 1963, LAC/MG 31 E59/vol. 1.19. During

the first few weeks of Pearson's premiership, Gordon Churchill, Diefenbaker's Veteran Affairs Minister and now opposition MP, read the letter to the House of Commons and, with Diefenbaker looking on, attacked Pearson for his collusion with the Kennedy administration: "Canada: The Letter," *Time*, Jun. 7, 1963.

113. "Hot Document Raps Tories, Says Writer," *Vancouver Province*, Apr. 6, 1963; Ottawa to State, no. 1317, Apr. 11, 1963, JFKL/NSF/box 18/folder Canada, General 4/11/63–5/3/63, and State to Ottawa, no. 1033, Apr. 12, 1963, JFKL/NSF/box 18/folder Rostow Memorandum and Related Materials 5/61–5/63; Telegram From the Embassy in Canada to the Department of State, Apr. 15, 1963, *FRUS*, 1961–1963, XIII, 1200.

114. M. Bundy Oral History #1, JFKL.

115. Ottawa to State, no. 1293, Apr. 6, 1963, JFKL/NSF/box 18/folder Canada, General 4/1/63–4/10/63.

116. B. Bradlee, *Conversations with Kennedy* (New York: Norton, 1975), 167; Ritchie, *Storm Signals*, 47.

117. "A New Leader," *Time*, Apr. 19, 1963; J. Holmes, "Canada in Search of Its Role," *FA* 41 (1963): 659–72.

118. Ottawa to State, no. 1313, Apr. 11, 1963, and covering letter Legere to Bundy, Apr. 11, 1963, JFKL/NSF/box 18/folder Canada, General, 4/11/63–5/3/63.

119. Transcript of a Telephone Conversation between President Kennedy and Prime Minister Macmillan, Apr. 1963, JFKL/POF/box 127/folder United Kingdom, Transcripts of Kennedy-Macmillan phone calls 1963.

120. Quoted in Nash, *Kennedy and Diefenbaker*, 307.

121. W. Armstrong, "Comment on Armament and Disarmament," *Fourth Seminar on Canadian–American Relations at Assumption University of Windsor* (Windsor: Assumption University, 1962).

122. Quoted in Stursberg, *Pearson*, 184–5.

123. Rusk to Butterworth, 9:15 pm, Jan. 31, 1963, NARA/RG 59/Rusk TTC/box 47.

124. K. McNaught, "Uncle Sam Again," *Canadian Forum*, May 1963.

## Epilogue

1. "Outlook for New Canadian Government and Possible U.S. Tactics," Apr. 11, 1963 and Tyler to Ball, "Relations with New Canadian Government," Apr. 17, 1963, NARA/RG 59/EUR-CDC/RRPM/box 3/folder Canadian Cabinet, 1961/62; NSAM 234, Apr. 18, 1963, JFKL/NSF/box 340.

2. Carter to A.E. Ritchie, Apr. 17, 1963, and A.E. Ritchie to Robertson, Apr. 16, 1963, LAC/RG 25/vol. 5030/file 1415-40-pt. 12.

3. Ottawa to State, no. 1331, Apr. 16, 1963, JFKL/NSF/box 18a/folder Canada, General 4/11/63–5/3/63.

4. Legere, "Meeting with the President on Canada," May 2, 1963, JFKL/NSF/box 18a/folder Canada, General 4/11/63–5/3/63; CC, May 9, 1963, LAC/RG 2/vol. 6253; Ritchie, *Storm Signals*, 48. See also: William Tyler Oral History Interview, Mar. 7, 1964, JFKL; English, *The Worldly Years*, 266–70; and Robinson to file, "General Colour of Hyannis Port Meeting," May 15, 1963, LAC/MG 31 E83/vol. 12.1.

5. Memcon, "Record of Meeting between the Prime Minister and the President, Hyannis Port, 10–11 May 1963," LAC/RG 25/vol. 5030/file 1415-40-pt. 12; and various Memoranda of Conversation in JFKL/NSF/box 19a/folder Canada, Subjects: Pearson Visit, 5/63—Memorandum of Conversation.

6. Washington to External, tel. 1403, May 9, 1963, LAC/RG 25/vol. 5030/file 1415-40-pt. 12.

7. Bundy to Rusk, May 13, 1963, JFKL/NSF/box 18a/folder 5/4/63–5/31/63; Butterworth Oral History Interview, JFKL; CC, May 13, 1963, LAC/RG 2/vol. 6253; Memcon, "East–West Relations and Soviet Reappraisal," May 21, 1963, JFKL/NSF/box 248/folder

Secretary of State's Trip—Ottawa 5/63 [1 of 2]; and Campbell to Dier, May 21, 1963 and attached "Summary Record," LAC/RG 25/vol. 5030/file 1415-40-pt.12.

8. W. Lippmann, "Today and Tomorrow," *WP*, May 16, 1963; "Report on Canada," *Atlantic Monthly*, Jul. 1963.

9. ConGen NY to External, NL-332, Jun. 14, 1963, LAC/RG 25/vol. 5030/file 1415-40-pt.12; "Good Relations Are Restored," *Calgary Herald*, May 14, 1963; "The return to sanity," *OC*, May 13, 1963; "Mr. Pearson's Diplomacy," *G&M*, May 13, 1963; "Pearson Negotiates Nuclear Warheads," *MG*, May 14, 1963.

10. Martin to Pearson, "Nuclear Weapons," May 20, 1963, LAC/MG 26 N6/vol. 42/file Nuclear Defence.

11. Legere, "Meeting with the President on Canada," May 2, 1963.

12. NSAM 248, Jun. 3, 1963, JFKL/NSF/box 341. The Johnson administration would later reopen these issues, but would encounter similar Canadian opposition: Donaghy, *Tolerant Allies*, 101–4.

13. Robertson to Ritchie, April 19, 1963, LAC/RG 25/vol. 5030/file 1415-40 pt. 12.

14. Summary Record, "Hyannis Port Meetings 10–11 May 1963," May 15, 1963, LAC/MG 32 B12/vol. 252/file 6.

15. Ottawa to State, no. 128, Jul. 25, 1963, NARA/RG 59/Subject Numeric Files 1963/box 3863/folder POL-CAN-US.

16. Schwarzmann to Ritchie, May 29, 1963, LAC/MG 32 B41/vol. 27.11.

17. Ottawa to State, no. 1562, May 27, 1962, JFKL/NSF/box 18a/folder Canada, General 5/4/63–5/31/63

18. HOC, Jun. 13, 1963, 997–1001.

19. "Step Backward for Canada?," *LAT*, Jun. 17, 1963; "Canada Waves the Flag," *NYT*, Jun. 18, 1963.

20. Robinson to file, "Canadian Budget," Jun. 21, 1963, LAC/MG 31 E83/vol. 12.2, Memcon, "Canadian Budget Resolutions," Jun. 21, 1963, and Klein to Bundy, "Financial Difficulties of the Pearson Government," Jun. 21, 1963, JFKL/NSF/box 18a/folder Canada, General, 6/63; Muirhead, *Dancing*, 54–60; Donaghy, *Tolerant Allies*, 21–5; and Azzi, *Gordon*, 95–110.

21. Memcon, Jun. 28, 1963, JFKL/NSF/box 18/folder Canada, General 6/63.

22. Martin to Pearson, Jul. 19, 1963, and Washington to External, tel. 2307, Jul. 19, 1963, LAC/RG 25/vol. 5005/file 171-B-40-pt. 1; Rusk from Ritchie, 12:29 pm, Jul. 19, 1963, NARA/RG 59/Rusk TTC/box 48.

23. Telcon Bundy, Ball 7/19/63, 12:20, SMML/MC031/box 149/folder 18; Memcon, "Canadian Reaction to US BOP Measures," Jul. 19, 1963, JFKL/NSF/box 19/folder Canada, General 7/12/63–7/30/63.

24. George Ball Oral History Interview, Mar. 29, 1968, JFKL; Memcon, "Meeting of Canadian and US Officials on the Proposed Interest Equalization Tax," Jul. 24, 1963, LAC/RG25/vol. 5005/file 171-B-40-pt. 1; Ritchie, *Storm Signals*, 72.

25. James A. Reed Oral History, Jun. 16, 1964, JFKL.

26. Telcon, Bundy-Ball Aug. 14, 1963, 10:35 am, SMML/MC031/box 149/folder 18.

27. Zeiler, *American Trade*, 48.

28. Memorandum for the Record, Apr. 24, 1963, JFKL/NSF/box 317/folder Meetings with the President, General, 4/63; Heller to JFK, "Canadian Deficits—Budgetary and Foreign," Jun. 30, 1962, JFKL/POF/box 74/folder July 1962.

29. Butterworth Oral History Interview.

30. Granatstein, "When Push Came to Shove," 103.

31. Rusk to Dillon, 12:18 pm, Jul. 19, 1963, NARA/RG 59/Rusk TTC/box 48.

32. C. Ritchie, *Undiplomatic Diaries, 1937–71* (Toronto: Emblem, 2008, 481; P. C. Newman, "The fall, more than ever, we're an economic satellite of the U.S.," *Maclean's*, Sep. 21, 1963.

33. Telcon, Bundy, Ball, Aug. 14, 1663, 10:35 a.m., and Telcon Kaysen, Ball, Aug. 14, 1963, 11:20 a.m., SMML/MC031/box 149/folder 18.

34. Vernon to Rusk, n.d., attached to Read to Bundy, Sep. 10, 1963, JFKL/NSF/box 19/folder Canada, General 9/5/63–9/10/63.

35. Summary Record of Joint Canada–United States Joint Committee on Trade and Economic Affairs, Sep. 20–21, 1963, LAC/RG 20/vol. 1977/file 20-310-pt.7.
36. Ibid.; And see D. Anastakis, *Auto Pact: Creating a Borderless North American Auto Industry, 1960–1971* (Toronto, 2005), 39–59.
37. HOC, Oct. 25, 1963, 3999.
38. Rusk to Ball, 11:05 am, Oct. 31, 1963, NARA/RG 59/Rusk TTC/box 49; Telcon, Ball-Fowler, Oct. 31, 1963, 9:10 a.m., MC031, box 149, folder 18; Hudec to Herter, Oct. 30, 1963, JKFL/Herter Papers/box 7/folder Canadian Automobile Parts.
39. Robinson to Ritchie, Oct. 4, 1963, LAC/MG 31 E83/vol. 12.5.
40. Bundy to Rusk, Nov. 11, 1963; Brubeck to Kennedy, Nov. 19, 1963, JFKL/NSF/box 19/folder Canada, General 11/9/63–12/2/63; and Donaghy, *Tolerant Allies*, 37.
41. R. A. Divine, "The Education of John F. Kennedy," in *Makers of American Diplomacy: From Theodore Roosevelt to Henry Kissinger*, eds. F. J. Merli and T. A. Wilson (New York: Charles Scribner's Sons, 1974), 317–44. On Kennedy as a maturing statesman, see J. G. Blight, J. M. Lang, and D. A. Welch, *Vietnam If Kennedy Had Lived: Virtual JFK* (Lanham: Rowman & Littlefield, 2009); M. J. White, "Introduction," in *Kennedy: The New Frontier Revisited*, ed. M. J. White (New York: NYU Press, 1998), 12–3; W. M. LeoGrande and P. Kornbluh, *Back Channel to Cuba: The Hidden History of Negotiations between Washington and Havana* (Chapel Hill: UNC Press, 2014), 64–78.
42. Ritchie, *Storm Signals*, 70.
43. P. Martin, "Canadian–American Relations," *Fifth Seminar on Canadian–American Relations at Assumption University of Windsor* (Windsor: Assumption University, 1963), 22.
44. Memorandum from Secretary of State Rusk to President Johnson, December 12, 1963 (Secret) in *FRUS 1961–1963*, Vol. XIII, 1217; Donaghy, *Tolerant Allies*; "Address before the Canadian Parliament in Ottawa," May 17, 1961, *PPP*.
45. M. Bundy, "Canada, the Exceptionally Favored: An American Perspective," in *Friends So Different*, eds. L. Lamont and J. D. Edmonds (Ottawa: University of Ottawa, 1989), 232.
46. D. Stairs, "Confronting Uncle Sam: Cuba and Korea," in Clarkson, *Independent Foreign Policy*, 68; and Bow, *Politics of Linkage*.
47. Ritchie, *Storm Signals*, 5.
48. "Interview with JL Granatstein, York University Oral History Programme," 41–2, CVA/ Add. MSS 903/605-D-1/file 2.
49. Robinson, *Diefenbaker's World*, 318.
50. M. Bundy Oral History #1, Mar. 1964, JFKL.
51. "Department of State Guidelines for Policy and Operations—Canada," Mar. 1962.
52. NIE 99-61, "Trends in Canadian Foreign Policy," May 2, 1961.
53. Bundy, "Canada," 232, 236.
54. Robinson to A.E. Ritchie, Jan. 11, 1963, LAC/MG 31 E83/vol. 9.2.
55. D. Kunz, "Introduction: The Crucial Decade," in *Diplomacy of the Crucial Decade*, 9.
56. Heeney to Merchant, Apr. 16, 1962, LAC/MG 30 E14/vol. 13.1.
57. A. Heeney and L. Merchant, *Canada and the United States: Principles for Partnership*, Jun. 28, 1965, LAC/MG 26 N6/vol. 29/file Canada–U.S. Relations 1954–1968. And see A. McKercher, "Principles and Partnership: Merchant, Heeney, and the Craft of Canada– US Relations," *ARCS* 42, no. 1 (2012): 67–83.
58. Cadieux to Martin, "Canada–United States Relations," Jun. 24, 1965, LAC/RG 25/vol. 8673/file 20-1-2-USA
59. R. Edwardson, "Of War Machines and Ghetto Scenes: English–Canadian Nationalism and The Guess Who's American Woman," *ARCS* 33, no. 3 (2003), 339–56; D. S. Churchill, "Draft Resisters, Left Nationalism, and the Politics of Anti-Imperialism," *Canadian Historical Review* 93, no. 2 (2012), 227–60; J. Cormier, *The Canadianization Movement: Emergence, Survival, and Success* (Toronto: University of Toronto Press, 2004).
60. Robinson, *Diefenbaker's World*, 103.

61. Bundy to Johnson, Mar. 22, 1965, LBJL/NSF/Memos to the President/box 3/folder McGeorge Bundy March 4/14/65 [2 of 3].

62. J. Blanchard, *Behind the Embassy Door: Canada, Clinton and Quebec* (Toronto: McClelland and Stewart, 2000), 147–8.

63. Bundy, "Canada," 233.

64. O. A. Westad, *The Global Cold War* (Cambridge: Cambridge University Press, 2005); J. Suri, *Power and Protest: Global Revolution and the Rise of Detente* (Cambridge, MA: Harvard University Press, 2003).

65. Bothwell, *Canada and the United States*, 70–1.

66. Edwardson, *Canadian Content*, 15, 137; Azzi, "The Nationalist Moment."

67. Doran, *Forgotten Partnership*; R. Bothwell, "Canada–United States relations: Options for the 1970s," *IJ* 58, no. 1 (2002–2003), 65–88, and "Thanks for the Fish: Nixon, Kissinger, and Canada," in *Nixon in the World: American Foreign Relations, 1969–1977*, eds. F. Logevall and A. Preston, (New York: Oxford University Press, 2008), 309–28; R. D. Cuff and J. L. Granatstein, *Canadian–American Relations in Wartime: From the Great War to the Cold War* (Toronto: A. M. Hakkert, 1975), 151–63; Bow, *Linkage*, 13–6.

68. Ottawa to State, no. 1328, Apr. 15, 1963, JFKL/NSF/box 18/folder 4/11/63–5/3/63.

# Bibliography

## Primary Source Collections

**DWIGHT D. EISENHOWER PRESIDENTIAL LIBRARY**

Ann Whitman File
Post-Presidential Papers
White House Office, Office of the Special Assistant for National Security Affairs
White House Office, Office of the Staff Secretary
John Foster Dulles Papers
James Hagerty Papers
Christian Herter Papers
General Lauris Norstad Papers

**JOHN F. KENNEDY PRESIDENTIAL LIBRARY**

Pre-Presidential Papers
President's Office Files
National Security Files
White House Central Subject Files
Harlan Cleveland Papers
Christian Herter Papers
Robert Kennedy Papers
Arthur Schlesinger Jr. Collection
Robert Eastabrook Papers

**LYNDON B. JOHNSON PRESIDENTIAL LIBRARY**

National Security Files
White House Central Files

**UNITED STATES NATIONAL ARCHIVES AND RECORDS ADMINISTRATION II, COLLEGE PARK, MD**

Department of State Records (RG 59)
Foreign Service Post Files (RG 84)

**LIBRARY OF CONGRESS, WASHINGTON, DC**

Stewart Alsop Papers

**SEELEY MUDD MANUSCRIPT LIBRARY, PRINCETON UNIVERSITY**

Livingston Merchant Papers (MC 095)
George Ball Papers (MC 031)

MASSACHUSETTS HISTORICAL SOCIETY, BOSTON
Richard B. Wigglesworth Papers

STERLING MEMORIAL LIBRARY, YALE UNIVERSITY
Chester Bowles Papers

RUSH RHEES LIBRARY, UNIVERSITY OF ROCHESTER
Kenneth Keating Papers

LIBRARY AND ARCHIVES CANADA
Privy Council Office Papers (RG 2)
Department of Finance Records (RG 19)
Department of Trade and Commerce Records (RG 20)
Department of External Affairs Papers (RG 25)
John Diefenbaker Papers
Gordon Churchill Papers (MG 32 B9)
Tommy Douglas Papers (MG 32 C28)
Donald Fleming Papers (MG 32 B39)
Walter Gordon Papers (MG 32 B44)
Howard Green Papers (MG 32 B13)
Douglas Harkness Papers (MG 32 B19)
Arnold Heeney Papers (MG 30 E144)
W. Arthur Irwin (MG 31 E97)
J. Waldo Monteith (MG 32 B29)
Lester B. Pearson Papers (MG 26 N6)
Escott Reid Papers (MG 31 E46)
Albert Ritchie Papers (MG 31 E44)
Norman Robertson Papers (MG 30 E163)
H. Basil Robinson Papers (MG 31 E83)
Arnold Smith Papers (MG 31 E47)
Peter Stursberg (MG 31 D78)

QUEEN'S UNIVERSITY ARCHIVES
Tom Kent Papers

CITY OF VANCOUVER ARCHIVES
Howard Green Papers (MSS 903)

THE NATIONAL ARCHIVES OF THE UNITED KINGDOM
Cabinet Office Records (CAB)
Dominions Office Records (DO)
Prime Minister's Office Records (PREM)

## Oral Histories

Laetitia Baldridge Hollensteiner: John F. Kennedy Library
McGeorge Bundy: John F. Kennedy Library
Walton Butterworth: John F. Kennedy Library
Angier Duke: John F. Kennedy Library
Livingston Merchant: John F. Kennedy Library
J.A. Reed: John F. Kennedy Library
Ted Sorensen: John F. Kennedy Library
William Tyler: John F. Kennedy Library
Howard Green: Dwight D. Eisenhower Library
Willis Armstrong: Foreign Affairs Oral History Collection, Library of Congress
Louise Armstrong: Foreign Affairs Oral History Collection, Library of Congress

## Secondary Sources

Acheson, Dean. *Power and Diplomacy*. New York: Atheneum, 1966 [1958].

Anastakis, Dimitry. *Auto Pact: Creating a Borderless North American Auto Industry, 1960–1971*. Toronto: University of Toronto Press, 2005.

Anderson, Benedict. *Imagined Communities: Reflections on the Origin and Spread of Nationalism*, Revised Edition. London: Verso, 1991.

Anglin, Douglas. "United States Opposition to Canadian Membership in the Pan American Union: A Canadian View," *International Organization* 15, no. 1 (1961), 1–20.

Aono, Toshihiko. "'It Is Not Easy for the United States to Carry the Whole Load': Anglo-American Relations during the Berlin Crisis, 1961–1962," *Diplomatic History* 34, no. 2 (2010), 325–56.

Armstrong, Willis. "Comment on Armament and Disarmament," in *Fourth Seminar on Canadian-American Relations at Assumption University of Windsor*, 79–84. Windsor: Assumption University, 1962.

Aronsen, Lawrence. "An Open Door to the North: The Liberal Government and the Expansion of American Foreign Investment, 1945–1953," *American Review of Canadian Studies* 22, no. 2 (1992), 167–97.

Aronsen, Lawrence. *American National Security and Economic Relations with Canada, 1945–1954*. Westport: Praegar, 1997.

Ashton, Nigel. *Kennedy, Macmillan and the Cold War: The Irony of Interdependence*. Basingstoke: Palgrave Macmillan, 2002.

Axworthy, Lloyd. *Navigating a New World: Canada's Global Future*. Toronto: Vintage, 2004.

Azzi, Stephen. *Walter Gordon & the Rise of Canadian Nationalism*. Montréal and Kingston: McGill–Queen's University Press, 1999.

Azzi, Stephen. "Foreign Investment and the Paradox of Economic Nationalism," in *Canadas of the Mind: The Making and Unmaking of Canadian Nationalisms in the Twentieth Century*, eds. Adam Chapnick and Norman Hillmer, 244–57. Montréal and Kingston: McGill–Queen's University Press, 2007.

Azzi, Stephen. "The Nationalist Moment in English Canada," in *Debating Dissent: Canada and the 1960s*, eds. Lara A. Campbell, Dominque Clément, and Greg. Kealey, 213–28. Toronto: University of Toronto Press, 2012.

Ball, George. *The Discipline of Power: Essentials of a Modern World Structure*. Boston: Little, Brown, 1968.

Barber, Joseph. *Good Fences Make Good Neighbors: Why the United States Provokes Canadians*. Indianapolis: Bobbs-Merrill Company, 1958.

Barkway, Michael. "Canada Rediscovers Its History," *Foreign Affairs* 36 (1958), 409–17.

Barry, Donald, and Duane Bratt. "Defense Against Help: Explaining Canada–U.S. Security Relations," *American Review of Canadian Studies* 38, no. 1 (2008), 63–89.

Bélanger, Damien-Claude. *Prejudice and Pride: Canadian Intellectuals Confront the United States, 1891–1945*. Toronto: University of Toronto Press, 2011.

Benvenuti, Andrea, and Stuart Ward. "Britain, Europe, and the 'Other Quiet Revolution' in Canada," in *Canada and the End of Empire*, ed. Phillip Buckner, 165–82. Vancouver: UBC Press, 2005.

Bergbusch, Eric, and Michael D. Stevenson. "Howard Green, Public Opinion, and the Politics of Disarmament," in *Architects and Innovators: Building the Department of Foreign Affairs and International Trade, 1909–2009*, eds. Greg Donaghy and Kim Richard Nossal, 191–206. Montréal and Kingston: McGill–Queen's University Press, 2010.

Berger, Carl. *The Sense of Power: Studies in the Ideas of Canadian Imperialism 1867–1944*. Toronto: University of Toronto Press, 1970.

Beschloss, Michael. *The Crisis Years: Kennedy and Khrushchev, 1960–1963*. New York: Edward Burlingame Books, 1991.

Bill, James. *George Ball: Behind the Scenes in U.S. Foreign Policy*. New Haven: Yale University Press, 1997.

Blanchard, James. *Behind the Embassy Door: Canada, Clinton and Quebec*. Toronto: McClelland and Stewart, 2000.

Blight, James G., Janet M. Lang, and David A. Welch. *Vietnam If Kennedy Had Lived: Virtual JFK*. Lanham: Rowman & Littlefield, 2009.

Borden, William S. "Defending Hegemony: American Foreign Economic Policy," in *Kennedy's Quest for Victory: American Foreign Policy, 1961–1963*, ed. Thomas G. Paterson, 57–85. New York: Oxford University Press, 1989.

Bothwell, Robert. *Canada and the United States: The Politics of Partnership*. New York: Twayne, 1992.

Bothwell, Robert. "The Further Shore: Canada and Vietnam," *International Journal* 56, no. 1 (2000/2001), 89–114.

Bothwell, Robert. "Canada–United States Relations: Options for the 1970s," *International Journal* 58, no. 1 (2002–2003), 65–88.

Bothwell, Robert. *Alliance and Illusion: Canada and the World, 1945–1984*. Vancouver: UBC Press, 2007.

Bothwell, Robert. "Thanks for the Fish: Nixon, Kissinger, and Canada," in *Nixon in the World: American Foreign Relations, 1969–1977*, eds. Fred Logevall and Andrew Preston, 309–28. New York: Oxford University Press, 2008.

Bothwell, Robert. *Your Country, My Country: A Unified History of the United States and Canada*. New York: Oxford University Press, 2015.

Bothwell, Robert, and John Kirton. "A Sweet Little Country," in *Partners Nevertheless: Canadian–American Relations in the Twentieth Century*, ed. Norman Hillmer, 43–65. Toronto: Copp Clark Pitman, 1989.

Bow, Brian. "Anti-Americanism in Canada, Before and After Iraq," *American Review of Canadian Studies* 38, no. 3 (2008), 341–59.

Bow, Brian. "Rethinking 'Retaliation' in Canada–US Relations," in *An Independent Foreign Policy for Canada? Challenges and Choices for the Future*, eds. Brian Bow and Patrick Lennox, 63–82. Toronto: University of Toronto Press, 2008.

Bow, Brian. *The Politics of Linkage: Power, Interdependence, and Ideas in Canada–US Relations*. Vancouver: UBC Press, 2009.

Boyko, John. *Cold Fire: Kennedy's Northern Front*. Toronto: Knopf, 2016.

Bradlee, Ben. *Conversations with Kennedy*. New York: Norton, 1975.

Bright, Christopher J. *Continental Defense in the Eisenhower Era*. Basingstoke: Palgrave Macmillan, 2010.

Brookfield, Tarah. *Cold War Comforts: Canadian Women, Child Safety, and Global Insecurity*. Waterloo: WLU Press, 2012.

Brooks, Stephen. *As Others See Us: The Causes and Consequences of Foreign Perceptions of America*. Toronto: University of Toronto Press, 2006.

Buckner, Phillip. "The Long Goodbye: English Canadians and the British World," in *Rediscovering the British World*, eds. Phillip Buckner and R. Douglas Francis, 181–208. Calgary: University of Calgary Press, 2005.

Bundy, McGeorge. "Diplomatic Strategy in a Nuclear Age," in *National Values in a Changing World*. Toronto: Canadian Institute of Public Affairs, 1957.

Bundy, McGeorge. *Danger and Survival: Choices about the Bomb in the First Fifty Years*. New York: Vintage, 1988.

Bundy, McGeorge. "Canada, the Exceptionally Favored: An American Perspective," in *Friends So Different*, eds. Lansing Lamont and J. Duncan Edmonds, 232–9. Ottawa: Universtiy of Ottawa Press, 1989.

Burtch, Andrew. *Give Me Shelter: The Failure of Canada's Cold War Civil Defence*. Vancouver: UBC Press, 2012.

Carroll, Michael. *Pearson's Peacekeepers: Canada and the United Nations Emergency Force, 1956–67*. Vancouver: UBC Press, 2009.

Casgrain, Thérèse. *A Woman in a Man's World*. Toronto: McClelland and Stewart, 1972.

Chapnick, Adam. "The Canadian Middle Power Myth," *International Journal* 55, no. 2 (2000), 188–206.

Chapnick, Adam. *The Middle Power Project: Canada and the Founding of the United Nations*. Vancouver: UBC Press, 2005.

Chapnick, Adam. "Peace, Order and Good Government: The 'Conservative' Tradition in Canadian Foreign Policy," *International Journal* 60, no. 3 (2005), 635–50.

Chapnick, Adam. "Running in Circles: The Canadian Independence Debate in History," in *An Independent Foreign Policy for Canada? Challenges and Choices for the Future*, eds. Brian Bow and Patrick Lennox, 25–40. Toronto: University of Toronto Press, 2008.

Churchill, David S. "Draft Resisters, Left Nationalism, and the Politics of Anti-Imperialism," *Canadian Historical Review* 93, no. 2 (2012), 227–60.

Clarkson, Stephen. "The Choice to be Made," in *An Independent Foreign Policy for Canada?*, ed. Stephen Clarkson, 253–69. Toronto: McClelland Stewart, 1968.

Coffin, Frank. "Opportunities for North American Economic Statesmanship," in *Third Seminar on Canadian–American Relations at Assumption University of Windsor*, 19–32. Windsor: Assumption University, 1961.

Conant, Melvin. "Canada's Role in Western Defense," *Foreign Affairs* 40 (1962), 431–42.

Conant, Melvin. *The Long Polar Watch*. New York: Harper, 1962.

Cook, Ramsay. *Canada, Quebec, and the Uses of Nationalism*, Second Edition. Toronto: McClelland and Stewart, 1986.

Cormier, Jeffrey. *The Canadianization Movement: Emergence, Survival, and Success*. Toronto: University of Toronto Press, 2004.

Costigliola, Frank. "The Failed Design: Kennedy, de Gaulle, and the Struggle for Europe," *Diplomatic History* 8, no. 3 (1984), 227–51.

Costigliola, Frank. "The Pursuit of Atlantic Community: Nuclear Arms, Dollars, and Berlin," in *Kennedy's Quest for Victory: American Foreign Policy, 1961–1963*, ed. Thomas G. Paterson, 24–56. New York: Oxford University Press, 1989.

Costigliola, Frank. "Kennedy, the European Allies, and the Failure to Consult," *Political Science Quarterly* 110, no. 1 (1995), 105–23.

Costigliola, Frank. "Culture, Emotion, and the Creation of Atlantic Identity, 1948–52," in *No End to Alliance*, ed. Geir Lundestad, 21–36. London: St. Martin's Press, 1998.

Costigliola, Frank. "'I Had Come as a Friend': Emotion, Culture, and Ambiguity in the Formation of the Cold War," *Cold War History* 1, no. 1 (2000), 103–28.

Cuff, R. D., and J. L. Granatstein. *Canadian–American Relations in Wartime: From the Great War to the Cold War*. Toronto: A. M. Hakkert, 1975.

Cuff, R.D. and J. L. Granatstein. *American Dollars, Canadian Prosperity: Canadian–American Economic Relations, 1945–50*. Toronto: Samuel Stevens, 1978.

Cullather, Nick. "Modernization Theory," in *Explaining the History of American Foreign Relations*, ed. Michael J. Hogan, 212–20. Cambridge: Cambridge University Press, 2003.

Dallek, Robert. *An Unfinished Life: John F. Kennedy, 1917–1963*. New York: Back Bay Books, 2003.

Dean, Robert D. *Imperial Brotherhood: Gender and the Making of Cold War Foreign Policy*. Amherst: University of Massachusetts Press, 2001.

Deutsch, John. "Selective Free Trade in the North American Bloc as a Defensive Concept," in *Third Seminar on Canadian–American Relations at Assumption University of Windsor*, 87–96. Windsor: Assumption University, 1961.

Diefenbaker, John. *One Canada, Three Volumes*. Toronto: Macmillan, 1975–1977.

Divine, Robert A. "The Education of John F. Kennedy," in *Makers of American Diplomacy: From Theodore Roosevelt to Henry Kissinger*, eds. Frank J. Merli and Theodore A. Wilson, 317–44. New York: Charles Scribner's Sons, 1974.

Dobson, Alan. *US Economic Statecraft for Survival, 1933–1991: Of Sanctions, Embargoes and Economic Warfare*. London: Routledge, 2002.

Domínguez, Jorge I. "The @#$%& Missile Crisis: (Or What Was 'Cuban' about U.S. Decisions during the Cuban Missile Crisis?)," *Diplomatic History* 24, no. 2 (2000), 305–15.

Donaghy, Greg. *Tolerant Allies: Canada and the United States, 1963–1968*. Montréal and Kingston: McGill-Queen's University Press, 2002.

Donaghy, Greg. "Coming off the Gold Standard: Re-assessing the 'Golden Age' of Canadian Diplomacy." Paper presented to the symposium A Very Modern Ministry: Foreign

Affairs and International Trade Canada, University of Saskatchewan, September 28, 2009.

Donaghy, Greg, and Bruce Muirhead. "'Interests but No Foreign Policy': Canada and the Commonwealth Caribbean, 1951–1966," *American Review of Canadian Studies* 38, no. 3 (2008), 275–94.

Donaghy, Greg, and Michael D. Stevenson. "The Limits of Alliance: Cold War Solidarity and Canadian Wheat Exports to China, 1950–1963," *Agricultural History* 83, no. 1 (2009), 29–50.

Doran, Charles F. *Forgotten Partnership: U.S.–Canada Relations Today.* Baltimore: Johns Hopkins University Press, 1984.

Dorn, Walter, and Robert Pauk. "Unsung Mediator: U Thant and the Cuban Missile Crisis," *Diplomatic History* 33, no. 2 (2009), 261–92.

Drake, Earl. *A Stubble-Jumper in Striped Pants: Memoirs of a Prairie Diplomat.* Toronto: University of Toronto Press, 1999.

Eayrs, James. *Canada in World Affairs, 1955–57.* Toronto: Oxford University Press, 1959.

Eaton, Mark A. "Canadian Editorial Opinion and the 1963 Nuclear Weapon Acquisition Debate," *American Review of Canadian Studies* 35, no. 4 (2005), 641–66.

Edwards, Fred. "Chinese Shadows," in *Canadian Among Nations 2008: 100 Years of Canadian Foreign Policy*, eds. Robert Bothwell and Jean Daudelin, 283–313. Montréal and Kingston: McGill–Queen's University Press, 2009.

Edwardson, Ryan. "Of War Machines and Ghetto Scenes: English-Canadian Nationalism and The Guess Who's American Woman," *American Review of Canadian Studies* 33, no. 3 (2003), 339–56.

Edwardson, Ryan. *Canadian Content: Culture and the Quest for Nationhood.* Toronto: University of Toronto Press, 2008.

Engel, Jeffrey A. "Of Fat and Thin Communists: Diplomacy and Philosophy in Western Economic Warfare Strategies toward China (and Tyrants, Broadly)," *Diplomatic History* 29, no. 3 (2005), 445–74.

Engler, Yves. *Pearson's Peacekeeping: The Truth May Hurt.* Vancouver: Fernwood, 2012.

English, John. *The Worldly Years: The Life of Lester Pearson, 1949–1972.* Toronto: Alfred A. Knopf, 1992.

Fetzer, James. "Clinging to Containment: China Policy," in *Kennedy's Quest for Victory: American Foreign Policy, 1961–1963*, ed. Thomas G. Paterson, 178–97. New York: Oxford University Press, 1989.

Flanagan, Ann. "The China Syndrome: External Economic Irritants in the Canada–US Relationship," in *The Diefenbaker Legacy: Politics, Law and Society Since 1957*, eds. Donald C. Story and R. Bruce Shepard, 15–25. Regina: Canadian Plains Research Centre, 1998.

Fleming, Donald. *So Very Near, Volume Two: The Summit Years.* Toronto: McClelland and Stewart, 1985.

Francis, R. Douglas. *The Technological Imperative in Canada: An Intellectual History.* Vancouver: UBC Press, 2009.

Freedman, Lawrence. *Kennedy's Wars: Berlin, Cuba, Laos, and Vietnam.* Oxford: Oxford University Press, 2000.

Friedman, Max Paul. "Anti-Americanism and U.S. Foreign Relations," *Diplomatic History* 32, no. 4 (2008), 497–514.

Friedman, Max Paul. *Rethinking Anti-Americanism: The History of an Exceptional Concept in American Foreign Relations.* Cambridge: Cambridge University Press, 2012.

Fulton, David. "Opening Address," in *Second Seminar on Canadian–American Relations at Assumption University of Windsor*, 1–9. Windsor: Assumption University, 1960.

Fursenko, Aleksandr, and Timothy Naftali. *"One Hell of a Gamble": Khrushchev, Castro, and Kennedy, 1958–1964.* New York: W. W. Norton, 1997.

Fursenko, Aleksandr, and Timothy Naftali. *Khrushchev's Cold War: The Inside Story of an American Adversary.* New York: W. W. Norton, 2007.

Gavin, Frank J. *Nuclear Statecraft: History and Strategy in America's Atomic Age.* Ithaca: Cornell University Press, 2012.

Gendron, Robin. *Towards a Francophone Community: Canada's Relations with France and French Africa, 1945–1968*. Montréal and Kingston: McGill–Queen's University Press, 2006.

Ghent, Jocelyn Maynard. "Did He Fall or Was He Pushed? The Kennedy Administration and the Collapse of the Diefenbaker Government," *International History Review* 1, no. 2 (1979), 246–70.

Ghent, Joceyln Maynard. "Canada, the United States, and the Cuban Missile Crisis," *Pacific Historical Review* 48, no. 2 (1979), 159–84.

Ghent-Mallet, Jocelyn, and Don Munton. "Confronting Kennedy and the Missiles in Cuba, 1962," in *Canadian Foreign Policy: Selected Cases*, eds. Don Munton and John Kirton, 78–100. Scarborough: Prentice–Hall, 1992.

Giauque, Jeffrey Glen. *Grand Designs and Visions of Unity: The Atlantic Powers and the Reorganization of Western Europe, 1955–1963*. Chapel Hill: UNC Press, 2002.

Gibson, David R. *Talk at the Brink: Deliberation and Decision During the Cuban Missile Crisis*. Princeton: Princeton University Press, 2012.

Gladman, Brian W., and Peter M. Archambault. *Confronting the "Essence of Decision": Canada and the Cuban Missile Crisis—Centre for Operational Research and Analysis Technical Memorandum 2010-250*. Ottawa: Department of National Defence, 2010.

Glazov, Jamie. *Canadian Policy toward Khrushchev's Soviet Union*. Montréal and Kingston: McGill–Queen's University Press, 2002.

Gloin, Kevin J. "Canada–US Relations in the Diefenbaker Era: Another Look," in *The Diefenbaker Legacy: Politics, Law and Society Since 1957*, eds. Donald C. Story and R. Bruce Shepard, 1–14. Regina: Canadian Plains Research Centre, 1998.

Gordon, Walter. *Troubled Canada: The Need for New Domestic Policies*. Toronto: McClelland and Stewart, 1961.

Granatstein, J. L. *A Man of Influence: Norman A. Robertson and Canadian Statecraft, 1929–68*. Ottawa: Deneau, 1981.

Granatstein, J. L. *Canada 1957–1967: Years of Uncertainty and Innovation*. Toronto: McClelland and Stewart, 1986.

Granatstein, J. L. "When Push Came to Shove: Canada and the United States," in *Kennedy's Quest for Victory: American Foreign Policy, 1961–1963*, ed. Thomas G. Paterson, 86–104. New York: Oxford University Press, 1989.

Granatstein, J. L. *Yankee Go Home?: Canadians and Anti-Americanism*. Toronto: HarperCollins, 1996.

Grant, George. *Lament for a Nation: The Defeat of Canadian Nationalism*. Montréal and Kingston: McGill–Queen's University Press, 2000 [1965].

Grasso, June. "The Politics of Food Aid: John F. Kennedy and Famine in China," *Diplomacy & Statecraft* 14, no. 4 (2003), 153–78.

Gwyn, Richard. *The 49th Paradox: Canada in North America*. Toronto: McClelland and Stewart, 1985.

Hafele, Mark. "John F. Kennedy, USIA, and World Public Opinion," *Diplomatic History* 25, no. 1 (2001), 63–84.

Haglund, David. "The US–Canada Relationship: How 'Special' Is America's Longest Unbroken Alliance?," in *America's Special Relationships*, eds. John Dumbrell and Axel Schäfer, 60–75. London: Routledge, 2009.

Hailey, Arthur. *In High Places*. New York: Doubleday, 1962.

Hart, Michael. *A Trading Nation: Canadian Trade Policy from Colonialism to Globalization*. Vancouver: UBC Press, 2002.

Haydon, Peter T. *The 1962 Cuban Missile Crisis: Canadian Involvement Reconsidered*. Toronto: Canadian Institute of Strategic Studies, 1993.

Heeney, Arnold D.P. "Washington Under Two Presidents: 1953–57, 1959–62," *International Journal* 22, no. 3 (1967), 500–11.

Heeney, Arnold D.P. *The Things That Are Caesar's*. Toronto: University of Toronto Press, 1972.

Heidt, Daniel. "'I Think That Would Be the End of Canada': Howard Green, the Nuclear Test Ban, and Interest-Based Foreign Policy, 1946–1963," *American Review of Canadian Studies* 42, no. 3 (2012), 343–69.

Herd, Alexander W.G. "A 'Common Appreciation': Eisenhower, Canada, and Continental Air Defense," *Journal of Cold War Studies* 13, no. 3 (2011), 4–26.

Herman, Ellen. *The Romance of American Psychology: Political Culture in the Age of Experts.* Berkeley: University of California Press, 1995.

Hershberg, James G. "The Crisis Years, 1958–1963," in *Reviewing the Cold War: Approaches, Interpretations, Theory*, ed. Odd Arne Westad, 303–25. London: Frank Cass, 2000.

Hershberg, James G. "The United States, Brazil, and the Cuban Missile Crisis (Part II)," *Journal of Cold War Studies* 6, no. 3 (2004), 5–67.

Hilliker, John F. "The Politicians and the 'Pearsonalities': The Diefenbaker Government and the Conduct of Canadian External Relations," *Historical Papers* 19, no. 1 (1984), 151–67.

Hilliker, John F., and Donald Barry. *Canada's Department of External Affairs, Volume 2: Coming of Age, 1946–1968.* Montréal and Kingston: McGill–Queen's University Press, 1995.

Hilliker, John F., and Donald Barry. "Uncomfortably in the Middle: The Department of External Affairs and Canada's Involvement in the International Control Commissions in Vietnam, 1954–73," in *Creating the Peaceable Kingdom*, ed. Victor Howard, 167–95. East Lansing: Michigan State University Press, 1998.

Hillmer Norman, and J. L. Granatstein, *For Better or For Worse: Canada and the United States into the Twenty-First Century.* Toronto: Thomson Nelson, 2007.

Hilsman, Roger. *To Move a Nation: The Politics of Foreign Policy in the Administration of John F. Kennedy.* Garden City: Doubleday, 1967.

Hollander, Paul. *Anti-Americanism: Critiques at Home and Abroad 1965–1990.* Oxford: Oxford University Press, 1992.

Holmes, John. "Canada and the United States in World Politics," *Foreign Affairs* 40 (1961), 105–17.

Holmes, John. "Canada in Search of Its Role," *Foreign Affairs* 41 (1963), 659–72.

Hunt, Michael. *Ideology and U.S. Foreign Policy.* New Haven: Yale University Press, 1987.

Hutchinson, Bruce. *The Unknown Country: Canada and Her People.* Toronto: Oxford University Press, 2011 [1942].

Hutchinson, Bruce. *Canada: Tomorrow's Giant.* Toronto: Oxford University Press, 2012 [1957].

Igartua, José. *The Other Quiet Revolution: National Identities in English Canada, 1945–71.* Vancouver: UBC Press, 2006.

Ilsaas Pharo, Per Fredrik. "A Precondition for Peace: Transparency and the Test-Ban Negotiations, 1958–1963," *International History Review* 22, no. 3 (2000), 557–82.

Jockel, Joseph T. *Canada in NORAD, 1957–2007: A History.* Montréal and Kingston: McGill–Queen's University Press, 2007.

Johnson, Harry G. "Canada in a Changing World Economy," in *Visions of Canada: Alan B. Plaunt Memorial Lectures 1958–1992*, ed. Bernard Osty and Janet Yalden, 99–134. Montréal and Kingston: McGill–Queen's University Press, 2004.

Jones, Matthew. "The Diplomacy of Restraint: Britain and the Laos Crisis, 1961–1962," in *The Failure of Peace in Indochina, 1954–1962*, eds. C. Goscha and K. Laplante, 159–77. Paris: Les Indes Savantes, 2010.

Jordon, Robert S. *Norstad, Cold War NATO Supreme Command, Airman, Strategist, Diplomat.* New York: St. Martin's Press, 2000.

Kent, Tom. "The Changing Place of Canada," *Foreign Affairs* 35 (1957), 581–92.

Keohane, Robert O., and Joseph S. Nye Jr., *Power and Interdependence: World Politics in Transition.* Second Edition. Boston: Little, Brown, 1989.

Keys, Barbara. "Henry Kissinger: The Emotional Statesman," *Diplomatic History* 35, no. 4 (2011), 587–609.

Kimball, Warren F. "The 'Special' Anglo-American Special Relationship: 'A Fatter, Larger Underwater Cable,'" *Journal of Transatlantic Studies* 3, no. 1 (2005), 1–5.

Kirk, John M., and Peter McKenna. *Canada–Cuba Relations: The Other Good Neighbor Policy.* Gainesville: University Press of Florida, 1997.

Kirton, John. "The Consequences of Integration: The Case of the Defence Production Sharing Agreements," in *Continental Community? Independence and Integration in North America*, ed. W. Andrew Axline et al, 116–35. Toronto: McClelland and Stewart, 1974.

Korinek, Valerie. "'It's a Tough Time to be in Love': The Darker Side of *Chatelaine* during the Cold War," in *Love, Hate, and Fear in Canada's Cold War*, ed. Richard Cavell, 159–82. Toronto: University of Toronto Press, 2004.

Kuffert, Leonard. "'Stabbing our Spirits Broad Awake': Reconstructing Canadian Culture, 1940–1948," in *Cultures of Citizenship in Post-war Canada, 1940–1955*, eds. Nancy Christie and Michael Gauvreau, 27–62. Montréal and Kingston: McGill–Queen's University Press, 2003.

Kunz, Diane. *The Diplomacy of the Crucial Decade: American Foreign Relations During the 1960s*. New York: Columbia University Press, 1994.

Kyba, Patrick. "Alvin Hamilton and Sino–Canadian Relations," in *Reluctant Adversaries: Canada and the People's Republic of China, 1949–1970*, eds. Paul M. Evans and B. Michael Frolic, 168–88. Toronto: University of Toronto Press, 1991.

Latham, Michael. *Modernization as Ideology: American Social Science and "Nation Building" in the Kennedy Era*. Chapel Hill: UNC Press, 2000.

Latham, Robert. *The Liberal Moment: Modernity, Security and the Making of Postwar International Order*. New York: Columbia University Press, 1997.

Legault, Albert, and Michel Fortmann, *A Diplomacy of Hope: Canada and Disarmament, 1945–1988*. Montréal and Kingston: McGill–Queen's University Press, 1992.

Lennox, Patrick. *At Home and Abroad: The Canada–US Relationship and Canada's Place in the World*. Vancouver: UBC Press, 2009.

LeoGrande, William M., and Peter Kornbluh. *Back Channel to Cuba: The Hidden History of Negotiations between Washington and Havana*. Chapel Hill: UNC Press, 2014.

Letner, Howard H. "Foreign Policy Decision Making: The Case of Canada and Nuclear Weapons," *World Politics* 29, no. 1 (1976), 29–66.

Litt, Paul. *The Muses, the Masses, and the Massey Commission*. Toronto: University of Toronto Press, 1992.

Lumsden, Ian. *Close the 49th Parallel Etc.: The Americanization of Canada*. Toronto: University of Toronto Press, 1970.

Lyon, Peyton V. "Problems of Canadian Independence," *International Journal* 16, no. 3 (1960–61), 250–59.

Lyon, Peyton V. *Canada in World Affairs 1961–1963*. Toronto: Oxford University Press, 1968.

Lyon, Peyton V. "Quiet Diplomacy Revisited," in *An Independent Foreign Policy for Canada?*, ed. S. Clarkson, 29–41. Toronto: McClelland and Stewart, 1968.

Macfarlane, Daniel. "Courting War Over a Rubber Stamp," *International Journal* 63, no. 3 (2008), 751–68.

Macfarlane, Daniel. "Caught Between Two Fires: The St. Lawrence Seaway and Power Project, Canadian–American Relations, and Linkage," *International Journal* 67, no. 2 (2012), 465–82.

Macfarlane, Daniel. *Negotiating a River: Canada, the US, and the Creation of the St. Lawrence Seaway*. Vancouver: UBC Press, 2014.

MacKenzie, Hector. "The ABCs of Canada's International Economic Relations, 1945–1951," in *Canada and the Early Cold War, 1943–1957*, ed. Greg. Donaghy, 215–50. Ottawa: Department of Foreign Affairs and International Trade, 1998.

MacKenzie, Hector. "Golden Decade(s)? Reappraising Canada's International Relations in the 1940s and 1950s," *British Journal of Canadian Studies* 23, no. 2 (2010), 179–206.

MacLennan, Hugh. "After 300 Years, Our Neurosis is Relevant," in *Canada: A Guide to the Peaceable Kingdom*, ed. William Kilbourn, 8–13. Toronto: Macmillan, 1970.

MacLennan, Jennifer. "Dancing with Our Neighbours: English Canadians and the Discourse of 'Anti-Americanism,'" in *Transnationalism: Canada–United States History into the 21st Century*, eds. Michael D. Behiels and Reginald C. Stuart, 69–85. Montréal and Kingston: McGill–Queen's University Press, 2010.

Macmillan, Harold. *At the End of the Day, 1961–1963*. London: Macmillan, 1973.

Maga, Timothy P. *John F. Kennedy and the New Pacific Community, 1961–63*. Basingstoke: Palgrave, 1990.

Mahant, Edelgard, and Graeme S. Mount. *Invisible and Inaudible in Washington: American Policies toward Canada*. Vancouver: UBC Press, 1999.

Maloney, Sean. *Learning to Love the Bomb: Canada's Nuclear Weapons During the Cold War*. Washington, DC: Potomac Books, 2007.

Martin, Lawrence. *The Presidents and the Prime Ministers: Washington and Ottawa Face to Face: The Myth of Bilateral Bliss, 1867–1982*. Toronto: Doubleday, 1982.

Martin, Paul. "Canadian–American Relations," in *Fifth Seminar on Canadian–American Relations at Assumption University of Windsor*, 21–29. Windsor: Assumption University, 1963.

Massolin, Philip. *Canadian Intellectuals, the Tory Tradition and the Challenge of Modernity, 1939–1970*. Toronto: University of Toronto Press, 2001.

May, Ernest R., and Philip. D. Zelikow. *The Kennedy Tapes: Inside the White House During the Cuban Missile Crisis*. Cambridge, MA: Harvard Belknap, 1997.

Mayers, David. "JFK's Ambassadors and the Cold War," *Diplomacy & Statecraft* 11, no. 3 (2000), 183–211.

McIlroy, Thad. *Personal Letters of a Public Man: The Family Letters of John G. Diefenbaker*. Toronto: Doubleday, 1985.

McKenzie, Francine. "A.D.P. Heeney: The Orderly Undersecretary," in *Architects and Innovators: Building the Department of Foreign Affairs and International Trade, 1909–2009*, eds. Greg Donaghy and Kim Richard Nossal, 151–68. Montréal and Kingston: McGill-Queen's University Press, 2009.

McKercher, Asa. "A 'Half-Hearted Response'?: Canada and the Cuban Missile Crisis, 1962," *International History Review* 33, no. 2 (2011), 335–52.

McKercher, Asa. "'The Most Serious Problem'?: Canada–US Relations and Cuba, 1962," *Cold War History* 12, no. 1 (2012), 69–88.

McKercher, Asa. "Southern Exposure: Diefenbaker, Latin America, and the Organization of American States," *Canadian Historical Review* 93, no. 1 (2012), 57–80.

McKercher, Asa. "Principles and Partnership: Merchant, Heeney, and the Craft of Canada–US Relations," *American Review of Canadian Studies* 42, no. 1 (2012), 67–83.

McKercher, Asa. "Diefenbaker's World: *One Canada* and the History of Canadian–American Relations, 1961–63," *The Historian* 75, no. 1 (2013), 94–120.

McMahon, Patricia. *Essence of Indecision: Diefenbaker's Nuclear Policy, 1957–1963*. Montréal and Kingston: McGill–Queen's University Press, 2009.

McPherson, Alan. *Yankee No! Anti-Americanism in U.S.–Latin American Relations*. Cambridge, MA: Harvard University Press, 2003.

McPherson, Alan. *Anti-Americanism in Latin America and the Caribbean*. New York: Berghahn Books, 2006.

Meren, David. *With Friends Like These: Entangled Nationalisms and the Canada-Quebec-France Triangle*. Vancouver: UBC Press, 2012.

Mills, C. Wright. *White Collar: The American Middle Classes*. New York: Oxford University Press, 1951.

Minifie, James. *Peacemaker or Powdermonkey: Canada's Role in a Revolutionary World*. Toronto: McClelland and Stewart, 1960.

Molinaro, Dennis. "'Calculated Diplomacy': John Diefenbaker and the Origins of Canada's Cuba Policy," in *Our Place in the Sun: Canada and Cuba in the Castro Era*, eds, Robert Wright and Lana Wylie, 75–95. Toronto: University of Toronto Press, 2009.

Mount, Graeme S. *Canada's Enemies: Spies and Spying in the Peaceable Kingdom*. Toronto: Dundurn Press, 1993.

Muehlenbeck, Philip. *Betting on the Africans: John F. Kennedy's Courting of African Nationalist Leaders*. New York: Oxford University Press, 2012.

Muirhead, Bruce. *Against the Odds: The Public Life and Times of Louis Rasminsky*. Toronto: University of Toronto Press, 1999.

Muirhead, Bruce. "The Development of Canada's Foreign Economic Policy in the 1960s: The Case of the European Union," *Canadian Historical Review* 82, no. 4 (2001), 690–719.

Muirhead, Bruce. *Dancing Around the Elephant: Creating a Prosperous Canada in an Era of American Dominance, 1957–1973*. Toronto: University of Toronto Press, 2007.

Munro, John. "Trials and Tribulations: The Making of the Diefenbaker and Pearson Memoirs," in *Political Memoir: Essays on the Politics of Memory*, ed. George Egerton, 242–56. London: Frank Cass, 1994.

Munton, Don, and David A. Welch. *The Cuban Missile Crisis: A Concise History*. New York: Oxford University Press, 2007.

Murray, Donette. *Kennedy, Macmillan and Nuclear Weapons*. Basingstoke: Macmillan, 2000.

Naftali, Timothy. *The Presidential Recordings—John F. Kennedy: The Great Crises, Volume One*. New York: W. W. Norton, 2001.

Naftali, Timothy, and Philip D. Zelikow. *The Presidential Recordings—John F. Kennedy: The Great Crises, Volume Two*. New York: W. W. Norton, 2001.

Nash, Knowlton. *Kennedy and Diefenbaker: Fear and Loathing Across the Undefended Border*. Toronto: McClelland and Stewart, 1990.

Newman, Peter C. *Renegade in Power: The Diefenbaker Years*. Toronto: McClelland and Stewart, 1963.

Ogelsby, J. C. M. "Canada and the Pan American Union: Twenty Years On," *International Journal* 24, no. 3 (1969), 571–89.

Oliver, Kendrick. *Kennedy, Macmillan, and the Nuclear Test Ban Debate, 1961–63*. New York: St. Martin's Press, 1998.

Palmer, Bryan. *Canada's 1960s: The Ironies of Identity in a Rebellious Era*. Toronto: University of Toronto Press, 2009.

Paterson, Thomas G. "Fixation with Cuba: The Bay of Pigs, Missile Crisis, and Covert War Against Fidel Castro," in *Kennedy's Quest for Victory: American Foreign Policy, 1961–1963*, ed. Thomas G. Paterson, 123–55. New York: Oxford University Press, 1989.

Pearson, Lester B. "Where is North American Going?," in *Fourth Seminar on Canadian-American Relations at Assumption University of Windsor*, 1–11. Windsor: Assumption University, 1962.

Pearson, Lester B. *Words & Occasions*. Toronto: University of Toronto Press, 1970.

Pearson, Lester B. *Mike: The Memoirs of the Right Honourable Lester B. Pearson*, Vol. III: *1957–1968*. Toronto: University of Toronto Press, 1975.

Perras, Galen Roger. *Franklin Roosevelt and the Origins of the Canadian-American Security Alliance, 1933–1945: Necessary But Not Necessary Enough*. Westport: Praegar, 1998.

Potter, Mitch. "JFK and Why Camelot Was a Living Nightmare for Canada," *Star Dispatches*. Toronto: Toronto Star, 2013.

Preston, Andrew. "Balancing War and Peace: Canadian Foreign Policy and the Vietnam War, 1961–1965," *Diplomatic History* 27, no. 1 (2003), 73–111.

Preston, Richard. A. "Introduction: National Imagery: The Canadian Image of the United States Today," in *Canada Views the United States: Nineteenth Century Political Attitudes*, eds. Sidney F. Wise and Robert Craig Brown, 3–15. Toronto: Macmillan, 1967.

Purdy, Al. *The New Romans: Candid Canadian Opinions of the US*. Edmonton: Hurtig, 1968.

Rabe, Stephen G. *The Most Dangerous Area of the World: John F. Kennedy Confronts Communist Revolution in Latin America*. Chapel Hill: UNC Press, 1999.

Rabe, Stephen G. "John F. Kennedy and the World," in *Debating the Kennedy Presidency*, eds. James N. Giglio and Stephen G. Rabe. Lanham: Rowman & Littlefield, 2003.

Rakove, Robert B. *Kennedy, Johnson, and the Nonaligned World*. Cambridge: Cambridge University Press, 2012.

Randall, Stephen J. "Great Expectations: America's Approach to Canada," in *Transnationalism: Canada-United States History into the Twenty-First Century*, eds. Michael Behiels and Reginald C. Stuart, 279–94. Montréal and Kingston: McGill-Queen's University Press, 2010.

Reford, Robert. *Canada and Three Crises*. Toronto: Canadian Institute of International Affairs, 1968.

Reid, Escott. *Radical Mandarin: The Memoirs of Escott Reid*. Toronto: University of Toronto Press, 1989.

Reynolds, David. "A Special Relationship? America, Britain and the International Order Since the Second World War," *International Affairs* 62, no. 1 (1985–86), 1–20.

Richter, Andrew. *Avoiding Armageddon: Canadian Military Strategy and Nuclear Weapons, 1950–63*. Vancouver: UBC Press, 2002.

Ritchie, Charles. *Diplomatic Passport: More Undiplomatic Diaries, 1946–1962*. Toronto: Macmillan, 1981.

Ritchie, Charles. *Storm Signals: More Undiplomatic Diaries, 1962–1971*. Toronto: Macmillan, 1983.

Ritchie, Charles. *Undiplomatic Diaries, 1937–71*. Toronto: Emblem, 2008.

Robertson, Paul, and John Singleton. "The Old Commonwealth and Britain's First Application to Join the EEC, 1961–3," *Australian Economic History Review* 40, no. 2 (2000), 153–77.

Robinson, H.B.O. *Diefenbaker's World: A Populist In Foreign Affairs*. Toronto: University of Toronto Press, 1989.

Rooth, Tim. "Britain, Europe, and Diefenbaker's Trade Diversion Proposals, 1957–58," in *Canada and the End of Empire*, ed. Phillip Buckner, 117–32. Vancouver: UBC Press, 2005.

Sayle, Timothy Andrews. "A Pattern of Constraint: Canadian–American Relations in the Early Cold War," *International Journal* 62, no. 3 (2007), 689–705.

Sayle, Timothy Andrews. "Canada, NATO, and the Berlin Crisis, 1961–1962: 'Slow-Boil' or 'Pressure Cooker?,'" *International Journal* 68, no. 2 (2013), 255–68.

Schild, Georg. "The Berlin Crisis," in *Kennedy: The New Frontier Revisited*, ed. Mark J. White, 91–123. New York: NYU Press, 1998.

Schlesinger Jr., Arthur M. *A Thousand Days: John F. Kennedy in the White House*. Boston: Houghton Mifflin, 1965.

Schlesinger Jr., Arthur M. *Journals, 1952–2000*. New York: Penguin, 2007.

Schoultz, Lars. *That Infernal Little Cuban Republic*. Chapel Hill: UNC Press, 2009.

Scott, L. V. *Macmillan, Kennedy and the Cuban Missile Crisis*. Basingstoke: Palgrave Macmillan, 1999.

Seaborg, Glenn T. *Kennedy, Khrushchev, and the Test Ban*. Berkeley: University of California Press, 1981.

Selverstone, Marc J. *A Companion to John F. Kennedy*. Chichester: Wiley, 2014.

Sévigny, Pierre. *This Game of Politics*. Toronto: McClelland and Stewart, 1965.

Simpson, Erika. *NATO and the Bomb: Canadian Defenders Confront Critics*. Montréal and Kingston: McGill–Queen's University Press, 2001.

Smith, Denis. *Gentle Patriot: A Political Biography of Walter Gordon*. Edmonton: Hurtig, 1973.

Smith, Denis. *Rogue Tory: The Life and Legend of John G Diefenbaker*. Toronto: MacFarlane, Walter and Ross, 1995.

Smith, Rufus. "Defence and North American Solidarity," in *Fifth Seminar on Canadian–American Relations at Assumption University of Windsor*, 117–20. Windsor: Assumption University, 1963.

Spencer, Dick. *Trumpets and Drums: John Diefenbaker on the Campaign Trail*. Vancouver: Greystone Books, 1994.

Spittal, Cara. "The Diefenbaker Moment." PhD diss., University of Toronto, 2011.

Spooner, Kevin. *Canada, the Congo Crisis, and UN Peacekeeping, 1960–1964*. Vancouver: UBC Press, 2009.

Spooner, Kevin. "Just West of Neutral: Canadian 'Objectivity' and Peacekeeping during the Congo Crisis, 1960–61," *Canadian Journal of African Studies* 43, no. 2 (2009), 303–36.

Stairs, Denis. "Confronting Uncle Sam: Cuba and Korea," in *An Independent Foreign Policy for Canada?*, ed. Stephen Clarkson, 57–68. Toronto: McClelland and Stewart, 1968.

Stairs, Denis. *The Diplomacy of Constraint: Canada, the Korean War and the United States*. Toronto: University of Toronto Press, 1974.

Steiner, Zara. "On Writing International History: Chaps, Maps and Much More," *International Affairs* 73, no. 3 (1997), 531–46.

Stevenson, Michael D. "'A Very Careful Balance': The 1961 Triangular Agreement and the Conduct of Canadian–American Relations," *Diplomacy & Statecraft* 24, no. 2 (2013), 291–311.

Stevenson, Michael D. "'Tossing a Match into Dry Hay': Nuclear Weapons and the Crisis in U.S.–Canadian Relations, 1962–1963," *Journal of Cold War Studies* 16, no. 4 (2014), 5–34.

Stewart, Gordon T. *The American Response to Canada since 1776.* East Lansing: Michigan State University Press, 1992.

Stewart, Gordon T. "'An Objective of US Foreign Policy since the Founding of the Republic': The United States and the End of Empire in Canada," in *Canada and the End of Empire*, ed. Phillip Buckner, 94–116. Vancouver: UBC Press, 2005.

Stursberg, Peter. *Diefenbaker: Leadership Gained, 1956–62.* Toronto: : University of Toronto Press, 1975.

Stursberg, Peter. *Diefenbaker: Leadership Lost, 1962–1967.* Toronto: University of Toronto Press, 1976.

Stursberg, Peter. *Lester Pearson and the American Dilemma.* Toronto: Doubleday, 1980.

Suri, Jeremi. *Power and Protest: Global Revolution and the Rise of Detente.* Cambridge, MA: Harvard University Press, 2003.

Sutherland, R. J. "Canada's Long Term Strategic Situation," *International Journal* 17, no. 3 (1962), 199–223.

Taffet, Jeffrey F. *Foreign Aid as Foreign Policy: The Alliance for Progress in Latin America.* London: Routledge, 2007.

Teigrob, Robert. *Warming Up to the Cold War: Canada and the United States' Coalition of the Willing, from Hiroshima to Korea.* Toronto: University of Toronto Press, 2009.

Thompson, John Herd, and Stephen J. Randall, *Canada and the United States: Ambivalent Allies*, Fourth Edition. Montréal and Kingston: McGill–Queen's University Press, 2008.

Trachtenberg, Marc. *A Constructed Peace: The Making of the European Settlement, 1945–1963.* Princeton: Princeton University Press, 1999.

Touhey, Ryan. *Conflicting Visions: Canada and India in the Cold War World, 1946–76.* Vancouver: UBC Press, 2015.

Underhill, Frank. "Canada and the North Atlantic Triangle," in *In Search of Canadian Liberalism*, ed. Frank. Underhill, 255–62. Don Mills: Oxford University Press, 2013 [1960].

Underhill, Frank. "The Image of Confederation," 1963 Massey Lecture. Toronto: Canadian Broadcasting Corporation, 1964.

Underhill, Frank. "Foreword," in *Nationalism in Canada*, ed. Peter. Russell, xvi–xx. Toronto: McGraw–Hill, 1966.

Ungerer, Carl. "Influence Without Power: Middle Power and Arms Control Diplomacy during the Cold War," *Diplomacy & Statecraft* 18, no. 2 (2007), 393–414.

Warnock, John. *Partner to Behemoth: The Military Policy of a Satellite Canada.* Toronto: New Press, 1970.

Webster, David. *Fire and the Full Moon: Canada and Indonesia in a Decolonizing World.* Vancouver: UBC Press, 2009.

Westad, Odd Arne. *The Global Cold War.* Cambridge: Cambridge University Press, 2005.

White, Mark J. "Introduction," in *Kennedy: The New Frontier Revisited*, ed. Mark J. White, 1–18. New York: NYU Press, 1998.

White, Mark J. *The Kennedys and Cuba: The Declassified Documentary History*, Revised Edition. Chicago: Ivan R. Dee, 2001.

Williamson, Richard D. *First Steps toward Détente: American Diplomacy in the Berlin Crisis, 1958–1963.* Lanham: Rowman & Littlefield 2012.

Young, John W., and Raj Roy. *Ambassador to Sixties London: The Diaries of David Bruce, 1961–1969.* Dordrecht: Republic of Letters, 2009.

Zeiler, Thomas W. *American Trade & Power in 1960s.* New York: Columbia University Press, 1992.

Zorbas, Jason. *Diefenbaker and Latin America: The Pursuit of Canadian Autonomy.* Newcastle: Cambridge Scholars Publishing, 2011.

# Index